The Triumph of Good

To Dr. Michael Vesnetka

Hoping you enjoy this book.

Best wishes,

The Triumph of Good

Cain, Abel and the End of Marxism

Thomas Cromwell

East West Publishing
Washington, DC

East West Publishing, Washington, DC
TriumphofGood.com

Library of Congress Control Number: 2021922213

ISBN Paperback: 978-1-7374418-0-9
ISBN Hardcover: 978-1-7374418-1-6
ISBN eBook: 978-1-7374418-2-3

First Edition

Printed in the United States of America

Contents

APPENDICES

There is but one good; that is God.
Everything else is good when it looks to Him
and bad when it turns from Him.

C.S. Lewis

Preface

We are witnessing a crisis of civilization. The values that have sustained free societies under the rule of law are being undermined by materialist ideologies that are leading to the destruction of traditional institutions of faith and family as well as foundational principles of honor, fidelity and patriotism.

This steady erosion of civilizational values may be difficult for some to recognize, given the marvels of science and technology that are simultaneously transforming the world around us. Yet there are signs aplenty: the promotion of immorality in our entertainment, the dishonesty of our mass media, the suppression of dissent in our democracies, the sexual confusion among many of our youth, the moral decline of our religious institutions, the irresponsibility of our educators who lead students to reject traditional values and norms, the promotion of depressing dystopian visions of our future, and the reckless spending of governments on socialist programs that our children and children's children will be forced to pay for.

What is the cause of this crisis? First and foremost, it is the steady spread of materialist ideologies into the very fabric of our culture, a metastasizing of destructive theories that are rotting our civilizational foundations. This is taking place despite the sincere efforts of good and conscientious people to stem the tide of these corrosive ideas, and despite the sacrifices by millions of our finest young people in the last century who defeated the totalitarian regimes built on these materialist ideologies.

We Thought Fascism and Communism were Defeated

With the Allied victory in World War II, we believed we had put an end to Fascism. And with the collapse of the Soviet Union forty-five years later, we believed we had finally discredited Marxism and defeated Communism. We were wrong. Both the Fascist and Communist regimes that caused so much destruction and suffering in the 20th century were based on socialist theories that put their trust and hope in powerful centralized governments rather than the virtues and abilities of individuals. These socialist ideas still flourish, and we are now faced with the imminent threat of the aggressive Marxist regime in China—which is more dangerous than the former Soviet Union—as well as the unprecedented infiltration and corruption of our societies by Marxist and Neo-Marxist ideologies. (See Glossary of Names and Terms on pages 490-505.)

Unlike Marxism, Fascism was never a theory of political economy; rather, it was simply an authoritarian ruling ideology that was eagerly adopted by dictators of all stripes, whether socialist or capitalist. Communism, however, was another matter altogether. It appeared in the 20th century as the incarnation of 19th century materialist theories developed by Karl Marx and Friedrich Engels—theories that justified violent revolution and totalitarian dictatorship. Its first true application was in the Bolshevik Revolution of 1917, after which many believers in the Communist promise of a materialist Utopia looked to Russia as the model society of the future.

Many of these believers were shocked, however, when the truth emerged about Soviet Russia and especially when the excesses of Stalin's Reign of Terror came to light in 1956. Nevertheless, despite the abysmal record of the Soviet Union and other failed Communist states, Marx's ideas survived the collapse of those regimes and have been infused with new philosophical life in our time. The first such infusion occurred when Marxism was combined with Freudianism in the Critical Theories developed by the Frankfurt School. Later, the French Postmodernists broadened the scope of Critical Theories to make them a comprehensive Leftist program of social transformation. It is the pernicious Neo-Marxism of Critical Theories that is now most responsible for destroying our civilization from within.

China's 100-Year Marathon to World Domination

The danger these theories pose is greatly heightened by the rapid development of a heavily militarized Communist China, a Marxist-Maoist regime that shares an ideological affinity with Leftist movements around the world. This affinity, coupled with an attitude of accommodation and appeasement towards China, is exploited by Beijing to advance its aggressive and expansionist international agenda, and intimidate and subvert governments and institutions everywhere. Shamefully, China's meteoric rise has been fueled by massive investments from an industrialized world that is morally bankrupt: It turns a blind eye to China's murderous history, its genocide of minorities, its persecution of religious groups and its suppression of individual freedoms just so corporations can profit from the vast Chinese market.

The West naturally looks at China through the lens of its own interests and history. But this is a fatal error. China has a totally different perspective, drawn from its own history and in particular the lessons from the period of Warring States (475-221 BC). In its more recent history, China experienced a century of international humiliation which, starting with the first Opium War (1839-1842), won by Britain, saw a series of foreign invasions and occupations that stoked national resentment towards the West and Westernized states. The Chinese Communist Party (CCP) believes that this era came to an end only when it took power in 1949. From that point on, the CCP has been pursuing a "100-Year Marathon" strategy to redress its past grievances by overtaking America as the world's superpower (by 2049 at the latest). The CCP claims it has assumed the Mandate of Heaven as the defender of Chinese honor. Its ideology is a clever combination of the ancient Chinese theory that there can be only one global hegemon (which they think is rightfully China) and the Marxist theory that history is an inexorable process of class warfare leading to the inevitable victory of the revolutionary class under the leadership of a Socialist dictatorship.

We Are Facing a Two-Headed Beast

China is no longer a distant threat. It has breached our weak defenses and is in our midst. Its agents, enablers and apologists are scattered throughout our society, and its network of allies is steadily encircling us, backed with Beijing's ever-growing financial and military power. In public, China espouses a multipolar world, but in practice it is working to achieve its own global hegemony. It is greatly aided in this by the Leftist movements around the world. Thus Communist China in the East, and Marxist and Neo-Marxist movements primarily in the West are two heads of the same beast that is slowly but surely killing our sacred traditions and trampling our civilization to death. This soulless and diabolical two-headed beast is our nemesis, our malignant enemy.

To confront and defeat the beast we have to know its nature and the nature of the threat it poses; we have to understand its motivation and strategy. In this endeavor we have the benefit of history, which amply reveals the nature of materialist ideologies in the record of their totalitarian predations. These ideologies may have evolved over time, but their core justification for hatred and conflict have remained.

Looking at the bloodshed of the last century, which is measured in the deaths of tens of millions of innocents, we really have no choice but to stand up and fight the beast we face today. The alternative is truly dark: It is a future similar to the present experienced by those living under the CCP today—privilege for those in the ruling class and persecution for anyone at odds with the regime. We should not be fooled by calming reassurances of peaceful intentions from Beijing or by the professions of idealism from the Leftists in our midst. Make no mistake. The beast is evil. It is our mortal enemy. If it succeeds, it will kill or enslave us all.

How Did We Get Here?

We find ourselves confronting today the most powerful and sinister ideology in history. How did we get to the point where our faith and belief systems have proven unable to stop the growth of Marxist ideologies and movements?

Britain's 1689 Glorious Revolution and the subsequent American Revolution of 1776 were historic milestones in the development of free and prosperous societies. These revolutions challenged monarchies, secured God-given rights for people to live in democracies and set in motion unprecedented advances for all humanity. But while successful, these revolutions did not anticipate the atheistic doctrines of Marx, Engels, Marcuse, Foucault and others, and they have not offered a convincing answer to the criticisms leveled against free and capitalist societies by the ideologues of the Left. This is because Marxist and Neo-Marxist theories challenge not only political systems, whether monarchies or democracies, but also the religion-based ideas and values that undergird our civilization and institutions. It is clear that neither Judeo-Christian principles and values of the West nor traditional Asian values and philosophies of the East have been able to successfully counter and defeat materialist ideologies or block the aggressive rise of Communist China. Consequently, the liberties we now enjoy are in grave danger.

Looking at the dire situation of the world today, people of faith and goodwill everywhere must recognize that despite their prodigious efforts to build free and just societies, they have not been able to stave off, let alone eliminate, the forces of materialism, violent revolution and totalitarian oppression. We must find a new frame of reference to address this manifestation of evil.

The Cain-Abel Paradigm

To understand evil in the world today, we must look to the beginning of human existence when evil was first introduced to the world. In the Biblical story, the first human family failed to fulfill its responsibilities and consequently introduced patterns of evil behavior into human relations that have bedeviled us ever since. This book uses that scriptural account of the origin of good and evil to explain how these two primordial but antithetical forces influence human nature and behavior, and how they have shaped ideas and history. Our particular interest is to identify how good and evil manifest in opposing attitudes and behaviors and explain the contradictory belief systems that emerge from them.

All people experience a struggle between conflicting forces within themselves: a desire to do good that is at war with a tendency to do evil. As Aleksandr Solzhenitsyn put it in *The Gulag Archipelago*: "The line dividing good and evil cuts through the heart of every human being. And who is willing to destroy a piece of his own heart?"[1] Our response to these conflicting impulses determines our behavior, good and bad.

The Genesis story of Cain and Abel reveals that members of the first human family inherited this internal conflict due to their alienation from the Creator. Thus the internal struggle between good and evil within individuals was externalized when Cain, the elder son, became bitter when his sacrifice was rejected by God and, in a fit of jealous rage, murdered his younger brother Abel, whose offering had been accepted by God. Cain's attitude and behavior established him as the archetype of evil while Abel became the archetype of good. Evil's domination of good in the first family established a pattern that has been repeated throughout history.

As Jordan Peterson pointed out in a 2017 lecture: Cain and Abel are "prototypical human beings... Humanity enters history at the end of the story of Adam and Eve, and then the archetypal patterns of human behavior are instantaneously presented... The first two human beings engage in a fratricidal struggle that ends in the death of the best one of them. That's the story of human beings in history."[2]

The importance of the Biblical story lies not in its historical accuracy but in the truth it reveals about human nature and behavior and about the nature of good and evil in general. In the Genesis account, Cain is jealous, resentful, accusatory, violent and murderous. Abel is faithful, patient, persevering, humble and obedient. These opposite-character types produce conflicting attitudes, ideas and behaviors that are reflected in fundamentally different worldviews.

This is the Cain-Abel paradigm: the principle that governs the relationships between people alienated from God, in history and the world. It recognizes that the world we live in is not the world of God's original intent but a world in which evil has dominion over good, after the pattern of Cain dominating Abel. And, since Cain was born first, in this world evil precedes good.

The problem caused by evil preceding good is exacerbated by evil typically masquerading as good, sowing confusion and mistrust. Consequently, many good people have been deceived into doing evil, often with the best of intentions. Understanding the Cain-Abel paradigm enables us to see clearly what is really taking place in history and the world around us—and to discern what is actually good and what is actually evil.

In this book we demonstrate how the Cain-Abel paradigm can be used to recognize the evil that lies behind Marxism and related materialist ideologies and how the forces of good can finally gain enduring supremacy over them. This is the triumph of good. It portends the demise of Marxism and an end to Cain's dominion of the world.

Cain and Abel in History and the World Today

Why is it that despite the tremendous advances of the past century, Marxism and its evil ideological offspring have been able to gain such a strong grip on the civilized world? The answer can be found within the Cain-Abel paradigm. As Winston Churchill said: "The story of the human race is war. Except for brief and precarious interludes, there has never been peace in the world; and before history began, murderous strife was universal and unending."[3] This history of violent conflict and war is a legacy of the conflict between Cain and Abel.

Although evil often dominates good, ultimately, through great effort, "Abel" has sometimes found the way to prevail over "Cain." Indeed, despite the prevalence of evil, history demonstrates that good advances incrementally as people of virtue sacrifice themselves for the sake of Divine providence.

For example, when Jacob won over his embittered elder twin Esau after twenty-one years of hardship in Haran, he was able to establish the twelve tribes as the foundation for the chosen nation of Israel. And when millions of good people made incredible sacrifices to defeat totalitarianism in the 20th century, they protected freedom and opened the way for liberty to spread around the world. Thus while Cain-type successes have resulted in setbacks for human progress, Abel-type successes have resulted in ever-increasing human enlightenment and progress.

Materialist ideologies—in particular Marxism and its offshoots—arose from Cain-type attitudes of jealousy and resentment. Therefore, these ideas appeal to and stimulate Cain-type nature. This is why a Marxist or other materialist is typically driven by insatiable envy and resentment and is willing to justify violence to achieve his ends.

We assert that Cain-type ideology has evolved over time as part of human development and reached its culmination in atheistic Marxism and its Neo-Marxist offshoots. These malignant theories advocate resolving differences and resentments through accusation and violence, as if Cain was right all along.

They promise an earthly Communist Utopia in the here and now, thereby exploiting the otherworldliness of Christianity and other religions that offer a reward for goodness in another, invisible world. Often well-meaning but naïve and misinformed people continue to follow the Pied Pipers of the Left because the evil in Cain's materialist ideologies is cloaked in the guise of virtue, and their advocates claim to have the interests of all people at heart. But the promises of the beast are always belied by its actions: Marxism and Neo-Marxism have not created a single example of a peaceful, prosperous or just society.

This is the Hour of Decision

Evil has always been with us, but never before has it been as successfully embodied in ideology as it is in Marxism and Neo-Marxism. This, compounded by the fact that these theories cleverly disguise their true nature and intent, makes this moment more dangerous for the future of humanity than the rise of Nazi Germany or the establishment and expansion of the Soviet Empire. We have reached this critical point because of the civilized world's naiveté or willful disregard for the imminence of the threat. As at the time of World War II, this is an hour of decision for the world—and especially for America, which continues to be the one nation on earth capable of withstanding and reversing the spread of Marxist ideology and power. Faced with this stark reality, it is time for the sleeping giant to awaken once more! We can no longer appease the beast.

To succeed, this task must be shared by all Abel-type people of faith and goodwill whose very existence is threatened by atheistic ideologies, just as Abel was threatened and murdered by Cain. There are some 4.3 billion members of monotheistic religions whose (Biblical and Quranic) scriptures include (almost identical) accounts of Cain and Abel. All these and other people of conscience should be able to recognize the threat posed by evil Cain-type theories and the movements inspired by them—and set aside what are ultimately petty differences to confront and overcome the common atheistic enemy. If allowed, this enemy will destroy our freedom and annihilate anyone who stands in its way. We must reject the seductions of the Left and work together to build a world in which every one of us can fulfill his or her true destiny under the mandate of Divine providence. This book sheds light on how that can be done.

Our Personal Responsibility

We contend that insufficient attention has been given to the importance of human responsibility in the shaping of providential history. As we will show, the providence advances when individuals fulfill their responsibilities and suffers setbacks when they fail to do so. The implication is clear: Divine providence is not dependent on God alone but on humanity participating in the realization of the Creator's purpose. Thus we cannot simply wait for God to solve our problems.

In today's world, our responsibility is to understand and confront the twin dangers of Leftist ideology and Communist China, to defeat the two-headed beast once and for all. Our response to their evil ideas and aggressive behavior must be spiritual and ideological as well as political. We have to reject their pernicious social justice agenda, with its wokism and "Cancel Culture," and restore faith to its proper place at the center of society. And we have to do whatever we can to stop the Communist regime in China from persecuting its own people and from spreading its evil influence abroad. As President John F. Kennedy said in the closing words of his 1961 inaugural address:

> Finally, whether you are citizens of America or citizens of the world, ask of us here the same high standards of strength and sacrifice which we ask of you. With a good conscience our only sure reward, with history the final judge of our deeds, let us go forth to lead the land we love, asking His blessing and His help, but knowing that here on earth, God's work must truly be our own.[4]

The importance of our personal responsibility in this work is articulated well in a line attributed to John Stuart Mill: "The only thing necessary for the triumph of evil is for good men to do nothing."[5] True as that is, it implies the broader meaning that we are advocating in this book:

> The only thing necessary for the triumph of good is for men and women to fulfill their God-given responsibilities.

Acknowledgements

After the collapse of the Soviet Union in 1991, I thought that the days of Marxism were numbered. I had visited the Soviet Union, many of its satellite countries and Communist China. All were wretched places to live in because of their oppressive policies and pathetic economies. Thus I believed that the utter failure of the totalitarian regimes that Marxism had spawned, combined with Communism's track record of mass murder, was sufficient evidence of the theory's gross inadequacies and lethal consequences to cause it to be rejected by humanity once and for all.

I was wrong. Since 1991, Communist China has supplanted the USSR as the most dangerous Marxist state in the world, while Marxism itself has metastasized into a broad range of Critical Theories that now threaten to destroy our civilization. This resurgence of Marxism and its offshoots, together with the expansionism of Communist China in recent years, is truly alarming. Clearly the world has not learned the lessons of the past century.

I have long thought that a book that examined Marxism from a spiritual perspective could help expose its most fundamental fallacies and make clear that it is not merely another materialist philosophy but the pinnacle of atheistic ideology. Furthermore, such a book would show that Marxism has its roots in the Biblical story of the Fall and the emergence of Cain as the archetypal representative of evil in society and history. Using the lens of the Cain-Abel paradigm, as this book does, people, ideas and movements take on new meaning—and providential patterns of history with major implications for the present can be seen.

The purpose of this book is not to gather more evidence for the prosecution of Marxism and its offshoots. In my view, we have all the proof needed for conviction. Its purpose is to cast the evidence in a new light, a light that dispels the materialist shadows that currently darken the skies of our civilization, a light that gives hope to those still living under totalitarian regimes, and a light that helps people everywhere understand where the line is drawn between good and evil.

My own renewed interest and concern in this topic resonated with several longtime friends who have been extremely helpful in bringing this project to fruition. Frank Kaufmann and I had often talked about the need "to do something" to address the resurgence of Marxism and rise of China. This led to us establishing The Settlement Project, which he heads, and which provides relevant information on Marxism and Neo-Marxism, and to me finally writing this book. (Frank is working on a related book that focuses on Postmodernism.) Frank had a significant impact on the subjects treated here, and I am grateful for his investment of time in reviewing drafts and making helpful suggestions.

Victor Jessop is an old friend whose concern for the present dangers posed by the Left and China caused him and his wife Tracy to leave their home in Australia and return to America in order to do what they can to fight the spread of Marxism and Neo-Marxist ideology and raise awareness about the dangers of an ever-more aggressive Chinese Communist Party. As he says, only America has the resources needed to lead a global effort to counter materialist ideology and Communism. Victor has spent many long hours reading and re-reading drafts of this book, making helpful suggestions and doing whatever he can to get it finished and get it known. The New America Initiative that he leads is a fruit of our collaboration and an organization that seeks to embody and promote the ideas discussed in this book.

David James likewise spent many long hours going over drafts and offering useful comments and suggestions. He also spent long hours assembling the Index. My son Alexander, who has been educated in university departments immersed in Postmodernism, gave valuable advice on the sections dealing with Critical Theories. Carl Hagen read an early draft and provided encouragement. Cheryl Wetzstein lovingly proofed every word and offered good advice on making the text as clear as possible. Jonathan Gullery designed the book and provided invaluable advice and assistance in getting it published. Other friends and family provided encouragement and both moral and financial support.

Finally, this book acknowledges that anything of worth contained herein is ultimately the work of our loving Creator and of the men and women who have left us a legacy of understanding and wisdom regarding the purpose of creation and the providential path towards its final fulfillment.

Thomas Cromwell

Washington, October 2021

Introduction

How can we understand our world of seemingly endless human suffering? Looking back over history, it is evident that human beings have only very slowly emerged from a state of primitive barbarism. How can this fact be squared with the religious view that we originated as creations of a good and loving God? According to monotheistic scriptures, the original world of Divine intent tragically never came into being because of human disobedience and consequent alienation from the Creator. Nevertheless, despite a long history of ignorance and brutality, humanity is undoubtedly endowed with a sense of good and evil, a capacity to recognize the existence of evil and yet believe our original purpose was good and that our ultimate destiny is also good. From this perspective, it is not sufficient to view history merely in terms of who did what when, but rather to gain an understanding of the root causes of human behavior and how these have shaped our past and predict our future.

In this book we address both the causal forces of history and the manifestations of those forces in the behavior of individuals and societies, past and present. The scope of this examination is necessarily limited, and our primary purpose is therefore to highlight the individuals and events that had the greatest impact in advancing what we believe is a Divine providence to enable humanity to fulfill its original purpose for being. To do this requires making certain assumptions about our origin and nature that might not be agreeable to some readers, but which we contend are a necessary basis for the interpretation of history from a providential perspective.

Good and Evil

Our starting point is this: The Creator is only good and endowed the original human beings with a nature that was an embodiment of Divine goodness. Thus human goodness means that which is true to God's design and purpose for our creation, while evil is that which is harmful to that design and purpose. Apparently, our ancestors violated the innate laws of goodness, and we now suffer the consequences of moral confusion brought about by conflicts between our original good nature and an inherited tendency to do evil. In this state of ignorance and separation from Divine love and truth, we too often do what is contrary to our original purpose and true self interest. Thus to do good requires us to reject our inherited tendency to do what is evil by reversing the patterns of thought and behavior that first caused human alienation from God. As C.S. Lewis pointed out in *The Great Divorce*, good and evil cannot coexist. They are irreconcilable opposites, and the conflict between them can be finally resolved only when evil is fully understood and totally rejected:

> Evil can be undone, but it cannot 'develop' into good. Time does not heal it. The spell must be unwound, bit by bit, 'with backward mutters of dissevering power' – or else not. It is still 'either-or'. If we insist on keeping Hell (or even earth) we shall not see Heaven: if we accept Heaven we shall not be able to retain even the smallest and most intimate souvenirs of Hell.[6]

The Biblical account of how human alienation first occurred in the Garden of Eden contains insights into the archetypal embodiment of good and evil in the character and behavior of Adam and Eve and their sons, Cain and Abel. Although both brothers were alienated from the Creator because of their parents' disobedience, Abel was relatively more faithful and responsible than Cain. This relative goodness was demonstrated when Abel's sacrifice was accepted, setting him up as an exemplar of relative goodness who could be used to advance the Divine providence.

Cain's murder of Abel abruptly ended the prospects for good gaining ascendancy in the first family and established the paradigm of typically destructive Cain-Abel relationships. The providence was delayed by the murder of Abel, but Abel-type figures (followed by Abel-type families, tribes and nations) would appear throughout history as humanity slowly advanced from the darkness of ignorance and evil into a more enlightened state.

Over the millennia, religions and philosophies that encourage goodness emerged to teach the Way of Abel, the path of responsiveness to the Divine and service to others. Always imperfect because of the presence of Cain-type attributes in individuals and organizations, religions nevertheless served to elevate human understanding and goodness. Throughout history, these efforts for good were opposed by Cain-type forces of resentment, selfishness and materialism. Capitalizing on the shortcomings of religion, these destructive ideas and movements drew people towards materialist alternatives that appealed to their innate sense of altruism but inevitably produced only more greed, jealousy and violence.

Nevertheless, the advancing enlightenment of humanity raises the hope that our fondest aspirations of achieving a world of goodness can be achieved once we finally learn to choose good and reject evil. This is the goal of spiritual growth. To borrow from C.S. Lewis once more:

> There is but one good; that is God. Everything else is good when it looks to Him and bad when it turns from Him.[7]

Marxism's Challenge to Christianity

After the crucifixion of Jesus, the establishment and growth of the church was marred by sectarian rivalries, persecution of dissidents and an inability to implement Christian teachings to create truly just societies. Unable to create a unified Christian realm, various branches of the church split off to pursue what they held to be truer interpretations of scriptures and better practices of the faith. The chief milestones of this history are the Great Schism between Rome and the Eastern Orthodox Churches in 1054, the

Protestant Reformation in 1517, and the migration of Pilgrims to America in 1620. Yet despite periodic reformation and renewal, none of the churches were able to maintain the high standards of Jesus or to create a model of godly life as taught in the Beatitudes. The Kingdom of Heaven remained an elusive goal the faithful hoped to achieve in a future end time.

This Christian sectarianism, combined with the inability of the churches to create a just and equitable society, has given critics of religion an opportunity to propose materialist alternatives. The most important of these critics was German philosopher Karl Marx (1818-1883). With his close collaborator Friedrich Engels, Marx spent most of his life blaming Christian and capitalist society for a range of injustices. The solution Marx and Engels proposed was based on an atheistic worldview that promised a pseudo salvation through the creation of a godless Utopia, a Communist state in which each would give according to their ability and receive according to their need.

Marx believed that existing economic systems and social institutions, from capitalist enterprises to religious organizations and traditional families, should be done away with. He prescribed violent revolution to bring about the changes he envisaged, believing that from the ashes of capitalist economies would rise Socialist states, which eventually would become Communist states. Marx claimed that, unlike Christianity, his theories were based on science.

Marx died a frustrated revolutionary, but his theories were picked up posthumously by Lenin, Mao and countless others to create violent revolutions and oppressive dictatorships around the world. These revolutions and the governments they spawned proved adept at making promises of a better world but would prove unable to build a single successful state. On the contrary, the radicals who carried out violent revolutions against existing governments became the leaders of ruthless dictatorships that were generally much worse than the regimes they replaced. The first Marxist revolution was led by Vladimir Lenin in 1917, leading to the establishment of the Soviet Union.

The sheer cruelty of Lenin and the other leaders of the revolution would become embedded in the ruling practices of the Soviet state. Furthermore, the "withering away of the state" under Socialism anticipated by Marxism never occurred. On the contrary, the Soviet state's insatiable lust for power became the driving force of the ruling Communist Party, shaping all its policies and practices at home and abroad.

A History of Socialist and Communist Failure

The Soviet Union lasted seventy years before its socialist economy collapsed, the Communist Party imploded, and the USSR's constituent and satellite states gained their freedom. As the Soviet Union passed into history and most of its client states abandoned Communism, China began to rise. Ruled by the ruthless Chinese Communist Party, the regime in Beijing has been able to survive for over seventy years by allowing its people a measure of capitalism. With relatively cheap labor and a market of 1.4 billion people, China has attracted massive amounts of capital from around the world, enabling it to become a major economic powerhouse that projects its influence and military might globally.

Over 170 years have passed since Marx and Engels published their *Manifesto of the Communist Party* in 1848. This twenty-three-page pamphlet explaining their theories would become the "Bible" of violent revolutionaries and totalitarian dictators alike. (See Appendix 1, pp262-297, for the full text of the *Manifesto*; in this book we use the short form, *The Communist Manifesto*.) However, despite the long passage of time and the many Marxist movements and regimes that have come and gone, none so far has created an economically prosperous state or a politically just society. On the contrary, the history of Socialist and Communist states has been abysmal. Workers (purportedly the main beneficiaries of Marxist revolutions) consistently fared much worse than their capitalist counterparts, with much of the population living close to or in poverty while the totalitarian ruling class enjoyed power and privileges reserved for the few. Furthermore, these dismal results were always purchased at the price of individual liberties and the ruthless suppression of dissidents. Tens of millions of lives have been sacrificed on the altar of the Marxist lie. (See Appendix 2, p298, for the death toll of Communism in the 20th Century.)

As we will show, the chronic failure of Marxism to deliver on its promises is not due to inadequate implementation of the theory but to the massive flaws in Marxism itself.

Evil's Ideological Empire

Marxism-Leninism's failure to turn Russia and its subject states into the promised land and the revelations of Stalin's bloody Reign of Terror, led many of its adherents to become disenchanted with the Soviet model of Communism. Nevertheless, many of these followers retained the theory's atheism and anti-capitalism and continued to use dialectical materialism as a tool for criticizing society and promoting revolution. Beginning in the 1920s, the Frankfurt School (discussed in Chapter 14) began to draw parallels between the Marxist rebellion against capitalism and the social status quo and Freud's theories on repression (especially in traditional families and society). They called their dialectic approach Critical Theory. Their influence was considerable in the West, especially during the 1960s through the work of Herbert Marcuse, Wilhelm Reich and others.

Later, in France, several Leftist thinkers, notably Michel Foucault and Jacques Derrida, sought to do away with traditional society altogether, rejecting all absolutes, including scientific laws. Their theory was that institutions were little more than social constructs devised to satisfy the human hunger for power and shaped by the language of the powerful. They then used Critical Theory to deconstruct these institutions, identifying and isolating their weaknesses before seeking to change or destroy the institutions themselves.

The leading personage in this movement was Foucault (1926-1984).

Rising to prominence by the end of the 1960s, today he is the dominant figure in the social sciences. His Postmodernist theories are widely employed in Western academia from where they have spilled over into school curricula, mass media, social media, entertainment, activism, corporate policy and politics. And while Marx was primarily interested in political and economic theory and especially class struggle, as he saw it, the range of issues addressed in Foucault's theories is far broader. Thus the scope of Critical Theories continues to grow and already includes anti-colonialism, critical race theory, anti-racism, white patriarchy, white privilege, white fragility, toxic masculinity, radical feminism, queer theory, gender studies, intersectionality, political correctness and social justice. The thrust of these theories is deeply anti-religious and anti-capitalist, feeding on Cain-type resentment, envy, victimhood and murderous anger. (For details on Postmodernist Critical Theories see Chapters 15 and 16.)

In the United States and many other developed countries, these theories are now entrenched in society and government. Those who oppose them in the name of traditional values and institutions are branded as racist, homophobic and fascistic. Politically correct language (that is the terminology of Postmodernism) is demanded of all. Most major media outlets and social media sites now accept the dictates of this radical Leftist movement, suppressing speech and cancelling alternative voices.

Marxism and the Neo-Marxism of the Frankfurt School and Postmodernism are the main theories of the Left and represent the culmination of Cain-type thinking and behavior. They made great inroads around the world because they provide an atheistic and materialist explanation for the conflicts in history, and they promise a solution to suffering and injustice in the here and now. However, just as Marxism-Leninism failed as it spread throughout the world, Neo-Marxism has also been unable to produce good fruit. The new theories justify violent revolution, but the violent rioters in the streets only produce mayhem and destruction, contributing nothing to society. In the meantime, the attacks on faith and the family are destroying moral values and producing social misery and chaos.

The Final Fulfillment of Human Purpose

This book exposes the Cain-type nature of the Marxist and Neo-Marxist theories of the Left and presents the Way of Abel as a desirable alternative. It looks at key Abel-type figures and entities in history that exemplified virtuous behavior and compares them with Cain-type figures and entities that tried to preempt the good with false imitations, leading to oppressive regimes. Most important among these Abel figures was Jesus, whose life of humility and service has inspired hundreds of millions of people across the globe to do good themselves. However, despite these virtuous efforts and those of other people of faith and goodwill, the challenge from the Left remains undiminished, threatening humanity with destructive forces of materialism and unending conflict.

This is the challenge that must be faced and overcome today. History demonstrates that forces of evil can be defeated and that the sacrifices of so many in the struggle with evil need not be in vain. To achieve an ultimate triumph of good, we can never accept the supremacy of evil. Rather, we must keep in mind our God-given destiny to live as a human family in a world of goodness and keep pressing on to achieve that goal.

The goal can be achieved through clear knowledge of the danger and a resolute commitment to return civilization to its spiritual roots, this time pursuing the Way of Abel to an irreversible conclusion. As always, the key to success lies in each person taking responsibility for his or her thoughts and actions.

In our view, America has a special role to play in this. From its founding to the present, America has pioneered a providential path that weaves together spiritual and moral principles with political and economic objectives. Traveling this path has made America a uniquely blessed nation that has inspired movements of personal liberty, democracy and free markets around the world. Thus America is destined to lead the world in the cause of good, which is why we are so concerned about the steady erosion of America's founding principles. Without those pillars, the ideological armies of the Left will relentlessly pull America down and turn it into a Socialist or Communist state in thrall to a malignant Communist China. America must be saved from this fate if it is to fulfill its larger providential mission for the world.

Chapter 1

The Crisis in Today's World

Marxism and Critical Theories are
Destroying Civilization

Despite the collapse of the Soviet Union and other Communist regimes at the end of the 1980s and beginning of the 1990s, Communism itself has not disappeared and in some respects is now stronger than ever. Given its immense wealth, Communist China is now more powerful than the USSR ever was. It is able to closely monitor its own people and brutally crack down on dissidents while expanding its pernicious influence throughout the world. And while the West played a critical role in the collapse of the Soviet Bloc regimes 30 years ago, this success bred complacency and blinded the world to the spread of Marxist and Neo-Marxist theories. These destructive ideologies are now established in a wide array of academic and social institutions, major media outlets and government bureaucracies.

Government bodies, including the military, educational institutions and even capitalist corporations, are now teaching Neo-Marxist Critical Theories, such as Critical Race Theory, Queer Theory and Intersectionality, all in the name of social justice. More sinisterly, governments and institutions are punishing people and organizations that do not conform to Critical Theory-based policies—even though these theories clearly undermine the foundations of traditional, religion-based civilization, especially the nuclear family, and sow chaos and confusion throughout society.

In America, the reality of this alarming development is now all too evident. The traditional values of America's founding, as enshrined in the Declaration of Independence and the Constitution, are suddenly no longer sacrosanct. Leftist ideologues and their allies in Big Media, Big Tech, Hollywood and Wall Street are now aggressively pushing their destructive agendas. They have largely taken over the Democratic Party and intimidated the Republican Party, enabling them to get their issues translated into government policy. On the streets, their activists attack innocents, burn cities and loot private businesses.

The presidential election in 2020 brought the American crisis into sharp focus. It exposed the power of the Leftist alliance as well as its ability to manipulate mass media and social media and to suppress dissenting voices through "Cancel Culture." Combined with sophisticated data manipulation and voter fraud, the Left managed to secure the presidency. For many Americans, this was a long overdue wakeup call. They suddenly realized that the unthinkable was unfolding before their very eyes, and that the future of their country as founded was in jeopardy of being destroyed by the radical Left.

With great foresight, in 1798, John Adams warned of just such a danger:

> Our Constitution was made only for a religious and moral people. It is wholly inadequate for the government of any other.[8]

More recently, in 1987, President Ronald Reagan warned that America's foundational values have to be constantly fought for:

> Freedom is never more than one generation away from extinction. We didn't pass it to our children in the bloodstream. It must be fought for, protected, and handed on for them to do the same, or one day we will spend our sunset years telling our children and our children's children what it was once like in the United States where men were free.[9]

The Threat of the Chinese Communist Party

The loss of traditional civilizational values that is so evident in the rise of Leftist ideologies is not only responsible for growing social chaos, but also serves to lower the nation's guard against the aggressive expansionism of the Chinese Communist Party. The CCP has shown itself adept at buying its way into vital institutions in America and other strategically important countries around the world; once ensconced, it corrupts officials and weakens their resistance to Chinese propaganda and subversion. In this very dangerous trend, venal individuals and interests in educational, media and political institutions, as well as corporations, are selling out their countries to this ultimate external enemy. When the influence of these corrupt people and entities shapes government policies, the future of the nation is indeed in jeopardy. In America, this harmful process is currently concentrated in the Democratic Party, which is adopting ever more radical policies, policies that strike at the religious and moral foundations of the nation and are therefore both inimical to the Founders' intent and conducive to Chinese subversion.

The Political Pendulum Problem

Given these alarming developments, and the warnings of great leaders like Adams and Reagan, how can people of principle and conscience respond to the destruction of American values from the inside and the rising threat of Communist China from without? The instinctive response of conservatives who see these dangers is to call for a return to traditional American and broader civilizational principles and values. But while this return to tried-and-true traditions is clearly advantageous, recent history has shown that this response is insufficient to solve the problem of endless political oscillations from right to left and back again. The truth is that this political pendulum does not maintain true political equilibrium.

As the 2020 American elections demonstrated all too clearly, the Left is gaining so much influence in society that it is fundamentally changing norms.

This influence is translating into the Federal Government granting itself powers that far exceed the scope envisioned by the Founders and threatens to transform America into an authoritarian state. More and more proof of this creeping power grab by the bureaucracy is coming to light as we learn that the institutions established to protect our rights have actually been engaged in subverting them on behalf of political interests (notably the Department of Justice and the FBI).

If elections can no longer be relied upon to pull the country away from the Leftist precipice, America could be dragged into Marxist Socialism or even Communism even though these systems destroy representative governments and the freedoms they secure. It was this terrifying realization that caused so many righteous Americans to recoil in dismay from the corruption of traditional American values that they witnessed in the 2020 election.

The challenge is to find a solution that does not merely give us another brief respite from the seemingly inexorable ratcheting up of influence from the Left that occurs when the Democratic Party is in power, but which finally and fully exposes the falsehoods of the Leftist promises and provides an effective and durable alternative. Thus we need more than a generational solution, let alone a quick political fix after a lost election. We must permanently bring the political pendulum of history to rest on the side of what is good and right.

A Durable Solution

Returning to the past and tradition is no longer an effective or sufficient response to the challenge posed by the Left. By this time, it is evident that Leftist ideologies have made deep inroads into civilized society due to the inability of civilization itself to provide a coherent and effective resistance to them. As in all contests, success comes eventually to the party with the best strategy and most effective plan of action. In the context of Left versus Right, this means that ultimate success will be achieved by the side that has the better prescription for social ills and can therefore offer the best path towards the realization of a world of enduring goodness and justice. As we have noted, it was the inadequacies of the Christian Church, and its inability to provide a path to a heavenly kingdom on earth, that opened the door for Marxism with its promises of an earthly Utopia. And, although Marxism and its offshoots have never succeeded in delivering on their promises, they nevertheless continue to spin a web of lies and deceptions that lure both the naïve and the cynical power seekers to their cause.

Communist Deceptions

The Communist Manifesto was remarkably blunt about its authors' hatred of capitalism, religion and the family. Being that candid, however, was not a very clever way to win support in societies primarily raised on Christian values, and over time the Communists realized that they had to disguise their real intentions behind idealist language and fine promises. Thus Lenin sold revolution to war-weary Russian workers, soldiers and peasants with the promise of peace, bread and land. Nevertheless, for more than a decade after the Russian Revolution Communist parties around the world invested much of their energies in attacking political and ideological rivals rather than enticing people with what "the masses" wanted.

This changed in 1934, when the Comintern (the Communist International, which was responsible for managing Moscow's relations with affiliated parties around the world) dramatically reversed course. It launched the Popular Front policy, which would be pursued through World War II and throughout the Cold War. The concept of the Popular Front was to use non-Communist organizations to advance the Communist (and in particular Soviet) agenda. The German Communist Party had made the mistake of attacking the ruling Social Democratic Party (SPD) as fascists during elections in 1932, thereby splitting the vote on the left and making way for Hitler and the Nazis to take power. Thus the first objective of the Popular Front was to form an anti-Fascist alliance that would be led by Communists.

This long-term strategy was broadened into the United Front approach to secure (often unwitting) support for world Communism from a wide range of individuals and groups dedicated to altruistic purposes. The range of humanitarian issues grew to include human rights, world peace, détente, the anti-war movement, nuclear disarmament, the environment and even ecumenism. Thus organizations with inspiring names and ostensibly laudable objectives of organizations, such as the World Peace Council and the World Council of Churches, consistently promoted Soviet policies due to the influence of Moscow. The deception of the United Front strategy was particularly insidious, since within Soviet bloc countries themselves human rights were virtually nonexistent, free speech was not allowed and no authentic religious, humanitarian or peace-making activities were permitted.

And Those Deceived

Nevertheless, many of the most upright and conscientious people on earth have believed Communist propaganda and dedicated themselves to Leftist causes, convinced that they are working to build a better world. To make these personal commitments to the Communist cause, they must accept the veracity of the promises made by the Left. As early as the 1920s, a number of Leftist Americans looked to Russia for an alternative to their own capitalist system, even though the Coolidge administration's laissez-faire approach to business resulted in burgeoning prosperity and unemployment rates as low as 1% and 2%. Some of those who visited Russia brought back mixed reports. Honest appraisals described the tottering economy and widespread poverty and oppression. But the Russians knew how to deceive their visitors, giving them VIP treatment that they likely never tasted back home even as they carefully controlled what the visitors were allowed to see.

One man eager to find Russia better than America was W.E.B. Du Bois, a leading American civil rights author and a founder in 1909 of the National Association for the Advancement of Colored People (NAACP). Du Bois believed that capitalism was the main cause of racism and therefore believed in socialism. After a 1926 visit to Russia, he expressed his admiration for the Soviet system:

> I stand in astonishment and wonder at the revelation of Russia that has come to me. I may be partially deceived and half informed. But if what I have seen with my eyes and heard with my ears in Russia is Bolshevism, then I am a Bolshevik.[10]

Du Bois would win the Lenin Peace Prize in 1959, indicating that the Soviet Union was well pleased with the work he was doing for their cause.

Another example of a committed American Communist clinging to his faith in the party—despite decades of evidence that Communism was an evil system—is folk singer Pete Seeger (1919-2014). In the 1960s, Seeger famously inspired the civil rights and peace movements with his crusading songs and activism. But earlier, in 1939, when he was a young man and Hitler entered into an alliance with Stalin (the Molotov-Ribbentrop Pact), Seeger campaigned for America to remain neutral and not support Britain and its allies (even after Germany and then Russia had invaded Poland). Then, a few years later in 1941, when Hitler turned on Stalin and invaded Russia, Seeger reversed himself 180 degrees—he now advocated for America to support the Allies against Germany because Russia now needed American help to fight Hitler. In other words, Seeger put the interests of the Communists and Stalin above those of his own country. He never abandoned his attachment to Communism, even after Khrushchev in 1956 revealed details of Stalin's Reign of Terror.

Addressing Communist Deception

The problem is, then, that while Marxism and other Leftist ideologies provide an atheistic roadmap to their idea of Utopia, albeit often deceptively wrapped in the language of altruism, Christianity and other religions and spiritual philosophies go only so far in setting out a credible alternative to these ideas. Thus, despite Marxism's unspeakably evil legacy, the Christian foundations of Western Civilization have as yet been unable to expose and decisively defeat the Marxist Utopian myth in the West, and in the East, the Asian traditions of Buddhism, Taoism and Confucianism have likewise been unable to stop and reverse the spread of the Marxist-Maoist Utopian myth.

The implication is clear: The movement to counter and defeat the Left needs to adopt a more robust and effective spiritual ideology. This new ideology must expose the lies and deceptions of Marxism and Neo-Marxism and provide a comprehensive alternative, an alternative that goes beyond the political dimension to embrace ideological and spiritual dimensions of truth. Ultimately, a new spiritual ideology must be fully aligned with Divine providence and show the way to establishing a good and just society on earth.

A Spiritual Ideology is Needed

We believe that the main purpose of a spiritual ideology is to explain good and evil and to show how good can triumph over evil. These two diametrically opposed categories of human behavior are often interpreted differently, based on differing beliefs and cultural traditions. But, in the main, the innate human sense of good and evil is facilitated by conscience and confirmed over time. Indeed, history is a record of conflict between good and evil that reveals the differences between the two. Goodness is the source of all justice, love and peace, while evil is the source of all injustice, suffering and war. The primordial struggle between good and evil has dominated, and continues to dominate, the lives of individuals and has shaped relationships among people, groups and nations from the beginning.

The universality of this struggle is reflected in the broad popularity of storytelling based on it, from Homer's epics and Shakespeare's plays to modern Westerns and movies like *Star Wars*. Why do people from all eras and all societies respond to these stories about good and evil? Surely it is because these dramatizations of what are in fact irreconcilable opposites resonate with our sense of what is right and wrong—and appeal to our natural desire for good to prevail over evil.

Why, then, are individuals and groups so wed to different beliefs as to what is good and evil? Are these categories only relative? To the extent that our knowledge of truth is always partial, there are bound to be differences in belief. These differences are deepened by education in opposing schools of thought, especially those based on materialist rather than spiritual principles. In an age of science, there should be less and less disagreement over important elements of the truth; yet here, precisely, is where the theories of the Left are problematic: They typically claim to have science on their side, when in fact they don't. Thus, for example, Marx and Engels claimed to have invented "scientific socialism," and radical environmentalists today claim to enjoy the support of a "scientific consensus." Both claims are false, as we will discuss in later chapters.

Today's Conflicts are Rooted in Ideology

Today, the world is facing ever more bitter conflicts caused by a moral divide that is tearing apart modern societies. This division reflects fundamental differences in how the two sides view human existence and purpose. In most modern states, both sides of the political divide claim to be guided by generally accepted norms of personal freedom and democratic government, but in fact the growing ideological conflicts point to very different beliefs about good and evil. To resolve these conflicts it is necessary to get beyond vapid platitudes claiming both sides are equally valid and recognize the very different outcomes produced by two very different ideologies that are at the root of societal divisions.

The impetus for the Left to reconsider its moral positions should come from the undeniable barbarity and economic failures of the socialist regimes in the 20th century. Both Hitler and Stalin established totalitarian regimes that inflicted unprecedented suffering on their own people and their enemies. Once crushed by the Allies, Nazism itself was put on trial at Nuremberg and has since become synonymous with evil to most people. Socialism and Communism, however, are more durable, and even though they are responsible for far worse crimes against humanity, have never been held to account. From Vladimir Lenin, Joseph Stalin, Nicolae Ceauçescu and Fidel Castro, in the West, to Mao Zedong, Kim Il Sung, Pol Pot and Ho Chi Minh, in the East, brutal Communist dictators are simply treated as historical figures of interest. Until humanity faces the truth of Communism and its history, and forcefully condemns it, we can expect more people to be deceived by it.

Although the sins of the Right pale next to those of the Left, it is nonetheless important to acknowledge that the record of the Right has often been shameful. Religious principles have been distorted to justify everything from slavery and the Crusades to the horrors of the Inquisition. And religious individuals and organizations have often supported evil ideas and regimes, including everything from torture to terrorism, often in the name of dubious ambitions, such as Jihad, or simply the political pragmatism of self-preservation.

The purpose of a spiritual ideology is to establish an intellectual and moral framework for separating good from evil and permanently replacing atheistic theories with the truth. Good and evil are abstract concepts that nevertheless produce very real consequences when acted on. Indeed, given our imperfect and conflicted state, we may not be able to recognize the differences between them until the results of the actions they cause become visible. Thanks to conscience, the moral values of individuals and societies have been able to evolve over time, resulting in advances in civilization. This is an encouraging sign, and it offers us the hope that the moral relativism of our experience can lead us to an absolute standard of morality, a standard that can secure the absolute dominance of good. After all, if there were no moral absolutes, there would be no hope of ever eliminating evil and replacing a world of injustice, suffering and war with one of justice, goodness and peace.

The divergence between spiritual and materialist ideologies is rooted in opposite beliefs about the origin and purpose of life and our existence. In the next chapter we will seek to compare theistic with atheistic beliefs in regard to the origin of life and answer the basic questions: What is the purpose of our existence, and how can we fulfill that purpose?

Chapter 2

In the Beginning

*Two Opposing Views of the Origin
and Purpose of Humankind*

The origin of human beings is an issue that divides people into two, often hostile camps. On one side are those who believe that we humans were created by a transcendent, divine being, whose nature is embedded in our own core being. On this side you find religion-based philosophies and the many cultural beliefs and institutions they have given rise to, including the belief that all goodness, truth and beauty flow from our Creator. On the other side are those who believe that we humans evolved from animals, and that the essence of human nature is found in instinctive and intellectual traits and behaviors that have evolved from more primitive lifeforms. On this side you find atheism and materialist philosophies that look to human intelligence and organization for goodness, truth and beauty.

It is easy to point to inadequacies on both sides. After all, neither would claim that the people and institutions on their side have reached a state of perfection. However, the characteristics, histories and trajectories of the two sides are radically different. Thus, for example, you can fault the religion of Judaism for the excesses of the Maccabees, Christianity for the predations of the Crusades, and Islam for Mohammed's ruthless beheading of Jews in Medina, but these atrocities do not compare in the extent of their evil with the murder of millions by the Nazis or tens of millions by the Soviet Union and Communist China.

Furthermore, religion itself does not approve of cruelty to others and censors selfish and malicious behavior, based on the belief that all people are created in the image of the Divine and therefore deserve respect. In contrast, the brutality of Nazism and Communism is prescribed by their ideologies, and historically the perpetrators of their violent and cruel revolutions and rulers of their brutal regimes have been rewarded with positions or power and influence.

Our purpose here, then, is twofold: to examine the foundational issues that divide spiritual from materialist views of life and then, in particular, to identify basic elements in Marxism that make it a theory antagonistic to a theistic belief in the origin and nature of humankind.

The Divine Purpose and Nature of Creation

It is a matter of logic that nothing is created by itself and that therefore we did not create ourselves. Indeed, creation is the manifestation of purpose in new existence: All creation, including humankind, has come into being with its purpose already established; it does not determine its own purpose. Thus in order to understand our purpose for existence we need to understand the purpose for which we were created. Having emerged from a state of gross ignorance, our understanding has unfolded only very slowly over centuries as enlightened individuals and groups have gained ever more knowledge of human nature and purpose.

Initially, the knowledge acquired was almost exclusively of a spiritual and religious nature. However, with the rise of basic science in Greece during the centuries before Jesus appeared, and then its full flowering in the wake of the Renaissance, our overall knowledge of the universe has increased exponentially. This explosion of knowledge gives us unprecedented power to influence the world around us, for good or evil, which makes it all the more important for us to understand our true, original purpose so that we can work to fulfill it by cultivating good and eliminating evil.

The most basic attribute of human nature is the desire for happiness. This is the driving force of life, from an infant's pursuit of its mother's milk to an adult's pursuit of love, wealth and power. Its universal manifestation in human nature tells us that happiness is the purpose for our existence and hence the purpose for which we were created. This is fully consistent with a Creator who is loving and good. It also explains the pleasure we experience in love and in the beauty of creation, with its infinite reflections of Divine purpose in the intricate designs and processes that make life possible.

The Harmonious Duality of Creator and Creation

How, then, do we fulfill our God-given purpose? In this book we contend that the human purpose to experience joy is accomplished when we establish harmonious relationships with our Creator, with other people, and with nature. This is achievable because all of nature is designed with complementary characteristics whose interactions are the basis for life. In simple terms, nature is composed of subject-object elements that engage in give-and-take action to exist and grow. These elements form harmonious dualities, such as male and female animals, stamens and pistils, and positively and negatively charged subatomic particles. Life requires the presence of these dual elements, and both subject and object fulfill their purpose through harmonious give and take with each other. (Note: This is not a duality of good and evil. Evil is antithetical to good: the perversion and nemesis of what is good. It can never be reconciled with good. It must be eliminated.)

That harmonious dualities are the basis for life implies that our Creator is likewise a being of dual characteristics, albeit in original, absolute and perfectly complementary form. As the central creative and organizing force of the universe, God made the whole creation in the image of Divine Nature and maintains order through laws that establish the order and proper behavior of its myriad elements. Human beings are the pinnacle of creation and most fully embody the Divine Nature. They are unlike the rest of creation in that they are endowed with an eternal spiritual being as well as a mortal physical being. This enables them to both enjoy an intimate relationship with the Creator and to exercise stewardship over nature; they mediate between the spiritual world of the Creator and the physical world of the rest of creation.

The Physical World and Spiritual World

The existence of an eternal human spirit points to the existence of an invisible spiritual world that complements and completes the physical world and is the eternal home for human spirits. The spirit is the internal embodiment of the Creator's dual nature; it is composed of both spiritual mind, or soul, and spiritual body. The eternal human spirit and mortal human body are a more fundamental aspect of duality than male and female attributes. In other words, we are spirit and body first, and man or woman second.

In this view, God is the source of both masculinity and femininity as well as both invisible causal and visible resultant elements in the creation. A human being grows through the interaction between spiritual and physical, a relationship in which the physical plays a limited yet vital role in enabling an individual to reach maturity and to reproduce. Eventually, the body dies, and the spirit continues its eternal existence in the spiritual world.

The existence of this invisible spiritual world is experienced in the life of every person, although most people never identify these experiences as such. Seeming coincidences, intuitions, flashes of insight, dreams, visions, moments of religious ecstasy and out-of-body experiences all derive from our contact with that intangible world. Many scientists, from Descartes and Mendeleev to Einstein, have spoken of this invisible influence in their lives and work. In 1927, Einstein explained his view:

> Try and penetrate with our limited means the secrets of nature and you will find that, behind all the discernible concatenations, there remains something subtle, intangible and inexplicable. Veneration for this force beyond anything

that we can comprehend is my religion. To that extent I am, in point of fact, religious.[11]

Another interesting perspective on the existence of an invisible, causal world is provided by Antony Flew, a life-long atheist philosopher who late in life reversed his position on God:

> I now believe that the universe was brought into existence by an infinite intelligence. I believe that this universe's intricate laws manifest what scientists have called the Mind of God. I believe that life and reproduction originate in a divine Source.
>
> Why do I believe this, given that I expounded and defended atheism for more than half a century? The short answer is this: this is the world picture as I see it, that has emerged from modern science. Science spotlights three dimensions of nature that point to God. The first is the fact that nature obeys laws. The second is the dimension of life, of intelligently organized and purpose-driven beings, which arose from matter. The third is the very existence of nature. But it is not science alone that has guided me. I have also been helped by a renewed study of the classical philosophical arguments.[12]

The Materialist View of Existence

For the atheist and materialist, there is no reason to believe in the existence of a universal desire for happiness, let alone a Divine design that enables human beings to achieve happiness. For them, the very existence of life and the characteristics of human beings and other creatures are nothing more than products of evolutionary forces governed by laws which have themselves emerged (magically?) from the chaos of the Big Bang. They assume that if they search long and hard enough, they will eventually discover the secret of life in the physical world, either on Planet Earth or elsewhere. But they won't succeed. Life cannot come from non-life. It can only come from life, whose origin is spiritual, not physical.

As a theory of existence, materialism is much younger than religion. It evolved in recent centuries after science began to break free from religious dogmas in the Renaissance, which began in the 14th century. From that time science has grown to become the most trusted form of knowledge, while in increasingly secular societies religion has been relegated to the realm of untrustworthy belief, tradition and superstition. Science is predicated on the ability to prove theories through experimentation and observation, based on the assumption that there are immutable laws that govern the universe.

Materialist philosophies typically claim science as the basis for their credibility. But what they can't explain are the intangible but very real phenomena of emotion, such as love, hate and empathy, and of intellect, such as reason, memory and imagination. These, as well as the even more mysterious spiritual phenomena of life, are said by materialists to be functions of the human brain and natural features of the physical world. Thus materialists believe in an arbitrary world devoid of transcendent purpose and absolutes, moral or otherwise. Their world offers no enduring hope or happiness.

Dialectical Materialism

The most influential materialist theories are Marxism and its Neo-Marxist offshoots in the Critical Theories of the Frankfurt School and Postmodernism. We describe the genesis and main features of Marxism in Chapter 10 and its offshoots in Chapters 14-16. However, at this point it will be helpful to briefly introduce the Marxist concept of what Stalin called dialectical materialism.

According to this theory, all beings are composed of contradictory elements, which naturally enter into conflict with each other as part of a process whereby the original entity (thesis) is challenged by its antithesis. Out of this struggle emerges the antithesis of the antithesis (the negation of the negation), which is called the synthesis. This synthesis is a new thesis that is also imperfect and so contains within itself conflicting elements that will inevitably engage in a new round of dialectical struggle. Marx and Engels believed that this dialectical process explained everything from natural evolution to human history. More importantly, it justified violent revolution by aggrieved classes against their rulers. (For a Marxist's explanation of dialectical materialism, see Appendix 3, p299.)

Dialectical materialism is essentially the materialist theory used to deconstruct language and social institutions in Critical Theories. These conflict-based theories of nature are fundamentally at odds with the view that all creation embodies harmonious elements derived from the Creator, as we have described above. As we will show, dialectical materialism and Critical Theories are themselves relatively recent constructs that rationalize what are in fact age-old characteristics of what we call fallen nature, that is of humankind in a state of alienation from God. Dialectical Materialism and Critical Theories are not scientifically sound explanations of nature or of human beings as originally created. As such they only serve to systematize and strengthen rebellion against the Divine and destruction of the beauty of creation.

Consequences of Atheistic Ideology

Marxism does not recognize the existence of an eternal human spirit, believing spiritual phenomena to be a function of the physical human being, mind and body. This view is also consistent with the Postmodernist idea that human beliefs and experiences are a function of societal influences. These materialist views are dehumanizing since they deny the spiritual core of our human nature and existence. They also excuse the brutalization of people in the name of ideological agendas that see men and women as nothing more than highly evolved animals. The lack of a moral compass based on an understanding of the eternal value of humankind is a common feature of totalitarian regimes— and is directly responsible for the cruel treatment inflicted on tens of millions of victims by Hitler, Lenin, Stalin, Mao, Pol Pot and other dictators who justified their brutality with materialist ideologies.

The Complementary Nature of Religion and Science

For most of human existence knowledge of the world and human existence was guided by observations that were filtered through religious beliefs and superstitions. This began to change when, in the centuries preceding the Christian era, ancient Greece gave birth to great thinkers, such as Pythagoras, Eratosthenes and Aristarchus, who studied the world around them with intense curiosity. They discovered basic laws of nature, including the fact that the earth is round, not flat, and that it circles the sun, not vice versa. At the same time, Greek philosophers like Socrates and Plato developed methods of intellectual inquiry based on reason and deduction, planting the seeds of science-based civilization.

These ideas would bear fruit some two millennia later when in the 16th century Nicolaus Copernicus, a Polish cleric, mathematician and astronomer, also argued that the earth circled the sun. He was followed by Galileo Galilei, who was tried for heresy by the Catholic Church. By this time the Renaissance was underway and the movement to explore the universe free from the constraints of religious dogma now led to the development of modern science, based on observation, reason and experimentation. In just a few centuries, science would emerge as the most trusted field of knowledge. In time, an overconfidence in science would cause many (especially materialist thinkers) to unwisely put all their trust in it, even though science has been unable to answer the deeper questions of life.

Marx and Engels wanted a complete divorce between religion and science. Lenin explained the Marxist antipathy to religion in his book *Religion*: "Atheism is a natural and inseparable part of Marxism, of the theory and practice of scientific socialism."[13] In *The Attitude of the Workers' Party to Religion*, Lenin elaborated: "Religion is the opium of the people: this saying of Marx is the cornerstone of the entire ideology of Marxism about religion. All modern religions and churches, all and every kind of religious organizations are always considered by Marxism as the organs of bourgeois reaction, used for the protection of the exploitation and the stupefaction of the working class."[14]

Yet the absolutist rejection of religion by Marxism makes no more sense than religion's earlier absolutist rejection of science. Religion and science should not be seen as antithetical but as fundamentally compatible and complementary. They both seek to understand the universe, which is a single existence endowed with its Creator's harmonious characteristics and single purpose. In maturity, human beings assume the responsibility of co-creators with God—a responsibility they can fulfill by developing the internal qualities necessary to exercise a wise dominion and stewardship over the internal, spiritual world of religious belief and knowledge, as well as the external, physical world of science and technology. Both the internal and external dimensions of our universe play vital roles in our existence.

Albert Einstein wrote about the complementarity of religion and science. Here is one of his statements:

> Now, even though the realms of religion and science in themselves are clearly marked off from each other, nevertheless there exist between the two strong reciprocal relationships and dependencies. Though religion may be that which determines the goal, it has, nevertheless, learned from science, in the broadest sense, what means will contribute to the attainment of the goals it has set up. But science can only be created by those who are thoroughly imbued with the aspiration towards truth and understanding. This source of feeling, however, springs from the sphere of religion. To this there also belongs the faith in the possibility that the regulations valid for the world of existence are rational, that is, comprehensible to reason. I cannot conceive of a genuine scientist without that profound faith. The situation may be expressed by an image: Science without religion is lame, religion without science is blind.[15]

There is an area within science that is exploring human experiences that cannot be explained as functions of a physical brain, namely those that relate to existence beyond the realm of the physical world. Through studying near-death experiences and other phenomena of human life that point to aspects of the mind that cannot be a function of physical existence and the human brain, scientists are challenging the materialism (or physicalism, as it is now more commonly called) that had been considered an axiomatic foundation of scientific knowledge. Two excellent books on this area of research that are, respectively, co-written and co-edited by Edward Kelly of the University of Virginia, are included in the Bibliography: *Irreducible Mind; Toward a Psychology for the 21ˢᵗ Century*, and *Beyond Physicalism: Toward Reconciliation of Science and Spirituality*.

Human Growth to Maturity

The human thirst for perfection, whether spiritual or physical, implies the possibility of its achievement. Whether we look back to the innocence of Eden before the Fall, or forward to paradise or heaven, we sense that the current state of human imperfection does not reflect our original purpose. In our view, the Biblical story of Adam and Eve succumbing to temptation implies that they were not yet spiritually and mentally mature at the time of the Fall. This leaves us with the obvious question: What would have likely happened if they had been obedient to God? In other words, what was their original, unfulfilled purpose? This is not merely a matter for academic speculation. It is our understanding that their existence itself represented the final stage of God's creative work, implying that we share with them an ultimate purpose and destiny. Therefore, determining exactly how they failed is extremely important for us, who inherited their nature and are continuously confronted with choices between good and evil.

Perfecting Love Through Three Blessings

Again, the Bible provides an answer: Human beings are endowed with a purpose in the form of Three Blessings. Adam and Eve were told: "Be fruitful and multiply, and fill the earth and subdue it; and have dominion over the fish of the sea and over the birds of the air and over every living thing that moves upon the earth." (Genesis 1:28). These blessings encompass the three main axes of human life: our vertical relationship with a parental Creator, our horizontal relationships with other people (especially family), and our stewardship of nature. By perfecting the Three Blessings we become true objects of Divine love, cultivating within ourselves a heart of love that enables us to understand and respond to our Creator's heart and to become co-creators with God.

The first blessing is foundational. It recognizes the fact of our creation as an embodiment of God's own attributes, which makes us co-creators with a capacity to love and reason. Unlike any other creature, we have free will, which is necessary for love, and which in turn is the basis for our relationships with our Creator, with other people and with nature. To be fruitful is to grow to maturity in love by exercising our free will responsibly.

The second blessing is the fulfillment of loving human relationships. Men and women reach maturity by learning to reciprocate the love they receive from their parents and then loving their siblings and others as brothers and sisters. On this foundation, they can enter into conjugal relationships and produce and raise children of their own.

The third blessing is extending mature love beyond other people to the rest of nature in the form of wise stewardship.

Free Will and Personal Responsibility

Human beings are endowed with free will, which enables us to choose between obedience and disobedience, good and evil. This uniquely human attribute is the basis for love, which by its nature must be freely given. It cannot be coerced. Thus fulfilling the Three Blessings is conditioned on us exercising our free will responsibly, in accordance with Divine purpose. Conversely, failing to fulfill our responsibility condemns us to a life of alienation from the Creator that is characterized by broken relationships and suffering.

In the next chapter we will put forward an explanation for the original reasons for this alienation, but at this point it is worth noting that the sadness and suffering we experience in life, and see all around us, are not what was originally intended for the creation by our Creator. We are living in a world that is very distant from the ideal we have described above, a world in which The Three Blessings remain unfulfilled. Suffice it to say that the tragedy of human alienation occurred because of failures by our first ancestors to exercise their free will wisely. Reversing their failures through the thoughtful exercise of free will became the central purpose of providential history and remains the primary goal of restoration today.

We can see, then, that the fulfillment of our Creator's purpose, from the original creation through the providence to restore fallen humanity, is dependent upon we human beings fulfilling our God-given responsibilities as co-creators. This is an unchanging law. It should be taught by all religions, and is taught by many. In the Bible, personal responsibility is first established in instructions given to the first people created, with the warning that disobedience will mean death. It was also the central tenant of the first laws revealed to the Israelites, the Mosaic Law, which clearly links the response of the Israelites to Divine instructions with the outcomes they can expect: If they are obedient they will be blessed; if disobedient they will be cursed. This message is repeated to them by Moses again and again. For example, he gave this warning from God to the Israelites before they entered the "Promised Land":

> See, I have set before you today life and good, death and evil. If you obey the commandments of the LORD your God that I command you today, by loving the LORD your God, by walking in his ways, and by keeping his commandments and his statutes and his rules, then you shall live and multiply, and the LORD your God will bless you in the land that you are entering to take possession of it. But if your heart turns away, and you will not hear, but are drawn away to worship other gods and serve them, I declare to you today, that you shall surely perish. You shall not live long in the land that you are going over the Jordan to enter and possess. I call heaven and earth to witness against you today, that I have set before you life and death, blessing and curse. Therefore choose life, that you and your offspring may live, loving the LORD

your God, obeying his voice and holding fast to him, for he is your life and length of days, that you may dwell in the land that the LORD swore to your fathers, to Abraham, to Isaac, and to Jacob, to give them. (Deuteronomy 30:15-20)

The Importance of Marriage and the Family

As seen from the Three Blessings described above, the family is the most important human institution. Through it, children grow in understanding and love, becoming good individuals, siblings and parents. Good societies and nations are built on good families and, inversely, broken families create dysfunctional societies of violence and crime. This underscores the importance and sanctity of marriage between a man and a woman—and ultimately elevates us to the status of wise co-creators with God.

Tellingly, Marx and Engels called for the abolition of the family. In *The Communist Manifesto*, they wrote: "Abolition of the family! Even the most radical [people] flare up at this infamous proposal of the Communists. On what foundation is the present family, the bourgeois family, based? On capital, on private gain. In its completely developed form, this family exists only among the bourgeoisie." (Appendix 1, p280.)

The twisted view that families are only a feature of oppressive classes reveals just how stilted and out of touch with science Marx and Engels were. The Communist war against the family is an integral element of a war against God, because good families are the place where love of God and other people is best nurtured. This pernicious Marxist teaching has remained a central part of all subsequent Neo-Marxist ideology; it is responsible for the wholesale destruction of families in Socialist and Communist countries as well as widespread social dislocation and human misery caused by Leftist movements to this day.

In its atheism and belief that families must be destroyed, Marxism is diametrically opposed to the Divine design for creation—but perfectly in line with the behavior of Lucifer/Satan who destroyed God's original family, as we will explain in the next chapter. More than any of its economic or political theories, the core anti-family beliefs of Marxism make it the greatest threat to a world of enduring love, justice and peace. Like Rousseau before him, Marx rebelled against the discipline of obedience to a higher authority. Believing in a godless world, he imagined that he himself could play god.

This mentality would become a characteristic of Leftist intellectuals, and especially those identified with the Neo-Marxism of the Frankfurt School and Postmodernism. As Paul Johnson describes so well in his book, *Intellectuals*, the typical thinker of the Left suffers from massive egoism and, from a perch far above the masses, prescribes solutions for the world's problems that never work when applied. Their love for abstract values of peace and justice never translates into caring for the individuals in their lives, and most are responsible for terrible treatment of family members and friends. All too often their anti-religious and anti-family theories serve as an excuse for their own immoral behavior. The broader result is, however, that they provide an ideological basis for society-wide abandonment of morality, as witnessed both in the brutal treatment of individuals by totalitarian regimes and in the collapse of moral standards in industrialized countries.

In this book we advocate for the strengthening of traditional family values as the basis for rejecting the prescriptions of the Left and reversing civilizational decline. As we will explain in detail, we believe that the attitudes and theories of the Left have deep roots in the origin of evil itself, and that Divine providence is aimed at reversing their influence and restoring godly values to the world.

We Hold the Key to Our Future

In the Introduction, we pointed out that good and evil cannot coexist. In this chapter we have shown that because of free will we are able to choose between good and evil. Our fulfillment of the Three Blessings, then, is determined by the moral choices we make. It's up to us to marshal our free will to accomplish our God-given purpose. This fact explains the paradox of a loving and omnipotent Creator existing while humanity remains rife with ungodly ideas and behavior. The Creator is restrained from removing evil from the world by the very nature and principles by which we humans were made. We will always be free to love or hate, but the future of a good and loving world that we long for can only be attained if we choose to love and reject hate.

The next chapter explains the cause for our alienation from God. This account also holds the key to understanding the process of restoring men and women to their original purpose that has played out over the course of human history.

Chapter 3

The Origin of Evil

Human Alienation from God

The Biblical Account of Evil's Origin

The Bible gives us an account of the original human failure to grow responsibly to maturity and the consequent disaster that befell humanity. It is a story about God's hope for creation; about the disobedience of Lucifer, Adam and Eve; and about their consequent loss of innocence and descent into evil. The relevance of this story is not in its literal authenticity but in its revelation of truths about behavior and relationships that apply to this day.

This is a story that materialists naturally dismiss because it is based on the existence of an invisible Creator and invisible angel, on the one hand, and prehistoric people, on the other. Yet truth undoubtedly resides in the unseen and the unknown, and materialists themselves have no good explanations for either the origin of life or the existence of evil.

All people relate to stories of good and evil, and much of popular literature and art is based on the age-old contest between them. In the case of religion, these stories also form an important element of belief and faith. The hugely popular *The Lord of the Rings* trilogy by J.R.R. Tolkien is a story about an epic struggle in a mythical land where the forces of evil threaten to destroy all that is good. As the two sides prepare for war, we get glimpses of a distant past when good prevailed, a past filled with tales of courage and nobility forgotten by most but still echoing in the memories of some. Tolkien, a man of faith, explained how myth can be the key to truth and to understanding an original world before human alienation from the Creator:

> Just as speech is invention about objects and ideas, so myth is invention about truth. We have come from God, and inevitably the myths woven by us, though they contain error, will also reflect a splintered fragment of the true light, the eternal truth that is with God. Indeed, only by mythmaking, only by becoming a 'sub-creator' and inventing stories, can Man ascribe to the state of perfection that he knew before the Fall.[16]

The sinless state that Adam and Eve enjoyed in the Garden of Eden before the Fall, referenced by Tolkien, is forever engraved on our (usually subconscious) hearts and minds. It is the original nature we too are endowed with. Thus the extent to which the Biblical account is myth, it is myth based on truth that resonates with our innate sense of what is good and what is evil. Our deepest nature yearns for the original state of innocence and is excited and inspired by glimpses of it in life, in literature and in art. The more we understand and taste it, the more we want it, which explains the universal allure of heaven. It also explains why false prophets and false ideologies have been able to tap into this ingrained idealism, leading sincere but naïve people astray by promising them fake facsimiles of heaven in the form of materialist Utopias.

Materialists reject the truth of the Biblical account of Adam and Eve in the Garden of Eden because it is predicated on the existence of an omnipotent Creator, whose existence they deny. In their view, humanity was not created by a loving God and is not seeking to regain a lost intimacy with the Creator, but rather is a highly evolved animal whose aspirations for a better life are based solely on satisfying human needs for intellectual and physical gratification. If they are correct in this, a reasonable person would expect the application of their ideologies to achieve significant progress against evil and injustice and the elevation of civilization's standards. In fact, history has shown that the opposite is true—wherever materialist theories have been applied, people have suffered, and civilization has been ravaged. We have to look much deeper than materialist ideology to find the real source of evil.

The Fall as a Perversion of Divine Love

Let us go back to the story of the Garden of Eden and reconsider the relationships among Adam, Eve and Lucifer. (See Appendix 4, pp311-315, for a transcript of relevant passages in Genesis.) According to the Genesis story, God told Adam and Eve that they could eat of any fruit in the garden except the fruit of the Tree the Knowledge of Good and Evil. However, the archangel Lucifer, symbolized as a serpent, tempted Eve to eat this very fruit, which she then gave to Adam to eat.

Taken at its face value, this story hardly provides a credible explanation for the likely origin of evil. The grip of fallen nature on human beings is much more powerful and deadly than the temptation to eat prohibited food. After all, Adam and Eve were warned: "…but of the tree of the knowledge of good and evil you shall not eat, for in the day that you eat of it you shall die." (Genesis 2:17) There must be a deeper meaning to this account, one that explains our alienation from God, our own struggles with evil, and the many manifestations of evil in history and the present world.

A more likely explanation is this. Lucifer was the being closest to God before the birth of Adam and Eve. As children they were under the archangel's care. As they grew to maturity, however, they received more and more of God's love, to the point when Lucifer saw his own position of privilege being overshadowed by them and believed the love he was receiving from God was diminishing relative to what they were receiving. In other words, he began to look at Adam and Eve from his own, selfish perspective, rather than sharing in the Parent's love for their children. Divine love is infinite. It flows to the creation that embodies Divine nature. The love Lucifer received as a trusted servant did not diminish, but it was of a different nature from that given to

Adam and Eve, God's children. When Lucifer began to entertain these divisive and ultimately destructive thoughts, he started down a path that would lead to the tragedy of the Fall.

As Adam and Eve became ever more fully the incarnation of Divine nature, they received ever deeper love from their Creator. Lucifer's erroneous viewpoint caused him to feel increasingly jealous and resentful towards Adam, and desirous of love from Eve, who was maturing in beauty. Unchecked, these impulses drove him to usurp Adam's role as the chosen spouse of Eve and to tempt Eve into an illicit sexual relationship. (Eve's spiritual body made this liaison possible.)

The First Lie

In order to win over Eve, Lucifer (the Serpent) deceived her with a lie, promising her that if she believed him rather than God she would not die but would become God-like:

> Now the serpent was more subtle than any other wild creature that the Lord God had made. He said to the woman, "Did God say, 'You shall not eat of any tree of the garden'?" And the woman said to the serpent, "We may eat of the fruit of the trees of the garden; but God said, 'You shall not eat of the fruit of the tree which is in the midst of the garden, neither shall you touch it, lest you die.'" But the serpent said to the woman, "You will not die. For God knows that when you eat of it your eyes will be opened, and you will be like God, knowing good and evil. (Genesis 3:1-5)

This was the first lie. It would make deception and dishonesty the hallmarks of evil and lead to the destruction of the first family. Lying became intrinsic to fallen nature, passing from parents to children and manifesting in what we call Cain-type thinking and action. As we will show, this nature has shaped the history of harmful ideologies, organizations and nations, and continues to characterize the forces of evil to this day.

But why would Eve respond to Lucifer's deception? The power of love is stronger than the fear of death, and she was not as yet sufficiently mature to control her own feelings and resist Lucifer's temptation. In the Old Testament, to know a woman meant having a sexual relationship with her. Genesis 24:16 says of Isaac's future wife Rebekah: "The maiden was very fair to look upon, a virgin, whom no man had known." Thus the Tree of the Knowledge of Good and Evil represented sexual experience that was not in accord with Divine law.

The preeminent power of love is by Divine design because love is the binding force of creation. It is more precious than life since it gives life purpose and meaning. Once subject and object are united in perfected love, nothing can separate them. At the time of the Fall, Adam and Eve were still growing, and their love was not yet perfected. To protect them against sinning while they matured, they had been told to not "eat of the fruit."

Lucifer's seduction of Eve violated his position of trust and caused him to lose his relationship with God. Eve, too, left her rightful position as spouse of Adam to pursue a relationship with Lucifer, and then to seduce Adam. Finally, Adam compounded these acts of disobedience by responding to Eve and entering into a relationship of love with her before they had reached maturity and could fulfill the responsibility of parents. Thus the violation of the Divine order through the misuse of love is the origin of evil.

Because of his role as instigator of this series of tragic events, Lucifer became synonymous with the serpent, the Devil and Satan. (Revelation 12:9)

We can relate this explanation of the Fall to our own life experiences, to what we know about our world, and what we know of human nature and history. Only for love will people risk their lives, whether it be love for a person, an idea, a possession or a country. Used wisely, love brings the greatest joy. Misused, it brings the greatest misery.

As with all the false promises that have deceived humanity and destroyed lives throughout history, Lucifer's promise to Eve—that she would become god-like—proved to be false. Instead, Eve found herself cut off from the love of God and beset with guilt inherited from Lucifer. She did indeed come to know evil by eating the fruit, but that evil was now planted deep inside her own nature and was impossible for her to remove by herself. From this position of alienation from God, she recognized her spiritual distance from Adam. But instead of seeking his assistance in overcoming the results of her fall, she encouraged him to "eat the fruit" as well. Thus instead of Adam rescuing Eve from her state of spiritual alienation from God, he joined her in that alienation.

We contend, then, that although wrapped in metaphorical language, Genesis actually describes an illicit relationship between Lucifer and Eve, which led to a premature relationship between Adam and Eve. Only after reaching maturity could the first couple fulfill the mission to establish a family at one with the Creator—and their inability to overcome temptation showed that they were as yet immature. Their misuse of Divine love explains why the Divine purpose for the first family and all humanity was thwarted at the outset of human existence. The first family became the dwelling of Satan—not God—and the descendants of Adam and Eve were likewise infected with sinful nature. The Fall of the first family was complete.

Jesus would make humanity's inheritance of a lying and murderous nature from Lucifer crystal clear:

> You are of your father the devil, and your will is to do your father's desires. He was a murderer from the beginning, and has nothing to do with the truth, because there is no truth in him. When he lies, he speaks according to his own nature, for he is a liar and the father of lies. (John 8:44)

Results of the Fall

Lucifer's jealousy and resentment towards Adam, his illicit love for Eve, and his consequent irresponsible, destructive and vengeful behavior towards both of them, became the core attributes of evil nature that we recognize in ourselves and the world around us. Acting on his self-centered impulses, Lucifer infected Adam and Eve with poisonous thoughts and feelings that alienated them from God. In effect, he was responsible for their spiritual murder. In addition, his fallen characteristics became the sinful essence of the first family and the inheritance of Cain and Abel and all their descendants. In the next chapter we will elaborate on the influence of this sinful inheritance and the way it can be rooted out of human lineage.

The traditional interpretation of the story of the Fall has never explained more than the importance of obedience to God. This is a meaningful lesson, but our contention that the real cause of the Fall was the misuse of love explains why sexual relations are so often the locus of temptations that lead to destructive behavior. On the personal level, cultivating godly love is the most important and challenging issue we face in our lives, while on the cultural level it is the key to establishing loving and healthy societies. Furthermore, history shows that civilizations decline when they abandon the moral values and discipline needed to retain the integrity of nuclear families. This is the essence of the problem facing our civilization today.

The perversion of love as the cause of the Fall also explains why so many exponents of atheistic or agnostic ideology, from Marx to Foucault, have personal histories of irresponsible sexual behavior and advocate for the abolition of traditional families. For them, disbelief in the Divine easily translates into disbelief in the value and sanctity of the nuclear family. In the last century, the sexual revolution initiated by the Frankfurt School led to social chaos and countless personal tragedies, a trajectory of human behavior that continues to reap a bitter harvest of broken relationships and shattered dreams. The Postmodernists have taken sexual liberation theories even further by challenging the basic order of nature, claiming that gender identity is different from biological sex. Tellingly, the most active Leftist groups in the West today, Antifa and Black Lives Matter, both embrace and advocate anti-family ideology and are led by people who do not adhere to traditional sexual norms.

Enduring Consequences

It is not difficult to see that separated from the Parent Creator and Teacher, our early ancestors were plunged into a primitive state of existence in which they suffered from a continuous conflict between their originally good natures, on the one hand, and their susceptibility to do evil, on the other. It is from this alienated state of spiritual and intellectual darkness and ignorance that human beings have struggled to understand themselves and their world, initially through religion and later through science as well. Ever since the Fall, the struggle for knowledge and wisdom has progressed in fits and starts as our ancestors have tried to understand the internal truths of existence and human relationships and the external laws that govern the natural world. This human state of confusion is a midway position between two competing influences: One is good, encouraging us to take the path of responsibility envisioned in the original creation; the other is evil, encouraging us to act on our self-centered impulses by blaming others and seeking revenge for perceived injustices.

The struggle to be good has been so difficult because evil has, from the time of our earliest ancestors, dominated good. This was demonstrated when Cain, the elder son, murdered his brother Abel. As the firstborn, Cain enjoyed the natural primogenital right to inherit his parents' legacy. However, this legacy was that of the Fall, not of a good family and world. Abel suffered under the domination of his brother, as have all Abel-type figures in our Cain-dominated world. As we will demonstrate, humanity progresses when Abel succeeds in winning over Cain, ideologically or practically, but is set back when Cain dominates and destroys Abel. According to this Cain-Abel paradigm, good has had to struggle against the dominance of evil, which offers a false facsimile of the good to seduce the vulnerable. However, history shows that with Divine providence on their side, wise and sacrificial Abels have advanced the cause of good.

As we will show, Marxism and Critical Theories are the culmination of a history of false ideologies based on Cain-type thinking and action, based on deceptions and outright lies. Marx and Engels looked at the world as if it was in its original state and not as a corrupt, Cain-type facsimile of the original. They never realized that this was not the world originally intended, and consequently they developed a theory that embodied the spirit and substance of evil that Cain inherited from his parents and, ultimately, from Lucifer. They misidentified capitalism as the source of evil and Communism as the good alternative. Their Critical Theory descendants went further by denying the biological basis of the natural order and the moral basis for social order, replacing traditional families with a chaotic, Luciferian hell.

The Creator's Parental Nature

In a state of ignorance, how can we ever regain the lost knowledge of the ideal world of Eden? And how can we ever restore Divine love to its rightful place at the center of our lives and society? Our hope lies in a Creator who cares, who is more eager than we are to see people restored to their true selves so that they can achieve their full potential. The characteristics that make us distinctly human reveal that our Maker must be the original source of love as well as having the capacity to experience the pain of separation and failure. This is not the distant Creator of Deism but the loving Parent of all humankind. The parental heart of our Creator is, then, the spiritual force behind the Divine providence that seeks to guide humanity to its proper place in the universe.

Most of us recognize that the love and heart of a parent for their children is the highest expression of human emotion. Indeed, it is the most profound aspect of this love that renders us, as parents, most vulnerable to the responses we receive from our children. If we have been endowed with the capacity for such sacrificial, all-embracing love for our children, might not our Creator/Parent be the origin of such profound love? And might we not conclude that our own capacities for great joy and profound grief reflect our Creator's own experiences of joy and grief with us?

We Are Not Alone

If so, there is reason to hope that we are not alone. A parental heart is broken by the suffering of children, but it is also determined to save them for better things, for the best possible future. If Almighty God were not parentally inclined, what would prevent the Creator from becoming the Destroyer: putting an end to human beings if not the whole of creation? Indeed, would that not be more merciful since human suffering would be curtailed? According to Genesis, there was such a time when God destroyed all but the family of Noah. That didn't work. Evil survived the flood. Since then, however, scriptures indicate that our Creator has been striving for millennia to save humankind from destruction. There must be an ultimately good telos, a good future for humanity that justifies this effort and the love for us it represents.

The other cause for hope is that we humans have free will. We don't need to repeat forever the disobedience of Adam and Eve or the murder of Abel by Cain. We can choose differently. Again, history confirms that when human beings choose to obey the Divine and do what is right, their efforts are rewarded with civilizational progress.

To begin to understand how the wrong of the Fall can finally be righted, we can look to the children of Adam and Eve. On one level, Cain's murder of Abel marked a repetition of the Fall in which the servant Lucifer destroyed God's children, Adam and Eve; yet their story also reveals a strategy for isolating and ultimately overcoming evil. This is what we will examine in the next chapter.

Chapter 4

The Way of Abel

A Divine Strategy for Human Restoration

To understand the process of restoration, or salvation, it is necessary to understand the principles that govern it. A starting point is to recognize that our Creator exists and creates according to divine law and therefore works through divine law to reverse the alienation of humankind. The object of the process of restoration is to separate evil from good and then to eliminate evil. And while this is ultimately an internal process of purification, persons infected with evil, as were Adam and Eve, are not able by themselves to recognize and eliminate the evil that is part of their spiritual and mental makeup. Thus good and evil are first separated by being externalized in representatives with differing levels of purity and goodness. Neither is perfect but one is closer to an absolute standard of goodness than the other and therefore is used to elevate both of them.

Cain and Abel Archetypes of Evil and Good

The Bible recounts the story of Cain's murder of Abel as follows:

> In the course of time Cain brought to the Lord an offering of the fruit of the ground, and Abel brought of the firstlings of his flock and of their fat portions. And the Lord had regard for Abel and his offering, but for Cain and his offering he had no regard. So Cain was very angry, and his countenance fell. The Lord said to Cain, "Why are you angry, and why has your countenance

fallen? If you do well, will you not be accepted? And if you do not do well, sin is couching at the door; its desire is for you, but you must master it." Cain said to his brother Abel, "Let us go out to the field." And when they were in the field, Cain rose up against his brother Abel and killed him. (Genesis 4:3-8)

A similar account is found in the Quran, in which the key figures of the first family are Adam, Hawa (Eve), Qabeel (Cain) and Habeel (Abel). Cain's murder of Abel is described as follows:

And recite thou to them the story of the two sons of Adam truthfully, when they offered a sacrifice, and it was accepted of one of them, and not accepted of the other. I will surely slay thee, said one. God accepts only of the god-fearing, said the other. Yet if thou stretchest out thy hand against me, to slay me, I will not stretch out my hand against thee to slay thee; I fear God, the Lord of all Being ... Then his soul prompted him to slay his brother, and he slew him, and he became one of the losers. (Sura 5:27-28, 30).

As the first offspring of humans after their alienation from God, Cain and Abel became the archetypal representatives of evil and good, respectively, and their relationship became the paradigm for the historical struggle between the opposing forces of good and evil. As the first born, Cain represented Eve's first relationship of love, with Lucifer, which was illicit, while Abel represented her second relationship of love, with Adam. This second relationship was premature and also forbidden, but it was less sinful since Adam and Eve were destined to be blessed in marriage by God. Thus Cain became the archetype of evil and Abel the archetype of good, albeit in a relative sense of good and evil.

When Cain's offering was rejected, he became angry and resentful, blaming God and Abel for his own failure. Unable to control his bitterness and rage, he killed his brother in a brutal attack. This murder repeated, rather than reversed, the spiritual murder of Adam and Eve by Lucifer and sealed the alienation of the first family from God. Consequently, the providence of restoration could not begin in the family of Adam and Eve but was postponed until a new central family could be chosen for that mission.

Thus the character of Cain became the model for attitudes and behaviors that we recognize as destructive and evil. It is a character that rebels against the supremacy of God and refuses to accept Divine authority. It is consequently arrogant, resentful of the success of others, and unwilling to take responsibility for its own mistakes and failures. Filled with bitterness and self-pity, the Cain-type character justifies vengeful and violent behavior, including murder. It is the root of greed and jealousy, of crime and warmongering.

All these unpleasant and harmful traits are displayed in the histories of Cain-type people, tribes, nations and ideologies. But they have never been as fully realized as in the Marxist and Neo-Marxist ideologies and the history of Socialist and Communist regimes. It is for this reason, too, that so many good and conscientious people today feel so oppressed by the Left with its dark theories and pernicious influence on society and the world as a whole. Like the black clouds of Mordor stretching across a once-blue sky, the prospect of continued ascendancy by the Left sends shivers of fear and trepidation through the hearts and minds of righteous people everywhere.

But what of Abel? Can we expect him to appear as our liberator in this dark hour? If so, how?

The Difficult Way of Abel

Abel is endowed with a character that is less burdened than Cain by the weight of fallen nature inherited from our ancestors. However, with this blessing comes a greater responsibility to set an example of virtue and self-sacrifice. Abel may receive Divine revelations, but he is then responsible for sharing them with the world and helping Cain find his way to God. Jesus understood, taught and demonstrated the way of Abel better than anyone in history. Asked which commandment of the Law of Moses was the most important, he said there were two that summarized all the teachings of the prophets and the law:

You shall love the Lord your God with all your heart, and with all your soul,

39

and with all your mind. This is the great and first commandment. And a second is like it, You shall love your neighbor as yourself. On these two commandments depend all the law and the prophets. (Matthew 22:37-40)

In the Beatitudes Jesus listed the virtues we should aspire to, including purity, humility, righteousness and peacemaking. (Matthew 5) Saint Paul described the way of Abel in terms of love:

Love is patient and kind; love is not jealous or boastful; it is not arrogant or rude. Love does not insist on its own way; it is not irritable or resentful; it does not rejoice at wrong, but rejoices in the right. Love bears all things, believes all things, hopes all things, endures all things. (I Corinthians 13:4-7)

But the way of Abel is never easy. History demonstrates that often the person or party called upon to represent Abel's position and fulfill the attendant responsibilities has failed to do so, resulting in the ascendancy of Cain. Why is this so? It is because the path of Abel is daunting, often requiring great courage and sacrifice. Abel is responsible not only for his own behavior but also for helping Cain to overcome his tendencies to do evil. In contrast, Cain is required only to confront his own fallen nature and accept the guidance of Abel. Although Abel is the younger brother, in effect he must become parent-like to Cain, winning him over to the side of good through humility and service and, if necessary, sacrifice of himself to stop Cain from harming others.

Historically, Abel's struggle to fulfill his purpose and win over Cain has often been a path of suffering and bloodshed. An evil and aggressive Cain must be confronted with clarity and resolve; it cannot be surrendered to. Sometimes Abel has to resort to force to contain and defeat Cain. For example, in recent history Britain had to commit all its human and material resources to the battle to stop Hitler's Germany, at the cost of hundreds of thousands of lives. America, too, reluctantly declared war against Japan and Nazi Germany, mobilizing all its resources to defeat these aggressive and murderous regimes, sacrificing hundreds of thousands of precious lives and great quantities of materiel. More recently, America has had to stand virtually alone in opposing Communist dictatorships, again sacrificing many of its finest men and women, as well as much treasure, on behalf of people suffering under totalitarian rule and in order to stop the spread of Cain ideology and power.

Reconciliation of Cain and Abel

The difference between Cain- and Abel-type character is revealed after they achieve a victory. Cain takes advantage of his success to punish and wreak vengeance on the vanquished, while Abel offers forgiveness and is magnanimous in helping Cain recover. Cain-type behavior never bears good fruit, either for Cain or his victims, while Abel-type behavior advances good for Abel and those he wins over. Put a little differently, when Cain wins, everyone loses, including Cain. When Abel wins, everyone wins, including Cain. So how can Cain and Abel be reconciled? The only way is for them to resolve their differences on Abel's terms: In other words, when Cain ceases to manifest fallen nature and himself becomes Abel-like.

After World War I, the Allies made the mistake of punishing Germany with draconian demands for reparations. These edicts fueled German resentment and gave Hitler a platform from which to launch his Nazi program of national restoration and revenge, leading to World War II.

After that war, there was greater cause for demanding reparations, based on the much greater damage done by the Axis Powers compared with the Central Powers, but the Western Allies wisely chose another course, providing humanitarian and financial aid for the rebuilding of Germany and Japan (through the Marshall Plan and other programs). This enabled the former Axis powers to become post-war allies of their erstwhile conquerors, leading to decades of peace among former combatants.

In contrast, Stalin and the Soviet Union took advantage of their contribution to victory in World War II by occupying several countries in central and eastern Europe, brutally crushing opposition, stripping factories of their equipment and taking other assets by way of financial reparations. Stalin then established puppet Communist regimes to force these countries into the Soviet Empire. Moscow would maintain this hegemony over these subject states for forty-five years, until the Empire collapsed at the end of the 1980s. After a wave of liberating revolutions, most former member states and satellites of the Soviet Union now enjoy full independence and freedom. However, Ukraine continues to suffer from annexation of its territory and other predations by an apparently unrepentant and Cain-like President Vladimir Putin. The Soviet empire cannot be said to have benefited any of its constituent or vassal states: All were eager to escape the stranglehold of Moscow. And today, shorn of its empire, Russia has few, if any, real friends.

The challenge for Abel is to be resolute in the face of evil. He cannot succeed through compromise, conciliation or appeasement. Evil must be defeated, but Abel cannot resort to the destructive behavior of Cain to achieve that victory. Abel's way is to win Cain to the side of good through service and love, if at all possible. However, Abel cannot surrender to Cain: He must employ all means necessary to prevent Cain from spreading evil. Nevertheless, after his victory, Abel can reconcile with Cain through magnanimity. Reconciliation on Abel's terms defeats evil and advances the cause of the providence of restoration, resulting in blessings for both Cain and Abel, as we shall see in history.

The Role of Religion

The primary role of religion is to reveal the often-hidden inner purposes and dimensions of providential history and the principles by which we can achieve our ultimate purpose. In other words, teach the way of Abel. Over time, the level of understanding communicated through religious teaching and example can be elevated as people mature in their thinking, understanding and behavior. This means that, as in science, we have to be open to ever deeper insights and change our thinking accordingly. The end goal of this process is not the perfection of religion but the perfection of human nature.

Until we get there, our thinking and understanding will always need further enlightenment.

In a broader sense, the purpose of religion is to create cultural environments that are conducive to enlightenment and to the creation of communities and nations that have the spiritual awareness and wisdom to participate in the creation of a good world. As we shall show, religion has often worked against this purpose by imposing dogmas that block the path of true enlightenment: censoring and persecuting those it deems heretics. This has seriously undermined religion and driven many from truths obscured by this Cain-type behavior.

Religion as a whole can redeem itself at this critical juncture in time by taking an unequivocal stand against the atheistic doctrines of Marxists and Neo-Marxists. People of faith espousing Marxist and related theories are deceiving their followers and contributing to a new type of inquisition, that of "Cancel Culture." Given the horrific history of the Left, there is no excuse for this perversion of religious truth.

In the next chapter, we will examine the historical process of enlightenment, based on the Cain-Abel paradigm and including the role of religious figures and doctrines. Evil first appeared in one family, and it is the history of the lineage of that family that tells us the most about patterns of human alienation from the Creator and the key steps that have been taken to end that alienation.

Chapter 5

The Struggle Between Good and Evil in History

Historical Materialism or Divine Providence?

Aprominent feature of Marxism is its theory that history is a record of the dialectic process working itself out over time, with its ultimate objective the realization of Communism, a materialist Utopia. For Marxists and most other Leftists, history is subject to inexorable forces that are propelling it towards a predetermined destination. This Marxist view serves not just as an explanation of history, but also as a justification for any program or activity that is deemed to hurry humanity towards the goal. This confidence in a Communist destiny is truly remarkable, given that Marxism itself admits to no overarching purpose for creation. What then gives Marx such confidence in a predetermined destiny? Clearly, his determinism is taken directly from monotheistic religions that teach a human telos in the advent of a Kingdom of Heaven.

The Providential Nature of History

As we pointed out in the previous chapter, we need to seek the truth of history in the revelations of Divine Providence, revelations that while shrouded in pre-history and legend nevertheless appeal to our innate sense of what is good and what is evil. Resorting to scriptures to discover the truth is, then, the best option open to us and the one taken here. What emerges are historical patterns of behavior that either advance or retard human progress and enlightenment. Furthermore, providential history advances behind a vanguard of virtuous leadership and sound teaching that spearheads the worldwide restoration of humankind. Following we will seek to identify this vanguard and explain its workings.

This is a very different account from the one proposed by Marxism, which sees history in the pseudo-providential light of a dialectical process that leads inevitably to a Communist state—itself a pseudo anticipation of the real end goal of providential history. We will examine the Marxist theory of history next, but it is worth noting upfront that it suffers from two huge problems. The first is that Marxism is clueless regarding the real nature of evil and therefore how it can be overcome, and second, as we demonstrate in this book, dialectical materialism is unscientific and therefore incapable of providing a credible explanation of the forces that have shaped history.

Historical Materialism

Marx, of course, rejected the religious base for an ideal world and developed his own "materialistic conception of history." Later called Historical Materialism, this theory looks at the world through the lens of class differences, the conflicts they cause, and the resultant changes in economic systems. The main body of *The Communist Manifesto* famously begins with this line: "The history of all hitherto existing society is the history of class struggles." (Appendix 1, p263.) To understand this theory, it is necessary to understand Marx's basic assumptions about the world and human existence, some of which we have already touched on.

Drawing on Darwinism, Marx believed that human beings emerged from the animal kingdom and that all human intelligence, ideas and spiritual experiences, including those of science, religion and culture, were essentially created out of the evolutionary human experience. For Marx, then, the fundamental nature of humans is material, and their most basic instincts and interests lie in their desire to survive and prosper.

This Marxist view is called Economic Determinism because it judges the way that people survive to be the fundamental force in history, shaping their ideas, behavior and organization. In Marxism, it is the base that shapes all human relationships and social structures in the superstructure. The base is comprised of the means of production, including labor and capital. These are the primary forces affecting the superstructure, which includes religious belief, science, the state, culture and social institutions, including the family. Thus in order to bring about social change, it is necessary to change the economic base, or system, of society (although Marx did recognize that the superstructure does have limited influence on the base).

For Marx, it is primarily the working out of the forces and relationships in the base that drives history. People are constantly looking to improve their situation in life and therefore reject the economic structures they inherit and seek to make better ones. In dialectic speak, an antithesis to the existing system emerges, negating the thesis. The antithesis itself, however, also contains contradictions and consequently is negated by its own antithesis, which emerges as a synthesis of the original thesis and antithesis. According to this theory, the synthesis is an improvement on the thesis, and thus this process is responsible for both natural evolution and human socioeconomic progress. The thesis-antithesis-synthesis process is not peaceful but characterized by violent struggle as the new economic system emerges from the old.

In Marxism, the dominant conflict within the base is that between economic classes. Since the distribution of wealth among people is never equal, there is a natural process of "survival of the fittest" in which some form a dominant class, and the rest are relegated to a subservient class. Thus Marx believed class struggle to be of primary importance in the shaping of history. (Later offshoots of Marxism, and especially Critical Theory, broadened the categories of causal dialectical struggle to include many aspects of society, as we shall discuss later.)

Marx believed that he could trace the dialectical workings of human existence beginning with the very first people, the hunters and gatherers. As they multiplied, their need for land forced the development of primitive agriculture. With further population growth, the competition for arable land increased, and a class of landowners and their slaves emerged, and the feudal system was born. The inequities of that system, however, resulted in resentment and agitation from landless peasants wanting to have ownership of property. Their revolt against feudal lords and nobility resulted in a new class of property owners emerging, a class that exploited workers to make profits. Thus capitalism was born.

Socialism as a Necessary Step to Communism

The inequities within capitalism doom it to failure, Marx believed. It was, he thought, nothing more than a stage on the road to Socialism and Communism. His role was to push along this process through a violent revolution of the working classes (the proletariat) against the wealthy ownership class (the bourgeoisie). In *The Communist Manifesto* he said: "The Communists disdain to conceal their views and aims. They openly declare that their ends can be attained only by the forcible overthrow of all existing social conditions. Let the ruling classes tremble at a Communistic revolution." (Appendix 1, p297.)

Marx believed that Socialism itself was a necessary step between capitalism and Communism. The Socialist state would introduce revolutionary, centrally planned economic measures and condition the people to appreciate Communism. In a Socialist state the workers would rule: They would confiscate all private property and concentrate all capital in the hands of the state. In turn, the state would invest its capital wisely and with the greatest benefit for "the people." The fruits of those investments would be distributed fairly according to need.

After watching the failure of the Paris Commune in 1871, Engels observed that it was necessary for the proletariat to be led to this promised land by an enlightened leadership. After all, their thinking had been spoiled by life under capitalism. Thus to "build Socialism," it was necessary to have a "dictatorship of the proletariat" that would guide the ship of state safely from its capitalist past to its Communist future. As the economy was transformed, so too would be all the superstructure ideas and institutions until the dictatorship would no longer be needed and there would be a "withering away of the state."

The Marxist Myth of Socialism 'Withering Away'

The notion of the state withering away is a glaring fault in Historical Materialism. It contradicts the basic precept of dialectical materialism, namely that all existence, all entities, are fraught with internal contradictions. These contradictions always give rise to conflict as the necessary process to achieve progress. How then is it possible for the Socialist state to simply wither away and the Communist state to emerge, free of contradictions and conflicts? Did Marx believe in magic?

As with all Marxist concepts, logic and science are neither the basis nor the objective of the theory. Violent revolution is the object, but Marx and Engels realized that beyond conflict there had to be a desirable destination for humanity, a materialist alternative to the heavenly kingdom. They were, after all, raised in a culture steeped in Jewish and Christian millennial beliefs, and they recognized that human aspirations are closely tied to achieving an eternal home of peace and happiness. So to be able to promise their version of heaven, they simply had the dialectic disappear into thin air once Socialism was established.

This is, of course, the ultimate indictment of the theory that dialectical materialism is the engine of existence and evolution. To say that it will cease to function in the form of class conflict, as Socialism withers away and a Communist state emerges, is to admit that it is not a principle of nature at all. As we have noted, Marxism offers no explanation for the non-conflictual interactions of natural elements that sustain life and suggest the possibility of peaceful coexistence among human beings. Their "science" mandates a constant state of conflict between diverse elements of nature. Thus the Marxist myth of a Communist Utopia was born, even though it contradicts Marx's own theory of existence and history.

And, in yet another extraordinary demonstration of wishful thinking, Marx expected violent Communist revolutionaries, who engage in the bloody destruction of existing authorities and institutions, to then form a wise and just dictatorial ruling class to govern a Socialist state—and finally to surrender their power voluntarily as they manage the transition to a perfect Communist state. Only a blind faith in the power of Socialism to transform ruthless and violent people into self-sacrificing saints can explain this fantastic theory.

However, Marx was right in one way. His prescriptions for society would attract a religious-like devotion from many, some even at a fanatical level. The Communist ideal does appeal to the religious nature of people, a nature we are endowed with that constantly aspires to an ideal state of existence. We want to believe in an ideal world that is better than the one we inherited. Even when Stalin was killing his own countrymen by the millions, many Communists around the world continued to believe in the myth that the Soviet Union was actually building an ideal state in which each would give according to their ability and receive according to their need. Many were only disabused of this lie when his Reign of Terror was made fully public in 1956.

But Marx, Engels, Lenin, Stalin, Mao and other Communist ideologues and dictators were not scientists dedicated to finding a factual basis for the theories they embraced. Rather they touted theories that provided a justification for violent revolution and were sufficiently fungible to justify totalitarian rule in the name of an imaginary underclass. This "theoretical flexibility" has meant that Socialist and Communist leaders have always been able to justify the contradictions between their promises and the reality of their regimes. As one long-suffering citizen of the former Socialist regime in Hungary commented sarcastically to this author: "They always tell us they are building Socialism. They never say when they will be finished."

The Marxist myth ignores a fundamental reality, namely that differences and even apparent contradictions will always exist in society. They are part of the true diversity and beauty of the creation, which embodies divine attributes in myriad permutations of subject-object relationships, as we have noted. The point is that for life to exist, there must be give and take between subject and object. To destroy one or the other is to destroy the fabric of life itself. Marxism fails to recognize the critical importance to life and history of the constructive relationships between subjects and objects.

The Real Legacy of Socialism

Indeed, history demonstrates how foolish the Marxist theory of development through conflict is. Violent revolutionaries naturally set up brutal and oppressive regimes. Their object is power, and once they have achieved it they are loath to relinquish it. This pattern has been repeated again and again. For example, in the Paris Commune itself, a motley assortment of radical leftists seized power and immediately used brutal means to suppress opposition. They were defeated quickly, but Marxist revolutions have proved more successful at retaining power: Lenin and the ruthless Bolshevik revolution spawned a brutal Communist regime in Russia; Mao Zedong and the Chinese Communist Party gained power through a bloody revolution and has kept it through tyrannical repression; Ho Chi Minh in Vietnam; Pol Pot in Cambodia; Kim Il Sung in North Korea; Fidel Castro in Cuba; and Che Guevara and his brutal insurgencies in Latin America... The pattern is consistent. No Socialist regime has ever been anything other than repressive and none has shown any potential to create an ideal state.

Yet despite this dismal and bloody record, the dogma of the godless Marxist religion is still believed by many, including well educated and widely experienced people who enjoy comfortable lives in free societies. The Marxist myth continues to lure them into believing that destruction of traditional societies is a path that inevitably leads to a better world.

As we will discuss in greater detail later, what Marx and Engels believed to be the inevitable demise of capitalism has never happened. Socialist dictatorships never succeed in investing capital efficiently or distributing wealth equitably. State control of capital is always less efficient than private control. The Socialist/Communist elites (the Nomenklatura of the Soviet Union) control all the power and all the property and do whatever they want with the rest of the population. Injustice is rampant. The state's lust for power and wealth is insatiable. It takes and takes and takes from the people until little or nothing is left. No idyllic Communist state has ever emerged from a Socialist system, and ultimately the Socialist states collapse from internal corruption and mismanagement. (Some, like China, have managed to prolong their existence by adopting limited levels of capitalism while retaining strict Communist rule.)

Marx's economic determinism and historical materialism are clearly flawed. They are theories built in ignorance of the purpose and principles of creation and true human aspirations. Furthermore, because they are rooted in an atheistic worldview, they are not anchored in any moral absolutes, making them susceptible to abuses. What Marx identified as institutions of the superstructure, most importantly religion and family, are far from being the products of economic systems. They are not governed by class relations but by moral law and spiritual purpose. They wield great influence over other institutions in civil society and it is ultimately from them that we can derive the most equitable economic systems.

Divine Providence Propels History

As we have shown, Marx's theory—that class struggle and violent revolution are the main engines for human progress in history—is patently erroneous. The actual legacy of class conflicts and violent revolutions has been disastrous, especially as evidenced in the establishment of Communist states in the Soviet Union and China, which have caused so much human suffering and destruction.

Consider the current state of the world compared to just a few centuries ago. For example, the standard of living enjoyed by billions of people today is far superior to that experienced by the vast majority of people in the 19th century. Thanks to the rapid advances in science and technology, the average lifestyle of the middle class today includes more comforts than the wealthy enjoyed just two centuries ago.

Did this transformation come about through a series of violent revolutions? Clearly not. This progress was achieved through the steady development of capitalist societies in which individuals were free to innovate and develop private enterprises. If anything, the Communist revolutions of the 20th century represented huge regressions in the forward march of human progress.

What, then, has been the true dynamic of historical progress? Humanity has advanced by people overcoming internal and external ignorance and achieving victories of good over evil, as part of a providential plan to restore human beings to their original purity, virtue and goodness.

Again, the Cain-Abel paradigm is instructive: It reveals the method and pattern of this historical process of human evolution. The killing of Abel by Cain was a huge setback, but Seth became the new providential ancestor and out of his lineage Noah and his family would emerge to restore the family of Adam and Eve. However, despite separating from the evil world through a flood, Noah's second son Ham made a mistake, and Shem became the new providential ancestor, out of whose lineage Abraham appeared. Thus Adam's family was replaced by Noah's family, which in turn was replaced by Abraham's family.

This is not the place to trace in detail the working out of Cain-Abel relationships in the providential history of restoration, as interesting as it is. Suffice it to say, that Abel-type figures, in religious and scientific fields of endeavor, have appeared again and again to bring enlightenment and hope to the world. They have always been confronted by reactionary, Cain-type resistance. When they have prevailed, human progress has advanced; when Cain has prevailed, it has suffered setbacks. In Appendix 5, pp316-331, there is a more detailed analysis of the Cain-Abel paradigm at work in the Old Testament era of the Bible, but there is one particularly important family that we will discuss now, that of Abraham and Sarah.

The Family of Abraham and Sarah

Abraham's first son, Ishmael, was born to Sarah's servant, Hagar, at the behest of Sarah, who was barren. However, when Sarah was later able to conceive, she had a son of her own, Isaac. Ishmael represented Cain, and Isaac represented Abel. However, when Abraham failed to complete a sacrifice of animals, the providence to restore Adam's family was postponed to the next generation, with Isaac taking Abraham's position. Isaac's twin sons, Esau and Jacob, inherited the Cain and Abel roles from Ishmael and Isaac. Esau was greatly angered when Jacob won the birthright and his father's blessing, and Jacob fled to Haran to escape being murdered by his brother. However, when Jacob eventually returned, he showered Esau with gifts, dissolving his elder brother's bitterness and resentment, and the twins were reconciled. This success enabled Jacob and his family to be blessed as the new providential ancestors. His twelve sons became the twelve tribes of Israel, the nation at the center of the providence of restoration.

There is another little-known yet significant aspect of this story. Ishmael, the elder half-brother of Isaac, who was born to Sarah's servant Hagar, also had twelve sons who became twelve tribes, the ancestors of the Arabs. It was from among these people that Mohammed would rise as a prophet some 500 years after the death of Jesus, establishing the religion of Islam. Thus Abraham became the father of the three great monotheistic religions: Judaism, Christianity and Islam. Although this topic lies beyond the scope of this book, history has shown that the relationship among these three faiths has had an enormous impact on the world and is pivotal to the ultimate dissolution of human resentments and the defeat of evil. Indeed, understanding the Cain and Abel dynamics at play in the relationships among these three faiths is critical to their peaceful reconciliation.

The Cain-Abel Paradigm Shapes Providential History

The dynamic of the Cain-Abel paradigm has been the driving force of providential history. It has played out starting on the individual and family levels, expanding to the tribal and national levels, and eventually reaching the global levels witnessed in the last century. As noted, it is spearheaded by a vanguard of Abel-type leaders and ideas that confront the status quo, based on its inadequate systems of belief and social order, and offers a better alternative. The histories of vanguard movements make up the core of providential history and therefore are of greatest interest to us here.

Looking at the world from this perspective, it is abundantly clear that Marx's theory that aggrieved groups should act on their anger and resentment by resorting to violent revolution is a politico-economic incarnation of Cain ideology. The results of its implementation have been predictably disastrous, causing death for tens of millions of people around the world and untold suffering for hundreds of millions more.

Compare the Marxist legacy with those of nations and governments established on a belief in the primacy of God-given rights and responsibilities and the sanctity of every life. It was these Abel-type countries that sacrificially confronted and defeated the Cain-type Nazi regime in World War II and, since then, have spearheaded opposition to the Cain-type Communist regimes in the Soviet Union, China and elsewhere.

That Cain was older than Abel established the pattern of evil preceding good, a phenomenon evidenced throughout history that offers hope for the true to follow the false, for light to follow dark. Thus the very prevalence of

Marxist and Neo-Marxist theories that today influence society and continue to justify totalitarian regimes suggests that it is time for a new Abel-type vanguard of leaders and ideas to emerge and show the way to replace these atheistic ideologies with godly alternatives.

The central providential path from Biblical history to the present is the next issue we will examine, beginning with the remarkable worldwide enlightenment of the Axial Age.

Chapter 6

The Axial Age: An Era of Global Enlightenment

Religious, Philosophical and Scientific Awakening

The history we have traced thus far focuses on a central lineage expanding from individual families into twelve tribes and ultimately the nation of Israel. Standing back from this account to look at the world more broadly, the centuries immediately preceding the arrival of Jesus 2,000 years ago were remarkable for their richness in religious, philosophical and scientific development. So pivotal was the period between the 8th and 3rd centuries BC, that German philosopher Karl Jaspers dubbed it the "Axial Age." Recognizing that many of its outstanding figures have had a global impact that affects our lives and the world to this day, in this chapter we will briefly examine some of the key people and main developments of this era.

The Rise of Asian Religions and Philosophies

After seventy years of humbling exile in Babylon, the people of Judah returned in stages to a ruined Jerusalem, triggering a worldwide period of spiritual renewal. Under the able leadership of the governor Nehemiah and guidance from Ezra, a scribe, they rebuilt the city and Temple. At the same time, important religious and philosophical movements were founded and growing in India, China and Persia. Building on the millennia-long foundations of Hinduism, both Buddhism and Jainism took root in India during the 6th century BC. In China, Confucianism was founded in the 6th century BC, followed by Taoism in the 4th century. Further west, Zoroastrianism was founded in Persia during the 6th century BC. (This religion would have a direct impact on the restoration of Jerusalem and the Jewish state when, in 538 BC, the Persian emperor Cyrus the Great conquered Babylon and freed the Israelite captives there, allowing them to return to their homeland.)

All these teachings brought fresh insights into the truth and guided followers to live a virtuous life. Following we look briefly at the founders and main ideas behind this age of enlightenment since they contributed very significantly to a process of positive global transformation and undoubtedly remain important to the realization of a world of enduring goodness and peace.

Buddhism

Siddhartha Gautama, the Buddha, lived from c. 563 to 483 BC. Born a prince into a wealthy family in what is now Nepal, he left the comforts of home to discover the reason for suffering in the world. He would develop four noble truths: the truth about suffering, the cause of suffering, the end of suffering and the path that frees us from suffering. This last is an eightfold path to achieve the virtues of right understanding, right thought, right speech, right action, right livelihood, right effort, right mindfulness and right concentration. There is no God in Buddhism, but the virtues he taught are those required to achieve spiritual maturity and to overcome resentment and hatred.

The teachings of Buddha, called Dharma, all contribute to a virtuous society based on the acquisition of wisdom and the practice of patience, kindness, generosity and compassion. Buddhism would prove a popular philosophy and way of life that spread throughout Asia, developing in three main branches: Theravada, Mahayana and Tibetan as well as some offshoots such as Zen. Today, there are some 470 million Buddhists worldwide. Buddhism is practiced most diligently in monasteries but is also a broadly popular spiritual path that can be woven into daily life.

Jainism

Mahavira was born as Vardhamana in northeast India in 599 BC and died in 527 BC. Like Buddha, he was a prince who left home to seek the truth. And, like Buddha, he achieved enlightenment, ultimately attaining "moksha" or liberation from the cycle of rebirth. He inherited a number of teachings from an earlier teacher, Parshva, such as no violence, no lying, no stealing and no possessions. To these, he added the principle of chastity. Jainism lost ground to Hinduism, Buddhism and Islam in India, but today has about 6 million followers. Most are concentrated in India, although some migrated to Africa and thence to Britain.

Confucianism

Living from 551 BC to 479 BC, Confucius was a Chinese philosopher who taught the importance of a good moral character as the basis for a virtuous society. This good character was to manifest in all human relationships, from those within a family to those between a ruler and the ruled. A good character was one that was respectful of others, humble and altruistic. Good people would make a good and harmonious world.

A key Confucian virtue is filial piety—respect for parents in particular and elders in general, including teachers. It extends to reverence for ancestors. Filial piety is a foundational virtue for maintaining harmony within the family by ordering relations between parents and children, brothers and sisters. Harmonious families are the building blocks of stable and peaceful societies, which themselves are structured in a hierarchical order.

Confucianism is the basis for traditional Chinese ethics and culture. Although it lacked an understanding and belief in a supreme being, it nevertheless recognized the importance of ancestors; in other words, it reveres inherited values and traditions. The ultimate spiritual power was described by Confucius as the Will of Heaven, implying belief in a transcendent existence that rules the world.

Taoism

The founder of Taoism, Lao Tzu, was born in China sometime between the 4th and 6th Centuries BC. His teachings complement Confucianism in that they focus on the importance of individuals being responsible for their own character and their relations with others. In addition to condemning killing, stealing, lying and sexual immorality, the teachings guide followers to virtuous personal behavior and interaction with others, from the family to community and state. Becoming a good person means that you will become a good member of your family, society and nation, which you can fulfill through the way of Tao. In other words, since efforts to change others often produce unintended results, it is better to pursue your own perfection rather than to try to change the world.

In this sense, Taoism is a system focused on individual maturity, without the need for an understanding of a broader, universal truth or mission towards others. The Tao itself is the ultimate principle of the universe, combining within itself the Yin and Yang. This is compatible with the idea of creation as an embodiment of Divine attributes of subject (Yang) and object (Yin), male and female.

Zoroastrianism

The dates of Zoroaster's life are not known. Called Zarathustra in his native Persia, his was a monotheistic religious teaching. Followers believe that he had a vision of a supreme being while engaged in a pagan purification ritual. He called this deity Ahura Mazda, ascribing to it characteristics that are immediately recognizable in Judaism, Christianity and Islam. Among these are omniscience, omnipotence and omnipresence, as well as an unchanging existence beyond human comprehension. Further, Ahura Mazda is Creator of life and the source of all goodness and happiness.

Many Zoroastrian beliefs are shared by Judaism, Christianity and Islam: heaven and hell, the existence of Satan (called Ahriman), the promise of redemption and a savior, and a final battle for human salvation between Ahura Mazda and Ahriman, resulting in victory for the side of good.

Zoroastrian teachings encourage followers to pursue a threefold path of virtue: good thoughts, good words and good deeds. These are not seen as a means to an end but rather as fulfilling human purpose in themselves. The spiritual qualities of men and women are equal, and both can best channel their goodness through charity, which spreads happiness among people.

Zoroastrianism took on a significant providential role when it emerged as a Persian state religion in the 6th century BC. Cyrus the Great was a devout follower, and Zoroastrianism would remain the official religion for the Achaemenid Empire he founded, as well as for the Parthian and Sassanid Empires that followed. It was replaced in Persia by Islam, which suppressed the older faith. Although much diminished since its days as an official imperial religion, remnants of Zoroastrian communities can still be found in India and Iran, with smaller groups in other countries. The total population of adherents (generally known as Parsis) is probably not very much above 100,000 worldwide and declining.

The Rise of Classical Greece

The flowering of Greece during the period between the 6th and 3rd centuries BC is one of the most amazing and significant events in history. Suddenly, as if out of nowhere, a small region of the world gave birth to a group of men who in a few centuries revolutionized human understanding of our universe. A brief sketch of that era shows how significant it was. In the big picture of human development over millennia, the ascendancy of Greece marked the first time that a group of thinkers (coming from various parts of the mainland and several islands) sought to discover truth by observing and analyzing phenomena in the world around them.

During this classical period, Greek thinkers made groundbreaking advances in philosophy and science, often through combining the two. Socrates, Plato and Aristotle are considered the leading philosophers, although Aristotle also contributed significantly to medicine. Pythagoras, Thales, Anaximander, Anaxagoras, Hippocrates, Eudoxus, Democritus, Theophrastus, Aristarchus, Euclid, Archimedes and Eratosthenes made revolutionary discoveries about the nature of the world and universe in fields ranging from botany, zoology and medicine to mathematics, astronomy and physics. These discoveries would form the foundations of modern science.

Pythagoras was typical of the Greek polymaths whose insights into existence cut across several fields of knowledge. In this, they foreshadowed Renaissance man. Although known primarily for the Pythagorean Theorem, he believed that the truth of the universe, as known through mathematics to astronomy and music, could be represented by numbers. He established a secret society in Croton Italy, then part of Magna Graecia, where he pursued science. He also established a community that held all property in common (as the early Christians would do six centuries later); practiced piety, moderation, respect for elders and the state (principles also found in Confucianism as well as Pauline Christianity); and advocated for monogamous families, a bedrock principle of Judaism and later Christianity.

Meanwhile, political leaders like Solon, Cleisthenes and Pericles pioneered early forms of democracy, while military leaders, notably Alexander the Great, helped establish a common cultural environment that included much of the known world. These facilitated the spread of enlightened thinking across traditional political and linguistic boundaries.

This remarkable period of enlightenment in Greece would have a major impact on the world, and Greece would become known as the cradle of

Western Civilization. The Greeks contributed to the ability of human beings to understand themselves and the natural world around them, giving the world a body of knowledge that was the precursor of science as we know it today.

Impact of The Axial Age

As we have shown, a significant feature of this period was the rise of both religious and philosophical movements as well as the development of the foundations of science. In principle, the revelations of truth that come through religion should be complemented by the discoveries of science since both seek to understand a single reality, our universe. The parallel advance of religion and science in the Axial Age foreshadowed what occurred 2,000 years later in the Renaissance and Reformation, which were secular and religious movements, respectively, that set in motion the transformation of the Middle Ages into the modern world.

Perhaps the best demonstration of the benefit derived from the parallel development of religion and science can be seen in the experience of scientists who have received critical insights from the invisible, spiritual world. One of the best-known cases of this is the account by the 17th century French scientist René Descartes, who famously credited a series of visions for his formulation of analytical geometry and his application of the scientific method to philosophy. More broadly, he believed that his pursuit of science was in fact a pursuit of truth itself.

Another scientist who had a similar experience was the Russian Dmitri Mendeleev, who woke from sleep one night with the solution for how to organize the periodic table of chemical elements.

Albert Einstein provided a useful explanation of the interdependence of religion and science and the spiritual grounding required of a "genuine scientist":

> Though religion may be that which determines the goal, it has, nevertheless,

learned from science, in the broadest sense, what means will contribute to the attainment of the goals it has set up. But science can only be created by those who are thoroughly imbued with the aspiration toward truth and understanding. This source of feeling, however, springs from the sphere of religion. To this there also belongs the faith in the possibility that the regulations valid for the world of existence are rational, that is, comprehensible to reason. I cannot conceive of a genuine scientist without that profound faith. The situation may be expressed by an image: science without religion is lame, religion without science is blind.[17]

These words resonate with the spirit of the Axial Age, which reappeared in the Renaissance, Enlightenment and Reformation. Marxism was a repudiation of that spirit because it specifically rejected the role of religion in the historical development of humankind. In other words, it was an arrogant, Cain-type reaction to the Abel-type phenomenon of complementary religious and scientific enlightenment. Marx famously wrote: "Religion is the sigh of the oppressed creature, the heart of a heartless world, and the soul of soulless conditions. It is the opium of the people."[18] He believed that "The more man puts into God, the less he retains of himself."[19] This atheistic view is not based on science but on a personal animus towards God and religion. As history has shown, Marxist doctrines do not provide people with the understanding they need to live a good life; they only incite them to hatred and violence and the destruction of good human relationships that are indispensable to stable and successful societies.

Just a few centuries after this first era of global enlightenment, Jesus appeared in Israel and revealed profound insights into the truth of creation and the purpose of existence, setting the stage for a truly revolutionary advancement for humanity. His teaching was not welcomed by most of the people, and their leaders put him to death after only three years of public life. Fulfillment of the promise of the Axial Age, centered on an Israel at one with Jesus, was postponed for many centuries as Christianity slowly evolved and spread around the world. We will examine that history in the next chapter.

Chapter 7

Jesus and the Christian Era

*Global Enlightenment Accelerates
the Mission of Jesus*

Jesus is the most significant person ever to have lived. Not only is he the source of truth for billions of Christians worldwide, he is revered and worshiped as the personal savior for believers who hope to achieve the Kingdom of Heaven. The moral teachings of Jesus form the internal basis for Western Civilization. Their great influence is due to the fact that he lived fully by his own precepts: He practiced perfectly what he preached. Thus, although he was killed at the young age of thirty-three, his words and deeds stand as the absolute standard of faith and virtuous conduct to this day.

Why was Jesus so significant? Essentially, he brought a new standard of purity and understanding into the world of alienated humanity. There was an unprecedented depth to his teaching that reflected his intimacy with God and consequent grasp of the profound meanings of life, human purpose and destiny. As Hebrews 3:5-6 puts it: "Now Moses was faithful in all God's house as a servant, to testify to the things that were to be spoken later, but Christ was faithful over God's house as a son."

However, neither Jesus' moral rectitude nor the many miracles he performed in healing people persuaded the religious or political establishments of Israel to accept him and his teaching. Why was this? In terms of the providential history we have traced thus far, the rejection of Jesus was consistent with the pattern of a faithful Abel being the target of Cain-type jealousy and resentment. As in Cain's murder of Abel, when the unrestrained self-centeredness of the people of Israel was fanned into full-blown rage, it ended in the murder of Jesus.

When looked at from this perspective, there is a fundamental and irreconcilable contradiction between two traditional Christian beliefs about Jesus: first, that Jesus came to be "king of kings and lord of lords" and to "sit upon the throne of David" (in fulfillment of Old Testament prophecies), and second, that he fulfilled this mission by dying on the cross. How can both be true? Surely the crucifixion of Jesus was a failure to fulfill the God-given responsibility to welcome and follow the Messiah. If so, how can one believe that it was God's will? The remorse and suicide of Judas after he realized the significance of having betrayed Christ gives us all the evidence we need to know that the crucifixion was not God's will but a failure of human responsibility. Nevertheless, it has been taken as axiomatic by most Christians that Jesus was supposed to die on the cross as a sacrifice for the sins of humanity so that we can be saved. (See Appendix 6, pp332-351, for a more detailed examination of the life and death of Jesus from the point of view of the Cain-Abel paradigm.)

The Global Impact of Jesus' Premature Death

It is not our purpose here to discuss the various beliefs and arguments about the nature of Jesus and the meaning of his crucifixion. Suffice it to say that the murder of Jesus was not only wrong but resulted in a very significant delay in the providence. There is no clearer indication of this than in the anguished words of Jesus himself as he neared death on the cross: "Father, forgive them; for they know not what they do" (Luke 23:34) This raises the question: What would have happened if Jesus had not been killed but instead was embraced by the people he came to save?

One obvious result of the crucifixion was that Jesus never married or had a family of his own. Given his role as a replacement for Adam, there was a need for a replacement for Eve to complete the restoration of the original family. Undoubtedly, Christian history—and world history for that matter—would have been very different had Jesus established a model family and sinless lineage to serve as prototypes for humanity. Instead, the legacy of Jesus became the Christian religion that has contributed a great deal to humanity but has always been vulnerable to the criticism that it falls short of achieving its own ideals. This inadequacy has resulted in a deep sense of frustration among the faithful, factionalism within the church and the rise of powerful rivals in Islam and Marxism.

This, then, is how we have to view the Christian era: It is a record of improvement, of better emerging from worse, but also of unprecedented conflicts and immeasurable human suffering. We have to be honest in recognizing that the conflicts within Christendom and between Christendom and other forces are to be blamed, at least in part, on the inadequate standard of Christian practice. Christian values were the primary moral force behind the Allies successfully confronting Nazism and Communism in the 20th century, but some features of Christian culture can be faulted for failing to prevent the rise of totalitarianism in the first place. Today, we face the fresh challenge of seasoned Marxist regimes (China, North Korea, Cuba) expanding in power while poisonous Neo-Marxist ideology spreads through Judeo-Christian cultures. This materialist onslaught is the new frontier for Christianity, which has not stemmed this evil tide so far. The reasons why this is so need to be understood.

In this chapter we will trace the progress of the Christian era over the past two millennia and in subsequent chapters examine some of the global developments related to this history.

The Birth of Christianity

Christianity was born the day that Jesus died. Without its founder and leader there to teach and instruct them, the disciples and early followers had to seek guidance from the Holy Spirit, from the remembered words of Jesus, and from those who had lived and worked with him. Inevitably, factions developed, and sectarianism has been a major feature of Christianity ever since.

One important issue the Church settled on early was that salvation belonged to everyone, not just the descendants of Jacob. This doctrine would empower the first great evangelist, Paul of Tarsus, who travelled through many parts of the Roman Empire planting Christian churches among Jewish and Gentile populations alike. His example would be the model for Christian outreach over the centuries, eventually taking the new religion to every corner of the earth.

A major milestone in the early history of the church occurred when Constantine became Roman Emperor in 312—and then, in 324, the sole ruler of the Eastern and Western Empires. Constantine ended the persecution of Christians and in 330 moved his capital to Byzantium, changing its name to Constantinople (now Istanbul). Under the influence of his Christian mother, he converted to Christianity on his deathbed in 337, becoming the first Christian emperor. Then, in 380, Eastern Emperor Theodosius signed a decree in front of Western Emperor Valentinian that made Christianity the state religion of the whole empire and punished the practice of pagan rituals.

The Great Schism

There were now five main Christian sees (jurisdictions): Jerusalem, Antioch, Alexandria, Constantinople and Rome. Jesus had appointed Peter to lead his followers after his death, and, since Peter died in Rome, it was the Roman church that claimed the mantle of Christian leadership. However, this claim was not accepted by the other four patriarchs, and in 1053 there was a formal schism between the Roman Catholic Church and the Eastern Orthodox

Churches, loosely centered on the Ecumenical Patriarch in Constantinople. The Catholic Church would become the largest and most influential Christian Church in the world, while the Eastern Orthodox Church would branch out primarily in Eastern, Southeastern and Central Europe and parts of the Levant.

However, there were several severe blemishes on the Catholic Church over the years, resulting in further divisions and conflicts. Two of the most damaging were the Crusades and the Inquisition, both of which contributed finally to the Protestant Reformation and the Catholic Counter-Reformation. A third blemish on the faith would come in the form of slavery, an inhuman practice that persisted for millennia and was exploited by Christian nations, both Catholic and Protestant, in pursuit of wealth and comfort.

The Folly of the Crusades

The Crusades were initiated by the Popes to regain control from the Muslims of the "Holy Land" of Jerusalem and the territory that had been Israel. Undoubtedly, many who led or participated in the crusades did so with good intentions, but the twelve major crusades between 1096 and 1291 were characterized by horrific bloodshed. Not only did some of the crusades target Jewish communities in Europe and the Levant (justified by blaming the Jews for Jesus' death) but also the Eastern Churches. In 1204, the Fourth Crusade attacked and sacked Constantinople, looting the churches, raping nuns and committing other atrocities.

The crusades were an erroneous manifestation of Christianity's mission to bring truth and goodness to the earth. They failed to do any good and only served to deepen divisions within Christianity and between Christianity and other faiths such as Judaism and Islam. These divisions are clearly counter to the true purpose of the religion, and they have created a legacy of resentment that casts a shadow over the relations among the three great monotheistic religions to this day.

The Evil of the Inquisition

The humbling of the Catholic Church through the seventy-year exile of the Papacy to Avignon (which started in 1309 and was brought about by conflicts between Rome and the French monarchy) did not lead to an end to one of its worst abuses: the so-called Holy Inquisition. From the standpoint of the Church, this was intended as a movement of purification: forcing confessions and repentance for divergence from the true faith. However, many who refused to recant their "heretical" beliefs were tortured and executed, frequently by burning at the stake.

The Inquisition started in 12th century France, when in 1231 Pope Gregory IX appointed the first "inquisitors of heretical depravity" targeting the Cathar and Waldensian heretics. The Inquisition, which ran its course for some 700 years, would later spread to Italy, Spain and Portugal. On the Iberian Peninsula, the primary target was converts from Judaism and Islam, many of whom had been coerced into conversion and were believed to be unreliable members of the church. Spain and Portugal even exported Inquisition courts to far-flung countries of their empires in Africa, Asia and the Americas, notably in Goa (India), Peru and Mexico.

This approach to heretics stained the Catholic Church and bled into wider society in the form of religious and ideological intolerance. Today, this prejudiced approach to the ideas of others has come full circle, and we now suffer from a "Cancel Culture" in which dominant academic, media and political institutions seek to control what people know and believe by preventing unwanted voices from being heard. And although the punishment for deviation from the accepted line has not yet reached Inquisition levels, those who write or say what is other than politically correct are made to suffer personal attacks, destruction of their character, loss of work and relegation to pariah status in society.

The Inhuman Practice of Slavery

One of the great stains on Christian civilization was the enslavement of pow-erless people by the powerful. This ancient and barbaric practice became of particular value to European powers as they expanded their empires. A pri-mary economic driver was the development of plantations in warmer climates outside Europe: in the Americas, Africa and Asia. These plantations required many workers, and often the colonial powers turned to slavery to supply the needed labor. Justification for Christians to tolerate or even participate in this ungodly practice was taken from Paul's letters, in some of which he encouraged slaves to be loyal ("submit yourselves") to their masters, in effect endorsing slavery. But for Christianity to accept rather than end the practice of one person owning another, especially when it preached that all people are children of God, was a very serious failure.

Slavery debased the European colonial powers as well as the colonies them-selves. In the British colonies of America, for example, where the trade in African slaves was introduced by settlers, the framers of the Constitution had to accommodate the slave-owning states in order to forge a unitary nation. Nevertheless, it was the Christianity of the abolitionists and the majority of the wider population that stirred the conscience of the nation to end slavery, even at the cost of a civil war that resulted in more American deaths than the nation suffered in any other war. And it was as Christian nations that coun-tries like Britain and America led the fight to end slavery around the world.

The Reformation and Counter-Reformation

The mistakes of the Catholic Church would inevitably lead to some believers calling for reform. Conscientious Christians could not accept the practices of the Inquisition or, more broadly, the anti-heretic policies of the Church in which dissidents were deemed damned and deserving of prison, torture or even death. There was definitely no basis for these policies in the teaching of Jesus, who had told his disciples they should love even their enemies. More and more critics of the Catholic Church emerged, and the Protestant Reformation movement was born.

One of the first and most articulate critics of the Papacy and Catholic Church was England's John Wycliffe. Among important contributions he made was a translation of the Bible from Latin into English. This made it widely available to the literate public and helped them access the teachings of Jesus directly, thereby freeing them from the need to depend on the Church's interpretation of Latin scriptures. Wycliffe was opposed by the Church, and after his death in 1384 the Council of Constance in 1415 declared him a heretic and ordered his books burned and his remains disinterred from church property.

John Huss, a Czech theologian and philosopher and rector of Charles University in Prague, was a sharp critic of the Papacy, the Catholic Church and many of its practices. In particular he was opposed to the practice of indulgences through which a sinner could purchase forgiveness. He was tried at the 1415 Council of Constance, sentenced to death for heresy and burned at the stake.

The persecution of these early reformers had the opposite effect of what was intended. Instead of spreading fear of rebelling against the church, it galvanized believers to pay attention to what the dissidents were saying. The Protestant Reformation movement really gained momentum when, in 1517, a German priest named Martin Luther nailed his "95 Theses" to a church door in Wittenberg, detailing criticisms of the practice of Papal Indulgences and other abuses by the Church. For example, Number 43 states: "Christians are to be taught that he who gives to the poor or lends to the needy does a better deed than he who buys indulgences." The message was clear: A true Christian life is one of love and service, not seeking to purchase one's own salvation. (See Luther's 95 Theses in Appendix 7, pp352-361.)

Luther was followed by other reformers, such as Ulrich Zwingli and John Calvin, both of whom lived in Switzerland. Churches that broke away from the authority of the Catholic Church became known as Protestant Churches, and the second major Christian schism was underway. Over time, Protestant churches would split off from one another to created hundreds of denominations, each with its own take on the scriptures and how they should be interpreted and practiced. Some of these offshoots would be small, but others became major international organizations.

A major feature of most Protestant churches would be pioneered by the anabaptists who insisted that the Catholic practice of child baptism was wrong: Only adults who could make a commitment of faith should be baptized. Some of the more radical anabaptists practiced communal living. In general, they were highly committed to a rigorous religious discipline, and many groups (Hutterites, Mennonites, Amish, Brethren) fled persecution in Europe by migrating to a more welcoming America.

Often the founders of new denominations were inspired and charismatic teachers who stirred the hearts of believers to make fresh commitments to the faith. Among the most prominent were John Wesley, who founded Methodism, and George Fox, who founded the Quakers. Some of the major denominations that became independent members of the Protestant family were Lutherans, Presbyterians, Anglicans/Episcopalians, Baptists, and a host of others. (See Appendix 8, p362, for a basic chart of major denominational families in Christianity.)

An organized response to the Protestant Reformation by the Catholic Church began with the Council of Trent (1545–1563). Although many of the practices that had driven believers into the Protestant churches were retained, this council signaled that the Catholic Church recognized the need for its own internal reformation or what would be called the Counter-Reformation. Among other short-term results, it led to the establishment of seminaries to provide better training for priests.

Christianity Goes Global

Thus the Protestant Reformation set in motion a process of renewal within Western Christianity that has been broadly beneficial. It introduced the notion that members of the clergy and lay believers alike have a right to question ecclesiastical authority, to study the Bible in their own language, and to decide for themselves how best to fulfill their obligations as followers of Christ. Over time, the changes in Christianity have been massive, and the church has grown to reach every corner of the world and to claim 2.4 billion adherents, making it the largest religion in the world. Christianity has inspired democracy and the rule of law as well as concern for the less fortunate. Nevertheless, despite its global presence, it has been only partly able to prevent wars, overcome crime and corruption and deliver full equality and justice to communities of its own followers, let alone to the world as a whole.

With a 2,000-year history, Christianity has come a long way, but its followers still long to attain the ideal world that was lost in the Fall and has been promised to them for the future. Jesus and his teachings provide the basis for their hope, but they do not anticipate some developments of the past two millennia that are, therefore, hard for Christians to understand and respond to. First among these is the rise of Islam, beginning with the birth of Mohammed in the 6th century AD. It too has grown into a worldwide religion and now claims some 1.9 billion adherents. It is currently growing more rapidly than Christianity. Second is the appearance of Marxism and later Neo-Marxism. When Marxism first appeared as a theory in the 19th century, it did not stand out as particularly important or threatening to Christianity. However, when it was used to justify violent revolutions and brutal dictatorships that conducted mass murder on unprecedented levels in the 20th century, it directly contradicted Christian ideals. We will now turn to a discussion of these phenomena, beginning with the rise of Islam.

Chapter 8

The Rise of Islam

A Challenge to Christianity

The Advent of Islam Changes the World

For Westerners immersed in Judeo-Christian culture, the emergence of Islam in the 7th century AD is an inexplicable phenomenon. Undeniably a monotheistic faith, it is based on scriptures contained in the Quran that align more closely with the Old Testament, including Mosaic Law and prophetic warnings, than with the teachings of Jesus. None of these differences were of great importance until Muslims began to conquer once-Christian lands in the Byzantine Empire and then European countries—and, in recent decades, began to resort to violence and terrorism to make their wishes known. Today, the global presence of some 1.9 billion Muslims has created a situation in which it has become vitally important to understand Islam in its providential context. Critically, Islam is a cousin religion to Judaism and Christianity, and, as with all family disputes, the differences among these three faiths should not be allowed to overshadow and outweigh the commonalities, let alone be allowed to provoke violence and the destruction of the whole family of descendants of Abraham.

In recent times, the terrorism of radical Muslim groups, in particular, has been a major obstacle to good relations among the Abrahamic religions. Al Qaeda (which used four civilian planes in terror attacks that, in New York alone, brought down the Twin Towers and killed almost 3,000 innocent people) and ISIS (which has gruesomely beheaded innocent victims in Iraq, Syria and Libya) have planted images of Islam as a religion of pure evil.

This dark image of Islam has been further compounded by the violations of human rights in Muslim theocracies, notably Saudi Arabia, Iran and Afghanistan under Taliban rule. The resurgence of the Taliban in 2021 has been accompanied by the brutal torture and execution of perceived enemies and the renewed repression of women and minorities. Such things remind the world of everything it finds reprehensible about Islam as a ruling ideology.

For non-Muslims who have lived well and peacefully in Muslim countries, or who have Muslim family members or friends, or who have found beauty in the words of the Quran or Rumi, the terror and oppression practiced by Muslim individuals, groups or states are an aberration, an ugly distortion of the faith on par with the perversions of Christianity in the Crusades and Inquisition of centuries past.

The Muslim concept of the world being divided into two competing spheres—the *Dar Al Islam* and *Dar Al Harb* (the Muslim world and the world that has to be conquered for Islam through *jihad* or holy war)—is not unlike the Communist view of a world divided between Communist states and states that have to be made into Communist states. The difference is that while Communism prescribes violent revolution and dictatorship to achieve its goals, Islam teaches its faithful to put God and a life of obedience to God above all else. If Muslims adhere to this principle and to the Quranic injunction, "There is no compulsion in religion" (Sura 2.256), there is no reason why Muslims cannot coexist peacefully with members of other faiths.

Islam Fulfills a Promise to Ishmael

How then can Islam and its role in history be understood? Perhaps the best place to begin is in the family of Abraham. As we mentioned in Chapter 5, Ishmael, as the elder half-brother of Isaac, was promised a blessing that was not given in his lifetime but that became a promise to his descendants. In an ideal world, had Jesus been embraced by Israel and expanded the reach of his work beyond Israel's boundaries, the first people to receive the blessing of his worldwide mission would likely have been the Arabs. However, although both Judaism and Christianity had established a presence in Arabia by the 7th century AD, it was then that Mohammed appeared as a prophet, teaching revelations from the angel Gabriel and establishing a religion that would spread throughout the world.

As with all religions, Islam has many diverse manifestations. The terrorists who cry *Allahu Akbar* (*God is Almighty*) as they detonate a bomb targeting civilians or pull a knife across the throat of an innocent person are disconnected from the true purpose of religion, which is to connect human beings to their Creator through truth and love. There should be no condoning of their actions, just as there should be no condoning of the slave trade—by Muslims or Christians—or of the Christian Crusades and Inquisition. If evil wraps itself in religious garb and uses religious language to appeal to good people, it is still evil—and perhaps the worst form of evil because it exploits good to achieve evil purposes.

But there are other manifestations of Islam. There are the ordinary people going about their daily life trying to make ends meet, trying to educate their children and give them a good future. For many of these people, Islam is a source of grounding, of purpose, of moral principles that guide their daily life in peaceful pursuits. And then there are the mystics, or Sufis, who seek a more intimate experience with God and are willing to dedicate their one day off work to prayer and *Dhikr* (devotional chanting of the names of God). This group has given rise to inspired poets, like Rumi and Hafez, as well as to many charitable endeavors, from serving one's family and community to providing food, education and health care to the needy.

An Early Chance for Reconciliation

In the early years of the new religion, there seemed a possibility for a reconciliation between Christianity and Islam. On the Christian side, in 800 there was a move to unify Christendom when Pope Leo III anointed Charlemagne first ruler of the Holy Roman Empire. At the same time, the Muslim world was largely united under the authority of its leading figure, the Caliph Harun Al Rashid, based in Baghdad. The emperor and the caliph exchanged gifts as gestures of friendship, but soon the relationship between the two great religions would sour, and they became outright enemies during the Crusades.

As Islam expanded out of the Arabian Peninsula, its main rival was the Byzantine Empire, with its capital city Constantinople. Several attempts were made to capture this fabled city, and eventually, in 1453, the Ottoman Turks under Sultan Mehmed II conquered it for Islam. The Sultan rode his horse into Hagia Sophia, the holiest church in the Orthodox world, and declared that he would make it into a mosque. Which he did, embittering Orthodox Christians for centuries.

This Muslim victory marked the end of a significant political role for the Orthodox Church in the Levant, as the Ottoman Empire extended to Egypt and much of North Africa, circled the Black Sea and reached all the way to the walls of Vienna in Europe. When the Ottoman Empire crumbled in World War I, much of the Orthodox world fell under Communist regimes, notably the Soviet Union in Russia and Ukraine, as well as similar dictatorships in Romania and Serbia. Following the collapse of the Soviet Union and the liberation of Central and East European countries from Communism at the end of the 1980s, the Orthodox churches have been able to rebuild. (The seat of the Ecumenical Patriarch remains in Istanbul, but there are only some 2,000 Greek Orthodox Christians in Turkey today.)

Global Expansion

Islam's rapid expansion often occurred in areas where Christianity had little success, such as west from its Arabian heartland along the arid lands of North Africa, and east and north into the Persian Empire, Asia Minor and Central Asia. Today, there are almost two billion Muslims scattered across the earth, with very large populations outside the Arab World in Indonesia, India and Pakistan, as well as in African countries like Nigeria and Senegal. It is the fastest-growing religion on earth.

The history of Islamic expansionism has sometimes been stained by violence and bloodshed. Often, conquered peoples were given a choice of converting to Islam or accepting the second-class status of *dhimmis* or non-Muslims who must pay additional taxes (*jizya*) in exchange for being allowed to practice their faith.

Encouragingly, the Muslim countries have not proved easy prey for Marxism, and some, notably Saudi Arabia, have been staunch opponents of Communism. Muslim societies to this day tend to be more outwardly religious than their Christian counterparts, and it is still rare to find citizens in Muslim-majority countries who espouse Marxist or Socialist ideas, as atheism is fundamentally antithetical to Muslim culture.

The main exception to this rule was seen in some newly independent Arab states—especially Syria and Iraq, both of which developed regimes based on *Baathism*. This socialist theory of government was developed primarily by Michel Aflaq (1910-1989), a Syrian Arab Christian who became a Communist while studying at the Sorbonne and who advocated for a one-party secular state. His interest was primarily Arab nationalism, and he believed the Arab states should form a single nation. The Baathist regimes of the Assad family in Syria and Saddam Hussein in Iraq were destructive of traditional Muslim societies and among the most tyrannical and brutal governments in human history.

Despite this history of resisting Marxism, a new danger has emerged with

Communist China's wooing of Muslim-majority states with lucrative investments and trade deals. Countries like Pakistan, Turkey and Iran have proven vulnerable to China's charms, especially given their desire for money to build their infrastructure and military, and for strategic alliances that help them achieve their own regional or larger goals. Whatever Beijing promises them (often soft loans as part of the Belt and Road Initiative) is likely to be fraught with risk, and the long-term price to be paid for playing along with a brutal, atheistic regime is likely to be high.

A Shared Mission for Abrahamic Faiths

Considering that Marxism poses a deadly threat to all authentic religions, there is good reason for Muslims, Christians and Jews to set aside their historical and theological differences and resentments from the past and work together to defeat Marxism and its atheistic offshoots. The beliefs that bind the members of these faiths together are far more significant and valuable than anything offered by materialist ideology or Communist regimes. If the members of these faiths are willing to view their differences in this context, they can work together to create a common front to defeat Marxism and its offshoots.

This is, of course, easier said than done. Religious differences have been responsible for countless disputes and wars in history and continue to make many believers look at members of other faiths with distrust and even hatred. Worse still, there are many religious leaders who build a following based on rallying the faithful to a crusade or *jihad* against members of rival faiths. This makes it all the more important for religious leaders to recognize the outcome of their teachings—and to make every effort to pursue the Way of Abel by reaching out to their brothers and cousins in faith so as to build an effective alliance against the destructive forces of the Left.

Chapter 9

Renewal and Revolution in Europe

Cain and Abel Movements Shape the Future

The Renaissance

The Roman Catholic Church persecuted not only those whose religious beliefs it deemed heretical but also those who put forward theories of human nature and the universe that did not fit with Church dogma. The reaction to the first type of persecution gave birth to the Protestant Reformation; the reaction to the second type of persecution gave birth to humanism and the Renaissance (French for renewal), which revived interest in the much earlier science of Greece and Rome.

The first notable Renaissance thinker and poet was 14th century Italian Francesco Petrarca (Petrarch). Once a priest, he would become known as the father of humanism and of the Renaissance. He believed that secular achievements did not preclude a relationship with God, pointing out that human intellectual and creative abilities were themselves an endowment by the Creator. Humanism enabled artists to glorify the human body and nature in their work, echoing their Greek and Roman forebears. Among these great artists were Leonardo da Vinci, Michelangelo, Raphael and Donatello.

In the 16th century, another religious man, Nicolaus Copernicus, discovered that the sun was at the center of the known universe and that the earth revolved around it, contradicting Church doctrine. A century later,

Italian Galileo Galilei agreed with Copernicus. He was arrested and accused of heresy by the Church and would die in prison while waiting to be tried. Nevertheless, seeds of scientific discovery planted by the Greeks two millennia earlier were now beginning to bear fruit as modern science.

The Renaissance was a reaction to the otherworldliness of Christianity. It relished the beauty of nature and celebrated human creativity in the arts. It was not anti-religion but rather helpful in translating some of the abstractions of religion into the reality of the physical world. It also helped remind people that they were responsible for their own actions and that exploring the universe and creating beauty through art and music were fully consistent with their purpose for being.

The Enlightenment

Freed from the censorship of the Church, science began to carve out its own realm of knowledge, based on observation and experimentation. This represented a wholly new way of looking at the world, and it would only grow in its attractiveness to rational human beings seeking to understand their existence. This growth of reason and science would spawn yet another movement, the Enlightenment of the 17th and 18th centuries. It represented a further move away from dependence on religion for understanding, and while not necessarily hostile to religion, it was increasingly skeptical of religious assumptions and beliefs, especially those related to the invisible world of spiritual existence and faith.

As with all human endeavors, the Renaissance and Enlightenment would spawn both Cain- and Abel-type offshoots: science used for evil, and science used for good; movements of violent revolution and oppression and movements of peaceful change and human liberation. Used wisely, science has proven to be of enormous benefit to humanity, enabling the development of a wide range of technologies that have enabled people to live longer and better than ever before. Harnessed efficiently by capitalist economies, science and technology have enabled a tremendous expansion of agriculture and food production and a radical reduction in poverty worldwide, promising an abundant life for all. In contrast, when science and technology are used for evil, they facilitate totalitarian rule, as we see in Communist China's surveillance of, and intrusion into, the lives of individuals and oppression of dissident individuals and groups.

Cain and Abel Revolutions in Europe

In the political arena, the Renaissance and Enlightenment had a dramatic impact on Western societies and ultimately the world. Encouraged by newfound freedoms inspired by a belief in individual rights, a new person was emerging, an individual who was educated and who sought to shape his or her own destiny. No longer could these enlightened people accept the primacy of any single church, the divine right of kings or the privilege of aristocracy. They wanted to have a say in their government and opportunities to better themselves. Given the reluctance of the establishment to relinquish power willingly, growing resistance to authority and, eventually, revolutions of some sort or another were inevitable.

However, the revolutions that occurred differed significantly from one another, resulting in very different long-term outcomes.

Britain's Glorious Revolution

In Europe, opposition to monarchical regimes and the desire for religious, political and economic freedom resulted in several revolutionary movements. In Britain, the steady development of the Common Law and individual rights led to King John relinquishing absolute power by signing the Magna Carta charter in 1215, thereby ceding power to wealthy landowners who established the first Parliament. The pressure to expand the powers of Parliament and limit those of the monarch would lead to outright civil war in 1642, when mainly Protestant rebels fought to seize power from King Charles I, a

Catholic. Under the leadership of Oliver Cromwell, who had wanted to join the pilgrims and emigrate to America, the "Roundheads" were victorious, taking control of the Parliament and executing the king in 1649.

After a decade of Regency under Cromwell, the monarchy was re-established in England under Charles II, the eldest surviving son of Charles I. However, the Civil War had brought about significant changes, and the monarchy would soon permanently relinquish many of its powers to the Parliament. This took place in the Glorious Revolution of 1688-1689, when Parliament forced King James II from power and replaced him with William III and Mary II. These joint monarchs took power on conditions set by Parliament, and in 1689 they signed a Bill of Rights into law that limited the power of the monarchy, elevated the role of the Parliament, and enumerated individual rights, thereby establishing a Constitutional Monarchy. (See the text of the English Bill of Rights in Appendix 9, pp363-371.)

The Glorious Revolution and the English Bill of Rights would play a significant role in inspiring the founding of America as an independent republic 100 years later. After the American colonies won their freedom from British rule, the Founding Fathers, who had initiated the anti-British revolt with the Declaration of Independence in 1776, devised a new, republican constitution. It was finally adopted on June 21, 1788, when New Hampshire became the ninth state to ratify it. Months later, on March 4, 1789, the new republican government started to operate. Once the Constitution had been adopted, a Bill of Rights in the form of ten amendments was added, echoing the English Bill of Rights. These amendments were ratified by the states in 1791.

Based on "Laws of Nature and Nature's God," as the Declaration of Independence put it, the American republic was established without a monarch or aristocracy and would become an Abel-type model of democratic government for the whole world.

The French Revolution

By contrast, in France, the people's bitterness towards the monarchy, nobility and Catholic Church would boil over into the violent, Cain-type revolution of 1789. The revolutionaries were bent on destruction of the existing order but did not have a specific, better alternative to offer. The main philosophical influence on the French Revolution came from Jean-Jacques Rousseau (1712-1778). Considered a Deist, his theory of the General Will was used as a justification for revolutionary, and later dictatorial, action on behalf of "the people." Rousseau was the primary inspiration for the Jacobins (named for the Saint Jacques Monastery where they first met), who were the driving force of the revolutionary movement founded in 1789 by Maximilien Robespierre—and led by him during the bloodiest phase of the French Revolution. Of Rousseau, Robespierre said: "Rousseau is the one man who, through the loftiness of his soul and the grandeur of his character, showed himself worthy of the role of teacher of mankind."[20] The Jacobins would become synonymous with violent revolutionaries. (See more on Rousseau's influence following.)

In a chilling foreshadowing of totalitarian regimes to come, Robespierre is credited with coining the movement's seductive slogan, "liberty, fraternity, equality," which proved a total deception given the violence and chaos the revolution produced for years. Again, in a pattern that would oft be repeated by tyrants, Robespierre abandoned his professed ideals once in power. He called for the execution of King Louis XVI even though he previously said he opposed capital punishment. "With regret, I pronounce this fatal truth: Louis must die so that the nation may live," he said.[21] On January 21, four days after the National Convention convicted the king, he was guillotined.

Foreshadowing tyrannies to come, the French Revolution became ever more extreme, entrusting the defense of the revolution and removal of its enemies to an innocuous-sounding Committee of Public Safety, led by Robespierre, which organized a Reign of Terror that lasted from 1793 to 1794. Aided by the Revolutionary Tribunal, it was responsible for several massacres and the official death sentences of 16,594, usually by guillotine. Another 10,000 died in prison without having a trial. Robespierre himself seems to have forgotten his ideals, justifying terror as a necessary guarantor of virtue, "an emanation of virtue":

> If the mainspring of popular government in peacetime is virtue, amid revolution it is at the same time [both] virtue and terror: virtue, without which terror is fatal; terror, without which virtue is impotent. Terror is nothing but prompt, severe, inflexible justice; it is therefore an emanation of virtue. It is less a special principle than a consequence of the general principle of democracy applied to our country's most pressing needs.[22]

As so often happens with violent revolutions, the French revolutionaries soon turned on their own. Thus it was that Robespierre himself fell victim to factional squabbles within the National Convention and was hauled off to prison, where he tried to commit suicide. On July 28, 1794, he was tried and convicted of "counter-revolution" by the Revolutionary Tribunal. He was guillotined that evening. The next day, seventy radical members of the Paris Commune (the city government), who were allied with Robespierre, were also guillotined. It would be another five years before the decade of revolution finally drew to a close. With the rise to power of Napoleon Bonaparte in 1799, France would turn from internal conflicts to external conquests, but for several decades it was intermittently troubled by violent revolts, culminating in the bloody Paris Commune of 1871, inspired by its Reign of Terror namesake.

The Long Shadow of Rousseau

In his insightful book, *Intellectuals*, Paul Johnson analyses the ideas of the main intellectual figures who shaped the dominant Leftist thinking of the modern era, starting from the 18th century. Johnson doesn't stop at the books they wrote but examines their lives to give context to their theories. First up is Rousseau, whom Johnson describes as:

> ...the first of the modern intellectuals, their archetype and in many ways the

most influential of them all. Older men like Voltaire had started the work of demolishing the altars and enthroning reason. But Rousseau was the first to combine all the salient characteristics of the modern Promethean: the assertion of his right to reject the existing order in its entirety; confidence in his capacity to refashion it from the bottom in accordance with principles of his own devising; belief that this could be achieved by the political process; and, not least, recognition of the huge part instinct, intuition and impulse play in human conduct. He believed that he had a unique love for humanity and had been endowed with unprecedented gifts and insights to increase its felicity. An astonishing number of people, in his own day and since, have taken him at his own valuation. In both the long and the short term, his influence was enormous. In the generation after his death it attained the status of a myth.[23]

Rousseau led a life of gross narcissism, handing over to a state orphanage (and almost certain death) every one of his five newborn children, despite his comfortable financial circumstances. As Johnson says, "By a curious chain of infamous moral logic, Rousseau's iniquity as a parent was linked to his ideological offspring, the future totalitarian state."[24] He elaborates:

> It was necessary to replace the existing society by something totally different and essentially egalitarian; but, this done, revolutionary disorder could not be permitted. The rich and the privileged, as the ordering force, would be replaced by the State, embodying the General Will, which all contracted to obey. Such obedience would become instinctive and voluntary since the State, by a systematic process of cultural engineering, would inculcate virtue in all. The State was the father, the *patrie*, and all its citizens were the children of the paternal orphanage.[25]

And further:

> Rousseau's state is not merely authoritarian: it is also totalitarian, since it orders every aspect of human activity, thought included. Under the social contract, the individual was obliged to 'alienate himself, with all his rights, to the whole of the community' (i.e., the State).

> 'You must, therefore, treat citizens as children and control their upbringing and thoughts, planting 'the social law in the bottom of their hearts.' They

then become 'social men by their natures and citizens by their inclinations; they will be one, they will be good, they will be happy, and their happiness will be that of the Republic.'[26]

At the same time, Rousseau criticized capitalism:

> The evil of competition, as he saw it, which destroys man's inborn communal sense and encourages all his most evil traits, including his desire to exploit others, led Rousseau to distrust private property, as the source of social crime. His fifth innovation, then, on the very eve of the Industrial Revolution, was to develop the elements of a critique of capitalism, both in the preface to his play *Narcisse* and in his *Discours sur l'inégalité*, by identifying property and the competition to acquire it as primary cause of alienation. This was a thought-deposit Marx and others were to mine ruthlessly, together with Rousseau's related idea of cultural evolution.[27]

Indeed, not only did Rousseau provide theories that were embraced by the Jacobins a decade after his death—and resulted in the French revolution devolving into a murderous bloodbath—he also proposed a solution to the world's ills that proved extremely useful to Marxism and would be translated into practices of both the Communist and Fascist revolutions and regimes of the 20th century:

> Hence—and this is the true revolution Rousseau's ideas brought about—he moved the political process to the very center of human existence by making the legislator, who is also a pedagogue, into the new Messiah, capable of solving all human problems by creating New Men. 'Everything,' he wrote, 'is at root dependent on politics.' Virtue is the product of good government. 'Vices belong less to man, than to man badly governed.' The political process, and the new kind of state it brings into being, are the universal remedies for the ills of mankind. Politics will do all. Rousseau thus prepared the blueprint for the principal delusions and follies of the twentieth century.[28]

Thus the French Revolution saw not only the first application of Rousseau's theories, its clumsy attempts at instituting a new, authoritarian system of government foreshadowed many of the grotesquely inhuman but much more successful totalitarian regimes of the 20th century. The chaos and bloodshed in France stand in sharp contrast to the American Revolution taking place around the same time on the other side of the Atlantic Ocean. Both revolutions marked the beginning of a post-monarchic era of representative government: In France, the trend led to regimes that concentrated power in the hands of government at the cost of individual rights; in America, the trend led to government ruled by a constitution designed to protect the rights of individuals against the predations of government.

The French Revolution Foreshadows Fascism and Communism

There were a number of aspects of the French Revolution that anticipated violent revolutions and oppressive regimes in the future. Briefly, one of these was the institution of state religions in the place of traditional Christian churches; the other was the terroristic character of the totalitarian state as it seized power and imposed its rule.

Hatred for the Catholic Church was deep among France's republicans, and a radical faction of the revolutionaries, including Jacques Hébert and Antoine-François Momoro, created an alternative, atheistic Cult of Reason to serve as the state religion. This was an anthropocentric system of belief without gods of any sort and was the official religion for a year during the Reign of Terror. Robespierre also despised the Church, but he believed that Christianity had value as a source of virtue. He devised a new state religion, called the Cult of the Supreme Being, that was adopted as the state religion by the National Convention in May 1794. He organized an initial Festival of the Supreme Being as an official state celebration, and took a leading role on the occasion, inviting accusations from his detractors that he had become a dictator. With Robespierre's execution, his religion soon faded, and Napoleon officially reinstated the Catholic Church in 1801.

Thus in a very short period, the French Revolution produced two statist alternatives to the Catholic Church, foreshadowing the exploitation and destruction of religion in the 20th century by totalitarian regimes. The atheistic Cult of Reason foreshadowed 20th century atheistic Socialist and Communist regimes (that in some cases, such as China, continue to the present) while the Cult of the Supreme Being foreshadowed state-sanctioned churches witnessed in the 20th century Fascist regimes in Germany, Italy and Spain, all of which used the church to oppress their citizens.

Second, Robespierre's justification for terror in the name of virtue and democracy, referenced above, was a perfect articulation of a totalitarian justification for ruthless suppression of all opposition, which is a hallmark of Socialism and Communism (most notably in Stalin's Reign of Terror) and Fascism (most notably in Hitler's Germany).

The Glorious Revolution Foreshadows Democratic Governments

As mentioned above, by contrast, the Glorious Revolution took place without the widespread cruelty, injustice and bloodshed of the French Revolution. It was an Abel-type, revolutionary transformation of society that built on English common law, Magna Carta and English Civil War. It championed individual liberty, democracy and the rule of law, and ultimately gave birth to the American republic and the US Constitution. By contrast, the French Revolution was Cain-like. It spawned more revolutions, violence and bloodshed in 19th century France, culminating in the 1871 Paris Commune, and it served as a prototype for Socialist, Communist and Fascist governments that emerged in the 20th century, beginning with Russia's Marxist-Leninist Revolution in 1917.

See the following table for a summary of the Cain- and Abel-type systems of government that originated with European revolutions.

Cain and Abel Revolutions and Their Outcomes

CAIN

Date	Revolutions	Date	Outcomes
1789	French Revolution		
1793	Jacobin Rule	1792	French Republic
	Reign of Terror	1871	Paris Commune
			Violent Revolutions: Socialism Communism
	Communism		Totalitarianism
1917	Russian Revolution	1922	Soviet Union
1927	Chinese Civil War	1949	Communist China
	Worldwide Revolutions		Worldwide Communism
1922	Mussolini		Worldwide Fascism
1933	Hitler		
1936	Franco		

ABEL

Date	Revolutions	Date	Outcomes
	English Revolution	1215	Parliament Established
1215	Magna Carta		
1642	Civil War	1649	Parliament Empowered
1688	Glorious Revolution	1689	Constitutional Monarchy
			Bill of Rights
	Republicanism		Democracy
1776	American Revolution	1789	Constitutional Republic
1788	US Constitution	1792	Bill of Rights
			Worldwide Democracy

Chapter 10

The Advent of Communism

Marxism Offers an Earthly Utopia

The Genesis of Marxism

There was much to concern a thoughtful person in the mid-19th century. The Industrial Revolution, which had started towards the end of the 18th century, was having a dramatic impact on how people worked and lived. Wealth was being created at an unprecedented pace. Initially, only owners and investors appeared to benefit from the development of capitalism, while the workers lived and labored in wretched conditions. The disparity in income and lifestyles is dramatically evident in the magnificent homes of industrialists of the era compared with the humble hovels of workers. However, as the 19th century progressed, there were several new workers' rights laws passed in industrial states, and the workers too began to see a very significant improvement in their standard of living.

It was against the backdrop of suffering among the poor classes, and especially workers, that Karl Marx developed his theory of Communism as the solution to social injustices. Working closely with his decades-long collaborator, fellow German Friedrich Engels, he developed a politico-economic theory that justified violent revolution by the poor against the wealthy. In their landmark 1848 treatise, *The Communist Manifesto*, Marx and Engels railed against injustices in Europe, blaming capitalism, religion, family and the state for human alienation and suffering. Believing that private property was the root of evil, they called for it—and the capitalist system based on it—to be abolished.

> In this sense, the theory of the Communists may be summed up in the single sentence: Abolition of private property. (Appendix 1, Page 277.)

Communism would become the most influential materialist and revolutionary ideology ever devised, inspiring numerous violent revolutions and the creation of many totalitarian Socialist and Communist governments. To this day, Marxism and its offshoots pose the greatest threat to civilizations around the world.

Karl Marx and Friedrich Engels

Marx and Engels were not accomplished scientists, despite their claim to have invented scientific socialism. Their economic theories were based on a narrow and inaccurate view of capitalism in 19th century Europe, as well as their personal resentments and hatreds for those more fortunate than them. (Ironically, foreshadowing a history of Communist hypocrisy, Engels was himself the son of an industrialist and supported both himself and Marx with income from those capitalist industries.) Their political views were developed to justify violent revolution to overthrow existing governments, the capitalist system and traditional social institutions, all in the name of the working classes or proletariat.

Most of their theories are contained in the three volumes of *Das Kapital* (Capital), a massive work started by Marx (the first volume was published in 1867) but finished by Engels after Marx's death in 1883. It is not an easy read. It features laborious argumentation for concepts of nature, economics, politics and theory that simply don't stand up to modern standards of scientific investigation and knowledge. Nevertheless, they claimed that the scientific basis for their central theories was confirmed when Charles Darwin came up with his theory of evolution based on natural selection. They believed that

"Survival of the Fittest," as it was labeled by Henry Spencer, was proof of their dialectical theory, in which inadequacies and contradictions within entities give rise to conflicts that ultimately produce new and better entities.

In a December 19, 1860 letter to Engels, Marx declared that Darwin's *On the Origin of Species*, "...is the book which *contains the basis in natural history for our view*."[29] And, in a January 16, 1861 letter to activist Ferdinand Lassalle, he elaborated: "Darwin's work is most important and suits my purpose in that it provides a basis in natural science for the historical *class struggle*."[30] Marx's chief dispute with Darwin was that the English scientist believed evolution was a very gradual process that unfolded over centuries and millennia. This contradicted Marx's dialectic theory, which predicted that species would develop through a progression of "revolutionary" leaps. Marx reasoned that as humans are merely evolved animals, their natural tendency to rebel against the status quo (as described in dialectical and historical materialism) is reflected in the evolution of the natural world.

The original concept of the dialectic is attributed to Aristotle and was demonstrated by his student in the *Dialogues of Plato* as an approach to validating knowledge. Georg Hegel elaborated on this concept with his theory that a proposition is a thesis that is contradicted by its antithesis, an interaction that is resolved by the emergence of a higher truth or synthesis. He saw this process guiding human development towards an absolute. Marx rejected Hegel's conclusion and adopted a Left Hegelian interpretation of the dialectic. He proposed that the reaction of the antithesis to the thesis was radical—and typically violent—due to their essentially contradictory nature. He described human beings as a composite of essence and existence who advance through dialectical action, ultimately creating a history of progress through repeated violent rejections of the status quo.

Marx and Engels borrowed another idea from Hegel, namely that dialectical action transforms quantitative change into qualitative change. As an example of this phenomenon, Engels explained that as water undergoes changes in temperature, it also transforms from solid to liquid to gas. For a biological example, he said that a barley seed naturally germinates (through an internal dialectical struggle) and becomes a plant. The seed no longer exists, but the plant then negates itself by producing seeds, and the sequence is repeated. This negation of negation results in more seeds and more plants. Engels speculated that through labor, apes were able to transition to humans, and that growth in human population resulted in changes in social structures. (Stalin embraced another example of negation of negation: French-Hungarian Marxist Georges Politzer said that when a chicken emerges from an egg, it negates the egg, but then the chicken grows into a hen and negates itself. See Appendix 3, p301, for this reference, and Appendix 10, pp372-375, for more of Engels' theories on nature, including the origin of life and history as process.)

But the dialectic doesn't explain the origin of life itself, unless we are to believe that life emerged as the negation of non-life. Furthermore, the argument that nature rewards conflict by emerging in a new and better synthesis of opposites through the dialectical process, is not supported by science. In fact, conflict is destructive. Nature rewards cooperation, as we see in human society where good emerges from constructive interaction among individuals and groups, whereas conflict results in suffering and destruction. (For a theory of science that codifies this notion of nature rewarding cooperation, see Appendix 11, pp376-377.)

Neo-Marxism: Frankfurt School and Postmodernism

For purposes of simplicity, we are using the term Marxism for those theories promulgated by Marx and Engels as well as for their direct ideological offspring—Marxism-Leninism and Marxism-Maoism, for example. For later theories heavily influenced by Marxism but generally not employing the label, we are using the term Neo-Marxism. In particular this term applies to the ideas developed by the Frankfurt School theorists and, later, the Postmodernists, which reincarnate dialectical materialism as Critical Theory and maintain Marxist atheism, anti-capitalism and socialism. Thus while Marx was primarily preoccupied with political and economic theory, especially what he called class warfare, and Neo-Marxists were more interested in the social sciences, both share a common overarching purpose: the destruction of traditional societies, including the nuclear family and religion, and ending private property. (For a detailed discussion of the Frankfurt School see Chapter 14, and for Postmodernism see Chapters 15 and 16.)

Is Marxism Scientific?

This leads to the question: Does Marxism qualify as science? While the theory seeks to justify violent revolution by pointing to conflict in nature, natural law itself does not comport with Marxism. The examples offered as proof of negation above prove nothing of the sort. Changes in the state of water brought about by the application or removal of heat have nothing to do with negation. Likewise, there is no negation in the life cycle of barley, which is based on the nurturing of seeds by soil, water and sunlight, leading to germination, growth and production of new seeds. The eggshell protects the chick until it can emerge into the world and sustain independent life. In these latter examples, it is not negation and conflict but the nurturing and multiplication of life that is the shared purpose of the biochemical interactions and the basis for transformation from one state to another.

Nature demonstrates that life is the object and result of an endlessly intricate process of one element or entity contributing to the existence of others. Simpler forms enable the appearance and success of more complex beings. In life, one existence may sacrifice to sustain the existence of another, sometimes in a hierarchy of life, as in food chains, or for the continuation of life within a species. For example, salmon spend most of their lives in the ocean, but they eventually return to the river of their birth, where they struggle upstream to reach a place where they spawn new life. Upon which they die, their bodies supplying food for the next generation.

Negation does not explain the origin of life or the mechanism of evolution. Life comes only from life, which is a product of purpose actualized through the dynamic of harmonious reciprocal interaction between subject and object in and between living beings. Thus a nucleus and cytoplasm interact to create a cell, and a male and female animal interact to create offspring. (In the inanimate world, this subject-object structure is seen, for example, in the formation of atoms based on interaction between the positively charged nucleus and the negatively charged electrons.) Evolution itself is a process of life building on prior life and not on negation of life.

Indeed, science is an evolutionary process of discovery in which one generation lays the foundation for the next. As Isaac Newton famously said: "If I have seen further it is by standing on the shoulders of giants." This was not the approach of Marx and Engels, neither of whom were scientists. They were academics who spent their lives in libraries looking for evidence to prove their revolutionary theories. They did no experiments, and there is no evidence that Marx even visited a factory, mine or other industrial workplace, although he claimed that workers, the proletariat, were his primary interest, both as the main victims of capitalism and as the world's best hope for a better future. And Marx was not above misquoting sources—or using references that were clearly out of date or irrelevant—to make a point. As Paul Johnson points out:

> [Marx} was not interested in finding the truth but in proclaiming it… there was nothing scientific about him; indeed, in all that matters he was an anti-scientist. [31]

> The kind of facts which did not interest Marx were the facts to be discovered by examining the world and the people who live in it with his own eyes and ears. He was totally and incorrigibly deskbound. Nothing on earth would get him out of the library and the study.[32]

The Absence of Science in Scientific Socialism

In 1880, Engels claimed that Marxism was "scientific socialism," but that was wishful thinking. Marx was not a real scientist. Neither was Engels. They were revolutionaries who sought to wrap their theories in science but failed: Their critique of capitalism is ill-founded and out of date; their labor theory of value has little relevance in today's developed economies; their dialectical materialism is a seriously flawed explanation of evolution and history, and, in truth explains nothing; their economic determinism is an erroneous analysis of societal forces; their debunking of religion is bigoted; and their criticism of the family is wildly erroneous in light of countless studies that demonstrate its vital importance to personal well-being and social stability.

Paul Johnson points out that Marx had an apocalyptic vision of impending global doom, a dystopian view that was often featured in his poetry and colored his philosophy. In fact, in all his studies and writings, Marx was seeking a philosophical and scientific basis for his theories, rather than developing theories based on facts and science:

> Marx, in short, is an eschatological writer from start to finish… Marx's concept of a Doomsday, whether in its lurid poetic version or its eventually economic one, is an artistic not a scientific vision. It was always in Marx's mind, and as a political economist he worked backwards from it, seeking the evidence that made it inevitable, rather than forward to it, from objectively examined data.[33]

In taking this backwards approach to formulating his ideology, Marx established a pattern that has been replicated by Marxist and Neo-Marxist theorists up to the present. They promulgate theories to justify their resentment, envy and prejudices as well as their immoral behavior.

Because Marxism provides a false justification for violent revolution, the record of its application in history has been abysmal. Socialism and Communism do not deliver the Utopia Marx and Engels envisioned. Quite the opposite, they deliver a kind of hell on earth. Instead of securing justice and equality, they justify oppression and inequality. Instead of freeing human minds to explore the truth on their own terms, they control information flows and dictate ideology. Detractors are punished on a scale that makes the Holy Inquisition look like the work of beginners. ("Cancel Culture" is the latest incarnation of this feature of Marxism: It is the first step in a Communist state's march towards total control of information and severe punishment for detractors and refuseniks.)

Perhaps the greatest irony of all (and indictment of the theory) is that while the whole point of Marxism is purported to be concern for workers, the proletariat, this class has fared the worst in Socialist and Communist states. Thus when, in the 1930s, avid Marxists Arthur Koestler and André Gide first visited the Soviet Union, they were shocked to find that workers there lived in wretched circumstances that were far worse than the condition of workers in the capitalist societies from which they had supposedly been saved by the Russian Revolution. (See their accounts in Chapter 12.)

Nevertheless, in our secularizing world, the notion that Socialism is scientific has proven attractive. Surely, its advocates insist, science can be trusted to guide us to the best possible economic and political system. But their wishful thinking would prefer not to look at the hard evidence of the 20th century, with its tens of millions killed at the hands of Socialist and Communist regimes (discussed in detail in the next chapter). Marxist apologists tell us that the Soviet Union and Communist China made mistakes, but the theory is sound; it just needs proper application. This is nuts. The Soviet Union and Communist China are two leading examples of the application of Marxism to the fullest extent possible.

The lack of sound science in Marxism and Neo-Marxism also explains another feature common to both: They prove nothing and therefore can be said to prove anything. (Karl Popper noticed a similar feature in Freud's psychoanalysis, which Popper determined was unscientific because it made no predictions that had the potential to be proved untrue; they were all compatible with every possible observation.[34])

As we shall show, the standard defense of Marxist ideologues and leaders, when confronted with obvious logical inconsistencies in their positions, has been to accuse their critics of being incapable of "dialectical thinking." The defense of Neo-Marxists is to accuse their critics of being incapable of "critical thinking." In the case of Postmodernism, Foucault and others abandoned science altogether, claiming that knowledge itself was a function of social structures shaped by the language of the powerful. This position creates a safe haven for nutty and dangerous ideas that are protected from science and rational debate. (Ironically, this position does not prevent the Left from claiming the mantle of science when convenient to do so, as, for example, when declaring that a consensus of scientists support global warming theories.)

The Marxist View of Evil

As noted, Marx believed that Darwin had provided the answer to the riddle of the origin of life, the process of evolution and the nature of human beings and society. Marx believed that class conflicts over property shaped history, and thus the root of evil was ownership of private property. In the case of capitalist societies, he believed that the accumulation of private property by the bourgeoisie at the expense of the proletariat was at the heart of social injustice and suffering. Thus capitalism itself is an evil system that can only be remedied by the transfer of private property to ownership by the proletariat-controlled state. He further believed that this remedy could only be achieved through the violent overthrow of the capitalist class since people would not voluntarily surrender their wealth and privilege.

The notion that capitalism is the source of evil has been preserved through generations of Marxist ideological evolution and adaptation and is a common thread that runs through Neo-Marxist and Postmodernist theories. It is supported by Marx's theory of alienation, which says that people are alienated from their true selves due to social stratification into classes, and the solution is to eliminate classes. This is an ultimately superficial and naïve theory that lost credence long ago. Capitalism has proved capable of spreading—rather than limiting—ownership and has created unprecedented wealth for an ever-expanding portion of humanity. Yet the Marxist theory continues to appeal to many who believe that injustice lies in the capitalist economic system, which they believe promotes greed. The inadequacy of the theory is evident in the fact that Socialist and Communist systems that have replaced capitalism have without exception failed to deliver social and economic equality and justice, let alone universal prosperity.

Marx's Cain Nature is Embodied in Marxism

Karl Marx was an unhappy man. Born in 1818 in the Prussian city of Trier (now part of Germany), his family was of Jewish ancestry, with both parents descended from lines of rabbis and Talmudic scholars. However, his father converted to Protestantism before Marx was born, joining the dominant Evangelical Church of Prussia, a Lutheran denomination, to get around a regulation preventing Jews from competing on an equal basis with Christians in the legal profession. Although Marx grew up in a comfortable, well-to-do home, and attended church and a Lutheran elementary school, he came to despise the church and society around him. As he grew into a young man, he saw inequities everywhere and came to believe that economic disparities were at the heart of human alienation and misery.

He often drank heavily and was poor at managing his finances—he constantly begged for money from his parents and, later in life, from his wife and friends. His own wasteful behavior also forced him to borrow money from lenders, often at usurious rates. This fueled his sense of economic injustice and made him a fierce anti-capitalist and anti-Semite (most of the lenders were Jews).

Marx epitomized ingratitude. Despite the sustained support of his parents, of his faithful wife Jenny, and of his partner in revolution, Engels, he never had a job of consequence and constantly complained about the system that failed to provide all of his needs as and when he wanted them provided. His was the archetypal Cain character: angry at the world, resentful and irresponsible. And he always blamed others for his own difficulties in life. An angry and bitter man, he created a miserable environment at home. Two of his daughters committed suicide, and all of his family, relatives and associates suffered from his mean-spirited disposition; endless, often caustic criticism; and refusal to take responsibility for any of his failings.

Marxism Perfects Cain Ideology

The Cain-type personality looks at the world through the myopic lens of self-interest. He is unable to recognize the benefit of mutual success and therefore always seeks to take from others for his own benefit. At the same time, he tends to project this attitude onto others, whom he accuses of possessing what are actually his own selfish interests. In this he epitomizes irresponsibility: blaming others for his own problems instead of taking responsibility for them himself. At this point, Cain will likely cloak himself in the virtue of Abel. He will lament his victim status and claim his innocence of any wrongdoing. Then, if others do not accept his accusations, he will attack them to try and force compliance. This is the point at which verbal abuse can turn to murder.

In essence, Marxism perfects the ideology of Cain, which itself was inherited from Lucifer's selfishness, envy and justification for murder. It is a theory. It is a theory critical of societies that are based on religious values of faith, fidelity and responsibility. It tells people that their troubles in life are not of their own doing but should be blamed on others, and that to end their misery, they need to do away with the individuals and institutions they accuse of making them suffer. In Marxism, the main antagonists are members of different economic classes. In his time, he identified these classes as the business owners (bourgeoisie) and the workers (proletariat). Marx believed that through violent revolution the proletariat would overthrow the bourgeoisie and establish a socialist state run by enlightened proletarian leaders. In its wisdom, this "dictatorship of the proletariat" would build Socialism and eventually oversee the "withering away" of the Socialist state, enabling a perfect Communist state to appear.

In Marxism, personal prejudices and resentments are translated into victimhood-based social agendas, justification for revolution and the destruction of traditional societies, as well as government policies that target social and political groups that are seen as standing in the way of "progress." Marxists and Neo-Marxists have long since expanded on the original, two-class, bourgeoisie-proletariat conflict that Marx and Engels believed was the fundamental problem of history and society. They now apply the dialectic to racial, gender, ethnic and a host of other social divisions. A Marxist only has to label a person or group as an "enemy of the people" to justify demonizing them and targeting them for revolutionary destruction or totalitarian oppression.

The Mentality of Bullies

Marxists have the mentality of bullies who blame others for their own problems, refuse to take responsibility for their own behavior and try to crush those who are actually better than them. They take what they want by intimidation and force and, if necessary, crushing their opponents, real or imagined. This explains the behavior of all violent revolutionary movements and all totalitarian regimes. Thus the Bolsheviks blamed the Tsarist regime, and then the Kerensky government, for all Russia's ills. They justified taking power from Kerensky by force, killing or imprisoning all the "enemies of the revolution" and executing the Tsar's family. Once in power, the Communist Party of the Soviet Union (CPSU) became expert at blaming the rest of the world for all its ills, from the arms race to colonialism and poverty. It also blamed the capitalist countries for its own lame economic performance and inability to provide a decent standard of living for its people.

For Marxists and bullies alike, the most difficult thing to do is to face one's own inadequacies, to admit failure or guilt, to ask for forgiveness and to change course. The Soviet Union accused the rest of the world of committing many sins, but these sins were in fact practiced more widely and lethally in Russia and other Socialist/Communist states. A perfect example of this accusatory mentality can be found in Nikita Khrushchev's speeches to the United Nations in 1960. (See highlights, Appendix 12, pp378-411.) He blamed the West for fomenting irresponsible nuclear policies and for continuing colonialist policies in the developing world. He claimed that the establishment of the Soviet Union was a model of peaceful integration of poor countries into the wonderful community of Soviet states, a much better solution for them than colonialism.

The facts, of course, tell the opposite story. In the Bolshevik revolution and the subsequent civil war, the CPSU crushed countries and ethnic groups—from Ukraine and Belorussia to the Baltic states, the Caucasus and Central Asia—and forced them into membership in the USSR. The Soviet Union wielded the threat of its nuclear arsenal in international affairs, fomented violent "national liberation" revolutions around the world, manipulated Western institutions, and worked tirelessly to subvert "enemy" states through agents of influence and espionage.

In Marxism, Ends Always Justify the Means

It is important to note that Marxism, whether as revolutionary or ruling ideology, always justifies its ruthless means by claiming its objectives are for the good of "the people" and consistent with the inevitable destiny of humankind—a Communist Utopia. As we discussed in Chapter 5, this destiny is the logical conclusion of historical materialism. However, Marxism is based on an erroneous theory of existence, dialectical materialism, that in practice can be used to justify any behavior since it recognizes no moral absolutes. In the world of Critical Theories, which employ dialectical materialism in a broader context, science itself is rejected as a source of absolutes, so that ultimately there are no axiomatic principles or even facts. All is subjective and open to interpretation, and justifies any words or deeds, however violent or destructive they may be. Only the end goal, as defined by the theorist, is important.

This subjective approach to truth explains Communism's bloody history of abuse and cruelty, of the murder of tens of millions of people in the name of "the people." In his book, *Judgement in Moscow*, Vladimir Bukovsky explains how Soviet laws, including Stalin's Constitution, were merely window dressing to provide an excuse for show trials, prison camps, psychiatric incarceration, forced exile and executions. He chronicles how the real decision-making was based on ideology, not law: The Central Committee of the CPSU, the main executive organ of the Party under the leadership of a secretary general, always chose the path that its members believed would best advance their agenda. And the CPSU agenda was, above all else, to expand and secure its power. Bukovsky points out that Marxist ideology cannot be a basis for law (or science or the economy, for that matter) since it lacks any grounding in scientific or moral principles or values. It is worth quoting his words at some length:

> ...ideology in general and the Marxist-Leninist version in particular are incompatible with the concept of law. Ideology is a legend, a myth, and thus unavoidably inconsistent, while the entire sense of the law lies in its internal consistency. Communist practice was all the more inconsistent, being a compromise between ideology and reality. And what was 'done' and what was not on any given day was known only at the top of the pyramid of power...

> The task of ideology is to explain everything on earth in veiled concepts, not amenable to precise definition; the task of the law is to determine everything with a maximum precision, leaving no loopholes. And how can these two things be reconciled? For instance, how can dialectical materialism be codified? The results would be something akin to the efforts of medieval scholars to calculate exactly how many angels can fit on the head of a pin.

> But the main reason for the incompatibility of the law with ideology in a totalitarian state lies in that here ideology, not the law, must dominate by definition, and if ideology cannot rule *through the law*, then it becomes *above the law, ruling from behind its back*, as it were. Just as the party – the

standard-bearer of the ideology – rules from behind the backs of other state structures and is a suprastate formation. Bearing in mind the global aims of this ideology (and with it, those of the party), the law simply transforms into a fiction, an offshoot of propaganda calculated to create an attractive image of 'the world's most democratic' socialist state. This was glaringly obvious in the example of the Stalinist constitution, written expressly for propagandistic purposes...

In practice, the law existed only on paper; the country was governed in accordance with an endless stream of departmental, state, and party instructions and resolutions, which were frequently contradicted and mainly confidential. To reduce all this to a single noncontradictory state was beyond even the party's ability. 'Telephone law' flourished; a call from the party boss would be the latest legislative act.

In all fairness it must be said that the ideology was just as incompatible with other areas of life such as economics, and science, for the very same reasons.[35]

The Marxist Criticism of Christianity

The attraction of Marxism was that it offered a "Kingdom of Heaven" on earth, a man-made Utopia that was attainable in your lifetime and hence much more alluring than the invisible, otherworldly Kingdom of Heaven promised in an ever-receding future by Christianity. In his 1894 *On the History of Early Christianity*, Engels emphasized this key "selling point" of Marxism:

> Both Christianity and the workers' socialism preach forthcoming salvation from bondage and misery; Christianity places this salvation in a life beyond, after death, in heaven; socialism places it in this world, in a transformation of society.[36]

This is precisely the vulnerability of Christianity that Marxism exploits with its fault-finding. It has been easy for Marxists and other materialists to point to imperfections and outright injustices in Christian societies (as well as those of other religions) and blame the religion itself for its failure to realize its own ideals in the here and now. And Christianity's promise of a good world sometime in an unknown future is simply not good enough for those afflicted with very real suffering in their lives. More than that, a righteous mind demands equality and justice in the present time. This is especially true in the world we live in now when science and technology have so dramatically been able to improve our lives. Surely, an equitable society should be within reach!

Indeed, in many respects, the attraction of Marxism has resided in its alignment with the global trends towards humanism and science over religion and faith. Marxism is an ideological offshoot of the anti-Church, anti-Monarchy French Revolution, which was the result of Renaissance and Enlightenment influences but lacked a cohesive revolutionary theory. Marx and Engels perfected just such a theory, providing an ideological base for violent revolutions into the future.

Marxism's Falsehoods Doom it to Failure

The obvious truth is that while society is more and more secular, human beings are eternally spiritual. The beautiful world pictured by Marx and Engels can never be delivered by Socialism and Communism or any other atheistic system built by totalitarians. Marxism and Neo-Marxism are bound to fail. Only enlightened, caring human beings can realize a real heavenly kingdom through understanding Divine laws and applying them to life, thereby growing ever more mature in giving and receiving love.

However, Marxism has continued to expand its influence after over a century of poisoning civilization with atheistic ideology and spreading violent revolutions around the world. Clearly, then, the existence of falsehoods and deceptions in the theory is not in itself a sufficient reason to trust in Marxism's demise. There must be a persuasive and effective alternative to Marxism that supplants it in our culture and in ruling ideologies.

Developing and planting that alternative deep into modern society is the most pressing task facing people of faith and goodwill today. After all,

Marxism has been criticized since its birth but it has not been thoroughly debunked and replaced with a credible alternative so far.

Developing an Effective Alternative to Marxism

Christianity and other religions have many of the essential truths needed to achieve a Godly alternative to Marxism, but this alternative has not yet been fully articulated. As Marxism built on the Renaissance and Enlightenment, a new articulation of religious understanding and belief can be built on the Protestant Reformation and the Great Awakening that took place in the 1730s and 1740s. A new and deeper understanding of the truth should make personal responsibility crystal clear: We should no longer wait for God to do what is in fact our responsibility and do everything in our power to contribute to the positive transformation of the world, as champions of truth, justice and goodness.

Both being part of an originally good creation, the Marxist and the bully know, at some deep level, that they are wrong. Yet they are unable to overcome their jealousy for the more blessed person, culture or nation. Their solution is to criticize and destroy as if this will actually benefit them. It never does. At best it offers fleeting gains—gains that are forever tainted by the injustice that they know they have indulged in to get what they want.

Only resolute opposition to their falsehoods by good people, good groups and good governments can enable the Marxists and the bullies to face this painful reality about themselves: the fact that they have acted in grievous error and must do something to rectify the injustices they have perpetrated. It is at this moment of self-realization that a sincere hand of help should be offered, to guide them on the path of virtue and goodness.

Appeasement, on the other hand, only feeds the beast of their selfish ambitions. That was the fundamental problem with détente, and it is the basic weakness of a policy of accommodation with Communist China today. We need to be clear in our opposition to Communism while appealing to the inherent goodness of the people and culture who are in fact its victims. We need to be confident that history is indeed on our side, that evil ultimately has no future because it exists in contradiction to the laws of creation. This is our responsibility.

Chapter 11

A Bitter 20th Century Harvest

Evil Unleashed: Socialism,
Communism and Fascism

Radical Ideas Spawn Totalitarian Regimes

This chapter is devoted to examining the tempest of evil and destruction unleashed by the 20th century application of 19th century socialist theories. As history demonstrates so vividly, once the falsehoods and deceptions of Marxist revolutionary theory were planted in the minds of power-hungry Communist leaders, they would produce unprecedented conflict and chaos that led to a terrible harvest of bloodshed and misery. Fascist leaders too would adopt socialist theories to create their own monstrous regimes.

In *The Communist Manifesto*, Marx and Engels claimed: "The charges against Communism made from a religious, a philosophical, and, generally, from an ideological standpoint, are not deserving of serious examination." (Appendix 1, p282.) This wishful thinking aside, what can we say of Communism as a practiced, revolutionary and ruling ideology? Surely Marx and Engels would agree that if their theories were sound, the implementation of their theories should produce wonderful, prosperous and happy societies characterized by perfect equality for all, with workers in particular enjoying the fruits of revolution. The history of Communism has, however, produced exactly the opposite. Since its first full application early in the last century,

Marxist ideology has produced nothing but brutal and bloody revolutions that have led to the establishment of oppressive dictatorships. In short, Marxism has been responsible for human misery, suffering and death on a scale never before seen in history.

A Century of Suffering

Indeed, in the 20th century, some 2,000 years after Jesus brought the hope of a new and better world, we witnessed an unprecedented flowering of evil on a global scale. Societies founded on religion-based values were crushed by the rise of Socialism, Communism and Fascism. The French Revolution of 1789 and the Paris Commune of 1871 had started the ball rolling for violent revolution in the modern era, but it was the addition of a comprehensive revolutionary ideology, Marxism-Leninism, that made the Bolshevik Revolution of 1917 so effective and lethal. For the first time, Marxism was applied in all its sinister and destructive force, and for the first time the real fruits of Marxist theory and practice were put on display for the whole world to see. By the end of the century, the toll of Marxist revolutions and regimes was some 100 million deaths and countless millions more lives destroyed. (Appendix 2, p298.)

Much of the 20th century would be dominated by Socialism, Communism and their totalitarian soulmate Fascism. These systems of government share certain tyrannical characteristics that cultivate and animate the very worst in human nature: dehumanization of others, violation of the rights of others, and the willingness to hurt, maim and kill anyone standing in the way of "progress." All these regimes were characterized by suppression of dissent, imprisonment of dissidents, torture and other forms of barbaric cruelty, and unbridled murder.

As Winston Churchill put it in his characteristically effective English, Communism and Fascism were little more than two sides of the same coin:

> There are two strange facts about these non-God religions. The first is their extraordinary resemblance to one another. Nazism and Communism imagine

themselves as exact opposites. They are at each other's throats wherever they exist all over the world. They actually breed each other; for the reaction against Communism is Nazism, and beneath Nazism or Fascism Communism stirs convulsively. Yet they are similar in all essentials. First of all, their simplicity is remarkable. You leave out God and put in the Devil; you leave out love and put in hate; and everything thereafter works quite straightforwardly and logically. They are, in fact, as alike as two peas. Tweedledum and Tweedledee are two quite distinctive personalities compared to these two rival religions.[37]

Following is a brief overview of 20th century totalitarianism and its human toll.

Socialism

There is often confusion about the terms being used here. Socialism is used to describe anything from a Scandinavian welfare state to the Soviet Union with its gulags. For our purposes, socialism with a lower-case "s" refers to democratic socialist governments that uphold private property rights and capitalism but also provide extensive government social programs for health care, retirement and other services. Socialism with a capital "S" denotes a politico-economic system based on state capitalism, central planning, a governing dictatorship and few, if any, individual rights. In Socialist states, these rights are sacrificed in the name of justice and equality for "the people." In Marxist theory, this Socialism is the improvement over capitalism that follows a violent revolution led by the proletariat against the bourgeoisie. It is the step between capitalism and Communism. (Although Hitler and the Nazis saw Communism as their chief rival in pre-war Germany, they adopted a Fascist variant of Socialism that is discussed further on in this chapter.)

Marx and Engels believed that Historical Materialism, as the driving force of history, would naturally produce revolutions against capitalist governments, such that the appearance of Socialist states was inevitable. However, the Paris Commune of 1871 demonstrated the need for a highly organized revolutionary movement if more than a brief upheaval was to be achieved. It was Lenin who saw this need most clearly, and he added to Marxist theory the need for a revolutionary party, a revolutionary putsch, and a dictatorship of the proletariat to guide the building of the Socialist state and its transition to a true Communist state. Thus most Communist revolutions were carried out in the name of Socialism, and the main task of the post-revolution regimes that replaced capitalist governments was to "build Socialism."

Remarkably, in a 1960 address to the United Nations General Assembly, Soviet leader Nikita Khrushchev described the wonderful world created by the Communist Party of the Soviet Union, claiming: "There is no greater freedom for man than the freedom to build and develop an independent State—and a Socialist State like ours into the bargain. The Soviet people have already completed the building of Socialism and have now turned to the building of Communism." (Appendix 12, p407.)

Khrushchev was comparing the Soviet Union with capitalist countries that had been colonial powers. He made the wildly false claim that the USSR had been a boon to formerly impoverished peoples that were forcibly assimilated into the Soviet Union. His words also revealed the arrogance of the USSR's foreign policy, with its justification for supporting so-called "wars of national liberation" in the name of anti-colonialism and Socialism, and its attempts to get the West to denuclearize when Moscow was developing its own nuclear capabilities as a matter of top national priority. In 1960, there were dozens of Socialist states around the world, with new ones being added almost every year. (See Appendix 13, pp412-413, for a map of Socialist and Communist states, by duration.) None of them would prove successful economically, all would crush individual rights, and all but a handful would eventually abandon Socialism.

With few exceptions, regimes that include "Socialist" in their official country name are of the radical, Marxist type. For example: the Union of Soviet Socialist Republics, the Socialist Republic of Vietnam and the Socialist Federal Republic of Yugoslavia. A popular variant is to substitute the euphemistic "People's" for "Socialist," as in the People's Republic of China, the

Democratic People's Republic of Korea, The People's Democratic Republic of Yemen, and so on. (Throwing "Democratic" or "Republic" into a title hides the regime's total lack of democracy or republicanism.)

Communism

The actual nature of a Communist state, as envisioned by Marx and Engels, is a mystery, despite Communists' claims to provide a real solution to the world's problems. In the abstract, Communism is a system in which citizens give according to their ability and receive according to their need. But how does Communism propose to get to that ideal state, especially if the Socialist state itself has withered away? Who will make decisions about the use of property and capital? Who will assure that participation in production is "according to ability" and distribution "according to need"? Even a society of morally perfect humans needs some level of organization, and the people produced by Socialist countries to date seem rather far removed from perfected men and women. Communism is mysterious in fact because it is a fantasy, a materialist dream of an imaginary world.

Although most Communist states disguise their real intentions with virtuous-sounding names, the ruling parties of these states typically use "Communist" in their names. Thus the Union of Soviet Socialist Republics was ruled by the Communist Party of the Soviet Union, the People's Republic of China is ruled by the Chinese Communist Party, and the Republic of Cuba is ruled by the Communist Party of Cuba. These parties have all committed atrocities on a massive scale in the name of creating Communist states, always justifying their cruelty as necessary to achieve a Marxist Utopia.

In addition, political movements dedicated to creating Communist states often use "Communist" in their name to distinguish themselves from democratic socialist parties, which don't share their ultimate objective. Thus the Communist Party of Germany was founded in 1918 as a radical offshoot of the ruling Social Democratic Party (SPD), which itself was a Marxist party from 1891 to 1959. And the Communist Party of the United States was established in 1919 after a split in the Socialist Party of America in the aftermath of the 1917 Russian Revolution.

The Soviet Union

After a revolt by angry citizens over unemployment and food shortages following Russia's disastrous defeats at the hands of the German Army in World War I, Tsar Nicholas abdicated on March 15, 1917, and a Provisional Government was established. In July, Alexander Kerensky, then minister of war, became prime minister.

Kerensky, a socialist, was in favor of pursuing the costly war against Germany and had members of the last Tsarist government arrested for incompetence and corruption. Lenin opposed the war, promising "Peace! Land! Bread!"[38] He saw weakness in Kerensky's coalition government, and on November 7 (October 25 in the Old Style Julian Calendar) the Bolsheviks mounted a coup against it. This started a five-year civil war in which the "Reds" ruthlessly eliminated rival reformists and revolutionary groups while pursuing a bloody war against the "Whites," the forces loyal to the Tsar. The "Reds" crushed all opposition in Russia and neighboring states, paving the way for the official establishment of the Union of Soviet Socialist Republics in 1922. The Communist Party of the Soviet Union (CPSU) would remain in power until 1991, when the USSR collapsed, and the party was abolished.

Winston Churchill described the arrival of Lenin in Russia, aided by the German government, which hoped (with good cause) that Lenin would take Russia out of the war:

> Lenin was sent into Russia by the Germans in the same way that you might send a phial containing a culture of typhoid or cholera to be poured into the water supply of a great city, and it worked with amazing accuracy.[39]

The salient characteristics of Marxist Socialism were set in stone largely by Vladimir Lenin when he added his own practical elements to Marxist theory to make it capable of mobilizing revolutionary forces to seize and hold power. Lenin established the Bolshevik Party in 1898 as a radical faction of the Russian Socialist Democratic Labor Party and the Vanguard of the Proletariat. (It would become the Russian Communist Party (Bolshevik) in 1918 and the Communist Party of the Soviet Union in 1952.)

Lenin introduced democratic centralism to the Party, a system of voting that kept any type of collective decision-making within the Party since only Party members were ever permitted to stand for election. (This system of "democracy" would be adopted widely by Communist Parties around the world.) While in power, the CPSU practiced almost every type of evil imaginable, with waves of persecution, oppression and purges that reached a crescendo in the 1930s under Joseph Stalin. Almost anyone could be accused of a crime against the state, arrested, tortured, sent to a prison camp in Siberia or executed outright. There were hundreds of prisoner camps and forced labor colonies established by the CPSU, as well as some 500 POW camps after World War II. According to *The Black Book of Communism*, some 20 million people died under CPSU rule. (Appendix 2, p298.)

Speaking of these huge numbers of victims tends to blur the actual extent and impact of the Communist horror. In a genocide called the Holodomor, some 6 million independent Ukrainian farmers, the Kulaks, would starve to death when they were forced to collectivize. Whole minority populations were forcibly transported from their native lands to remote regions of the Soviet Union, like Siberia. For almost everyone living in the USSR, fear was a normal part of life, spreading suspicion about everyone they knew and poisoning even close family ties. Anyone could be picked up by the authorities in the middle of the night, for any reason, real or made-up. They would likely be thrown in prison, tried and sentenced to prison camps in Siberia or execution. The laws were meaningless. Dialectic thinking and rationalization were used to justify any decision or action.

Individuals were simply powerless in the face of government oppression.

Even some of the founders of the Soviet Union, such as Leon Trotsky and Nikolai Bukharin, would fall foul of Stalin's secret police. Trotsky was chased across the world until caught in Mexico City, where he was killed with an ice axe by an agent of Stalin. In Moscow, despite international pleas for his life to be spared, Bukharin was sentenced to death for treason and shot, while his wife was sent to a labor camp. Their crimes? Falling out of favor with Stalin.

Creation of the Soviet Empire

The aggressive nature of the CPSU was evident from the outset. When the USSR was established by treaty on December 30, 1922, there were four founding members: Russia, Ukraine, Belorussia and Transcaucasia. By 1940, the number of USSR states had increased to fifteen and included Moldova; the Transcaucasian states of Armenia, Azerbaijan and Georgia; the Central Asian states of Kazakhstan, Kyrgyzstan, Tajikistan, Turkmenistan and Uzbekistan; and the three Baltic states: Latvia, Lithuania and Estonia. All were conquered by the Soviet Red Army and forced to assimilate into the USSR.

Further afield, the Soviet Union exported its revolutionary ideology and repressive methods of rule throughout the world. Largely because of American assistance through Lend-Lease during World War II, Moscow was able to withstand and reverse the Nazi invasion and four-year occupation. It then mounted an invasion of Eastern and Central European countries, several of which (notably Romania, Slovakia and Hungary) had fought with the Nazis. The Soviets set up client states in East Germany, Poland, Czechoslovakia, Hungary, Romania, Bulgaria, Albania and Yugoslavia, although these last two would forge policies that were often independent of Moscow.

In Asia, Moscow switched its initial alliance with Chiang Kai-shek's nationalist government fighting the Japanese to Mao's Chinese Communist Party and later backed Kim Il Sung's takeover of North Korea in 1948. Later too, Moscow supported the North Vietnamese in their war against the South, their Pathet Lao allies in Laos, and the North Vietnamese-created

People's Republic of Kampuchea in Cambodia. In addition, the USSR supported so-called movements of national liberation around the world, from Latin American countries (especially Cuba) to Arab countries and almost half the newly independent African states, who gained independence from their previous colonial masters. The last Soviet conquest was of Afghanistan, which it invaded in December 1979, ostensibly at the request of the People's Democratic Party of Afghanistan.

These successful Communist insurgencies and conquests were supplemented by the activities of a network of Communist parties in non-Communist countries. The CPSU recognized 95 Communist parties worldwide and considered support for them a high priority. These included Communist parties in West European countries and America. Many of these parties were directly controlled by Moscow through the Communist International, or Comintern, which operated from 1919 to 1943. (It was shut down by Stalin to calm the fears of his Western World War II allies who worried about Soviet expansionism. It was partially replaced by the Cominform in 1947, but this was also dissolved, in 1956, when its activities were relocated to the International Department of the Central Committee of the CPSU.)

As the Soviet Union inspired and backed violent revolutions across the globe, sent its armies to occupy countries and its agents to penetrate and undermine foreign governments—including those in West Europe and the United States—Moscow worked hard to maintain the pretense that it was merely acting on behalf of "the people" who appealed for its help, and that it was deeply committed to peace. As typical of Leftist movements and governments, Moscow made an art of blaming others for its own sins (and those of its allies), always claiming it was not responsible for any of the atrocities perpetrated by its own government, by other Communist governments, by Marxist national liberation organizations or by Marxist terrorist groups.

Moscow also became adept at disguising its real expansionist agenda by, beginning with the 7th Congress of the Comintern in 1935, to employ the

"United Front" strategy. It would create or support fine-sounding initiatives and organizations in collaboration with credible—but ultimately gullible—individuals or organizations, all the while using those entities as Trojan horses to advance its own interests. Thus it ran the World Peace Council and infiltrated the World Council of Churches. It encouraged the nuclear disarmament movements and exploited détente to lull the West into believing that it really wanted peace in Europe when its actual agenda was to dominate Europe. It signed the Helsinki Accords in 1975 because they provided *de facto* recognition of Soviet boundaries in Europe and a basis for the Soviet Union to claim moral equivalence with the West. (The real international intentions of the CPSU are laid out in Vladimir Bukovsky's *Judgement in Moscow*, which reproduces transcripts from meetings of the Central Committee and Politburo of the CPSU in which the top Soviet leaders openly discuss their strategy.)

China Surpasses Russia in Cruelty and Destruction

The most important offshoot of the CPSU was the Chinese Communist Party (CCP), founded on July 1, 1921 as a Marxist-Leninist party. Mao Zedong gained increasing influence in the party in the late 1920s, when he became a guerrilla leader. He originally agreed with Marx in despising peasants (farm laborers), as a class. But he eventually came to see them as a better source for a revolutionary party in China than the much smaller Chinese proletariat (factory workers). This difference in revolutionary focus would become a central feature of Maoism that distinguished it from the original theory. In 1931, Mao helped create the Jiangxi Soviet (Chinese Soviet Republic), becoming its chairman. However, holding on to this "republic" proved untenable against the superior forces of Chiang Kai-shek's Kuomintang, and Mao initiated the Long March of the CCP's Red Army, which would establish itself in Yan'an, in China's northwestern Shaanxi Province.

In 1937, the Communists made an official United Front pact with the Kuomintang to fight the Japanese occupation. As in so many of these alliances, the Communists used a period of cooperation with their real enemy to gain territory and support in anticipation of the moment when they could seize power. (See, for example, Nicholas Gage's book, *Eleni*, about how this strategy worked in Greece during World War II.) In 1943, Mao became the unchallenged leader of the CCP. He continued to use the United Front tactic with Chiang Kai-shek while he consolidated power and cultivated the interest and support of international Communists, including some key figures in the US State Department and other American institutions.

By the time Japan surrendered to the allies on August 15, 1945, the Red Army had grown to a force of 1.3 million, supplemented by a militia of 2.6 million. At this point, it would change its name to the People's Liberation Army (PLA). During the war it had used the fighting to take control of large swaths of the Chinese countryside, gaining support from peasants by using guerrilla tactics against the Japanese occupiers. At the very end of the war, per an agreement with US President Franklin Delano Roosevelt made at Yalta, the Soviet army entered the Asian theater, defeating the Japanese in Manchuria. At this point, Stalin handed over weapons confiscated from the Japanese to Mao's forces, greatly strengthening their capabilities in their fight against the Kuomintang.

In 1946, any pretense of an alliance between Mao and Chiang Kai-shek evaporated, and the country entered into an outright civil war, which ended in the defeat of the Nationalists, who escaped *en masse* to the island of Formosa (Taiwan), where they established their Republic of China, based in Taipei. On October 1, 1949, the People's Republic of China was established on the mainland, with Mao as its chairman.

Although Mao had made adjustments to Marxist theory by replacing the proletariat with peasants and the bourgeoisie with landowners and industrialists, Marxism-Maoism was just as cruel and murderous as the Soviet system. Rather like Stalin's 1932-1933 forced starvation of the Kulak farmers in Ukraine, from 1958 to 1962 Mao forced farmers to contribute to the "industrialization" of China as part of the "The Great Leap Forward." Estimates of the death toll from this coerced "industrialization"—which featured forced labor, torture, execution, starvation and suicide—reach as high as 55 million Chinese people, making this the deadliest non-wartime campaign of mass killing in history.[40]

It is truly impossible to imagine the suffering this astronomical death toll represents—the fear, the terror, the horror of watching loved ones, including helpless infants, die from starvation. (A gripping personal account of this famine and the later suffering of Chinese in the Cultural Revolution is found in Jung Chang's *Wild Swans: Three Daughters of China*. See the Bibliography.)

Later, in 1966, despite China's never-ending economic problems, Mao launched the Cultural Revolution to purge the country of "impurities"—its traditional beliefs—and establish Maoism as the ideology of the masses. Once more, Communist efforts at ideological purification resulted in massive suffering and as many as 20 million deaths. In a truly grotesque twist, the CCP mobilized students for this anti-civilizational campaign. They turned against their own parents, teachers and neighbors, accusing them in public denunciations of betraying the revolution and committing a host of "crimes" against the state.

The incitement to this cruel behavior by the CCP was intended to destroy the Confucian foundations of Chinese society, which were rooted in respect for parents, elders and teachers. The abused and terrified victims were forced to make confessions and renounce imaginary wrong thinking, on pain of death. The Cultural Revolution created hardened, callous creatures of the CCP regime. It would last ten appalling years, until Mao's death in 1976. The cost in human lives was enormous but so too was the societal cost of destroying Confucian ethics and morality.

The estimates of the total death toll inflicted by the CCP vary, but all agree that it is in the tens of millions. *The Black Book of Communism* estimates the total death toll for the two greatest crimes of the CCP, the Great Leap

Forward and the Cultural Revolution, at 65 million. (See Appendix 2, p298.) But many millions more have fallen victim to the CCP, beginning with the long civil war and continuing through the brutal persecutions that continue to this day. On July 1, 2021, the 100th anniversary of the founding of the CCP, *The Epoch Times* estimated that the total CCP death toll is 80 million. (Appendix 14, p414.)

The CCP has never taken responsibility for the unprecedented slaughter of 80 million of its own people.

The Evil of Communism's Global Specter

The Communist Manifesto begins with this sentence: "A specter is haunting Europe—the specter of Communism." Marx and Engels wrote their *Manifesto* to dispel the mysteries surrounding Communism, to "publish their views, their aims, their tendencies." (Appendix 1, p262.) At the time, Communism was indeed a specter, a dark spirit of evil possibilities. No longer. Since the beginning of the 20th century, the specter has become a reality, an unprecedented force for evil that has destroyed the lives of hundreds of millions of people around the world and continues to oppress hundreds of millions to this day. And although Communism reached its global high-water mark in the last century, given the ascendancy of the CCP today, it could cause even greater suffering in this century.

In the Preface we call the Specter of Communism a two-headed beast because it not only operates as a diabolical and soulless force that corrupts the beliefs, principles and politics of civilization, but because it also serves as the ruling ideology of totalitarian regimes, in particular Communist China.

The USSR and China are the main exemplars of the evil of Communism, but there are plenty of other examples of the harm wrought by Socialism and Communism wherever they have been tried. In 2021, China, North Korea, Vietnam, Laos and Cuba remain outright Communist countries, while Cambodia, Venezuela and Nicaragua were still ruled by dictatorial Socialist regimes. In the Middle East, only the Assad regime in Syria continues in its Socialist ways, albeit based on a new alliance with Russia instead of the USSR. Countries like Algeria, South Yemen and Iraq had all experienced the evils of Socialism and rejected it. Across Africa, one by one, countries that had embraced Communism as the answer to colonialism found that it was a disastrous economic system that brought cruel dictatorship and typically greater suffering than they had experienced under European rule.

Nevertheless, the dream of a Communist Utopia lives on around the world. Although only a handful of Communist countries remain, there are still Communist parties in many countries, including most industrialized nations. A reflection of Communism's success, 115 Communist and anti-capitalist parties have been elected worldwide to parliaments in fifty-six different countries. And despite the dismal record of Communism in the 20th century, die-hard Communists still cling to the false promises of Marx and Engels in countries everywhere.

More serious than small Communist parties scattered around the world, however, is Marxism's metastasizing into various Neo-Marxist and Critical Theory offshoots. These typically claim to reject Marxism—or at least its Soviet legacy—but continue to offer the seductive promise of a better world through atheism and violent revolution, albeit a revolution now focused on destroying traditional social institutions, especially religion and family, in addition to the capitalist states. We will discuss some of these Marxist trends in Chapters 14-16.

Fascism: A 20th Century Brand of Socialism

Often mistaken for the antithesis of Socialism and Communism, Fascism is in fact a branch of the same Socialist tree. It lacks the ideological underpinnings that have enabled Communism to endure as a ruling ideology for decades, but it has the same characteristics as Socialist and Communist states, namely totalitarian government with centralized planning and denial of individual rights. One key difference is that while Socialism and Communism are overtly anti-religion, Fascism often uses religion as a tool of control and repression. Fascism is not a global movement tied together by a common ideology. Rather, it is a name for individual statist regimes that manifest fascistic characteristics. These traits are typical of Socialist and Communist movements and states as well as those officially labeled Fascist.

Fascism reached its peak influence in the mid-20th century, when Fascist parties in Italy (under Mussolini) and Spain (under Franco) rose to power, in part by exploiting the support they received from the Catholic Church. Both were dictatorships, but neither rose to the level of totalitarianism practiced by the Nazis in Hitler's Germany or by the Communist regimes in the Soviet Union and China.

In his seminal book, *The Road to Serfdom*, written in the late 1930s, Friedrich Hayek pointed out that Germany was the European country that had advanced furthest towards socialism at the time. A key marker of this socialist tendency was the tendency towards central planning, believed by many on the Left to be the answer to the apparent failings of capitalism. Central planning was also considered essential for a war economy, and Hitler's Nazi Party used it to pull Germany out of post-World War I hyperinflation while simultaneously establishing a powerful *Reich* and preparing for revenge against Germany's rivals.

Socialism was well entrenched in Germany by the time the Nazi Party was established in 1919. The Social Democratic Party, the SPD, had been established as early as 1863 and adopted Marxism as its leading ideology in 1891. From the 1890s into the early 20th century, the SPD was the largest Marxist party in Europe. In 1914, during World War I, a radical Marxist faction of the SPD, headed by Rosa Luxemburg and Karl Liebknecht, broke away and formed the Spartacus League, named after the leader of the Roman slave revolt. On December 30, 1918, Luxemburg and Liebknecht established the German Communist Party.

The Socialism of Nazi Germany

Hitler embraced many of the anti-capitalist and anti-bourgeoisie principles of German socialism, but he was also explicitly anti-Semitic and anti-Communist, the latter in part because the rise of Communism in Russia appeared to threaten Germany. A low-ranking officer in World War I, Hitler joined the German Workers Party in 1919. Months later, in 1920, it would become the Nationalist Socialist German Workers' Party (in German the *Nationalsozialistische Deutsche Arbeiterpartei*, or NSDAP) otherwise known as the Nazi Party. The Nazis were aligned with the Freikorps paramilitary, which was formed largely of World War I veterans and used by the SPD-controlled Weimar Republic to suppress the nascent German Communist Party. (To win the support of German industry, the Nazis would later downplay their anti-capitalism.)

As with Communism, Nazism held a strong attraction for young people. Hitler tapped into strong nationalist sentiments, which drew on a long history of pan-German idealism. As the Nazi Party grew, it capitalized on these sentiments, stoking them with bitterness towards France, thanks to the harsh penalties imposed on post-World War I Germany by the Treaty of Versailles. Churchill captured the German romanticism of the Hitler Youth:

> I think of Germany, with its splendid clear-eyed youth marching forward on all the roads of the Reich singing their ancient songs, demanding to be conscripted into the army; eagerly seeking the most terrible weapons of war; burning to suffer and die for their fatherland.[41]

As seen with the Fascist governments in Italy and Spain, when the Nazi government took power in 1933, it sought to co-opt religion to serve its purposes. In some of his earlier speeches, Hitler recognized Christianity as the foundation of German values. He also claimed to support Christianity as a way to distinguish Nazism from atheistic Communism, his political rival in prewar Germany and, later, his great enemy to the east. But Hitler's interest in the church was not to follow the teachings of Jesus but to use it to support his regime. The dominant German Evangelical Church largely supported the Nazis, although a dissident "Confessing Church" insisted that Christians owed allegiance to God and scripture, not the Nazi Party. (Notable members of the Confessing Church were Martin Niemöller, who spent seven years in concentration camps, and Dietrich Bonhoeffer, who was executed for his part in a plot to kill Hitler.)

Like Marx, Hitler drew on Darwin's theory of natural selection to justify his racist theory, albeit without direct reference to the British scientist. In his book, *From Darwin to Hitler*, Richard Weikart writes:

> No matter how crooked the road was from Darwin to Hitler, clearly Darwinism and eugenics smoothed the path for Nazi ideology, especially for the Nazi stress on expansion, war, racial struggle, and racial extermination.[42]

Richard Overy elaborates on this in his book, *The Dictators: Hitler's Germany, Stalin's Russia*:

> Truth lay in natural science, and for Hitler that meant the truths of racial biology—natural selection, racial struggle, 'identity of kind.' Hitler was politically prudent enough not to trumpet his scientific views publicly, not least because he wanted to maintain the distinction between his own movement and the godlessness of Soviet Communism. Nor was he a thorough atheist. His public utterances are peppered with references to 'God' and 'Spirit.' For Hitler the eschatological truths that he found in his perception of the race represented the real 'eternal will that rules the universe'; in the infinite value of the race and the struggle to sustain it men find what they might call God, an inner sense of the unity and purposiveness of nature and history... Such views could be detected in the development of critical theology in Germany before the First World War, which suggested that God should be experienced as inner feeling rather than as external morality... What Hitler could not accept was that Christianity could offer anything other than false 'ideas' to sustain its claim to moral certitude.[43]

Hitler's Cain Nature is Embodied in Nazism

As with Marx, Hitler was driven by personal hatreds and biases. These he channeled into a ruling ideology that combined state Christianity, anti-Semitism, socialism and German nationalism in an unholy alliance that was responsible for tens of millions of deaths and the ruin of millions more lives. Above all, Hitler was driven by an overwhelming lust for power. He was willing to put his anti-Communism aside to enter into the August 1939 Molotov-Ribbentrop Pact with Stalin, in which they agreed to jointly carve up Poland. This gave Hitler the green light to invade Poland, which he did on September 1, starting World War II.

Hitler exploited a long-standing, virile streak of anti-Semitism in Christianity. This anti-Semitism was based on blaming the Jews for killing Jesus. The Nazis went further, blaming Jews for Germany's woes and dehumanizing them as a race. However, this hatred of the Jews was totally counter to Christianity's mandate, which in following the teaching of Jesus required believers to embrace all people, regardless of their beliefs or heritage. Jews are older brothers in faith to Christians and the extermination of 6 million Jews by "Christian" Germany was a gross abuse of Christianity's heritage and a total repudiation of its true mission.

Hitler's fascist Germany and Stalin's Communist Russia were all too similar. Both leaders were obsessed with power, and both attached no value to human life. They created two evil regimes on a world scale. Nazism would fail with the defeat of Germany, but Communism would continue to expand after World War II, as Stalin engineered Communist takeovers throughout Central and Eastern Europe and continued Communist expansion throughout the world.

Why Communism is More Dangerous than Fascism

As we have seen, the essential difference between Communism and Fascism is that the former is based on a comprehensive ideology while the latter is little more than a theory of dictatorship that is practiced by strongman rulers.

History has shown that Communist regimes are generally much more durable than their Fascist counterparts because the ruling ideology of Communism enables a succession of Communist leaders, whereas a Fascist state typically dies with its dictator.

Benito Mussolini was in power for twenty years, from 1925 to 1945; Adolf Hitler was in power for twelve years, from 1933 to 1945; and Francisco Franco was in power for thirty-six years, from 1939 to 1975. All three regimes shared several features, including: dictatorship supported by a personality cult, single-party rule, ruthless suppression of opposition, demagoguery, co-opting of religion and the dehumanization and devaluation of individuals by an all-important state.

These features of Fascism are also evident in Communist dictatorships as well, which is why Hitler and Stalin loomed over 20th century history as such similar monsters. But the list of Communist dictators who exemplified Fascist behavior is considerably longer than the short list of Fascists above. It includes Vladimir Lenin, Joseph Stalin, Nikita Khrushchev and Leonid Brezhnev in the Soviet Union, Mao Zedong in China, Pol Pot in Cambodia, Ho Chi Minh in Vietnam, Fidel Castro in Cuba, Enver Hoxha in Albania, Nicolae Ceauçescu in Romania... the long list goes on.

Many Communist regimes have lasted for decades. The Soviet Union was formally established in 1922, after five years of revolution and civil war. It lasted until 1991, about seventy years. The Chinese Communist Party took power in 1949, when it established the People's Republic of China, 28 years after the CCP's founding in 1921. The PRC turned seventy in 2019. The Cuban revolution brought Castro to power in 1959 and the Communist Party of Cuba remains in power to this day, sixty-two years on, despite a neighborhood of largely democratic countries (with the exception of Venezuela and Nicaragua).

All of these regimes were responsible for massive violations of human rights, for the destruction of innocent lives, and for the creation of horribly grotesque regimes masquerading as authentic governments. How silly and misleading it is, then, to attach the "Fascist" label to leaders of democracies who have been freely elected and who advocate for individual rights and the rule of law.

Lessons That Must Never Be Forgotten

In summary, 400 years after the Protestant Reformation and a little over 100 years after the French Revolution, the 20th century witnessed the advent of the worst regimes to ever appear on earth. The stark reality of Socialism, Communism and Fascism were on full display, and they were clearly visible for any reasonable person to recognize as evil. Only the resolute resistance of Britain, America and other allies stopped a total victory for totalitarianism. Given their record in the last century, there is no excuse for anyone today to believe in these pernicious and destructive ideologies. Yet millions of people still do. And while today Fascism is almost universally decried, Socialism and Communism are still able to seduce the naïve with their Utopian promises.

It should not be necessary to point this out, but humanity cannot afford to go back to the evil days of totalitarian regimes causing massive suffering and destruction around the world. How wrong it is, then, that so many people and institutions are enabling Communist China's spectacular rise today. In the next chapter we analyze the continued attraction to Marxist and Neo-Marxist ideology, and in Chapter 13 we examine China's growing power and what lies behind its global ambitions.

Chapter 12

The Communist Seduction

Waking Up to a World of Broken Promises

A Predatory and Seductive Ideology

The spirit informing Marxism and its offshoots is both predatory and seductive. What we have called the Two-Headed Beast is typically cloaked in the fine clothes of idealistic and aspirational language, but it targets two types of human prey with its seduction:

The first is a humble, innocent "Eve-type" of a person who is sincerely concerned about injustices in the world and is looking for a real solution to human suffering. These people are often willing to sacrifice for Socialism or Communism, committing resources and putting in long hours to create a new society and state. Most of the naturally idealistic young people drawn to Leftist movements are of this type. As Whittaker Chambers, one of America's most famous ex-Communists and the former head of a network of Soviet spies, explained:

> They feel a great intellectual concern at least, for recurring economic crises, the problem of war, which in our lifetime has assumed an atrocious proportion, and which weighs on them. What shall I do? At that crossroads, the evil thing, Communism, lies in wait for them with a simple answer.[44]

The second is an arrogant "Lucifer-type" of person who is resentful and bitter about his or her life, blames others and seeks vengeance. The primary attraction of Socialist or Communist revolutions and regimes for these people is that they offer a pathway to gaining power and wreaking vengeance on those they blame for depriving them of their due in life. These are the Lenins, Stalins, Maos, Pol Pots... They are the leaders of violent revolutions and, once in power, they become part of the "dictatorship of the proletariat," oppressing others and turning Socialist states into totalitarian regimes that will never relinquish their power willingly.

The first type often comes to realize that they have been seduced and taken advantage of by Communist leaders of the second type, who do not share their idealism but exploit them as "useful idiots." In this circumstance, the first type can easily become disillusioned by the reality of Communism, leave the movement or party or start to oppose the regime. It is this first type that interests us in this chapter.

At this point in history, when we know so much about the wretched record of Socialism and Communism, it is important to understand why good people end up committing themselves to evil enterprises. What is it about Marxism that attracts them? What is it that eventually disillusions them? And how can one avoid the pain of committing to a cause that is later shown to be based on false promises and must therefore be abandoned?

For more than a century now, tens, if not hundreds, of millions of people—many of them well educated and deeply concerned about the problems of humankind—have been drawn to the Marxist and Neo-Marxist prescriptions for the world's ills and lured into a religious-type devotion by the Left's promises to create an earthly Utopia. For example, the Americans who in the last century signed up to betray their country in the belief that they were serving the higher purposes of world Communism, were typically well educated and came from "good" homes. Many graduated from Ivy League universities and had excellent jobs in government and industry. Yet they voluntarily gave their allegiance to Moscow. The young people who today participate in riots and various forms of violence on America's streets are also typically students or graduates who come from middle class or wealthy homes. They clearly believe that they are literally fighting for good and just causes.

It should be noted that while the Communist Party USA is now aligned with Beijing, rather than Moscow, and continues a tradition of slavish servitude to the most powerful dictatorship on earth, most espionage for China by Americans today is based on the seduction of money, not participating in a Communist Chinese Utopia. Nevertheless, the American Left seems always eager to praise the PRC for its wonderful infrastructure and superior management of society. They also encourage the strengthening of US-China relations, echoing the tired and long-discredited moral equivalency arguments used in the last century to justify détente with the Soviet Union.

The Problem of Blind Faith and Delayed Consequences

The problem with Communist and Postmodernist promises of a better world is that it usually takes decades for believers to realize they have been duped. Thus, while today many Critical Theories are offered to young people as fresh solutions to long-standing social ills, the full consequences of the implementation of these theories will remain shrouded into an indeterminate future. This makes it all too easy for (often idealistic) people to be lured into devoting themselves to radical Leftist agendas that promise positive change for society and the world. And, indeed, the zeal of the Left can only be understood as blind faith in Utopian promises—promises that time will show can never be fulfilled. For those making the promises, the delay in their realization can always be explained away by blaming the entrenched institutions that the revolution is seeking to overthrow as being too resistant to change.

Faith in the promise of a better, or even ideal, future is, of course, not unique to Leftists. It is a feature of our original nature, which is endowed by the Creator with the desire for perfection, the achievement of a state of personal fulfillment, harmonious relations with others and nature, as well as ideal societies of peace and love. Religion promises to fulfill this desire by leading believers to Paradise, the Kingdom of Heaven or Nirvana. Marxist and Neo-Marxist theories exploit this innate human desire by promising their own versions of Utopia, making them pseudo-religious ideologies.

For any system of belief, faith is a powerful motivator; but with the science and knowledge available to us now, there is no excuse for blind faith, regardless of its basis. For those on the Left, there is really no good excuse for claiming ignorance of the likely outcome of Marxist and Neo-Marxist theories and programs. As we will elaborate in chapters 14-16, Critical Theories, whether of the Frankfurt or Postmodernist schools, are direct descendants of the Marxist dialectic. As such, their outcome is highly predictable.

Learning the Lessons of the Past

With this in mind, it is instructive to look at the last century for defining examples of people who were captivated by the ideals and promises of Marxism and devoted their lives to the Marxist cause—but ultimately realized they were contributing to a monstrosity, a global empire built on the suffering and blood of hundreds of millions of people. Nevertheless, even after disillusionment set in (especially at times like the signing of the Nazi-Soviet pact in 1939 and Khrushchev's 1956 revelations of Stalin's Reign of Terror), many ex-Communists clung to their Marxist beliefs while criticizing certain leaders and regimes for failing to implement the theory correctly. In other words, they failed to recognize that the evil they abhorred was not an aberration of Communism but an inevitable consequence of its practice.

France: Profound Disenchantment

Only a few publicly professed contrition that they had likely been responsible for leading well-intentioned people into hell. One who did was Frenchman André Gide (1869-1951), perhaps Europe's foremost author in the first half of the last century. He became an avid Communist and a believer in the Soviet Union as an ideal state. That was until he actually visited the country in 1936 and saw the wretched lives of most Soviet citizen—lives that his government hosts tried to hide from him. Later, he remembered his earlier enchantment with the USSR:

> Some years ago I wrote of my love and admiration for the Soviet Union, where an unprecedented experiment was being attempted, the thought of which inflamed my heart with expectation and from which I hoped a tremendous advance, an impulse capable of sweeping along the whole of humanity. It was certainly worth-while to be alive at such a moment to be able to witness this rebirth and to give one's whole life to further it. In my heart I bound myself resolutely, in the name of future culture, to the fortunes of the Soviet Union.[45]

> Far more than the country of my choice, an example and an inspiration, it represented what I had always dreamed of but no longer dared hope—it was something toward which all my longing was directed—it was a land where I imagined Utopia was in process of becoming reality.[46]

As a man of considerable influence (why else would the Soviets have rolled out a thick, red carpet for him?), Gide realized that he had a responsibility to warn his readers of the mistake he had made. Referring to a speech he had given in Russia describing the USSR in glowing terms, he said:

> This speech belonged to the early part of my visit, to the time when I still believed—still had the naiveté to believe—that one could seriously discuss questions of culture with the Russians. I wish that I could still believe it. If I was mistaken at first, it is only right that I should recognize my error as soon as possible, because I am responsible for those at home whom my opinions might lead astray. No personal pride must hinder me—I have little in any case—there are matters far more important than myself and my personal pride, more important than the Soviet Union. The future of humanity and the fate of its culture are at stake.[47]

Gide was one of the most articulate critics of Communism after he "saw the light." There are many others who have added to his insights. The accounts following may seem more numerous than necessary, but by invoking examples from America, Germany, Italy and elsewhere, the point is made that

Communism has a truly global appeal. It is hoped that those now promoting Leftist theories and activism, or contemplating doing so, will consider these lessons from the past relevant to the here and now.

America: A Romance Sours

Founded in 1921, the Communist Party USA (CPUSA) was created through the merger of two rival communist parties established in 1919 that were inspired by the 1917 Bolshevik Revolution in Russia. A membership organization requiring dues, CPUSA never topped 20,000 members until 1933, when President Franklin Delano Roosevelt established diplomatic relations with the Soviet Union for the first time, thereby normalizing Communism as just another system of government. By 1939, the CPUSA membership had surged to 69,000. It then started to decline, thanks to the Nazi-Soviet pact of August that year that disillusioned many members. (Everyone on the Left seemed to agree that Hitler and the Nazis were bad, and Fascism had to be opposed by the world.) Membership growth recovered when the United States and Russia became allies against Hitler, in 1941, peaking at 75,000 in 1947.

The CPUSA's aims included establishing "Soviet America" by spreading the ideas of Marxism-Leninism and helping (through its underground apparatus) Soviet espionage agencies, including the GRU (military intelligence) and precursors of the KGB. When Whittaker Chambers, a 1920s convert to Communism, in 1939 revealed the existence of Soviet spy networks in America to FDR (through his advisor Adolf Berle), there was little if any official interest shown, and no action was taken. (See details of the Chambers' story in Appendix 15, pp418-420.) This official disinterest at the highest levels of the US government continued throughout FDR's time in office and even after his death in 1945. President Harry Truman famously called Congressional investigations into Soviet espionage a "red herring" designed to disguise a partisan political agenda.[48]

However, by the time Elizabeth Bentley, an American running an extensive network of Soviet agents, recanted her treachery and in 1945 went to the FBI to report what she knew, concern for the extent of Soviet penetration of sensitive US agencies was beginning to grow among some official circles in Washington.

As World War II came to an end and Stalin's brutal occupation of East and Central European countries made a lie of his declared peaceful and democratic intentions for post-war Europe, public opinion in America began to turn against Communism. Hearings by the House Un-American Activities Committee (HUAC) took on new life, and the FBI under anti-Communist J. Edgar Hoover began to more actively pursue Communist agents and spies in the US government, in the Manhattan Project and in various other arenas.

This work was assisted by a secret project named "Venona," which was started in 1943 to decrypt Soviet cables sent between Moscow and Moscow's agents in the United States. Finally declassified in 1995, these cable transcripts corroborate the revelations of Chambers and Bentley and reveal the extent of Stalin's duplicitous relations with his most important ally in the war against Hitler. They also make it clear that the CPUSA was intimately involved in providing agents to the Soviet spy networks.

Over 300 Soviet agents have been identified as having worked actively for Moscow in the 1930s, 1940s and 1950s. Dozens were in sensitive government positions, including the White House, State Department, Treasury Department, the World War II Office of War Information and Office of Strategic Services, (later the Central Intelligence Agency). Remarkably, while many government officials kept their membership in the CPUSA secret, to avoid detection and likely firing, they faithfully paid their Party dues through their handlers. (See the Bibliography, PX, for books on Soviet espionage and influence operations during this period.)

Among the most prominent agents exposed by Chambers and Bentley was Alger Hiss, a Harvard Law graduate who held several senior government posts. While at the State Department, he attended Yalta with Foreign Secretary Edward Stettinius and FDR, and later played a leading role in the establishment of the United Nations. On his way back from Yalta, he stopped in Moscow, where he received a high Soviet decoration for his service to the USSR. Hiss steadfastly denied ever being a member of the CPUSA and a Soviet agent, but due to massive evidence of his treachery, he was convicted of perjury in 1950 and sentenced to five years in Federal prison.

Another notable Soviet agent was Harry Dexter White, a Stanford graduate in economics and a top official at the Treasury Department who would play a leading role at Bretton Woods, helping shape the post-war global financial system. He became the first US director of the International Monetary Fund.

Several agents provided information about the top-secret World War II Manhattan Project to build a nuclear weapon. The most famous, but likely not the most important, were Julius and Ethel Rosenberg. Several members of their network testified that they were spies for Moscow (confirmed by Venona cables), but the Rosenbergs never admitted their guilt and never recanted their treachery. They were executed in 1953, the only Soviet spies in the US to face that fate.

For many Americans drawn to Communism during this period, Party membership and political beliefs were entwined with personal, even romantic, emotions and aspirations. For example, a key couple in the Rosenberg spy network were Ethel's brother, David Greenglass, and his wife, Ruth. As described in *Venona: Decoding Soviet Espionage in America*, by John Earl Haynes and Harvey Klehr:

David and Ruth Greenglass… were both fervent Communists who had joined the Young Communist League as teenagers… After [David] entered the Army, the young soldier's letters to his bride mixed declarations of love and longing with equally ardent profession of loyalty to Marxism-Leninism. One letter declared, "Victory shall be ours and the future is socialism's." Another looked to the end of the war when "we will be together to build—under socialism—our future." In yet another, David wrote of his proselytizing for communism among his fellow soldiers: "Darling, we who understand can bring understanding to others because we are in love and have our Marxist outlook."

And in a June 1944 letter, he reconciled his Communist faith with the violence of the Soviet regime:

'Darling, I have been reading a lot of books on the Soviet Union. Dear, I can see how farsighted and intelligent those leaders are. They are really geniuses, every one of them... I have come to a stronger and more resolute faith in and belief in the principles of Socialism and Communism. I believe that every time the Soviet Government used force they did so with pain in their hearts and the belief that what they were doing was to produce good for the greatest number... More power to the Soviet Union and a fruitful and abundant life for their peoples.[49]

In 1935, a CPUSA spokesman wrote that Stalin "has directed the building of Socialism in a manner to create a rich, colorful, many-sided cultural life among one hundred nationalities differing in economic development, language, history, customs, tradition, but united in common work for a beautiful future... [He is a] world leader whose every advice to every Party of the Comintern on every problem is correct, clear, balanced, and points the way to new, more decisive class battles."[50]

This loyalty to Communism, and to Moscow and Stalin in particular, is inexplicable without remembering that Marxism exerts a religion-like pull on many of its adherents, making them truly blind to reality, as we have noted above. They believed in its veracity, and they looked to it for purpose in life. They excused the bloodshed and torture by the Soviet leadership, including Stalin himself, and they accepted his justifications for brutal purges and the incarceration of millions of innocent Soviet citizens as necessary steps towards establishing the Communist ideal. Apparently, these loyalists were unable to grasp the meaning of millions of people being killed or imprisoned and many millions more being starved to death. The extent of Stalin's terror would not become widely known until 1956, but there were enough reports to know that Stalin was exacting a very high price in human suffering to "build Socialism."

This faith in the Communist movement and child-like trust in "Uncle Joe" Stalin is reflected tellingly in one of the Venona cables sent to Moscow by Iskhak Akhmerov, the spy chief in the United States during much of World War II. He reports that the head of one of the most significant spy networks in Washington, Robert Silvermaster, was delighted with Moscow's decision to give him an award and a book:

> Robert is sincerely overjoyed and profoundly satisfied with the reward given him in accordance with your instructions, as he says his work for us is the one good thing he has done in his life. He emphasized that he did not take this only as a personal honor, but also as an honor to his group. He wants to see the reward and the book.[51]

Disillusionment Deepens

In 1935, Vivian Gornick was born into a working-class family of Ukrainian émigrés in New York. In her book, *The Romance of American Communism*, she describes how her Communist parents and many of their friends and colleagues would gather in her home to speak eagerly about the movement of the international workers they believed the Communist Party represented. They were excited to be Party members. It gave them a religious-like sense of purpose in life. They thought the Party could do no wrong, that Marx was a messianic figure for the workers, and that Stalin was a great and wise leader of the masses. Gornick writes:

> What I remember most deeply about the Communists is their passion. It was passion that converted them, passion that held them, passion that lifted them up and then twisted them down. Each and every one of them experienced a kind of inner radiance: some intensity of illumination that tore at the soul.[52]

However, in February 1956, Nikita Khrushchev gave an earth-shattering speech to the 20th Congress of the Communist Party of the Soviet Union in which he condemned Stalin for creating a personality cult and conducting massive purges in a Reign of Terror. This revelation destroyed the Communist myth, at least as far as Stalin was concerned. (See Appendix 16, pp421-437, for the text of the speech.) Although initially given in secret, the text would soon be known, and it sent shockwaves throughout the Soviet Union and around the Communist world. That wave hit the United States when *The New York Times* published a shortened version of the text in June that year.

Gornick reports the devastating effect of these revelations on her family and friends. They said to themselves: "For this? Have we sunk to this? Those who are dead, those who are dying in prison, have sacrificed themselves for this?"[53] She adds: "Overnight, the effective life of the Communist Party in this country came to an end. Within weeks of the report's publication, 30,000 people left the Party. Within a year, the Party was as it had been in its 1919 beginning: a small sect, off the American political map."[54] Gornick noted that the hopes and dreams of dedicated Communists were shattered in a way "... that can be understood only, perhaps, by those who have loved deeply and suffered the crippling loss of that love."[55] (See Appendix 17, p438, for the rise and fall of the CPUSA membership from 1922 to 1950.) By the end of the 1950s, membership had cratered. The bitterness was deep because the expectations had been so great. For decades, the Communist faithful had been fed lies about Stalin and the glorious future he was building in the Soviet Union.

Gornick's book is based on a series of interviews she conducted in the 1970s with some of those active in the Communist Party USA in the 1930s, 1940s and 1950s. Most looked back on their days in the Party as the most important chapters in their lives. They had experienced purpose, comradery, discipline in the Party. They believed they were building a new world.

Diana Vinson was a successful actress who had joined the Communist Party USA in 1941 and remained in it for twelve years. She told Gornick:

"They were good years, very good years. Rich, alive with the sense of everything coming together, a fusion of world and being that made you drunk with life. And the bond created through work done in comradeship. What a powerful bond that is! I never understood that properly until the Communist Party."[56]

One of the most thoughtful ex-Party members interviewed by Gornick was Anthony Erhenpreis. He put his experience in the CPUSA into historical perspective: "For myself, it was the best life a man could have had. I feel that as a Communist I have lived at the heart of my times. The most problematic sense of man's life is embodied in the history of twentieth-century Communism. It was through Communism that, in our time, one could grapple most fiercely with what it means to be a human being. Four-hundred years ago it was through Christian doctrine and the politics of the church, but in our time it was, without question, through Marxism and the Communist Party. For my money, it still is."[57]

Still a believer, Erhenpreis is comparing the rise of Communism with the Protestant Reformation of 400 years earlier. And, indeed, it was exactly 400 years from Martin Luther's 95 Theses of 1517 to the Russian revolution in 1917. But to think that Communism could be the natural heir of Protestantism, or of Christian renewal in general, reveals the power of Marxism-Leninism to win hearts and minds—and to hold onto them despite mountains of evidence proving the theory wrong and the source of immeasurable suffering.

Disenchantment with the Party came through various means. For some it was the Kafkaesque disciplinary hearings in which a member faced a "court" of peers who sat in judgment over some infraction of Party discipline. Colleagues would turn into accusers as brotherhood was transformed into dictatorship. For many, it was the Khrushchev speech in 1956.

But strangely, few blamed the ideology itself for the sins of Communism. It was as if the religion of Marxism was sound but the church of Communism and its leaders—men like Lenin and Stalin—had unfortunately gone astray.

This explains why, despite this disillusionment, Marxism and its offshoots continue to be able to tap into the intrinsic goodness and idealism of people, and the Leftist faithful continue to believe that materialist ideas are the key to building an earthly Utopia.

Germany: Waking Up With Leah

Arthur Koestler (1905-1983) was one of the most articulate writers to go through a powerful conversion to Communism, a painful awakening to its reality and final disillusionment. A Hungarian by birth, he joined the German Communist Party in 1931. As with so many good people of that time, he was preoccupied with the rise of Fascism under Hitler. It was a confusing period politically. The three main political forces in Germany during the early 1930s were all socialist: the ruling Social Democratic Party (SPD), the rising National Socialist German Workers' Party (Nazi Party) and the Communist Party of Germany (KPD). Koestler saw the KPD as the only party capable of taking on the Nazis and fascism. In *The God That Failed*, he explains his conversion to Communism:

> Even by a process of pure elimination, the Communists, with the mighty Soviet Union behind them, seemed the only force capable of resisting the onrush of the primitive horde with its swastika totem. But it was not by a process of elimination that I became a Communist... I began for the first time to read Marx, Engels and Lenin in earnest. By the time I had finished with *Feuerbach* and *State and Revolution*, something had clicked in my brain which shook me like a mental explosion. To say that one had 'seen the light' is a poor description of the mental rapture which only the convert knows (regardless of what faith he has been converted to). The new light seems to pour from all directions across the skull; the whole universe falls into pattern like the stray pieces of a jigsaw puzzle assembled by magic at one stroke. There is now an answer to every question, doubts and conflicts are a matter of the tortured past—a past already remote, which one had lived in dismal ignorance in the tasteless, colorless world of those who *don't know*. Nothing henceforth can disturb the convert's inner peace and serenity—except the occasional fear of losing faith again, losing thereby what alone makes life

worth living, and falling back into the outer darkness, where there is wailing and gnashing of teeth. This may explain how Communists, with eyes to see and brains to think with, can still act in subjective *bona fides*, anno Domini 1941. At all times and in all creeds only a minority has been capable of courting excommunication and committing emotional hara-kiri in the name of an abstract truth.[58]

Koestler would lose his job as an editor in the leading publishing house in Germany after they found he was passing information to the KPD, but by that time he anyway wanted to devote himself completely to the Party. (He even offered to go to the Soviet Union as a much-needed tractor driver!) He watched as the Comintern insisted that the KPD call the SPD "Socialist Fascists," and went it alone in the critical 1933 national elections rather than aligning with the SPD to defeat the Nazis. At the time, Stalin was most afraid of an invasion by Japan, and the KPD campaigned with the idiotic slogan: "The defense of the Chinese proletariat against the aggression of the Japanese pirates."[59] The Comintern's insistence that the KPD use this slogan demonstrates the extent to which Moscow tried to control world Communism, and the inevitable limitations of this incarnation of central planning.

Koestler learned to set aside his own rational criticisms of Communist thinking and policies in pursuit of becoming like a proletarian himself, the almost mythical Communist ideal of a plain-spoken worker. "We craved to become single- and simple-minded. Intellectual self-castration was a small price to pay for achieving some likeness to Comrade Ivan Ivanovich [a Russian John Doe; in this case a proletarian]."[60] He accepted that his was "mechanistic thinking" that he should abandon in favor of the far more productive "dialectical thinking" of the Party, which could explain all contradictions between word and action, including moronic Party decisions:

Gradually I learned to distrust my mechanistic preoccupation with facts and to regard the world around me in the light of dialectical interpretation. It was a blissful state; once you had absorbed the technique you were no longer disturbed by facts; they automatically took on the proper color and fell into their proper place. Both morally and logically the Party was infallible: morally because its aims were right, that is, in accord with the Dialectic of History, and these aims justified all means; logically, because the Party was the vanguard of the Proletariat, and the Proletariat the embodiment of the active principle in History.[61]

The ability of intelligent and well-educated people like Koestler to trust in a party that so clearly made decisions that defied all reason and logic is echoed today in the willingness of educated young people to vest their trust in radical movements based on nothing more than the promise that those movements are doing the right thing and fighting for a better world. Once they accept the ideology as true, it is very easy for the Leftist faithful to accept that the owners of that ideology are trustworthy leaders whose wisdom is not to be questioned.

After the KPD committed political suicide by spurning the ruling SPD in 1933, it was forced to go underground in the face of Nazi suppression. At this point, Koestler finally got a visa to his beloved Soviet Union, where he spent a year travelling much of its vast territory, ostensibly to write a book on the wonders of the current five-year plan. Even employing "dialectical thinking," he could barely explain away the disastrous reality he witnessed. He would write: "My faith had been badly shaken, but thanks to the elastic shock-absorbers [of dialectical thinking], I was slow in becoming conscious of the damage."[62] He found a renewed reason to believe when, in 1934, the Comintern introduced the new Popular Front for Peace and Against Fascism. This reversed the policy of rejecting and condemning rival movements on the Left and advocated for a united front against the common enemy of Fascism. For Koestler, this was "a second honeymoon with the Party."[63]

It wouldn't last. Like so many other starry-eyed Communists of that time, he went to Spain to support the anti-Franco effort but became disillusioned after being captured and imprisoned. In prison, he daily expected to be shot and naturally feared the torture that might precede death. He came to see his fellow inmates as individuals who did not fit into the Marxist classist categories. He realized,

> … that man is a reality, mankind an abstraction… that end justifies the means only within very narrow limits; that ethics is not a function of social utility, and charity not a petty-bourgeois sentiment but the gravitational force which keeps civilization in its orbit… yet every single one of these trivial statements was incompatible with the Communist faith which I held.[64]

It is worth noting that another Leftist who famously became disenchanted with Communism by his experiences in the Spanish Civil War was George Orwell. He went to fight Fascism in Spain in 1936, joining the Workers' Party of Marxist Unification (POUM) in Barcelona. He became aware of the real nature of Communism when pro-Soviets accused POUM of collaborating with the Fascists and then labeled it a Trotskyist organization—the ultimate Stalinist smear of a rival on the Left at that time. On returning to England, Orwell would write *Animal Farm* and *Nineteen Eighty-Four*, two hugely popular novels that brilliantly exposed Communism, and Stalinism in particular, as a totalitarian ideology. He became a good friend of Koestler and greatly admired *Darkness at Noon* for its authenticity and insights.

After Spain, Koestler still didn't make a break with the Communist Party, although Stalin's purges, which destroyed the lives of many he had known to be dedicated Communists, further eroded his faith in Communism. He observed: "At no time and in no country have more revolutionaries been killed and reduced to slavery than in Soviet Russia."[65] Even so, when he wrote a letter of resignation to the Central Committee of the KPD,

> I stated my opposition to the system, to the cancerous growth of the bureaucracy, the suppression of civil liberties. But I professed my belief that the foundations of the Workers and Peasants State had remained unshaken, that the nationalization of the means of production was a guarantee of her eventual return to the road of Socialism; and that, in spite of everything, the Soviet Union still "represented our last and only hope on a planet in rapid decay."[66]

The last straw for Koestler, as for many other wavering Communists, came with the Molotov-Ribbentrop Pact of August 23, 1939. Protected by this agreement from Soviet military reaction to its aggression to the east, on September 1, 1939, Nazi Germany invaded Poland, and World War II was launched in earnest.

In closing the saga of his romance with Communism, Koestler compared his seven years in the Party to Jacob's seven years laboring for his uncle Laban in Haran to win Laban's daughter, Rachel, as a wife. "When the time was up, the bride was led into his dark tent; only the next morning did he discover that his ardors had been spent not on the lovely Rachel but on the ugly Leah."[67]

Italy: Too Many Betrayals

At age 17, Ignazio Silone (1900-1978) joined the Italian Socialist Party, rising to become a leader. In 1921, he co-founded the breakaway Communist Party of Italy (PCI). Later known for his anti-Fascist novels, he would play a leadership role in the PCI and the Moscow-based Comintern. It was in dealing personally with Stalin and other Russian leaders that he experienced duplicity and profound prejudice against non-Russian Communists. After voicing these criticisms, in 1930 he was ejected from the PCI.

In 1949, he reflected on his time in the Socialist and Communist parties in Italy:

> For me to join the Party of Proletarian Revolution was not just a simple matter of signing up with a political organization; it meant a conversion, a complete dedication... The Party became family, school, church, barracks; the world that lay beyond it was to be destroyed and built anew. The psychological mechanism whereby each single militant becomes progressively identified with the collective organization is the same as that used in certain religious orders and military colleges, with almost identical results. Every sacrifice was welcomed as a personal contribution to the 'price of collective redemption'; and it should be emphasized that the links which bound us to the Party grew steadily firmer, not in spite of the dangers and sacrifices involved, but because of them. This explains the attraction exercised by Communism on

certain categories of young men and of women, on intellectuals, and on the highly sensitive and generous people who suffer most from the wastefulness of bourgeois society. Anyone who thinks he can wean the best and most serious-minded young people away from Communism by enticing them into a well-warmed hall to play billiards, starts from an extremely limited and unintelligent conception of mankind.[68]

Observing the situation of workers in Russia, Silone noted: "Most of the much-vaunted rights of the working class were purely theoretical."[69] However, despite his sharp observations on the many failings of Soviet Communism, his departure from the Party was wrenching: "The truth is this: the day I left the Communist Party was a very sad one for me, it was like a day of deep mourning, the mourning for my lost youth."[70]

The Religious Allure of Communism

Religion has the power to motivate people to sacrifice themselves for a higher cause because the ultimate reward is the Kingdom of Heaven, a state of enduring peace and happiness. The essence of the Communist lie is that it promises an alternative, atheistic path to a similar destination, a path that leads through violent revolution and a dictatorship of the proletariat to a Communist Utopia. Animated by that belief, Communists have been willing to sacrifice themselves for their cause while often practicing deception or committing atrocities along the way. Most of the Americans who spied for Russia did so without monetary compensation. In fact, they secretly paid dues to the CPUSA to hide their political affiliation while they held sensitive positions in the US government.

Stalin killed millions and imprisoned tens of millions; yet at his death, many millions in the USSR and abroad wept, including many of the Gulag inmates. At his funeral, the crowds were so enormous that several hundred people were crushed to death. A naïve, 31-year-old Andrei Sakharov, who was one of the USSR's leading nuclear scientists before becoming a famous dissident, was caught up in the moment, writing to his wife: "I am under the influence of a great man's death. I'm thinking of his humanity."[71] Later he would admit: "It was years before I fully understood the degree to which deceit, exploitation and outright fraud were inherent in the Stalinist system."[72]

As we have shown, the path leading to enchantment with Marxism and Communism, followed by disillusionment and revulsion for what Communism does, is well-trodden. It is similar to the disillusionment with religion that follows unethical behavior by ecclesiastical leaders. Both experiences can be bitter. The real difference lies in the fact that Marxism has not a single example to show of good results produced by its application. Religion, however, has a rich history of virtuous activity that produces undeniable benefits for people. For those who might entertain the notion that scrapping religion in favor of Marxism is a good idea, the message is clear: Marxism and its offshoots are not a solution to the problems and suffering of the world; they have made the world's many ills infinitely worse.

A Remarkable Resurgence of Socialism

Remarkably, seven decades after Khrushchev's speech, the popularity of socialism is on the rise in America and elsewhere, once more attracting those too young to know its true legacy. A 2020 Gallup poll showed that 39% of Americans have a positive view of socialism. Among millennials and Gen Zers, this number rises to 59%. Among baby boomers, however, "only" 32% have a favorable view. Gallup attributes these high numbers to the popularity of self-professed American socialist political leaders, notably Vermont Senator Bernie Sanders and New York Representative Alexandra Ocasio-Cortez, both of whom deceptively (ignorantly?) reference Scandinavia—rather than the Soviet Union, Communist China or Venezuela—as models of the socialism they are advocating.[73]

This is a stunning result. It proves that Socialism and Communism have continued their march through various educational and cultural institutions, as well as political parties, despite the disastrous record of Marxism around the world. As in the past, the destiny of the current generation of young people who are tempted by the allure of Leftist promises will be determined by their ability to see through the deception and recognize the reality of what the Left has to offer. The seduction of the Marxist and Critical Theory myths will continue to snare those who fail to approach the proffered Utopia with a rigorously critical and questioning mind. Ultimately, only a comprehensive and compelling alternative to Marxism and Neo-Marxism, based on transcendent principles and values, will be able to debunk these bankrupt theories and replace them with a compelling and durable alternative.

Chapter 13

The Rise of Communist China

Casting a Dark Shadow Across the Earth

The Most Dangerous Nation on Earth

The rise of Communism in China was once a distant phenomenon of little importance for Westerners. But that has changed as China has rapidly become a global superpower, aggressively expanding its international role. It has now replaced the Soviet Union as the most dangerous Communist nation in history and is using its massive wealth to buy influence and advance its agenda. The Soviets projected power and influence through supporting violent revolutions, on the one hand, and "united front" organizations, on the other, including those advocating for an end to nuclear arms and war itself. The Chinese Communists have not been able to adopt a similar strategy: The attraction of Maoism has weakened as the revolutionary spirit of the last century has morphed into a less-focused social and political activism. Now it's all about money. There are always those who are naïve—or willing to sell their souls for money—and the Chinese Communist Party (CCP) is masterful at using their new-found wealth to exploit this naiveté and greed.

In discussing the rise of Communist China, it must never be forgotten that the CCP is a blood-drenched organization. As we have pointed out, it is responsible for the death of as many as 80 million of its own people and the indescribable suffering of so many millions more, including persecuted religious and ethnic minorities. On July 1, 2021, the CCP celebrated its 100th anniversary without a hint of remorse for its record of unparalleled cruelty. (See Appendix 14, pp414-417, for an excellent synopsis of the CCP's evil history so far.)

Capitalism Saves Communist China

The Great Leap Forward and the Cultural Revolution both exacerbated the trenchant economic problems of Communist China, which, like the Soviet Union, could not feed itself. It was only after the death of Mao in 1976 that the CCP figured out how to remain in power and avoid economic disaster. The main architect of this strategy was Deng Xiaoping, who became China's supreme leader in 1978. Over the next decade, he set the country on a new and prosperous course. The key to this success was simple: allow the Chinese people to own property. Although this policy directly contradicts Marxist theory, it relieved the restless and rebellious pressure of ordinary people seeking political change by channeling their energies into wealth creation for themselves and their families.

The results are dramatic. China has transformed itself from a Third World economic backwater to the second-largest economy in the world, after the United States. It is far wealthier than the Soviet Union ever was, and it has used this wealth to enforce control of its people while extending its political and economic reach to every corner of the earth. There are other features of Communist China that make it a more powerful nation and greater threat than the USSR, and we will discuss them in this chapter.

China's State Capitalism

The nature of China's capitalist system is not the same as we are accustomed to in the West. In the Western model, corporations are independent of government ownership and/or control, although they are regulated by government. In the Chinese model, the CCP is heavily involved both in ownership and control of business enterprises, especially in strategic industries. More specifically, the People's Liberation Army (PLA) is a major player in industry. This arrangement means that all significant business activity is bent to the will of the CCP, and Chinese investments abroad are an integral and essential element of its strategic power projection.

For smaller enterprises, the right to ownership of property and business assets is a huge advantage enjoyed by Chinese citizens compared with citizens of most Communist states, including the Soviet Union in the past and Cuba and North Korea to this day. State ownership has always proved disastrous for economies for two main reasons. First, it is inefficient. Central planners are never smart enough or nimble enough to anticipate, let alone keep up with, markets so their allocation of capital resources is necessarily clumsy and unproductive. Second, ownership is a deep-seated attribute of the human nature we are endowed with by God. Therefore, private property is not evil but a necessary precondition for us to exert our dominion over creation wisely. We are responsible for what we own, and we are motivated by the desire to better ourselves and our families by developing the property we own.

With China, the CCP's strategy of allowing limited private ownership and economic independence from the government—while retaining ultimate control of industry and infrastructure—has worked so far. However, that success has been possible only because international capital markets have invested heavily in the Chinese economy and continue to underwrite its ambitions. If this stream of financial support stopped, the Chinese system of semi-independent, ultimately state-controlled industry is likely to founder, especially when individual interests start to compete with the meta-ambitions of the state.

Capitalism Enables China's Surveillance State

The true nature of the regime in Beijing is best demonstrated by the way it treats its own people. It has perfected the surveillance state, with cameras everywhere monitoring every individual, giving it excuses to punish anyone straying from CCP loyalty. It has violated its 1997 agreement with Britain, which granted Hong Kong fifty years of relative autonomy, and it is constantly threatening Taiwan with military conquest. It has cracked down ruthlessly on the Uyghur population of Xinjiang Province, incarcerating millions of these minority Muslims in "re-education" camps where they are subjected to sterilization and rape and forced to renounce their faith and swear allegiance to the CCP.

This religious repression continues a tradition started by Mao, who hated Taoism and Confucianism, the two most important philosophical bases for traditional Chinese society. Both those traditional belief systems were brutally targeted during the rise of the CCP, particularly during the Cultural Revolution between 1966 and 1976. The Catholic Church in China has faced constant interference from the state, which insists on the right to appoint or approve ecclesiastical leaders (something the Vatican under Pope Francis has appeared to compromise on). Protestant and other churches have faced constant harassment, and many have been forced underground.

Perhaps the most egregious and brutal policies have been directed at the indigenous Falun Gong (also known as the Falun Dafa) movement, founded by Li Hongzhi in the early 1990s. With its membership reported to be in millions or tens of millions, the movement incorporates meditation, traditional Chinese *qigong* practices and a moral philosophy that stresses virtuous living. In 1999, Chinese authorities estimated Falun Gong membership at 70 million and began a crackdown, labeling the movement as a heretical cult. Tens of thousands have been arrested and imprisoned, and state authorities from the highest levels of the CCP have targeted Falun Gong members for organ harvesting for profit, an evil and gruesome practice that involves the sale of organs to customers while the "donors" are still alive. Many Falun Gong believers have been forced to flee their native China, and the group is currently based in the United States, from where it seeks to expose the abuses of the CCP by publishing *The Epoch Times* in many countries and several languages.

Capitalism Funds China's Expanding Global Reach

Overseas, China is using its growing wealth to purchase influence and to extend its penetration of economies around the world. Already in place is a vast Chinese diaspora, which stretches from the United States to Australia. Chinese people naturally feel affinity for their homeland, and Beijing seeks to exploit this sentiment by encouraging loyalty to their traditional roots— rather than to their current nationality or place of residence—and reinforcing this policy by holding their relatives hostage in China. This global network can help expand Chinese investment and trade around the world—or force Chinese living abroad in a more subversive role as agents of Beijing.

China's growing wealth has meant that it can sustain a massive effort to track down Chinese dissidents and other Chinese who have fallen foul of the regime in Beijing, often on the pretext (and sometimes legitimate basis) that those who have fled China did so to escape prosecution for corruption. On February 4, 2021, Freedom House published a report on transnational repression, the illegal activities of various governments pursuing their citizens overseas, from torture and assassinations to intimidation and forced repatriations. Of China, the report says: "China conducts the most sophisticated, global, and comprehensive campaign of transnational repression in the world." It adds: "All told, these tactics affect millions of Chinese and minority populations from China in at least 36 host countries across every inhabited continent." The message to all Chinese people is clear: Criticize the government and we will track you down and punish you, wherever in the world you try to hide.[74]

China also exerts tremendous pressure on corporations that are heavily invested in its economy, seeking to control the content of their public statements and social media posts about China, and, for example, censoring the movies they invest in. The danger is that the tension between free market forces and CCP totalitarianism is likely to be resolved in favor of the latter. The CCP cannot afford to grant freedom to the point where the Party will no longer retain political control, and Western governments have erroneously assumed that engaging in commercial activity with the CCP would inevitably lead to it becoming more open and democratic. They are learning the hard way that this is not so. On the contrary, Communist China is wielding its economic power to press democratic states and free institutions to sacrifice their principles of independence in exchange for financial gain.

Communist China is today the greatest threat to freedom and peace in the world. Its huge population, now empowered by ever-growing economic and military might, is harnessed to an ambitious expansionist program of world domination, making China a deadly force to be reckoned with. Never chosen by the people, the CCP has to maintain its grip on power by keeping control of restless minorities at home while flexing its threatening muscles on the world stage. As with the Soviet Union before them, this may well result in verbal belligerence being converted into military adventurism in the name of defending the new Chinese nationalism. China has replaced the Soviet Union as superpower sponsor of smaller Communist and Socialist states, notably North Korea, Cambodia and Laos, providing it with pretexts to meddle in overseas affairs. And it has made major inroads in the developing world, especially in Africa, where governments have often foolishly accepted Chinese "aid" with its entangling and costly strings attached.

Nevertheless, the CCP's ultimate weakness lies in its dependence on ruling by force. Its claim to be the heir to Han nationalism and the Chinese heritage in general through its authoritarian rule is a propaganda sleight of hand that works in good times only, but is unlikely to be a successful strategy over the long haul. When the economy weakens, cracks in Han support for the CCP appear. And as China's international reach grows, its Han racism and totalitarian methods make it a global pariah that is only able to secure allies through dollar diplomacy. Because it has adopted capitalism (albeit a corrupt form), China may avoid the economic death spiral that pulled the Soviet Union to its destruction, but it cannot avoid forever the consequences of the falsehoods inherent in its flawed founding ideology and its legacy of brutal behavior.

China's Global Influence and Subversion Campaign

As with the many Communists around the world who were attracted to Stalin as a strongman, believing that he was taking the difficult but necessary steps to "build socialism," there is a growing international cadre of Leftists, or simply opportunists, who are attracted to China's growing wealth and military power. Typically, they believe that China today is setting an example for a progressive society. For them, the attraction is not so much ideological as practical: They see in China a strong nation that has achieved remarkable economic success recently and therefore offers opportunities for them to make money for themselves. They are drawn into Beijing's orbit by China's willingness to spend vast amounts of money to curry favor and secure allegiance.

Just in America alone, which is undoubtedly China's primary target for subversion and influence, the quiet spread of Beijing's influence has reached massive proportions. And while this influence has largely gone unnoticed, that has begun to change as the consequences are starting to have a serious impact on society. For example, a 2021 release of emails between Dr. Anthony Fauci, the head of NIAID (the National Institute of Allergy and Infectious Diseases, a division of the National Institutes of Health), and academics engaged in epidemiological research, reveal a strong connection between American scientists (in government, non-profits and academia) and the CCP. Fauci became the national, and to some extent international, guru doling out advice concerning the COVID-19 virus that by mid-2021 had caused some 4 million deaths worldwide, and over 600,000 deaths in the

United States alone. The emails reveal that Fauci had all along downplayed the likely scenario that the virus originated in the Wuhan Institute of Virology, something the CCP was determined to hide from the world.

Fauci was compromised because his agency had provided funding to the Wuhan lab, which was engaged in "gain of function" research, a dangerous field in which scientists tinker with animal viruses to make them better able to infect human beings. In other words, Fauci himself was implicated in being at least partially responsible for the death of millions of people. Strongly encouraged by the agents of the CCP, he chose to mislead Americans rather than admit to the truth. The Chinese read him right: He was more concerned for his own prestige and reputation than for the millions of people suffering and dying from COVID-19.

A July 1, 2021 *Fox News* article on this issue explains that the Chinese manipulation of Fauci is part of a very extensive CCP scheme to influence and subvert the United States.[75] The author, Joe Schoffstall, explains:

China conducts numerous influence campaigns within the United States, including targeting institutes of higher learning.

He continues with a quote from Brian Fitzpatrick, a member of Congress and veteran of the FBI's counterintelligence and counterterrorism departments:

…what China does (and other countries do the same) is they identify what they call the spheres of influence. China's identified five [spheres of influence] essentially in the United States. It's academia; it's the media, it's Big Tech, it's Hollywood and professional sports. They view those as the five influencers of human behavior in American culture. Essentially what they try to do is silent sabotage, a soft influence whole government approach where they nestle in and engrain themselves in these institutions financially to make people economically dependent on them, and then they use that as a platform to get their message out—mainly through propaganda.

The article points out that one of the key contacts of Fauci regarding the

COVID-19 coverup was Walter Ian Lipkin, a professor of epidemiology at Columbia University. Lipkin has had extensive contacts with senior Chinese scientists and officials and thanked Fauci in an email for publicly downplaying the possibility that the virus originated in the Wuhan lab. Lipkin has been a beneficiary of NIH grants as well as money from China. The article points out that:

> Columbia has received millions in foreign funding from China. According to the College Foreign Gift and Contract Report database, which relies on universities self-reporting their foreign cash, the university has raked in at least $17.7 million from China for research, facilities and professorships.

The Fauci affair is the first major revelation of nefarious Chinese meddling in American affairs that has gained wide public attention. It has been treated as anomalous by much of the media, but unlike some of the other proven cases of Chinese espionage and influence peddling, the COVID-19 pandemic disrupted the life of every American and resulted in the death of hundreds of thousands of loved ones. It seems the brazen behavior of the CCP is finally starting to be noticed!

So far, China has found the targets of its influence campaign easy game, especially since the beneficiaries in American academia, media, sports, the corporate world and government have faced little censure and are rarely punished at all. This record of success has made Beijing appear cocky, confident that with its billions of dollars it can buy its way into any society. It combines the carrot of financial payoffs with the stick of intimidation: It forces companies, media groups, sporting organizations and government bodies to toe the CCP line or face an end to the gravy train and exclusion from the lucrative Chinese market.

For countries targeted for its Belt and Road initiative, Beijing's strategy is a little different. It typically combines bribes to officials in client countries with punitive clauses in the contracts it signs that enable it to take control of infrastructure projects if the client defaults on repayment of loans for the project.

There is really no excuse for continued Western ignorance of China's true nature and ambition. When Communism was taking hold in China decades ago, and later in the Cultural Revolution, little was known about Mao's ruthless suppression of Confucianism, Taoism and Christianity (imitating the Soviet destruction of the Russian Orthodox Church). Recognizing that, without their traditional faiths they lack a basis for cultural exchange with the West, the CCP would now have us believe that it is the inheritor of traditional Chinese culture. They are peddling this deception through a global network of state-sponsored Confucius Institutes. The atheistic CCP, with its 94 million members, has no real interest in spreading religious or spiritual principles. Its sole interest is to use traditional culture as a cover for CCP propaganda. In the meantime, the true face of the CCP is seen in its ruthless campaign against the Muslim Uyghurs, Christians and Falun Gong practitioners.

China Practices Genocide

The destruction of the Uyghur population has now become outright genocide. In an April 2021 article in *Foreign Policy*, Peter Mattis points out: "Under the *Convention on the Prevention and Punishment of the Crime of Genocide*, to which both China and the United States are signatories, genocide has two parts. The first is the commission of any of the following acts: 'killing members of the group, causing serious bodily or mental harm to members of the group, deliberately inflicting on the group conditions of life calculated to bring about its physical destruction in whole or in part, imposing measures intended to prevent births within the group, or forcibly transferring children of the group to another group.' The second part is intent. Any of those acts 'committed with intent to destroy, in whole or in part, a national, ethnical, racial or religious group' would constitute genocide." Mattis concludes: "China's actions very clearly meet four out of five conditions of genocide—and remember, they only need to meet one."[76]

On June 10, 2021, Amnesty International published a 160-page report on the CCP's systematic persecution of the Uyghurs, concluding:

> The evidence Amnesty International has gathered provides a factual basis for the conclusion that the Chinese government has committed at least the following crimes against humanity: imprisonment or other severe deprivation of physical liberty in violation of fundamental rules of international law; torture; and persecution.

> The government's abuses are ongoing. Large numbers of people are still arbitrarily detained in Xinjiang. Moreover, the government has devoted tremendous resources to concealing the truth about its actions. It prevents millions of people living in Xinjiang from communicating freely about the situation and denies journalists and investigators meaningful access to the region. People living abroad are often unable to obtain information about family members in Xinjiang who are missing and presumed to be detained. [77]

A key strategy of the CCP is to break the Muslim faith of the Uyghurs and replace it with loyalty to the Communist Party. The tactics employed include denying the Muslims access to their scriptures, preventing them from worship and suppressing their language. Uyghurs are prisoners in vast internment camps where they are forced to suffer indoctrination in the CCP's Marxist theories. Physical torture, sleep deprivation and other forms of coercion are used to compel them to renounce their faith and pledge loyalty to the CCP. The CCP also attacks the traditional Uyghur family unit, which is the center of their culture, through surveillance of family life by Han Chinese government monitors, who may spend days at a time in private homes. Other inhuman practices include sterilization or rape of Uyghur women by Han Chinese men.

Marxism is Antithetical to Traditional Chinese Faiths

Mao Zedong and his Chinese Communist Party despised Confucianism and sought to eradicate its influence from Chinese society. They labeled it backwards, counter-revolutionary and reactionary. This campaign was stepped up during the Cultural Revolution (1966-1976) when Confucian teachings were banned and Confucian scholars were tortured and killed. Worse still, the CCP did its best to destroy the Confucian foundation of Chinese society by getting children to turn on their parents and teachers, in a direct repudiation of filial piety. This turned Chinese youth into inhuman monsters.

Today, there are only some 6 million Confucianists in a country of 1.4 billion people. However, in typical Communist style, the regime in Beijing has used some of Confucius's teachings about loyalty to rulers to encourage obedience to the CCP and co-opted the sage's name for a network of Confucius Institutes around the world that peddle Communist propaganda within a broader program of language and cultural education.

Taoism's concept of harmony between Yin and Yang is also directly contradicted by the Marxist dialectic, which is based on conflict between opposites. Banned by the CCP, Taoism was suppressed on the mainland but flourished in Taiwan. It is now cautiously being allowed back into the Mainland under the watchful eyes of the CCP, which believes that, as with Confucianism, it can play a constructive role in society and ultimately serve the interests of the Party. There are an estimated 12 million Taoists worldwide.

It must be remembered that all religious and philosophical movements in China are subject to the strict control of the CCP: Any freedom they enjoy is only because the Party recognizes elements in them that can be appropriated to serve its interests, which include maintaining social stability and peace. After all, there is nothing in Marxist doctrine that can be used to cultivate good families or harmonious and constructive relations among people in general. Tolerating spiritual traditions is also good for propaganda purposes: It deceives the world into believing China respects spiritual traditions.

China Crushes Authentic Religions

As with all Communist regimes, the CCP has from its founding been dedicated to crushing or co-opting religious organizations, both Eastern and Western in origin. For example, many of the established Christian churches outside China have been happy to cozy up to the CCP despite its terrible record in persecuting Christians in China. Pope Francis himself caved to the CCP's insistence that it have veto power over appointments of Catholic bishops, and the World Council of Churches (WCC) has shunned authentic Christian groups while courting the CCP. A book that is extremely critical of the CCP, *How the Specter of Communism is Ruling Our World*, traces the WCC's long-standing relationship with Communist states:

> On a global scale, one organization that was infiltrated by communism in Eastern Europe was the World Council of Churches (WCC). Established in 1948, the WCC is a worldwide interchurch Christian organization. Its members include churches of various mainline forms of Christianity, representing around 590 million people from 150 different countries... It also was the first international religious organization to accept communist countries as members during the Cold War and to accept financial support from them.

> Based on a released KGB file from 1969, Cambridge University professor and historian Christopher Andrew wrote that during the Cold War, five KGB agents held seats on the WCC Central Committee, exerting covert influence on the WCC's policies and operations. A released KGB file from 1989 shows that these KGB-controlled agents ensured that the committee issued public communications that aligned with socialist aims.

> The WCC also was infiltrated by the CCP through the China Christian Council. The council is the only official representative of communist China in the WCC, yet, due to monetary and other influences, the WCC has for years gone along with the CCP's interests.

> The general secretary of the WCC officially visited China in early 2018 and met with several Party-controlled Christian organizations, including the China Christian Council, the National Committee of Three-Self Patriotic Movement of the Protestant Churches in China, and the State Administration

for Religious Affairs. In China, the number of members of non-official Christian groups (underground churches) is far greater than the official ones, yet WCC delegates didn't arrange to meet with any non-official Christian groups, in order to avoid friction with Beijing.[78]

Christianity and other faiths should lead the world in rejecting the Communist seduction, but all too many religious bodies have believed that they can make common cause with Communism, turning their other cheek towards the greatest perpetrator of evil over the past century. The result has been that these organizations are used by the Communists to cover their own evil behavior while authentic believers suffer under totalitarian oppression.

CPUSA Now Serves CCP Interests

True to its history of obsequious subservience to international Communism, the CPUSA realigned itself with Beijing after Moscow ceased to lead the worldwide Communist movement. A much-reduced American Party (probably with about 5,000 members in 2020) in 2018 sent a delegation to China, led by chairman John Bachtell, to celebrate the 200th anniversary of Marx's birthday. Those returning from this and similar CPUSA missions to China reported how impressed they were with Chinese Communism and offered enthusiastic support for the CCP. (See cpusa.org for information on this and other China-related activities of the CPUSA.)

The CPUSA website carries a January 6, 2020 article by Norman Markowitz, describing his visit to China for a "Conference on Marxism and Socialism in the 21st century." He reports that, "most scholars from capitalist countries used Marxist analysis to show the continued destructive effects of capitalist policy on both the physical environment and the education and social welfare of the people throughout the capitalist world. My own presentation dealt with capitalist responses to China's new direction, and I also gave two presentations to undergraduate and graduate students: 'The Recycling of Cold War Ideology toward the People's Republic of China' at the Central Wuhan

Normal School, and 'The American Way of Imperialism' at the School of Marxism of Wuhan University; both led to interesting questions and lively discussions."

He concludes with this stirring comment: "As the People's Republic of China seeks greater engagement with communist parties and socialist and anti-imperialist movements, we should welcome those engagements and build upon them as we work for a shared socialist future for humanity." As we saw in the mid-20th century, American Communists' loyalty to Communism and Communist states trumps their loyalty to their own nation, making the CPUSA a treasonous organization. For its adherents, the Soviet Union used to be the model of a virtuous nation, and America an evil capitalist state. Today, Communist China is the model, a place where American Communists give lectures on topics like "The American Way of Imperialism."

The American Communists no longer field their own candidates for president, and John Bachtell told *Gawker* that he had enthusiastically campaigned for Barack Obama's two presidential bids. This demonstrates that the Democratic Party has now moved so far left that American Marxists are completely comfortable in its fold. For China to have such an eager ally in one of America's two dominant political parties is indeed a triumph for Communism and signifies that China is a much more dangerous foe to America than the Soviet Union ever was.

Why China is so Dangerous

In this chapter we have discussed some of the salient characteristics of Communist China, both in terms of its bloody history and in its current oppression of minorities and projection of power internationally. But we should not let its many unpleasant features distract us from the reality of its strength. With 1.4 billion people, China is still the country with the largest population in the world, although a declining birthrate will cause it to slip from that perch. China has a massive diaspora of some 40 million people in 130 countries. Many of these people identify as Chinese in a way that enables Beijing to use them as agents of influence or spies. With rapid growth fueled by massive foreign investment, China has the second-largest economy in the world behind the United States and is on track to overtake America.

China's ambition is to achieve an economy double or triple the size of America's by 2049 and to increase the gap from there. [79] Much of the Chinese population is on board with this government's project to restore the nation's dignity and to make it the dominant country in the world. China has stolen or copied or created the technology to accomplish this goal, beginning with a massive build-up and modernization of its military power. All these aspects of China's current strength take on new significance in the light of its national ambition to achieve what it considers its destiny. That destiny is world domination, and it is the object of what the Chinese call the 100-year marathon.

China's 100-Year Marathon

In 2015, Michael Pillsbury published a book with the title: *The 100-Year Marathon: China's Secret Strategy to Replace America as the Global Superpower*. In it, he reveals China's long-term strategic thinking and the motivation behind it. Essentially, the CCP considers 1949 as a pivotal year in the history of the world. It was in that year that the People's Republic of China was established after the CCP victory in the long civil war. The Party teaches that from 1949 China finally began its return to global prestige and dignity after a century of humiliation that had begun with the Opium War of 1839-1842, in which Britain had defeated China, reducing it to the status of a second-rate nation. For the next century, China would be subjected to invasion and occupation and never rose above being a minor player in world affairs.

The 100-year marathon is the CCP strategy to gain global supremacy by 2049. By that time, it plans to have surpassed America in every significant area, so that China no longer has to look up to any other power. This overarching ambition explains the regime's willingness to do literally anything to achieve its goal. For example, Mao believed that his Great Leap Forward would in the span of a few years raise China's steel production to the level of America's. That it failed miserably was a setback. That it cost tens of millions of lives was incidental. As we've noted several times, the Communist system of centralized planning never works well, and the Great Leap Forward was only one in a long series of CCP economic failures. The Chinese marathon was not making progress.

This all started to change when the United States dropped its recognition of Taiwan in favor of the mainland government on January 1, 1979. This coincided with Deng Xiaoping's economic reforms of 1978, which allowed private ownership of property and businesses in a "socialist market economy." Normalized relations facilitated investment and trade, and in 2001, China was admitted to the World Trade Organization as a developing country that could now enjoy favorable trade terms. The capitalist scramble for China was on, and the economy grew by leaps and bounds, freed from the chokehold of centralized planning.

Most China experts in the West considered all of this development a good thing. Their assumption was that if China was brought into the world community of international trade, the Communist government would see the benefits of democratic government and moderate its policies to make them compatible with those of other industrialized nations. It's only now that some of these experts, like Pillsbury, realize that America and other developed countries have been played by Beijing. The CCP has no intention of becoming just another modern state.

The actual long-term objectives and strategies of the CCP are revealed in nine core principles of the 100-Year Marathon:[80]

1. Induce complacency to avoid alerting your opponent.

2. Manipulate your opponent's advisers.

3. Be patient—for decades, or longer—to achieve victory.

4. Steal your opponent's ideas and technology for strategic purposes.

5. Military might is not the critical factor for winning a long-term competition.

6. Recognize that the hegemon will take extreme, even reckless, action to retain its dominant position.

7. Never lose sight of *shi*: deceiving others into doing your bidding for you and waiting for the point of maximum opportunity to strike.

8. Establish and employ metrics for measuring your status relative to other potential challengers.

9. Always be vigilant to avoid being encircled or deceived by others.

Not listed here is another central idea from China's ancient past, namely that the world order is hierarchical. This means that there can be only one supreme power, one superpower. That country is now America, which is why China is so determined to surpass the United States. In line with its policy of keeping its real intentions hidden, this is not its commonly stated public policy:

> China's leaders claim to want a multipolar world in which the United States will be first among equals. Put differently, they do not want to ask the weight of the emperor's cauldrons. In truth, however, they see a multipolar world as merely a strategic waypoint *en route* to a new global hierarchy in which China is alone at the top. The Chinese term for this new order is *da tong*, often mistranslated by Western scholars as "commonwealth" or "an era of harmony." However, *da tong* is better translated as "an era of unipolar dominance." Since 2005, Chinese leaders have spoken at the United Nations and other public forums of their supposed vision of this kind of harmonious world. [81]

That the CCP took most of these ideas from books based on insights from *The Art of War* by Sun Tzu and other sources that explain winning and losing strategies employed in the Warring States era of ancient China (475-221 BC) does not diminish their potency. On the contrary, using these ideas has enabled the CCP to present itself as the authentic representative of Chinese traditions. Furthermore, while many of these stratagems are considered dishonorable or criminal in many other countries, they are perfectly consistent with Marxist ideology, which holds that the end always justifies the means.

This explains why the CCP has so far managed to stay in power without too many challenges from the people. The Party has convinced many Chinese that its leadership is the key to both preserving ancient Chinese traditions and restoring China's prestige in the world. Thus the Chinese government promises to make China great again by employing its special brand of state-controlled capitalism, combined with strategies drawn from China's distant past, all overseen by a heavy-handed dictatorship.

The Marathon Picks Up Speed

Beginning with the new millennium, China's fortunes have greatly improved, and its economy has expanded dramatically until it is now the second-largest economy on earth. The CCP has become buoyant, and on the June 1, 2021 centennial of its founding, it let the world know how it felt. Standing at a podium emblazoned with the Communist Hammer and Sickle above the portrait of Mao that always looks out over Tiananmen Square from the Gate of Heavenly Peace, President for Life Xi Jinping, dressed in a Mao suit, spoke to a crowd of 70,000. As reported by *The Guardian*, he "praised the ruling party for lifting China out of poverty and humiliation and pledged to expand China's military and influence." Xi continued:

> We will not accept sanctimonious preaching from those who feel they have the right to lecture us. We have never bullied, oppressed, or subjugated the people of any other country, and we never will.
>
> By the same token we will never allow anyone to bully, oppress, or subjugate [China]. Anyone who tries will find themselves on a collision course with a steel wall forged by 1.4 billion people. [82]

This is classic Communist propaganda with a Chinese twist. Or, as the CCP would itself say, it is "Socialism with Chinese characteristics." It reveals a Cain-type attitude of victimhood and resentment while claiming to be innocent of ever committing an offense. Tell that to the Tibetans. Tell that to the Uyghurs or the Falun Gong. Tell that to the people of Hong Kong and Taiwan. Tell that to the 80 million Chinese who have died cruel deaths at the hands of the CCP.

China claims to have peaceful intentions and, no doubt, would rather conquer the world through the peaceful surrender of the United States and all other powers. But—as we've now heard from China's new Mao—if the rest of the world doesn't get with Beijing's "peaceful" program, it can expect to be buried along with those 80 million who have already lost their lives to the Chinese Communist cause.

Typical of Communism's bullying behavior, China has done its utmost to catch up with the West by devious means. It has forced investors seeking access to its vast markets to share their technology with Chinese partners, which are often, directly or indirectly, the CCP or the PLA. When unable to secure proprietary information that way, it has resorted to international corporate espionage to steal the blueprints of a modern economy: its science, technology and military capabilities. In the meantime, cynical Chinese propagandists have tried to exploit issues of racism and other social problems in the West to intimidate democratic governments into remaining silent over the far more egregious behavior by China itself, such as its Uyghur genocide and outright repression of the Falun Gong and other religious organizations.

Liberating Communist China

As discussed in Chapter 10, at its root Marxism is an ideology of aggrievement, jealousy, resentment and vengeance. Xi's aggressive speech could have been made by any of the Soviet leaders. However, for all its constant bluster, the Soviet Union knew that the West was far ahead in science and technology and offered a far higher standard of living to its people than did the Communist bloc countries. Communist China, too, was long in a similar position. However, unlike the USSR, China has been successful in convincing the West that it is not an enemy and that it is a worthy business partner, thereby attracting the economic engagement the Soviets long wanted but never secured. Communist China is also a nation of bluster, but thanks to its economic and military power, it has to be taken seriously and recognized as a real threat to a free and peaceful world.

Communists like to think of themselves as on the side of history, thus justifying their dictatorship of the proletariat. The CCP has been able to marry this concept with the traditional Chinese concept of the Mandate of Heaven such that Xi Jinping believes he is now ruling the People's Republic with the full blessing of "heaven" and history.

China does have a great history with a rich culture and several early contributions to human progress, such as the inventions of paper and gunpowder. It is also the birthplace of two of Asia's most important spiritual traditions, Taoism and Confucianism. But Communism is not a natural progression from that past: It is a total rejection of traditional Chinese virtue. As such, it can never be a successful vehicle to restore China's true greatness.

The other problem the CCP faces is the fact that Marxism-Maoism offers nothing of lasting value to the Chinese people or the world. Totalitarianism is hardly a system of government sought out by people longing for a better life, and even an economy that provides opportunities for wealth creation is still no substitute for a free society in which individuals can pursue their own interests and worship according to their own beliefs.

As we have noted, the principles of how to deal with Communist China are the same as for all other totalitarian regimes. There can be no détente, no appeasement. The West must be absolutely resolute in its condemnation of the inhuman practices of the CCP at home and its rogue and ruthless behavior overseas. The West, and America in particular, must maintain a deterrent military supremacy, preventing China from engaging in any sort of adventurism and circumventing the spread of its pernicious influence around the world.

At the same time, there is no need to downplay China's global importance. Rather, it is up to the industrialized nations to realize that they are not just dealing with a large and lucrative market but with an ideological enemy that is willing to do anything to gain global ascendancy. We must not forget that China's current success has been achieved by nefarious means, including the theft of intellectual property and the bullying of anyone who engages in business with them.

Ultimately, we have to believe in the Chinese people and not in the CCP. The majority of Chinese people may accept the CCP for the time being because it has given them greater prosperity than before. But the destruction of their traditional culture means that they now lack the values that actually make life worth living. No Communist state has ever been successful in providing a truly good life for its citizens, and the shiny skyscrapers in Shanghai are a poor disguise for the reality of life under Chinese Communism. Those of us in free nations need to always remember this and to work diligently towards the liberation of the people of China from the tyranny of the Chinese Communist Party.

Chapter 14

Marxism Metastasizes I

*American Marxists Find a Trojan Horse
and The Frankfurt School Marries Marx
with Freud in Critical Theory*

Collapse of the USSR Exposes the Evils of Marxism

With the collapse of the Soviet Union in 1991, the web of Soviet secrecy began to unravel. Already in 1973, Aleksandr Solzhenitsyn's monumental *The Gulag Archipelago* had exposed the evil of the Soviet prison camp system and the ruthless regime that fed it with victims. In the 1990s, for the first time, international researchers were able to explore the archives of the Central Committee of the Communist Party and the Politburo, the Comintern and some of the security agencies. These documents confirmed the cruel callousness of the Soviet leadership's decision-making, its support and manipulation of Communist parties throughout the world—and its exploitation of naïve Western individuals, organizations and governments who took the Soviets at their word when they said they believed in peaceful coexistence, détente and nuclear disarmament.

For Americans, long-held assumptions about extensive Soviet espionage in their country during the World War II era were generally confirmed by the US Government's 1995 public release of the Venona cables. "Venona" was the code name for a secret project to decrypt cables between Moscow and its secret agents in the United States. Started in 1943, it would provide valuable proof of espionage activities by the CPUSA, its network of underground members, and many of the individuals who had been engaged in spying, such as Alger Hiss and the Rosenbergs.

Even for faithful Marxists, the mountains of evidence that came to light after the collapse of the Soviet Union could not be ignored. They had to admit that the Soviet Union had been a monumental failure, a macabre incarnation of Marxist theory. However, many thought the fault lay in the Soviet application of Marxism-Leninism and not in the theory itself. They wanted to believe that Marxism continued to have value and could be used beneficially to address social ills. They reasoned that the failure manifest in the Soviet Union lay primarily in Marxism-Leninism's focus on economics and politics, at the expense of personal and social issues.

The Frankfurt School, established in the 1920s, had already laid the groundwork for a new application of Marxism by combining it with Freudianism, a theory that enjoyed widespread acceptance in academia and society at large. They dubbed their approach Critical Theory. Several French scholars would take Critical Theory further, essentially rejecting the absolutes of science in favor of ascribing beliefs and theories to social influences shaped largely by the language of dominant social groups.

But Marxism Survives the Demise of the Soviet Union

Thus the widely held belief that Communism died and went to hell after the collapse of the Soviet Union, and that Marxism lost its relevance and appeal from that time, is not true. Marxism-Leninism as a revolutionary and ruling ideology is alive and well in China (and a handful of small countries). In many respects, it is now a greater danger to the world than ever before because of China's great wealth, growing military prowess, and ever-increasing international aggression. Meanwhile, the ugly intellectual offspring of Marxism, known collectively as Neo-Marxism, continue to spread their poison throughout academia, infecting general education, mass media, government policies and corporate decision-making. Marxism is not dead. It is very much alive.

Communism Finds a Home in the Democratic Party

There were thousands of Communist and Communist front organizations during the Cold War, some international, some national, and some local. Generally, they were formed with innocent-sounding names, such as the International Organization of Journalists (IOJ), a United Front tactic the Communists used to recruit support from people who would not consider themselves Socialists or Communists but generally agreed with the aims of the front organizations. Most of these groups folded with the collapse of the Soviet Union, but some merged with other groups or morphed into new entities that continued to pursue Marxist-Leninist or Maoist objectives.

For example, in America the New Communist Movement (NCM) of the 1960s and 70s included groups like the Organization for Revolutionary Unity (ORU), which was itself formed from a merger of the Committee for a Proletarian Party (CPP) and the Communist Organization, Bay Area (COBA). In 1986 the ORU and other elements of the NCM became part of the Freedom Road Socialist Organization (FRSO), which is still active today.

The result of decades of this splintering, merging and renaming of Communist and Communist front organizations has resulted in the creation of a plethora of organizations that have Marxist or Neo-Marxist roots, but which often hide the fact. Some are linked directly or indirectly to the Communist Party of China (CCP). Many advocate for ostensibly worthy causes, such as justice, human rights, worker rights, minority rights, etc. The Communist Party USA, which barely survived a great loss of members when Khrushchev revealed some of the evils of Stalin in 1956, switched its allegiance from Moscow to Beijing after the Soviet Union collapsed. Since then it has become a tool of the CCP and actively promotes the radicalization of the Democratic Party.

Indeed, the Communist strategy in America is to use the Democratic Party as a Trojan Horse to infiltrate its radical agenda into the American mainstream. Thus the CPUSA no longer puts forward its own candidates for election but now works to get Democratic Party candidates elected. There are dozens of radical Left organizations doing similar work. Typically, they target minority communities, exploiting resentment to stir up anger and action (protesting, rioting and looting), as well as harassing targeted individuals, groups and institutions, all the while promoting radical Democratic Party candidates who claim they can address minority grievances—something they never actually do. Black Lives Matter and Antifa are two of these groups that are well known, and are discussed in some detail in Chapter 16. However, most of the groups are not widely known at all. (For a list of currently active US-based groups with a Socialist/Communist agenda, see Appendix 18, pp439-447.)

To take over America, the Communists are working from an old playbook: use democratic elections to gain power, and then replace authentic democracy with democratic centralism in a one-party state. The American version of that strategy is to control enough "blue" states to win every presidential contest and keep a majority in both the Senate and House. If successful, this will make America a de facto one-party nation. Reaching that destination starts at the local level by getting Democrats elected as city, county and state representatives. The next goal is national elections. Prime targets are major "red" and "purple" sates (like Texas, Virginia, Georgia and Florida) which through this process can be turned "blue".

In addition to funding flowing from the CCP, many of these organizations receive very significant funding from wealthy individuals (George Soros and Mark Zuckerberg come to mind) and corporations that either benefit from big government alignment with business or that don't want to be targeted by radicals. Some of these backers are members of Democracy Alliance, which claims to raise over $100 million a year for "progressive" causes.

This strategy is proving successful. The "old" Democratic Party was patriotic and fundamentally aligned with America's founding values. It enjoyed support from a broad cross-section of American society, and many of its leaders, like presidents Harry Truman and John F. Kennedy, were strong opponents of Communism. No more. The Party today presents itself as a patriotic champion of American values, but its policies tell a different story. Increasingly it is becoming the home of radical Left ideologies and the instrument to translate those ideologies into government policies and programs that are causing enormous damage to America's traditional principles and institutions.

If it is allowed to achieve its ambitions, a radicalized Democratic Party will bring permanent change to America. That change will be for the worse, making America a big-government state with few personal freedoms that is unable to maintain its role as a global champion of liberty.

Marxist Threads Run Through Neo-Marxist Offshoots

There are several theoretical threads connecting Marxism with its Neo-Marxism offshoots. These threads are rooted in the nature, attitudes and actions of Cain, including his envy towards Abel, his resentment towards God and Abel for the Divine order of creation, his refusal to take responsibility for his own situation, his desire to dominate Abel and his use of violence to achieve his objective. Thus the core ideas of both Marxism and Neo-Marxism, dialectical materialism and Critical Theories, share several attributes: they both feed on envy and resentment towards the more fortunate and successful (they are anti-private property and anti-capitalist), they both reject the order of creation (in particular the nuclear family established by a Supreme Being), they both refuse to take responsibility for their own situations and blame others for their difficulties, and they both believe the world develops through conflict between opposites rather than cooperation between complementarities, a view which justifies violent destruction of the existing order by the aggrieved.

Intrinsic to these theories is their shared belief that human consciousness, reason and beliefs are the product of physical and social conditions. As articulated in *The Communist Manifesto*: "Does it require deep intuition to comprehend that man's ideas, views and conceptions, in one word, man's consciousness, changes with every change in the conditions of his material existence, in his social relations and in his social life?" (Appendix 1, p282.)

This is the essence of the materialist answer to the religious view that human existence originated with the incarnation of Divine attributes in the substance and form of man and woman. Without belief in a Creator, human beings are alienated from their roots and endlessly seek to explain their existence in humanistic and materialistic terms. The pursuit of truth is undoubtedly laudable, but when its assumptions are faulty the results can only be faulty as well. This explains why dialectical materialism and Critical Theory produce endless deconstructive explanations of history and society but never succeed in increasing human wisdom. On the contrary, they produce more confusion and conflict.

An Inexcusable Embrace of Socialism

It is truly remarkable that anyone who knows the history of the 20th century or is familiar with the Socialist and Communist countries today, such as China, Cuba and Venezuela, can advocate for Socialism or Communism in any incarnation. Yet, as we showed in Chapter 12, a large percentage of young people in America (and elsewhere) think that socialism is a good thing and preferable to capitalism. These are not young people who grew up in Bedouin tents in the Sahara, straw huts in Africa or Brazilian slums; they were raised in the freest and wealthiest country ever to exist. How could they possibly want to see their country become a Venezuela, Cuba, China or North Korea? The answer is that the Pied Pipers of socialism are themselves inexcusably ignorant or outright liars. The academic avatars of Critical Theory insist that they long since divorced themselves from Marx and have a whole new solution to the problems of injustice and inequality. Not true.

This deception needs to be identified and debunked. The way that Marxism has metastasized into seemingly endless shades of Neo-Marxism needs to be tracked and exposed. Critical Theory is creating societal chaos at an unprecedented level and threatens to undermine the good that has been achieved through the evolution of personal freedom and representative government based on Judeo-Christian teachings and the spread of capitalism. Allowed to fester and spread further, it will cause inestimable damage to the world. It must be stopped and replaced with a morally sound ideology.

Religion's Failings Do Not Justify Its Destruction

Thus while Marxism and Critical Theory are able to identify inadequacies in religion and religion-based culture, they are unable to offer a better understanding of our existence and world. It is irrational to destroy an existing set of ideas and cultural norms if you don't have a better one to replace them. But that is precisely what the dialectic and Critical Theory do through the process of deconstruction. After all, so long as humans are imperfect, their beliefs and ideas will be imperfect too. Thus religion should be understood as a work in progress. There is no justification for trying to destroy it because of its imperfections and incompleteness. A wise approach is to recognize religion's shortcomings, learn from its past mistakes, and find ways to improve it. This rational approach has historically been frustrated by condemnation of religious critics as heretics by ecclesiastical authorities, stifling legitimate ideas and suppressing movements of reform. Nevertheless, the outright condemnation of religion itself has been even more harmful to humanity, as the record of Marxism shows.

Major Neo-Marxist Theories and Movements

Although we have already touched on several Neo-Marxist movements, they have come to supersede Marxism in their ability to wreak havoc in societies around the world and therefore need a much closer look. In this chapter we delve into the critical theories of the Frankfurt School and in the next look at the many harmful theories that have grown out of Postmodernism.

The Frankfurt School and Critical Theory

One of the earliest and most important of the Neo-Marxist scholarly endeavors was concentrated at the Institute for Social Research at the Goethe University Frankfurt. Here, in the 1930s, a group of academics, who had for a decade been developing what they would call Critical Theory, sought to influence social theory. Among the notable names associated with this school were Max Horkheimer, Theodor Adorno, Wilhelm Reich, Eric Fromm and Herbert Marcuse.

Members of the Frankfurt School were influenced by Freud's theories of repression, seeing in them a theory analogous with Marx's analysis of classist oppression (as in the oppression of the proletariat by the bourgeoisie). However, they believed that culture was not part of the Marxist superstructure but a separate force influencing society. They used Critical Theory to attack virtually all established cultural institutions, including the family, employing the Marxist practice described by Arthur Koestler as "dialectical interpretation" of the facts.[83]

Max Horkheimer explained it this way: Critical Theory is "suspicious of the very categories of better, useful, appropriate, productive, and valuable, as those are understood in the present order."[84] Indeed, as elaborated by the Frankfurt School, Critical Theory would prove a handy tool for deconstructing traditional social institutions, thereby negating the values they embodied. As with dialectical materialism, it provided a theoretical basis for analyzing the constituents of conflict in society, isolating them, and then attacking the elements believed responsible for dysfunction and injustice. In practice, it meant that any ideas or institutions identified as "enemies of progress" should be subjected to criticism and elimination. Thus Critical Theory leads to strident, often violent, opposition to "non-progressive" elements of society in the name of realizing a world aligned with the progressive ideals of an imaginary secular Utopia.

As we have noted, Marx himself had identified the traditional family as an oppressive institution of the bourgeoisie that needed to be destroyed, and in the early years of the Soviet Union, a free sex philosophy was tried, in line with this Marxist theory. An article in *The Atlantic* of July 1926, by "A Woman Resident in Russia," is titled: *The Russian Effort to Abolish Marriage.* It notes that:

> When the Bolsheviki came into power in 1917 they regarded the family, like every other 'bourgeois' institution, with fierce hatred, and set out with a will to destroy it. 'To clear the family out of the accumulated dust of the ages we had to give it a good shakeup, and we did,' declared Madame Smidovich, a leading Communist.[85]

Madame Smidovich had written in *Pravda* in March 1925:

> Every member, even a minor, of the Communist Youth League and every student of the Rabfak [Communist Party training school] has the right to satisfy his sexual desire. This concept has become an axiom, and abstinence is considered a bourgeois notion. If a man lusts after a young girl, whether she is a student, a worker, or even a school-age girl, then the girl must obey his lust; otherwise, she will be considered a bourgeois daughter, unworthy to be called a true communist.[86]

The Atlantic author describes the social chaos brought about by this free sex culture, where many young people had multiple partners, resulting in tens of thousands of children without homes. (To address this problem, the Soviets simply abolished the notion of illegitimate children.) "Men took to changing wives with the same zest which they displayed in the consumption of the recently restored forty-per-cent vodka," she wrote. Divorces could be had in minutes, which is why a bill to end marriage altogether was being debated. However, with total social chaos looming, the bill was not passed. Instead, the Soviets reversed course and the family was reinstated as a source of social stability. (With dialectical thinking, anything is possible.)

This history of disastrous anti-family policies did not deter the Frankfurt School, and its scholars eagerly pursued their theories of sexual repression and the psychological and social problems they attributed to it. And while these writers generally believed that the Soviet Union was a failure (especially due to Stalin's Reign of Terror in the late 1930s), they retained the atheism, anti-capitalism and anti-family positions of Marxism.

Frankfurt's Poison Infects America and the World

With the arrival of Hitler, most of the Frankfurt School left Germany, with several settling in the United States. The most prominent was Herbert Marcuse, whose writings would become popular in the mid-1960s, when he became known as the "Father of the New Left." In his book critiquing secular humanism, author Morris Bowers looked closely at Marcuse' book, *Eros and Civilization*. He noted that Marcuse argued "that by freeing sex from any restraints, we could elevate the pleasure principle over the reality principle and create a society with no work, only play." Bowers further noted that Marcuse believed that the working class would not lead the revolution because it had become part of the middle class, the bourgeoisie; their place would be taken by "a coalition of blacks, students, feminist women and homosexuals."[87] Marcuse also wrote that the new revolutionary groups opposed Western Civilization "with all the defiance, and the hatred, and the joy of rebellious victims, defining their own humanity against the definitions of the masters."[88]

Marcuse summed up his agenda: "One can rightfully speak of a cultural revolution, since the protest is directed toward the whole cultural establishment, including the morality of existing society... What we must undertake is a type of diffuse and dispersed disintegration of the system."[89] He supplemented this broad program of radical social destruction with a concept of "partisan tolerance" that is now all too prevalent in the Left's Cancel Culture. He wrote that the "realization of the objective of tolerance would call for intolerance toward prevailing policies, attitudes, opinions, and the extension of tolerance to policies, attitudes, and opinions which are outlawed or suppressed."[90] This is precisely the point of the Cancel Culture, as we are experiencing it today.

The Destruction Wrought by the Sexual Revolution

An Austrian writer, Wilhelm Reich, studied and worked with Freud. He sought to address his own sexual issues by combining Freudian and Marxist ideas and prescribed sexual liberation as the solution to neurosis. His 1936 book, *The Sexual Revolution*, was influential and provided a theoretical argument for a libertine lifestyle. (Freud would later reject Reich's theories.) In a taste of Reich's insights, he wrote this dismal evaluation of marriage: "Marital misery, to the extent to which it does not exhaust itself in the marital conflicts, is poured out over the children."[91]

In 1956, there was an influx of American Marxists into academia and influential organizations after tens of thousands of members of the CPUSA broke with the Party out of disgust with Stalin (when exposed by Khrushchev), as discussed in Chapter 12. Many of these Americans kept their Marxist faith and easily transferred their revolutionary interests to the Critical Theory movement brought to America by Marxist refugees from Nazism. Thus Marxist refugees from Stalinism and Nazism provided fertile soil for Leftist radicalism to take root in America during the 1960s.

It was the work of Marcuse, Reich, et al., that provided a theoretical justification for the sexual revolution of the 1960s and played a major role in the American embrace of Postmodernism. This French-based school of thought began to gain popularity in America in the late 1960s and is the dominant ideology of the Left today. It has come to dominate social theory in American academia and much of the West. Together, these two branches of Critical Theory (the Frankfurt School and Postmodernism) have transformed society in the West and many other parts of the world.

In their Critical Theories, the religious values that make the relationship between a man and woman a sacred bond of love are seen as obsolete. Self-gratification in the name of personal liberation has taken their place. Avatars of the sexual revolution treat it as if it was a scientific discovery of global and historical significance. In fact, "free sex" theory is the intellectual rationalization of men and women seeking justification for their own unprincipled and destructive behaviors. There is nothing new about these practices at all; it is just that now we have academic courses explaining what an important advance in science the sexual revolution represents. And we have a media and culture that embrace and promote it, despite the undeniable evidence of the enormously harmful effect the breakdown of traditional families has had on society, from increases in poverty and crime, to a wide range of psychological problems.

Alinsky Codifies A Radical Program for the Left

It is worth looking briefly at Saul Alinsky, the Pied Piper of the America Left who was politically active from the late 1930s to early 1970s. Born in 1909, he grew up in America when the Communist Party had made significant inroads, especially in labor unions and through a network of agents and Soviet spies in the government. Alinsky helped organize unions within the labor giant CIO (Congress of Industrial Organizations) and raised funds for the Comintern's International Brigade that fought against Franco in Spain. But his primary interest was community organizing: working within less fortunate communities to get them to "shake off the shackles" of the capitalist system. Unlike Reich or Marcuse, he was a man of action who translated Marxist revolutionary theory into a program of radical change.

His 1971 *Rules for Radicals* educated readers in how to leverage minority group grievances to bring about change. His was a classical Marxist approach of identifying targets for resistance, isolating and then attacking them, all as part of a program to wrest power from established capitalist individuals and institutions. His work would prove influential: Presidential candidate Hillary Clinton wrote her college thesis on his writings, and President Barack Obama followed him into community organizing.

Here are his rules:[92]

1. Power is not only what you have, but what the enemy thinks you have.

2. Never go outside the experience of your people.

3. Wherever possible go outside of the experience of the enemy.

4. Make the enemy live up to their own book of rules.

5. Ridicule is man's most potent weapon.

6. A good tactic is one that your people enjoy.

7. A tactic that drags on too long becomes a drag.

8. Keep the pressure on.

9. The threat is usually more terrifying than the thing itself.

10. The major premise for tactics is the development of operations that will maintain a constant pressure upon the opposition.

11. If you push a negative hard and deep enough it will break through into its counter side.

12. The price of a successful attack is a constructive alternative.

13. Pick the target, freeze it, personalize, and polarize it.

These prescriptions explain the tactics of the Left, whatever the cause, from environmental movements to anti-racism and Cancel Culture. Perhaps the most used of all these "rules" is the last, the politics of personal destruction. Again and again the Left slanders its enemies, and again and again it is successful in shutting them up, getting them to resign, destroying their careers and lives. These Alinskyite principles for action are the inverse of a virtuous response to human differences. In what we call the Way of Abel, a righteous response to a rival demonstrates firm resolve to oppose evil but always seeks first to address inequities and injustices through peaceful means—take responsibility for the situation oneself, to the greatest extent possible. Only after all such efforts have been made is the use of force on behalf of the vulnerable and defenseless justified.

Alinsky tellingly dedicated his *Rules for Radicals* to Lucifer: "Lest we forget at least an over-the-shoulder acknowledgment to the very first radical: from all our legends, mythology, and history (and who is to know where mythology leaves off and history begins—or which is which), the first radical known to man who rebelled against the establishment and did it so effectively that he at least won his own kingdom—Lucifer."[93] Yes, it was a Luciferian ideology that Alinsky used to promote revolution in America, an ideology used by social justice warriors to divide and radicalize society, to attack and destroy the traditional institutions that they hate.

Zinn Spreads Marxist Lies About America

In 1980, Howard Zinn published *A People's History of the United States*, a Marxist polemic that paints the European settlers and America's founders, starting with Christopher Columbus and the Pilgrims, as rapacious, bloodthirsty, capitalist conquerors and oppressive rulers. Cherry picking sources and facts, and omitting vitally important elements of the country's history, Zinn weaves a damning account of America as an oppressive and unjust nation on a par with Hitler's Germany. Incredibly, this fallacious account has been widely accepted in academia, and is taught in many schools and universities, where it is promoted by radical teachers and administrators. It is responsible for a whole generation of religion-hating and America-hating people on the Left, who embrace its cynical account and its justification for violent revolution by the groups it claims to be victims of the American monstrosity.

In 2019, Mary Grabar came out with a comprehensive critique of Zinn's book: *Debunking Howard Zinn; Exposing the Fake history That Turned a Generation against America.* Grabar depicts Zinn as a fraud who lifted whole sections of other's work, almost verbatim, who ignored many of the most important events in American history, and consistently interpreted the American story from a hostile, Marxist perspective. (Both the original book by Zinn and the Grabar critique can be found in the Bibliography.)

Marxism in Any Form Cannot Succeed

From a religious perspective, Lucifer's rebellion and alienation from the Creator resulted in the first family being established under Satan instead of God. Thus a legacy of the Fall is the pattern of evil preceding good, of a Satanic imitation of the original ideal usurping the true embodiment of Divine love and truth. As we discussed in Chapter 5, in history this pattern is repeated again and again, beginning with Cain, the first son of Adam and Eve, who after inheriting Satan's nature murders his younger brother Abel. The Satanic forces that led to this murder are the same forces that have inspired Marxist revolutions and Marxist oppression and which propel Critical Theory today. They are destructive to their core. As Saint Paul described these forces:

> For we wrestle not against flesh and blood, but against principalities, against powers, against the rulers of the darkness of this world, against spiritual wickedness in high places. (Ephesians 6:12)

The good news is that Satan can create nothing himself; he can only pervert and disfigure what God makes. In this lies the hope that Satanic ideologies will ultimately be exposed for what they really are and relegated to the dustbin of history. Marxism and Critical Theory represent the final stage of Satanic ideological development in that they so completely embody Satan's atheistic, anti-family credo, and do so on a global scale.

Once the evil nature of Marxism and Neo-Marxism are exposed and discredited, they can be replaced by the final stage of an ideology that incorporates a Divinely inspired alternative to materialism, with a credible promise of a good, just and peaceful world. The explanations in this book are part of that alternative.

Chapter 15

Marxism Metastasizes II

Postmodernism Takes Critical Theory Global

Foucault and Postmodernism

Meanwhile, in post-World War II France, a new school of thought was emerging from the shadows of the Marxist-Leninist horrors of Stalin's Soviet Union. Leading figures of this school were Michel Foucault and Jacques Derrida. As with the Frankfurt School, Foucault retained the essence of Marxist dialectical materialism while addressing social and cultural issues far beyond the boundaries of Marx's class warfare categories. His true radicalism, however, wasn't limited to using a dialectical analysis for deconstruction of society, as had Marx and the Frankfurt School. He questioned the very basis of science and the existence of universal absolutes.

True to the essential gospel of materialism, Foucault believed that knowledge and social institutions were the product of power relationships in society, not of a working out of relationships between Creator and creation. For his part, Derrida was particularly interested in the role of language in this process. He pointed out that dominant classes or groups have a larger role than weaker groups in establishing the prevailing language of society, thereby reinforcing the power status quo. (This explains the Left's persistent and oppressive efforts to get everyone to use its politically correct terminology.)

As with the Marxist dialectic, these theories led inevitably to the conclusion that power structures must be broken down for change to occur. This, in turn, led inevitably to violent revolution since those with power are always reluctant to relinquish their positions of privilege. By rejecting the absolutes of truth and science, Foucault had no reference point to justify his prescriptions for social change, no starting point for cogent argumentation. Instead, he depended on nothing more than his own instincts and insights to argue for the changes he wanted to see take place. Given this perfectly unscientific approach, it is truly remarkable that much of the social science taught in Western universities today is based on Foucault's theories and assertions.

An Amoral Theory from an Immoral Man

Noam Chomsky, one of the most radical Leftist academics in America, was stunned during a 1971 televised debate with Foucault to find that he had no belief in science or absolutes whatsoever.[94] Specifically, Foucault disagreed with the possibility of a fixed human nature. He also rejected the notion that human reason is the basis for justice, claiming there is no universal basis for a concept of justice. [95]

Following the debate, Chomsky expressed his amazement at Foucault's rejection of a possibility for the existence of a universal morality:

> He struck me as completely amoral, I'd never met anyone who was so totally amoral... I liked him personally, it's just that I couldn't make sense of him. It's as if he was from a different species, or something. [96]

If science and reason are not the basis for Foucault's theories, what is? It would seem nothing more than his own subjective experiences and ideas. How, then, is it possible for Foucault to be the last word in the social sciences today? And how is it possible to have a rational debate with anyone who embraces Foucault's theories? Finally, if Foucault accepts no moral absolutes, doesn't that make him immoral by most civilized standards of morality, rather than merely amoral? His personal life of sexual promiscuity and his advocacy for homosexual, underage and pedophile sex would seem to indicate so.

Despite basing their assertions on this fundamentally flawed foundation for the theories of Foucault and Postmodernism in general, faithful followers of the French theorist very often get extremely agitated if you do not accept their "facts" and their language. Most peculiar of all, very often Leftists of the Postmodernist school claim that science is on their side and that those with rival ideas are anti-science. With a straight face, they tell us to "follow the science." Thus if you question the Left's assertions that gender and biological sex are not necessarily related, you are a bad person who refuses to accept the "science" of the Left because you are a heteronormative bigot (and probably a racist to boot). Or if you don't believe that global warming will become irreversible and destroy the planet in twelve years—unless we throw trillions of taxpayer dollars at Green New Deal programs—you are likely to be labeled a "science denier" who refuses to accept the verdict of a worldwide consensus of scientists.

In this deeply flawed parallel universe, truth itself is deemed to be a function of language and the power relationships operating in society. Truth belongs to no one (certainly not God) and is forever incomplete and imperfect, inviting the disciples of Foucault and Derrida to keep hacking away at it in the name of progress.

Today, Foucault is the most influential thinker in the social sciences, and his approach is employed to deconstruct, criticize and destroy an ever-wider range of traditional beliefs and social institutions. This school of Critical Theories is now called Postmodernism. It is responsible for many of the academic programs that together make up the dominant Leftist view of the world and the "progressive" ideas that spill onto the streets and into schools, media and corporations. They are also increasingly the basis for government policies.

Some of the specific Postmodernist theories, as they are used today, are summarized and commented on here. Some clearly build on Marxist or Frankfurt School theories; others are additions. (We can't blame Marx for transgenderism or anti-racism, but we do hold him largely responsible for the Critical Theory approach that produced them.) Taken as a whole, Postmodernism amounts to a materialist movement that can only be described as deceitful and evil. It is deceitful in hoodwinking good people with false promises of justice and virtue, and it is evil in its very real destruction of the values and norms upon which good societies are based. Postmodernism threatens the very foundations of civilization and must be exposed and excised from our culture and world.

Anti-Religion Theory

The Leftist worldview asserts that religion is a force in history and society and responsible for shaping language that has considerable influence on both. This sterile, arms-length view of religion keeps it remote from hearts and minds and safely in academia, where it can readily be dissected and relegated to abstract obscurity. All that remains is a legacy of ideas and language that are seen by Marxists and Postmodernists as obstacles to "progress." Marx and Engels articulated this view with their description of religion as an "opiate"— in other words, as something that people indulge in to avoid facing the realities of life. As most modern democracies are based on a secular state (that is, a state without an official religion), Leftists with an anti-religion agenda can use secularism to justify pushing religion out of all public institutions altogether: Prayer is banned in public schools; religious symbols are removed from the public square; faith and devotion are scoffed at.

Within the secularized world of industrialized states, there has been a steady drop in the percentage of people who believe in a deity or the primacy of spiritual values. Those who worship and believe faith should be a basis for life and a source of values for government decision-making are often met with disdain and mockery.

But the religious impulse is deeply rooted in human nature. As "children of God," our "spiritual DNA" connects us to Divine love, truth and purpose. We have shown how this impulse has been co-opted by Marxism, which replaces the Creator and the Kingdom of Heaven with Marx and a Communist Utopia. In Postmodernism, religion is a central player in traditional societies and therefore a prime target for deconstruction and destruction. Furthermore, morality is viewed not as the basis for personal and social virtue, but as an arbitrary code of conduct imposed by religion for religion's sake, not the well-being of people. As such, religion-based morality is part of the oppression by dominant social forces of ordinary people. Foucault himself had rebelled against Christian morality, especially in his personal life as a gay man, which explains, in part at least, his criticism of the church and its rules for life. (In addition to being a gay activist who left the French Communist Party because of its anti-gay policies, Foucault was a vocal proponent of adult-child sex and pedophilia.)

The thrust of Critical Theory is clearly anti-religious on purpose. After all, in the West at least, Judeo-Christian precepts are reflected in everything from legal codes to social mores, and therefore removing religion from society undermines the whole societal edifice. This is exactly the Postmodernist objective: It is a movement that aims to undercut the pillars upon which modern society has been built, plunging it into a state of chaos that is uncoupled from religious or scientific absolutes.

Although many good people are drawn to Postmodernism because they are truly concerned for injustices in the world, destruction for destruction's sake is a dangerous path to follow. Postmodernism offers no credible alternative to religion, only destruction of what is. What improvements to human understanding and life can Postmodernism claim? It produces bitter and resentful people who see themselves as victims and are eager to criticize the world they inherited while insisting that you agree with their analyses and their descriptive language. They are not happy. They bring no joy to the world, and their political correctness gets ever more extreme as they seek to cancel all voices of faith and the love of family and nation.

Anti-religion theory seeks to rip from history and society that which is eternal and transcendent—the very heart of human existence. Without these, meaning and purpose and the basis for morality are lost. In a world of conflicting ideologies, religion always points in one direction, towards what is transcendent and good. It is the most important force shaping family and society. This is not to say that religion needs no renewal; it surely does, constantly. But because of its materialism, Postmodernism cannot reform religion. Its diagnoses might be be accurate, or relevant, but its prescriptions are deleterious and often lethal.

Marxism Perverts Christianity in Liberation Theology

One subtle and harmful effort of the Left has been to attempt to reconcile Christianity with Marxism by suggesting that Marxism offers a program of social transformation that translates Christian idealism into practical action. The best-known such program is Liberation Theology, which became popular in Latin America during the 1960s, following the liberalization of Catholicism under Vatican II. The argument for this theory is that the church has not succeeded in addressing social ills, and therefore it should adopt Marxist theories of oppression and injustice as the basis for its own social programs. Liberation Theology condemns capitalism as nothing more than an economic system based on greed, thereby naturally aligning the church with Socialist agendas and regimes.

This focus on social activism may seem laudatory, and to the extent that it enables people of faith to concern themselves with the less fortunate on earth, it is. However, it can just as easily be a disservice to believers. Liberation Theology encourages believers to see activism as the primary responsibility of Christians rather than doing the work of cultivating a life of faith in order to become a better person and serve others. What's more, the atheism of Marxism always makes it incompatible with religious belief. Marxist revolution does not lead to improvement of society but to the exact opposite—violence and misery. Few would disagree that a life of faith should translate into a life of caring for others, but believers should not be tricked by the alluring platitudes of Marxist propaganda into endorsing an atheistic program of violent revolution and oppression.

A somewhat similar Marxist subversion of Protestant Christianity in America can be found on the CPUSA website (cpusa.org), published as a PowerPoint presentation in early 2021. Titled *Understanding and Confronting Christian Fascism: The Structure and Danger of the White Evangelical Movement*, this piece of propaganda is produced by Dr. Paul Scholl, a medical doctor who identifies himself as a "Marxist and a Christian and an ordained minister." It targets in particular the evangelical churches in America, although it doesn't spare the Catholics. Believing that the goal of evangelicals is to create a "fascist theocracy," Scholl makes this statement: "The opiate of the masses has become toxic, and it will take a massive "United Front" against Christian fascism to defeat it." If he believes Christianity is the opiate of the masses, isn't he simply a Marxist and not a minister of Christ?

Erroneously Conflating Marxism with Buddhism

Incredibly, Tibet's Dalai Lama—whose Buddhist religion has been ruthlessly suppressed by the Chinese Communist Party and who has had to live in exile from his Tibetan homeland because of China's brutal occupation—has spoken positively of Marxism. During a visit to France in 1993 he said:

> Of all the modern economic theories, the economic system of Marxism is founded on moral principles, while capitalism is concerned only with gain and profitability. Marxism is concerned with the distribution of wealth on an equal basis and the equitable utilization of the means of production. It is also concerned with the fate of the working classes—that is the majority—as well as with the fate of those who are underprivileged and in need, and Marxism cares about the victims of minority-imposed exploitation. For those reasons the system appeals to me, and it seems fair… The failure of the regime in the former Soviet Union was, for me, not the failure of Marxism but the failure of totalitarianism. For this reason I still think of myself as half-Marxist, half-Buddhist.[97]

This is a remarkable statement for one of the most revered religious leaders in the world today. To say that Marxism is "founded on moral principles" demonstrates a profound lack of understanding. What are the moral principles of Marxism? What is their source? Indeed, it is Marx's failure to recognize transcendent moral principles and virtues that makes his theories so thoroughly violent and destructive. Marx's atheistic, anti-religion and anti-family beliefs are at the heart of Communist ideology and its history of violent revolution and tyranny. These beliefs explain Communist China's brutal oppression of the people of Tibet and refusal to give them their freedom. Does the Dalai Lama not see that?

While Marxism and Postmodernism may well identify real deficiencies in religion, they are no better qualified to improve religion than a wrecking ball is to improve the condition of a house in need of repair. In truth, the best they can do is to inadvertently reveal the inadequacies of their own theories by applying them as alternatives to religion. Indeed, this has been the pattern of Leftist movements: The Socialist and Communist regimes of the last century were infinitely worse than any society based on religion, and the behavior of "liberated" Leftists today is characterized by hedonistic lifestyles that are personally and socially destructive.

Denial of Science and Anti-Family Theory

Whereas Marx and Engels claimed the mantle of science for their theories, the Postmodernists reject science as an absolute, believing it to be, along with all other knowledge, a product of language shaped by social forces over time. As we have noted, this evolution in Leftist thinking enables Postmodernists to dispense with the Marxist claim to "scientific socialism," to claim independence from Marxism, and to justify their positions purely on the basis of subjective criteria. In the Postmodernist world, then, the traditional family is little more than a temporary ordering of human relations around the animalistic sexual urges of men and women.

The sexual revolution advocated by Reich and other members of the Frankfurt School, and now by truly radical theories of gender and sex, have their root in Marxism. In *The Communist Manifesto,* Marx said that the family is an institution of the bourgeoisie and alien to the proletariat:

> The proletarian is without property; his relation to his wife and children has no longer anything in common with the bourgeois family relations; modern industry labor, modern subjection to capital, the same in England as in France, in America as in Germany, has stripped him of every trace of national character. Law, morality, religion, are to him so many bourgeois prejudices, behind which lurk in ambush just as many bourgeois interests. (Appendix 1, pp273-274.)

As we have shown, the denial of a biological basis for the existence of just two sexes strikes at the very root of our existence and the role of science. To deny this first principle of nature is to undermine the basis of modern science and to invalidate the human record that points to millennia of social development around nuclear families. The traditional human family, which provides nurture and protection to new life, is not only the most stable structure for multiplication of our kind, it is also the carrier of the knowledge and values on which societies are built. In its mature form, it is the best environment for a growing person to learn to love others and, ultimately, produce children of their own.

It is only ignorance of our original purpose and the design of nature that explains advocacy for destruction of the family. As we discussed in Chapter 2, nature itself demonstrates no confusion over the basic biological order of sexual and social organization, albeit within the parameters of a very wide diversity of species. Procreation and multiplication are achieved through the interaction of male with female, stamen with pistil. In the atom itself, order is maintained through the relationship between positively charged protons and negatively charged electrons. This order, in itself, points to an overarching purpose for all existence, enabling all creation to contribute to an ever-expanding universe.

Withering Away of the Human Race?

Birthrates in most developed countries are plummeting. For a world that has long worried about overpopulation, this is an unexpected new challenge. The United Nations projects that by the end of this century, global population will level off at around 11 billion people. However, the demographic trajectory is extremely uneven, with the vast majority of countries expected to see rapid population declines while a few grow dramatically. Significantly, China's current 1.4 billion people population is expected to be cut in half by 2100. Africa, by contrast, is expected to triple its current 1.3 billion population to an estimated 4.3 billion, with Nigeria projected to become the second-largest country in the world after India. (See Appendix 19, pp448-449, for UN population projections to 2100.)

These projections are, of course, based on changes in lifestyles which produce changes in birthrates. When the birthrate drops below 2.1 children per woman, the population begins to shrink. If this downward trajectory is sustained, it tends to lead to an acceleration in decline. (See an article on this in *The New York Times* of May 22, 2021.[98]) The global trend is for families in economically developed countries to have fewer children, in part so that they can sustain a desirable standard of living, but also because government policies often disincentivize childbearing. Furthermore, the trend of fewer children being welcomed into the world is one consequence of the anti-family theories of Marxism and Neo-Marxism, as they encourage sexual self-indulgence in relationships that do not produce children. If the trend of developed countries losing population continues, we can expect that Africa, too, will begin to experience population decline as it progresses economically.

Many governments already have programs to encourage childbearing. These typically include everything from tax breaks to direct payments to women willing to have more children. Ultimately, the driving force to form families and expand populations will be the love and inborn desire of a man and a woman to have children. Whatever the ideal birthrate is for the world, it can best be achieved by policies that are unequivocally pro-family, that address the economic pressures on a family, and that teach the personal and social benefits of parenthood and family.

Queer Theory, Gender Studies and Transgenderism

The essence of queer theory is that there is no God-made natural order for sexual relations within a family. Rather, sexual needs and desires are natural, and traditional families are restrictive and oppressive structures that have no relevance in today's world. Thus morality takes on a completely different meaning. It is based on acceptance of whatever sexual relations a person chooses as their own. There are no absolutes. The radical Lesbian, Gay, Bisexual, Transgender and Queer (LGBTQ) agenda is to get society as a whole to accept and normalize this perverted concept of morality.

The idea that sex and gender are not necessarily aligned has been pursued using Postmodernist deconstruction and criticism of the traditional family. Foucault himself was an actively gay man who obviously developed his theories in part to rationalize his own lifestyle. As with Marx, who all his adult life sought to justify his resentments against society and desire for violent revolution, Foucault's self-indulgence is a purely subjective standard that is totally inconsistent with a scientific approach to knowledge.

Gender dysphoria results from a person believing his or her gender is other than what their biological sex says it is. Thus, for example, a woman can believe she is actually a man in a woman's body. Today, this transgender theory has resulted in a whole new movement seeking "gender equality," that is, insisting that people have a right to determine their own gender and that other people should accept their determination and treat them accordingly, even though this contradicts biology. Thus a man who believes he is actually a woman trapped in a man's body has the right to be called by female pronouns and allowed to use women's bathrooms. In a fascistic twist, a number of governments and institutions now prescribe punishments for those who do not conform with these dysphoric pronoun demands or do not allow men to use women's bathrooms (or vice versa).

Meanwhile, men who self-identify as women are being allowed to compete with biological women in sports—perhaps the most illogical (and frankly insane) outcome of gender theories as they are not even remotely attached to scientific truth. (In sports, practically all the abuse of transgenderism favors biological male athletes who enjoy natural physical advantages.) In the upside-down world of Leftist values, the media, corporations and politicians are urged to support these policies and punish any person or institution that does not allow biological men to compete against women.

More sinisterly, transgenderism has become a movement within the sexual revolution that encourages immoral people to play God. Children who are confused about their sexual identities are encouraged in this confusion by counselors and transgender activists who promote the notion that gender dysphoria is normal and it can be solved through sex-change treatments. Irresponsible doctors prescribe hormonal treatments that encourage the dysphoria, and finally recommend surgery to align physical characteristics with the patient's believed gender identity. Such drastic, sterilizing surgery can never truly be reversed.

The results have been catastrophic. Many young children and teens have been advised all too hastily into making such sex-change decisions. It is not unusual for them to struggle with their male or female identity, but once they have embarked on hormone therapy or surgery, they are doomed to live under the shadow of that decision for the rest of their lives. It's not surprising, then, that suicide rates are astronomical among transgender children, as demonstrated by the following 2018 data from a study by *Pediatrics*, the official journal of the American Academy of Pediatrics:

Nearly 14% of adolescents reported a previous suicide attempt; disparities by gender identity in suicide attempts were found. Female to male adolescents reported the highest rate of attempted suicide (50.8%), followed by adolescents who identified as not exclusively male or female (41.8%), male to female adolescents (29.9%), questioning adolescents (27.9%), female adolescents (17.6%), and male adolescents (9.8%). Identifying as nonheterosexual exacerbated the risk for all adolescents except for those who did not exclusively identify as male or female (ie, nonbinary). For transgender adolescents, no other sociodemographic characteristic was associated with suicide attempts.[99]

Perhaps more alarming still, the *Pediatrics* study found that, "female to different gender and female to male adolescents report higher rates of suicide ideation (ie, 73.9% and 62.5%, respectively) and previous suicide attempts (46.4% and 18.4%, respectively) compared with all other groups." In other words, almost three-quarters of all female adolescents who have undergone a sex change have thought about committing suicide, and almost half have actually attempted suicide.

Considering these alarming and heartbreaking statistics, how can anyone advocate for a sex change to solve the experience of sexual dysphoria? Half of all adolescents who have gone through sex change procedures have tried to commit suicide! Is this activity not tantamount to murder in the guise of transgender advocacy? The perpetrators and enablers of this cruel and inhuman practice should be held to account for the consequences of their words and deeds.

Tellingly, these erroneous theories on gender are making great headway in many societies that have lost, or are losing, their religious culture. Thus in cities around the world, Gay Pride Week celebrates the new morality: LGBTQ people parade in the streets, their rainbow signs displayed everywhere, with businesses and institution encouraged to show their support for the cause.

Many places of worship have been co-opted into championing the LGBTQ agenda. During Gay Pride Week celebrations, and sometimes continuously, these places of worship display rainbow signs and pro-gay slogans to show support for LGBTQ people and organizations. This surrender of traditional values by religious groups is due in part to the spread of homosexuality within the church—especially in the Catholic Church, which does not permit marriage for priests and has a dark history of homosexuality and pedophilia in its seminaries and among its clergy.

Radical Feminism, White Patriarchy and Toxic Masculinity

In its first wave, women's liberation was about women gaining the right to vote, to hold office, to get equal pay, and generally to be treated the same as men under the law. In America, this first-wave feminism followed close on the heels of the Civil War and the Constitutional changes that ended slavery, giving African Americans the same rights as whites.

The rise of Neo-Marxist and Postmodernist theories of race and gender, however, have inevitably led to a feminist movement that goes much further. As with anti-racism, women's liberation and the radical feminist movement have become a great deal more aggressive, envisioning a world that inverts male domination by instituting policies that favor women over men. Thus radical feminist movements are no longer satisfied with equal treatment for women: They insist that discrimination against women can only be solved by women receiving preferential treatment through discrimination against men. This is, of course, a sexist policy that is not likely to foster peace and goodwill between the sexes.

As with all Marxist-derivative theories, and especially Postmodernism, deconstruction is based on identifying the cause of the problem within society, isolating it, and then destroying it. In this case, the Left has identified what they call white patriarchy and toxic masculinity as the sources of injustice to women and "people of color." In other words, simply being male and white makes you toxic and guilty of anti-woman bias and racism. To rectify the wrongs of the past, white males are singled out from among all other groups in society, condemned for the presumed injustices they have perpetrated, and punished by stripping them of their traditional roles and privileges.

Ironically, this analysis in itself is necessarily sexist and racist in that it assumes white men are prejudiced against women and "people of color" solely because they are male and white. You can't solve the problem of sexism with more sexism or racism with more racism. Thus the approach of the Left only makes the situation worse. It does not eliminate negative sexist or racist resentment and bitterness; it deepens and broadens their poisonous influence in society. Do the radical feminists really believe that attacking men on the basis of their sex and color will create a less sexist and less racist world? Of course not. The whole point of the Leftist agenda is to divide people against one another so that existing social institutions will collapse, making way for them to take power.

Nevertheless, to a large extent, the roles and contributions of men and women in history have been determined by their biological differences. Men are generally larger and stronger, making them better able to hunt, cultivate the earth, fell trees, cut stone for buildings, dig ditches, build homes and fix things when they break. And they make more powerful warriors to defend families, communities and nations. Women complement these qualities, giving birth to children, nurturing their growth, guiding their development and managing the home environment. In today's professional world, women excel, for example, in education and health care, in the legal professions and counseling. Other natural skills and capabilities often make women particularly adept at employing technology to good advantage. (And do they really want to take from men the jobs of plumber, electrician, mechanic, laborer and garbage collector?)

Most important, however, in the realm of mind and spirit, men and women contribute equally to life and family, to the creation of beauty and goodness. From the Creator's parental point of view, men and women are of equal value, which is why in a union of love they can experience mutual joy, pleasure and satisfaction. The natural differences between men and women do not detract from the achievement of this goal, they make it possible. Men and women are not intrinsically rivals, but partners who by design complement and complete each other.

The Right to Infanticide

One of the most destructive theories of radical feminism is that children in the womb are not human beings but merely extensions of the mother, appendages over which she has the "right to choose" life or death. This belief is only credible if you ignore the basics of creation and biology, namely that every baby has a father as well as a mother, and that women are endowed with a Divine quality as co-creators of new life. The newborn emerges complete from its mother's womb and is an entirely new person who is completely dependent on the love and nurture of its parents, especially its mother.

A number of animal species are known to kill and eat their own babies, including polar bears, cats, chimpanzees and rabbits. Witnessing this stirs a natural sense of disgust in us. How worse is it, then, when human beings kill their own progeny? Abortion has long been used to escape personal responsibility for "unwanted children," especially in Communist states where ideology dictates that a human being has no transcendent value. But the fact of killing a child in the womb is not an abstraction; it is an irreversible act of choice for which the mother is bound to experience repercussions.

The extremes to which the pro-abortion movement has descended has been demonstrated recently by several states in America passing legislation that allows abortions up to the time of birth. In Virginia, State Delegate Kathy Tran introduced a bill in January 2019 that would allow abortions at any time during a pregnancy with the approval of a single doctor, a change from the current law requiring three doctors to consent. Governor Ralph Northam, a pediatrician (!), told *WTOP* radio what would occur to a fetus under the bill:

> When we talk about third-trimester abortions… it's done in cases where there may be severe deformities, there may be a fetus that is nonviable. If a mother is in labor, I can tell you exactly what would happen. The infant would be

delivered. The infant would be kept comfortable. The infant would be resuscitated if that's what the mother and the family desired, and then a discussion would ensue between the physicians and the mother.[100]

In other words, after a child is born, the mother and her doctor would discuss whether or not to kill it. The bill did not pass, despite its supporters insisting it was only for exceptional cases. The real point is that if a law permits a mother to kill her newborn child for any reason, in practice it can be used for all reasons.

We should know better. We are created in the image of our Creator, with a spirit and body, and as parents we participate in the creation of new life. Every new life is a gift that should be treasured, from conception and gestation in the womb through life on earth and into eternity. Being a mother is magnificent, a blessing of co-creatorship with God that has eternal value. Radical feminism's antipathy towards men and irreverence for life is a recipe for human misery, for women as much as for men. After all, the greatest joy in life derives from love experienced within the family, between husband and wife, parents and children, and among siblings; this fact is demonstrated by the lifelong ties that bind members of families to one another. Although humanity has not yet fulfilled the ideal or full potential of the family, it remains by far the most important and successful social institution in history.

What are Human Rights?

The Left has used the concept of human rights as an absolute moral imperative against which societies and policies must be judged. But what is the basis for determining human rights? What, for example, are women's rights? Who can grant them? In a Marxist world, human rights are those granted by the dictatorship of the proletariat. In a Critical Theory world, human rights are subjective, meaning they are whatever the aggrieved believe them to be. Combined with revolutionary atheistic ideology, these views of human rights lead to criticism, intolerance and suppression of those who disagree with your concept of morality. This is a dangerous attitude that breeds social and political conflicts, and ultimately totalitarian government in which those in power impose their morality on all.

From a religious point of view, without absolutes of good and evil, there are no moral absolutes and therefore no basis for determining human rights. The human sensibility of what is right and wrong comes from an original nature that is aware of these opposites. The purpose of religion is to help people become ever more attuned to this innate sensibility through the cultivation of conscience, and to provide understanding and support for living an ever-better life. Ultimately, this process of spiritual growth should lead to the full alignment of human morality with the absolute standard of Divine morality.

Even nature exhibits characteristics consistent with human morality. Consider, for example, the mutual benefit of symbiotic relationships compared with predatory, parasitic or mutually destructive relationships. In fact, it is the notion that human rights are natural rights granted by the Creator— and that governments exist to protect those rights—that made America's founding significant and unique among nations. These natural rights were evoked in the Declaration of Independence and elaborated in the Constitution, especially the Bill of Rights. (See American Bill of Rights, Appendix 20, pp450-453.) That these rights are not fully realized is because imperfect people inevitably create imperfect societies. Nevertheless, the formal recognition and inclusion of natural rights in founding and governing documents has been an incredibly important development in the human path towards a truly just and equitable society. Articulating shared aspirations is a critical first step in achieving them: We cannot hope to reach a goal that is not clearly understood and articulated.

Radical Environmentalism

Just as the Left has co-opted authentic, Godly concern for justice and human rights to advance its radical agendas, it has also co-opted the God-given human concern for nature to further its radical environmentalist agenda to destroy capitalism and vastly increase the power of government. Any sensible person will agree that we should be good stewards of nature, and that we need clean water and air, as well as wise policies for agriculture and economic development if we are to preserve the environment we need to sustain life. And any sensible person will acknowledge that there have been many human activities that have been extremely harmful to nature, such as deforestation, dumping chemicals into rivers, lakes and seas, and polluting the air with industrial and vehicle emissions.

But most of these abuses have long since been addressed, at least in developed economies. London is no longer a grimy, soot-covered city spewing toxic fumes into the air and lethal chemicals into the River Thames. Just ask the fish. Realizing this, the Left has transformed environmentalism from a virtuous movement of concern for the environment into a political movement serving a revolutionary agenda. The main focus of this new incarnation of environmentalism has been global warming or, more flexibly, climate change.

Led by people with questionable-to-no scientific backgrounds, such as former Vice President Al Gore, climate doomsayers give us just ten or twelve years before the environmental damage caused by humans is irreversible. Their solution? Governments must spend astronomical amounts to reduce carbon emissions and cool the planet. They insist this will work, although to date there is no evidence that government intervention makes any difference at all. When the decade passes and we find our world little changed, they make new prophecies that are even more terrifying than the previous round. In the meantime, scientists who doubt the "scientific consensus" around global warming are dismissed as "climate deniers," a sub-breed of Neanderthals, and have their research grants cancelled.

As with so many Leftist nostrums, a simple examination of facts throws their environmental theory into doubt. Among many reasons to question their so-called climate science is this: Scientists believe that there have been only four periods in the life of our planet during which ice-covered parts or all of the Earth (Ice Ages). During the rest of its existence, the Earth has been free of ice. How then can human activity be the primary cause, if a cause at all, for the disappearance of ice caps? And, by the way, why is the absence of ice on Earth considered such a grave threat to human existence? A much warmer and wetter climate would still be highly livable. Just ask the dinosaurs.

To illustrate what the above science tells us, as recently as 18,000 years ago, during the last Ice Age, the Wisconsin Ice Sheet was as much as two miles in depth over parts of North America. New York City was covered with a layer of ice estimated at over 2,000 feet thick, deep enough to bury the Freedom Tower today.[101] Where did all that ice go since there were no SUVs pumping out global warming emissions? And why would we impoverish our planet now through confiscatory taxes to fund the trillions of dollars in global warming mitigation that the Left wants us to spend? Only a love for big, all-controlling government can explain this Leftist obsession.

Climate change activism is a deceitful appropriation of a genuine concern for the world by conscientious people—and especially young people—who naturally care for the environment. Its purpose is not to fulfill a role of true stewardship but rather to justify deconstruction of society and imposition of totalitarian rule.

Chapter 16

Marxism Metastasizes III

Social Justice Theory Infects Every Aspect of Life

What is Social Justice?

In Critical Theory, social injustice is structural. In other words, it is built into the institutions of society to unfairly award privilege and power to certain classes or groups. Social justice, then, means identifying these structural inequities—these illegitimate centers of power—as the root of injustice and destroying them. More specifically, this concept of justice requires that people be sorted into victim classes and groups so that the oppressors can be identified and opposed.

In the absence of an absolute standard, a relative morality of this nature quickly becomes subjective. In the Social Justice world, morality has come to mean caring for the plight of those who are identified as part of approved victim groups. This is in contrast to the approach taken by the American Declaration of Independence and the Bill of Rights, which establish universal rights that should be available for all individuals and all groups. Not every grievance is justified by a human right, and not every desire of every person can be justly fulfilled, especially if that fulfillment means loss of rights for others. The pursuit of happiness is a very broad expression of human rights consistent with our original purpose.

Thus the rule of law should protect our freedom and our right to pursue happiness within a fair system, but it cannot guarantee outcomes. Trying to make the law guarantee equity of outcomes can only create further injustices because no person, organization or government can ever determine true equality of outcomes, let alone guarantee it. This is what Communism promises to do—and fails to deliver—at huge cost to the people forced to participate in its macabre experiments. (Central planning has sometimes been helpful, especially in times of crisis and war, but it is not a sustainable system of government over significant periods of time.) And since Postmodernism does not recognize universal absolutes, its Social Justice warriors only have subjective standards to go on—standards that are forever changing and can never be the basis for a durable system of justice.

For example, are we to believe that the 2020 death of African-American George Floyd at the hands of the police in Minnesota justified months of rioting, looting and attacking innocents, resulting in at least fifteen deaths, over $2 billion in damage and the destruction of hundreds of minority-owned businesses?[102] The only reasonable conclusion is that the rioters were not interested in justice for anyone—least of all for the members of minority communities who were the main victims of their predations and who suffered the greatest losses. The rioters were simply carrying out their revolutionary program, for which Floyd's death while in police custody provided a convenient pretext.

Following are some of the main Critical Theories that support the Left's Social Justice agenda and are being taught in schools and universities and translated into government policies.

Intersectionality and Identity Politics

Looking at people as the victims of social forces has inevitably led to the concept that any given individual is the product of a number of such forces. This analysis of victimhood goes far beyond Marx's underprivileged class of proletarians and Mao's underprivileged peasants. It includes categories for race, ethnicity, religion, and gender. From the point of minorities, or victims of injustice, this "intersection" of victimhood has become a study in its own right.

According to this theory, a woman who is black has at least two strikes against her in a white, male-dominated society. If she is lesbian, she has a third. This can, necessarily, get complicated. How do you weigh the importance of one social deficit over another? How do you measure the cumulative effect of several deficits? How do you assess the just compensation for these deficits? And, perhaps most critical, who is to pay this compensation?

As with all Critical Theories, the real object of intersectionality is not to establish a logical or rational basis for determining objective social justice and appropriate remedies. It is instead a means for multiplying victimhood as a basis for seeking retribution and restitution for grievances. On its face, that is an impossible task, better left for God. Society should limit itself to punishing crimes—such as murder, rape and theft—that clearly violate laws that have been enacted by democratically elected legislators.

The practical use of intersectionality is to divide people into victim groups and then build political power around agendas that purport to represent those groups' interests. This is called "identity politics," and it is a critical tool in the Democratic Party of today. Its actual effect is not to ameliorate the challenges faced by minorities and other groups that actually suffer the consequences of being less fortunate than most, but to get people and politicians to think of society and constituencies in sexual, racial and ethnic categories. In other words, its real effect is to awaken the very prejudices that it claims to be driving from the minds and hearts of the people and nation. Sadly, many minority religious and political leaders have embraced this false theory instead of standing up to it and promoting an authentic explanation for injustices.

Postcolonial Theory

The Postmodernist method first gained a following through its postcolonialism theories. It was not difficult to pin the injustices and suffering of the people of colonies, or former colonies, on the colonists, who were primarily whites from Christian European countries. Few would disagree that colonialism was rife with prejudices born of the assumed superiority of white Europeans over darker inhabitants of Africa, South America and Asia. Thus anti-colonialism is widely accepted on the basis that all people have a right to self-determination and equal treatment. Postcolonialism theory points to the failure of the colonial powers to recognize the injustices of their unjust policies and rectify these shortcomings by taking responsibility for the well-being and development of the former colonies.

But the history of colonialism and postcolonialism is not that simple. For one, Marxism played a major role in the anti-colonial movements that rose after World War II. The Soviet Union and its allies and surrogates presented themselves as the great champions of the victims of colonialism, nurturing and encouraging nascent Socialist and Communist parties and revolutionary movements throughout the developing world. They offered themselves to newly independent countries as a desirable alternative to the colonial, or former colonial powers, with great success. Almost half of all African independence movements took the path of aligning with Moscow; many established Socialist dictatorships of one stripe or another, as Marxism-Leninism, pan-Africanism and tribalism worked out uneasy compromises. (See Appendix 21, p454, for a map of African countries that tried Socialism post-independence.)

The Postmodernist analysis of the racist component of colonialism tends to blur some of its features that, in the long run, changed the dynamic between colonists and colonies in a positive way. One of these was the sincere desire of Christians to benefit the less fortunate of the world. Missionaries not only taught the gospels but also built and operated hospitals and schools, sometimes at the risk of their lives, and generally played a constructive role in the development of the colonies. In the postcolonial era, it was often the churches that shouldered the responsibility for continuing or increasing their aid to poor countries.

Also, the colonial governments were not all equal. The worst simply enslaved the native people for use on their plantations and exploiting mineral resources for their own economies. Better governments, however, built hospitals and schools, introduced transportation and communications infrastructure, provided modern technology and established efficient government administration.

Indeed, the worst postcolonial outcomes were those produced by violent revolutions and the institution of Communist or Socialist governments. Take, for example, countries like Benin, Guinea Bissau, Angola and Equatorial Guinea, all of which turned to the Communist bloc for assistance once they gained independence. Their attempts at building Socialist states all ended in disaster. The best postcolonial transitions were produced by peaceful transfers of power followed by continued cooperation between former colonial powers and their former colonies. A good example of postcolonial amity in general is the British Commonwealth—to this day, former colonies are partners with Britain in an organization that promotes mutual development among all its members.

Slavery was endemic in the earliest human societies and persisted over the millennia. Colonialism often encouraged slavery, especially as European nations sought labor for their colonial plantations. But it was eventually the Christian conscience of Europeans (and later Americans) that ended the practice in the West and ultimately worldwide. In 1807, the British outlawed the slave trade and used its navy to enforce it. In 1833, Britain abolished slavery altogether, a decision followed decades later in America with President Abraham Lincoln's Emancipation Proclamation of 1863.

Critical Race Theory, Anti-Racism, and White Privilege, Fragility and Supremacy

Perhaps the most damaging of all Critical Theories are those related to race. Racism has become a useful issue to divide society and is the favorite label the Left attaches to its targets. After all, to be labeled a racist is to be smeared with the worst possible character. If you accept the Critical Theory assumption that racism is structural—a prejudice built into society and reinforced by a long history of white oppression—you naturally look for culprits to identify, isolate and attack. It is no surprise, then, that Critical Race Theory goes so far as to castigate all whites simply for being white: If you are a white person, you must be a racist, and the onus is on you to prove that you are not. Ironically, this is the definition of racism: judging people by the color of their skin instead of by the content of their character, as Martin Luther King put it so well.

The racist lens through which these anti-racism theories look at the world identifies privileged white people ("White Privilege") as the scourge of the earth and the source of the world's worst problems, from colonialism and capitalism to the unjust wielding of political and economic power. The latest theory in this genre is "White Fragility," explained in a popular 2018 book of that title by Robin DiAngelo. As with its predecessors, a key assumption of this theory is that racism is systemic in America—at least among whites, who are unable to talk about it frankly because of their complicity in it.

The Left is quick to point to violence perpetrated by whites against non-whites as proof of systemic white racism and a belief in white supremacy. In other words, the racism that is so embedded in white people because they are white is bound to manifest in violence against non-whites. According to this theory, racial differences themselves—not acquired bigoted attitudes—are the cause of racist attitudes and behavior. The only logical conclusion to draw from this theory is that racism is systemic among whites—it is inevitable and cannot be eradicated. However, if this is the nature of white racism, why would it be any different for races of other colors? And isn't it the epitome of racism to associate specific negative characteristics with specific colors?

In fact, anti-racist theories are patently false and dangerously racist ideas themselves because they conflate skin color with character. There are a few white supremacists, but their influence in the wider American society is insignificant. Their racism is no worse than those of other purveyors of racist theories. All are harmful and should be rejected.

Of course, races do exhibit differences. This is part of the great and wonderful diversity of the human family in which there are not even two people who are fully identical. There is nothing wrong with group affinity, whether based on skin color, religion, nationality or other factors. It is a natural characteristic of the creation that can serve to build a sense of identity, belonging and community. Racism is the corrosive inverse of positive group affinity; it exploits natural differences in the cause of conflict and destruction. In this, it fits perfectly into the dialectical and Critical Theory views of societal contradictions and divisions, lending itself to radical Leftist prescriptions. And although Marx himself had little to say about racism—he was obsessed with class differences—sadly, it has now become a primary weapon in the arsenal of the Left, which uses the racist label to dehumanize and attack those it opposes.

It is important to acknowledge that racism has caused great harm to many, especially as a justification for slavery. However, in the past two centuries, great strides have been taken to rectify the systemic, structural aspects of slavery and the prejudices that justified it. In the American Civil War, hundreds of thousands of white men gave their lives to see that America put an end to slavery once and for all.[103] Before buying into the all-too-easy anti-racist accusation of whites, it would be wise to remember the sacrifice of the young men who left home and family to risk their lives at Antietam, Gettysburg, Vicksburg and Cold Harbor so that America could remain one nation under God, free from slavery. Their sacrifices deserve to be honored, not ignored and buried in the bloody fields of battle, wretched prisons and ill-equipped hospitals where they gave their all.

Today, anti-racism theory, including Critical Race Theory, White Privilege and White Fragility, has itself become a racist doctrine that is being spread far and wide by academia, media and government. It is an insidious and destructive theory that provides an ideological construct that justifies attacking whites for being white and advocates for radical measures by institutions and governments to address what it sees as systemic racism. Meanwhile, "diversity" directors at companies and organizations encourage policies designed to punish whites for being white and to elevate "minorities of color" to achieve equity. They have left behind the ideal of equality of opportunity and embraced equity of outcomes. This does not solve racism; it merely reverses the categories of racists and its victims. Racism cannot solve the problem of racism.

What racism remains in the hearts and minds of Americans, and people everywhere, is the consequence of the unfinished journey towards the destiny that belongs to all humanity. But the Abel solution to human inadequacy and imperfection is not to kill or oppress, but to educate, enlighten and uplift. Racial, ethnic, religious and other differences will always be part of the mosaic of humanity. The conflicts that exploit these differences will only be eliminated when society is composed of mature individuals who fully embrace the beauty and goodness of creation's diversity.

Wokeness, Political Correctness and Cancel Culture

The Left believes it is uniquely aware of the injustices of this world. Using Critical Theory, it believes it has discovered a wide range of social inequities, which it claims to be addressing. Accordingly, people on the Left think they alone are awake to the problems of capitalism, racism, sexism, etc. Their "wokeness" enables them to see clearly both the problems and the solutions— insights they insist you agree with.

In their state of wokeness, only they have the proper language to define problems and rectify them. Thus they ride the waves of Critical Theory through academia, media and government, dictating correct interpretations and suitable terminology for the revolutionary categories they have established. Their "thought police" in social media and mass media jump on any use of language that violates their politically correct lexicon. And any comments, articles, programs or books that stray from their intellectual compound are attacked as dangerous and in need of cancellation. They go further, heckling speakers they disagree with, attacking "enemies" on social media and harassing them in public places and at their homes.

The irony of their fascistic attitudes and actions seems to be lost on them, since they claim to be anti-fascists. As all Marxists before them, their rigid conformity to Leftist ideology casts an ever-expanding and ever-darkening cloud over the world of ideas, including genuine scientific theories. Their attacks on those with whom they disagree cause perfectly innocent people to be fired, de-platformed or worse. In 2020, the Cancel Culture warriors reached a peak of aggressive behavior when social and news media censored unwanted articles about Joe Biden's son, ignored or suppressed unwelcome information about voter fraud, castigated anyone who suggested that the COVID-19 virus originated in a Wuhan lab, and vilified authors and pundits for providing any information or opinions counter to the Left's narrative.

The Left need only look to China to see itself in the mirror. In 2020, the Chinese Communist Party tightened surveillance of its people and continued the ruthless genocide of its Uyghur minority, forcing them to abandon their Muslim faith, imposing the state's Communist ideology, and forcibly sterilizing many to prevent the expansion of their community. (See Endnotes 72 and 73) At the same time, it continued its brutal persecution of the Falun Gong and other religious groups; it suppressed free speech and democracy in Hong Kong; and it ratcheted up its pressure on Taiwan by blocking its access to COVID-19 vaccines while increasing its military intimidation of the island state. Oh yes, and it has denied any responsibility for the COVID-19 virus that spread around the world, killing millions, instead claiming the virus originated in the United States.

The woke agenda of political correctness and Cancel Culture is designed to achieve results similar to what we see in China. The Democratic Party has embraced most of the Left's ideas and is seeking to translate them into government policy. If this continues, and the influence of the Left in government is unchecked, who's to say that it will be any different from the government of Communist China?

Language as Violence, Hate Speech and Hate Crimes

One of the most pernicious theories of the Left is that language itself can be violent, as demonstrated in their efforts to impose politically correct terminology and to prevent anyone they disagree with from speaking. This unhealthy view of language is derived from Postmodernist concepts about the role of language in shaping society—including that some structures need deconstructing to remove inequities and injustices. A handy label for unwanted speech is "hate speech." As with racism, if you attach this label to what someone says, you condemn them as a bad person and justify censoring them or seeking their prosecution for hate crimes.

The notion that language can be violent and therefore must be censored is inimical to traditional liberalism, which welcomes the free flow of ideas as essential to learning and science. Because the importance of freedom of speech is almost universally recognized and accepted, it is protected in most constitutions, even those of regimes that in fact suppress free speech. Thus, for the Left and for totalitarian regimes, the way to get around constitutional guarantees of free speech is to criminalize unwanted speech by classifying it as speech that is outside the protections of the law. For the Leftist movements, this "unprotected speech" is likely labeled hate speech (or insurrectionist speech). In totalitarian regimes, unprotected speech is labeled reactionary, subversive, anti-revolutionary or treasonous speech; these are all punishable by the regimes.

Somewhat strangely in America (and many other countries as well), the censorship of language on behalf of the Left these days is often initiated by private sector companies that apparently see themselves as morally superior and wiser than the general public. Thus major news companies (Associated Press, Reuters, ABC, NBC, CBS, CNN, MSNBC, *The New York Times*, *The Washington Post* and others) and social media companies (Facebook, Twitter and Google in particular), who enjoy an almost monopolistic control of news and information flows, are now voluntarily doing what used to be the exclusive work of government censors in authoritarian and totalitarian states. These big companies don't yet have the means or authority to round up and punish the perpetrators of unwanted speech, as censors do in totalitarian states, but with their extensive data on individuals and organizations and through their close relations with the Democratic Party and many in government, that limitation may soon be gone.

The Fusion of Marxism and Critical Theory

Some of the most active groups who claim to be fighting racism, sexism, homophobia, fascism, capitalism and other forms of structural injustice believe that violence on behalf of their cause is justified. For a Marxist, this is natural: Violence is a core part of the prescription for revolutionary change. And, as with many Marxist movements of the past, the names these modern activist groups choose, both for their organizations and for their agendas, are typically innocuous and above reproach.

Black Lives Matter, which fuses traditional Marxism with Postmodernist Critical Theories, is such an organization. Using a name that no one can disagree with, it has managed to win the support of many Americans as well as the bulk of mass media and social media, many major corporations and droves of educators and government officials—even though its leaders are self-declared

Marxists. Young people in particular are attracted by BLM, seeing the organization as championing ideals that they identify with. However, in 2020, BLM was behind many attacks on police and innocent individuals, as well as the burning and looting of small businesses, all carried out in the name of outrage over the death of a black man, George Floyd, as discussed above.

The Left has always been violent, believing that change cannot be achieved without it. In the 1960s, the Leftist group Students for a Democratic Society (SDS) was active in organizing demonstrations and protests. When these did not deliver hoped-for results, a radical offshoot, the Weather Underground, began a campaign of violence, setting off bombs at strategic locations. Several people were killed.

One of the chief activists of SDS and the Weather Underground was Eric Mann, who spent time in prison for his violent behavior. He would transition to the radical Labor/Community Strategy Center. A protégé of his in that organization was Patrisse Cullors, one of three co-founders of BLM. In 2015, Cullors told the Real News Network: "The first thing, I think, is that we actually do have an ideological frame. Myself and Alicia in particular are trained organizers," she said. "We are trained Marxists. We are super-versed on, sort of, ideological theories." Alicia Garza is the second co-founder of BLM. (See Appendix 22, pp455-458, for these references and for the other information on BLM presented here.) Given BLM's tactics and behavior, should we be surprised by this revelation?

Both Cullors and Garza are not only self-identified Marxists but also self-identified queers, and BLM's 13 Principles include a number of Critical Theory ideas that would never have been included in *The Communist Manifesto*, reflecting the influence of Critical Theories on the Left today. Here are two of the 13 Principles:

Queer Affirming: We are committed to fostering a queer affirming network. When we gather, we do so with the intention of freeing ourselves from the tight grip of heteronormative thinking or, rather, the belief that all in the world are heterosexual unless s/he or they disclose otherwise.

Trans Affirming: We are committed to embracing and making space for trans brothers and sisters to participate and lead. We are committed to being self-reflexive and doing the work required to dismantle cis-gender privilege and uplift Black trans folk, especially Black trans women who continue to be disproportionately impacted by trans-antagonistic violence.

BLM has received tens of millions of dollars in donations from supporters and corporations trying to signal their virtue or simply to protect themselves from attack as racists. With this money, BLM has drawn up curricula for schools, grades 1-12, based on its radical 13 Principles. Graduates of this type of Leftist education—plus Critical Theory education in universities— are filled with disdain for their society and country, believing, for example, that America is systematically racist, sexist and imperialist. They want to tear down the existing order in the belief that a better one will emerge if they are in charge. Violence is their natural recourse. (In what appeared to be a demonstration of hypocrisy, Cullors was in 2021 found to have purchased four residences worth a total of $3.2 million![104] In fact, this type of behavior by leaders on the Left is typical, as evidenced by the lives of relative luxury enjoyed by the Soviet Nomenklatura.)

Antifa is a frequent partner with BLM in street violence. This organiza- tion takes its name from the original German short form of *antifaschistisch* ("anti-fascist") and was the nickname for *Antifaschistische Aktion* (Anti-Fascist Action), an organization set up by the German Communist Party (KPD) in 1932. Its original purpose was to engage in the street warfare between the Nazi Party and the KPD, which intensified at the time of the 1932 national elections that would lead to Hitler ascending to power in 1933. The Nazi "Brownshirts" were known for their violent intimidation tactics, and the KPD, which spurned the ruling Social Democratic Party (SPD) as "social fascists," created Antifa to fight the Nazis using similar violent tactics.

The current incarnation of Antifa has all the unpleasant and dangerous hallmarks of the original. It is anarchistic and employs violence to intimidate and harm those it identifies as its enemies. For months during 2020, we witnessed Antifa in cities like Portland, Seattle and Washington, DC burn buildings, attack police and their vehicles, and loot and burn private businesses of all types. Their violence was responsible for a number of deaths, including a man who was shot by one of their activists. Anyone their mobs considered an "enemy" was liable to be beaten, sometimes severely. The same was true of journalists deemed unfriendly to their cause. Andy Ngo, a journalist who has covered many Antifa demonstrations and riots and written a book exposing their tactics, was severely beaten, suffering brain injuries. No police came to his rescue. He would later tell the *New York Post*:

> I was chased, attacked and beaten by a masked mob, baying for my blood. Had I not been able to shelter wounded and bleeding inside a hotel while they beat the doors and windows like animals, there is no doubt in my mind I would not be here today. It seemed obvious they intended to make good on hundreds of threats over the past two years to kill me. [105]

According to a 2017 article in *The New York Times*, Antifa is "the diverse collection of anarchists, communists and socialists…"[106] Ironically, although anarchists are supposed to be against state power, this group (like most other ostensibly anarchist organizations) is actually led by the leading advocates for authoritarian big government: Socialists and Communists. Ironically too, this supposedly anti-fascist movement exhibits all the hallmarks of Fascist and Communist movements and regimes. They use force to intimidate anyone they disapprove of from being able to speak in public or distribute their publications. They also employ a nasty, fascistic practice of "doxing" anyone they target for intimidation, publishing private addresses and contact information, and sometimes organizing demonstrations at those private locations.

Their behavior is the epitome of the ruthless authoritarianism they claim to be fighting. Hiding behind masks and helmets, they take to the streets armed with clubs, knives, bricks and crowbars and sometimes high-tech weapons like lasers; they use the latter to blind police. They show no regard for the civil rights of people they attack, whether their victims are police protecting the public, seniors eating in a restaurant, small-business owners, or ordinary people going about their daily business. They are eerily like Hitler's Brownshirts—but now armed with the far more dangerous Marxist ideology.

A conservative activist, who was curious to know more about Antifa after some of her friends had been attacked by the group, dressed up in a black outfit and joined a "demonstration" to see how they operated. She found that they were disciped in their "black bloc" tactics, provoking their archenemies, the police, with brazen attacks, pushing them to the point where they had to respond:

> That's why all the "press" is there, the sympathetic press. [Antifa is] trying to create propaganda. They know how the police are going to react, so they carefully calibrate what they do to try to provoke the police into reacting and then filming it. They want to try to push public opinion in favor of removing the police.[107]

As with BLM, Antifa demonstrates a fusion of Marxist and Postmodernist influences. The revolutionary ideology is Marxism, but some of their main objectives are right out of Critical Theories. Prominent among these is their interest in transgenderism. At a recent presentation at Hillsdale College, Andy Ngo shared some of the police reports on Antifa rioters in Portland, Oregon, where Antifa spearheaded over 100 days of riots in 2020.[108] He found evidence of an outsized role of transgender people in the organization, much as the leadership of BLM self-identifies as queer.

False Divisions and True Diversity

All of the above Neo-Marxism theories and movements are based on identifying parties the Left holds responsible for divisions in society, and then isolating and attacking them. This cynical endeavor is, ironically, frequently carried out in the name of promoting diversity. There is no subtle paradox at play here; the Left's attack on diversity in the name of diversity is simply a symptom of what is fundamentally wrong with Marxism and Critical Theory.

First, the beauty of creation lies in its diversity and the harmony that characterizes its order. Shades of blue make oceans beautiful; shades of green make forests fascinating. Nature exhibits a kaleidoscope of colors and an endless variety of shapes, sizes and behaviors. As the pinnacle of creation, human beings are the most diverse species of all: Each person possesses unique features, characteristics and capabilities. Within this diversity, the more important differences are internal, those of character rather than gender, race or ethnicity. And if we are indeed the product of Divine creation, the most important human nature is the image of the Divine imprinted on the original hearts and minds of all people, endowing them with absolute value.

It is important to distinguish this true diversity from differences between good and evil. As noted in the Introduction, good and evil are fundamentally incompatible and cannot coexist. Good exists as an attribute of the Creator, who is only good, whereas evil is simply the perversion of good. Thus evil is antithetical to good and must be thwarted and defeated. Marxism and its offshoots mistakenly conflate natural diversity with good and evil, and thus look at people as members of groups, good or bad, rather than as individuals. To wit, Marxists and Critical Theorists see people as members of classes, races, sexes, sects and ethnicities. These groups are assumed to be in conflict with one another, as per dialectic or critical theories, and these conflicts that can only be resolved through violent resistance and rebellion by the aggrieved group.

The Left's Grievance Industry

Thus diversity has become an industry of the Left that deals with visible differences of class, race or gender as if these categories were a legitimate basis for separating good from evil (as in all whites are automatically racist). This erroneous concept of good and evil is often used by the Left to punish true diversity, based on natural, God-given differences. Wealthy individuals and corporations pour money into organizations that advocate for diversity on Leftist terms, including LGBTQ rights, racial minority rights, gender rights, and similar causes. Thus a Leftist industry is created that provides jobs for radicals. And because this industry depends on the existence of grievances, it is in its interest to keep these grievances coming. Thus real or manufactured social problems are inflated into major national issues, which justify new demands for money—and so the cycle continues.

Many politicians of the Left see constituencies in terms of race or class and shape their campaigns accordingly. In this world of identity politics the politically ambitious exploit group grievances and differences to gain support and get elected. Once in office, they work to retain the support of constituencies by promoting or supporting legislation that promises to address the groups' grievances. Rarely do these prescriptions bring positive change, and often they make situations worse. But repeating the promises works, which is why this practice is continued by the unscrupulous.

For their part, corporations are fearful of being labeled racist or the like, or of facing discrimination lawsuits from the Left. They hire diversity executives who are responsible for seeing that all aggrieved groups are treated equally or that they are assured equity of outcomes in positions and pay. They also see to it that the corporate social responsibility programs and corporate donations satisfy Leftist social justice criteria, keeping critics at bay. This perversion of fair policies logically leads to people being given jobs and compensation based on their color, sex or other group identity rather than their capabilities. It is discrimination that inevitably penalizes those who meet real criteria for employment by working hard to gain educational qualifications and work experience.

Increasingly, government and private institutions and corporations boast about their diversity programs, proudly announcing how many minority groups are represented in their management and workforce. Apparently blind to the irony, this approach takes them full circle to the bad old days of discrimination when people were looked at based on their group identity rather than being treated as individuals deserving of respect based on their qualifications and merits. Diversity programs reverse decades of law and policy that require government and private organizations and businesses to hire based on merit—not on color, gender, ethnicity or the like.

The fruits of the Civil Rights movement, the Civil Rights Act of 1964, and the many other advances in legislation and other guarantees of equality in the eyes of law, should not be abandoned so easily. The world is a better place if people are treated on the basis of their character and not the externalities of race, sex, ethnicity or religion. As we have shown in this chapter, the prescriptions of Critical Theory lead to conflict and violence. They exploit the goodwill of good people and offer nothing of value in return. Marxism and Neo-Marxism are theories barren of life, liberty and happiness. They offer no food for the spirit and soul. It's high time they were exposed and replaced with positive and productive alternatives.

Chapter 17

Making Fallen Nature the Law

Governments Side with Lucifer and Cain

Evil is Codified in Legislation and Regulations

As our explanation of Marxism and Neo-Marxism reveals, these materialist theories advocate for what we consider to be Satanic beliefs regarding faith, human relationships and the family. They go beyond the fallen nature manifest in Cain to the very root of evil, Lucifer's seduction of Eve and the consequent destruction of the original family. Taken together, these theories are a prescription for hell on earth.

We have already witnessed Marxist ideology being translated into laws in Socialist and Communist countries. But now we are facing a much more subtle subversion of our civilization through Neo-Marxism, and especially Postmodernist Critical Theories, being used as the basis for laws and regulations in governments and institutions. Every conscientious person should be deeply concerned by this development and should do whatever they can to put an end to it.

Examples of this trend are proliferating worldwide, always under the pretext of protecting minority rights or human rights in general. What is actually happening is that traditional values of faith and family are being demonized and condemned while the nostrums of the Left are being made into law and regulations.

For example, United States government agencies, including the military and public educational institutions, are mandating education in Critical Race Theory for all employees, rank and file members or students. In Canada, Bill C-16 was passed in 2017 to amend the Canadian Human Rights Act and Criminal Code to enforce the use of preferred pronouns for transgender people. This means Canadians can be legally punished for not complying with the language of the Left.[109] Similar legislation has been passed on state or municipal levels in the US, Canada and elsewhere, including a law in New York City that imposes fines of up to $250,000 for "mis-gendering" people (referring to people by any other than their preferred pronouns).[110]

Mandating Evil Worldwide

Leftist activists are rarely satisfied with domestic policy changes and laws in their favor. They want the whole world to be forced to follow their dictates. Thus Leftists policies are often translated into foreign policy guidelines by Left-leaning governments, regardless of the wishes of other countries—including those directly affected by such policies and those that are in desperate need of assistance. Thus in December 2011, President Barack Obama instructed US officials to link foreign aid to compliance with US laws on LGBTQ rights.As quoted by *The Guardian* in its article on this, Texas Governor Rick Perry rightly noted that this "was just the most recent example of an administration at war with people of faith in this country… President Obama has again mistaken America's tolerance for different lifestyles with an endorsement of those lifestyles."[111]

In a more recent example, the European Commission, the EU's top administrative body, on July 15, 2021 threatened member states Hungary and Poland with legal action because of laws they had passed to protect families from harmful Postmodernist theories being promoted by LGBTQ activists. (See Appendix 23, pp459-463.)

These are just a few examples of a terrible trend. When governments and institutions promote evil ideologies through policies, laws and regulations, they cease to enjoy the right to represent the people. They must be restored to virtue or replaced.

Chapter 18

America's Providential Mission

*Divine Providence and the
Rise of a Worldwide Abel*

> For the support of this Declaration, with a firm reliance on the Protection of
> Divine Providence, we mutually pledge to each other our Lives, our Fortunes
> and our sacred Honor.
>
> US Declaration of Independence (Appendix 24, p468.)

God's Providence Spans the Atlantic

These stirring words from the Declaration of Independence capture a central belief among America's Founders. They saw their departure from Europe and establishment of a government that secured their God-given rights as part of a larger Divine providence—the plan of their Creator to establish a heavenly state on earth in which every person could practice his or her religion freely. This vision inspired Americans to be their best and do their best, and establish institutions that were designed to avoid the injustices and problems of the societies they had left behind. As we have seen in the history of the Christian era, this vision continued the trend towards an ever-finer expression of Christ's teaching, free from the corruption of Christian institutions that persecuted heretics, turned on rival churches, engaged in the Crusades, failed to end slavery and resisted reformation movements.

Thus the Pilgrims were an Abel-type movement within Christianity. They rejected both the deeply political Catholic Church and Papacy as well as the Church of England, the state religion headed by the English monarch. In 1609, they left England for Holland, the only European country offering freedom of worship at the time. Not wanting their children to be raised speaking Dutch, they turned their eyes to "those vast and unpeopled countries of America," as William Bradford wrote in his *Of Plymouth Plantation*.[112] By moving to America they would be totally free to believe and worship as they wished, and to contribute to the establishment of a godly society on earth:

> ...they cherished a great hope and inward zeal of laying good foundations, or at least of making some way towards it, for the propagation and advance of the gospel of the kingdom of Christ in the remote parts of the world, even though they should be but stepping stones to others in the performance of so great a work.[113]

Arriving in what is now Plymouth, Massachusetts, in 1620, the 102 Pilgrims set about building a Christian community. The English investors who had funded the venture had insisted on communal ownership of all property, treating the colony as a single corporation to facilitate profit-sharing. And although the English investors' system seemed similar to the early communitarian idealism of the earliest followers of Jesus (as described in Acts of the Apostles, they held all property in common), it required a voluntary pooling of property. This was something the Pilgrims did not agree with, as they rightly recognized that it compromised their personal freedom to live and worship as they wanted.

Bradford, the second leader of the colony, described how the initial communal approach failed. The Pilgrims felt themselves part of an unjust, slave-like system that fostered an unwillingness to work and general confusion. He pointed to the problem—seen later with Communism—which was the lack of correlation between effort and rewards: If people shared equally in the fruits of communal work, regardless of what they had contributed to their production, they worked less. In Bradford's words:

> "For the young men who were most able and fit for service objected to being
> forced to spend their time and strength in working for other men's wives and
> children, without any recompense."[114]

This unfair system pushed the new colony toward extinction. But under Bradford's leadership, a decision was made in 1623 to assign "every family a parcel of land, according to the proportion of their number."[115] As each family took responsibility for its own welfare while continuing to support the community as a whole, there was a dramatic improvement in overall outcomes: "This was very successful. It made all hands very industrious, so that much more corn was planted than otherwise would have been…"[116] Thus the seeds of American capitalism were sown more than 150 years before Adam Smith in published his groundbreaking work on capitalism, *The Wealth of Nations*, in 1776.

The combination of individual liberty and private ownership would prove a powerful driving force behind the rapid growth and ultimate ascendancy of America.

The Pilgrims in Massachusetts would be followed by other religious exiles from Europe who settled along America's Atlantic coast, as well as immigrants motivated by commercial interests, the desire to own property or simply to escape poverty. Some colonies had charters that encouraged settlement by particular church denominations or were havens for members of those churches. Maryland was established in 1632 under a charter from Catholic King Charles I and was a preferred destination for Catholics. Pennsylvania was established by William Penn who received a charter to create a Quaker settlement from King Charles II in 1681.

The Great Awakening

As with the creation of European empires abroad, America's expansionist impulse combined internal, religious aspirations and sense of mission with external, capitalist ambitions. For European nations, especially Britain, Holland, Spain and Portugal, missionizing the world was a sacred duty, while mercantilism provided an economic incentive to establish outposts in far-flung lands. As demonstrated in the founding of America, religious motivation sustained the courage to venture into uncharted territories, but economic interests often came to dominate the relationship between colonial power and colony.

Within America itself, the rapid expansion west into the interior (and eventually all the way to California, Alaska and Hawaii) was increasingly driven by material interests: the desire for land to farm and natural resources to exploit. From the 1607 founding of the settlement in Jamestown, this commercial drive had overshadowed the religious mission in Virginia and other southern colonies, and it would fuel land rushes west of the Mississippi and gold rushes in Nevada, Colorado, Oregon, California and elsewhere.

A hundred years after the landing at Plymouth Rock, America was ripe for religious renewal. This came in the form of the Great Awakening, a movement of fervent Christian renewal in both Britain and America. Powerful preachers like Jonathan Edwards (1703-1758) and George Whitfield (1714-1770) called Christians to return to a pure faith, to repent of their sins and seek forgiveness and renewal.

This movement marked an important response to the Enlightenment, with its emphasis on science and the material world. It brought acknowledgment of a higher purpose back to the center of American society and culture, underscoring the importance of Christians establishing a personal relationship with God and taking responsibility for their behavior. And it served as an important refocusing of the Pilgrim effort to break away from established churches with their ecclesiastical hierarchies and political entanglements. Religious freedom and responsibility became matters of personal conscience rather than denominational allegiance. The result was the rapid growth of new Protestant churches, like the Baptists and Methodists, and ultimately a society in which every person could choose his or her own path to God.

The Great Awakening was an important movement of internal enlightenment and religious resurgence that helped prepare America for the next stage in its separation from the Old World: independence from Britain. This rejection of European rule was yet another step in the long process of enlightened movements breaking away from ossified and often corrupt institutions. It was a western movement that saw Rome separate from the Orthodox churches, the Protestants separate from Rome, and the Pilgrims leave England for America.

The American Revolution

England's Glorious Revolution, with its Bill of Rights, had a profound effect on the American colonies. It represented the convergence of Renaissance and Reformation, or the rise of science *and* renewal of religion. Especially after the Great Awakening, America had become a more religious country than Britain, and religious fervor mixed with a strong belief in liberty and independence would lead to the American Revolution against Britain.

Many Americans objected to laws imposed on the colonies by King George III, who, despite being restrained by the Bill of Rights that granted significant powers to Parliament (See Appendix 9, pp363-371.), still wielded significant powers as the British monarch. The Americans came to see monarchies themselves as unjust. They wanted their Creator—not a monarch—to be recognized as the ultimate arbiter of justice. This sentiment was expressed by some of the colonial revolutionaries as "No king but Jesus." As Thomas Paine wrote in his hugely popular pamphlet, *Common Sense,* published early in 1776:

> But where, say some, is the King of America? I'll tell you, friend, he reigns above, and doth not make havoc of mankind like the Royal Brute of Great Britain.[117]

As Abraham Lincoln would put it in his 1863 Gettysburg Address, Americans wanted "government of the people, by the people, for the people."[118] Inspired by British writers like John Locke and Edmund Burke, and French philosopher Montesquieu, as well as by examples of democracy from as early as Classical Greece, the Founding Fathers declared independence from British rule on July 4, 1776.

In the Declaration of Independence, Thomas Jefferson wrote: "We hold these truths to be self-evident, that all men are created equal, that they are endowed by their Creator with certain inalienable rights, that among these are life, liberty and the pursuit of happiness. That to secure these rights, Governments are instituted among men, deriving their just powers from the consent of the governed." (See the Declaration of Independence, Appendix 24, p464.)

The formal recognition of our Creator as the source of natural rights was truly revolutionary, and probably the most important statement on human rights in history. It gave the American Revolution a uniquely spiritual and providential character, and it led to the creation of a Constitution that enshrined God-given natural rights as the basis for individual liberty within a system governed by the rule of law, not the rule of men.

The combination of individual liberty founded on religious principles with the economic liberty of the capitalist system became the engine of American success and growth. It precipitated the American Revolution and saw America rise rapidly in the world after independence. By the 20th century, America would eclipse its old colonial master Britain as the wealthiest and most powerful nation on earth. The American republic would become the model for democracies everywhere, and the freedom and prosperity enjoyed by Americans would be sought after by people fleeing poor or oppressive governments around the world.

However, as with any human venture, America was flawed and would be forced to face internal weaknesses and injustices. One of its most important challenges came through the institution of slavery, an evil practice that had been imported with some of the settlers. In the 1861-1865 Civil War, America paid dearly to rid itself of slavery and to set an example for the world.

Some 750,000 Americans, from both sides, were killed in the fighting or died of related diseases—more than in any other war that involved America, before or after.

Britain abolished slavery in 1833, and in 1865, with the adoption of the 13th Amendment to the US Constitution, America finally caught up with this unequivocal language: "Neither slavery nor involuntary servitude, except as a punishment for crime whereof the party shall have been duly convicted, shall exist within the United States, or any place subject to their jurisdiction."[119] Other injustices had to be dealt with, from lingering racial prejudice to the unequal treatment of women under the law, but the system has—until now—proven robust and able to adapt without losing its principled base.

Today's Challenge

America's ability to overcome internal challenges while pursuing a constructive leadership role in the world has now come under an unprecedented threat. The year 2020 marked the 400th anniversary of the Plymouth landing. Four hundred years is a time period that has frequently been significant in providential history, from the 400-year period of Jewish slavery in Egypt to the 400 years of Judges that preceded the establishment of a unified Kingdom of Israel, and the four centuries between Luther posting his 95 Theses in 1517 and the Russian Revolution in 1917.

America is a blessed land, but its blessings should not be taken for granted. The blessings flow as a result of faith and righteous action. The Pilgrims left the security of their homes in Europe to come to America in pursuit of freedom to practice their faith as they chose and to shape their own destiny. The nobility of this intention is at the heart of the American spirit, which has guided the country through independence and civil war, rapid expansion and incredible growth in population and wealth. It aroused America to fight sacrificially on the side of the Allied Powers in World War I and against Nazi Fascism and Japanese Imperialism in World War II. It kept America resolutely opposed to Communism during the Cold War—a resolve that led to the collapse of the Soviet empire.

Unlike Nazi Germany and the Soviet Union, America engaged in wars abroad not to build an empire but to protect the victims of aggression. Young men, often still in their adolescence, volunteered to go to distant lands to fight against truly evil empires and terrorist organizations, shedding their blood so that total strangers could be saved from death and destruction. This rare quality of selfless sacrifice represents the best of America and is one reason it is so blessed.

This does not mean that America is destined to be the world's policeman, defending the democracy it has long exported. But it does mean that America's great wealth and power continue to be of global significance: It is an endowment that is not for America's benefit alone. And, since the overarching challenge facing the world today is the internal threat of civilizational decline brought about by the spread of Marxist and Neo-Marxist ideology—plus the external threat of an ever-more powerful, wealthy and aggressive Communist China—America undoubtedly continues to have a leading mission to expose, oppose and finally defeat global Marxism and Communism.

Since the collapse of the Soviet Union and its Communist empire in the late 1980s and early 1990s, America's providential mission has become blurred. With the fall of the Berlin Wall and the liberation of one Communist country after another, it seemed that the world had finally had enough of Marxism and its oppressive and aggressive regimes that couldn't even feed their own people. As the Soviet threat seemed to melt away, Americans were lulled into a complacency so widespread that they did not see the stealthy march of Leftist ideology through Western institutions. As we have shown, this complacency has brought America and much of the world to a very dangerous moment: Since the Left has successfully corrupted society and much of the political establishment and undermined its traditional values, the will to confront the Communist China juggernaut has become severely weakened.

Regaining America's Sense of Providential Purpose

As underscored by international events, America still is the one country in the world with the resources needed to confront and defeat forces of evil. From the war against Al Qaeda and the Taliban in Afghanistan, to the ongoing containment of the radical Islamic regime in Iran and the wider war against terror, the United States is the only country that can effectively project its power anywhere in the world. However, its containment of Communist China is haphazard at best, and America is constantly being tested by the aggressive regime in Beijing. Moreover, just as voices in Europe once urged England to capitulate to Hitler, voices in American media, business and government constantly advocate for passivity and appeasement in the face of Chinese aggression.

The first challenge for America, then, is to address its compromised institutions. Communist China is no friend, let alone ally, of America. It is a global rival as dangerous as any we have faced in the past, including Nazi Germany and the Soviet Union. Would any American company have considered investing in Nazi Germany to reach the German and European markets during World War II? Would any American company have considered investing in Stalin's Soviet Union at the height of the Cold War? The answer is yes, a few, but they were deservedly outliers; some self-interested businesspeople will do anything to enrich themselves, including betraying their country.

On many American university campuses, French theorist and sexual libertine Michel Foucault is now considered to be the single most important social scientist in history. His Postmodernist deconstruction of traditional societal institutions is embraced as the most brilliant analysis of, and prescription for, what ails our imperfect world. The sexual revolution started by Foucault, Wilhelm Reich, Herbert Marcuse and others of the Frankfurt School—based on merging Marxism and Freudianism—has been broadened through Postmodernism. Today, gender theories not only challenge traditional beliefs about marriage and family, they reject the biological basis for human sexuality and social organization. Meanwhile, the Internet has facilitated the pernicious spread of pornography, accelerating the destruction of morality and replacing it with total sexual chaos.

The Leftist influence in academia is no longer a fringe phenomenon, and the Left itself is no longer a fringe movement in America. It is now mainstream, dominating Hollywood, mass media, tech giants, sports, corporate boards trying to be "woke," Federal and state bureaucracies, and the Democratic Party. These forces are arrayed against a weakened conservative movement that is fighting a rear-guard action to preserve traditional American values.

The Judeo-Christian foundations of America are indeed under deadly assault. In truth, we have to recognize that the level of understanding and practice of faith in American society has failed to stem the tide of Marxist and Neo-Marxist ideologies. Christianity predates Marx, and the teachings of Jesus therefore provide Christians with no specific theoretical basis for countering Marxism and other derivative ideologies. (In fact, in the name of "social justice," many sincere Christians have unwisely allied themselves with Marxist and Neo-Marxist ideas and movements.)

The implication of this obvious truth is that we cannot solve the problem of Marxism by reverting to earlier incarnations of our Christian faith, since they were unable to prevent the rise of Marxism in the first place. Nevertheless, as believers we bear the responsibility to build on the Judeo-Christian values that underpin our society and create an effective counter to the ideologies of the Left. To succeed in this endeavor, it is vitally important for Americans to regain their sense of providential purpose and an understanding of what that purpose means for today and for the future.

Confronting the Chinese Bully

On the world level, China is like a playground bully who intimidates everyone into submission. America is the only country with the capacity to confront the bully and protect the vulnerable of the world. This means standing up to China's economic coercion of smaller countries through its Belt and Road initiative, which is later coupled with growing military intimidation. As we learned during the Cold War, the policies of appeasement and détente only fueled the aggression of the Soviet Union and prolonged the suffering of its oppressed people. This mistake must not be repeated with Communist China.

America's noble mission also requires substituting China's malicious influence with genuine economic partnerships based on mutual respect and mutual benefits. Americans have been outstanding in helping the less fortunate of the world, both through private charitable donations and government assistance. But the inroads China has made in Africa in recent years point to the need for a much more robust program of engagement with developing countries. Paralleling the failure of détente, during the Cold War the West largely stood by as the Soviet Bloc and other Communist countries extended their influence in Africa and throughout the developing world. This led to numerous civil wars in the name of "national liberation" and the creation of Socialist states that fostered brutal dictatorships and economic impoverishment. We must not let this pattern be repeated with China as the prime mover behind the global expansion of Communism.

Ike Articulated the American Mission Well

Dwight Eisenhower reminded us of America's virtuous role in the world with poignant words on the 20th anniversary of D-Day. Filmed at a Normandy cemetery for Americans who died during the invasion to liberate Europe from Nazism, the former Supreme Allied Commander during World War II and later a US President, made the following comments:

> D-Day has a very special meaning for me. I'm not referring really to the anxieties of the day, anxieties that were a natural part of sending in an invasion where you knew that many hundreds of boys were going to give their lives or be maimed forever. But my mind goes back so often to this fact. On D-Day, my own son graduated from West Point. And after his training with his division, he came over, with the 71st Division. But that was some time after this

event. But on the very day he was graduating, these men came here, British and our other allies, Americans, to storm these beaches, for one purpose only. Not to gain anything for ourselves, not to fulfill any ambitions that America had for conquest. But just to preserve freedom, systems of self government in the world. Many thousands of men have died for ideals such as these. And here again, in the 20th century for the second time, Americans—along with the rest of the free world, but Americans—had to come across the ocean to defend those same values.

My own son has been very fortunate. He has had a very full life since then. He is the father of four lovely children that are very precious to my wife and me. But these young boys, so many of them, over whose graves we have been treading, looking, wondering and contemplating about their sacrifices. They were cut off in their prime. They have families that grieve for them. But they never knew the great experiences of going through life, like my son can enjoy. I devoutly hope they will never again have to see such things as these. I think and hope, pray, that humanity has learned more than we had learned up to that time. But these people gave us a chance. They bought time for us. So that we can do better than we had before. So every time I come back to these beaches, or on any day that I think about that day, 20 years ago now, I say, once more, we must find some way to work for peace, and really to gain an eternal peace for this world.[120]

These words are a perfect reminder of America's history as a blessed nation that has sacrificed for the sake of others. They also remind us that these sacrifices were final. They ended the lives of young men and women who would never again taste the joys of life on earth and have families of their own. Finally, they remind us that the end goal of sacrifice is the creation of a world of enduring peace. This high purpose remains the providential destiny of America. It is a unique goal that Americans can rightly be proud of. The Left in America and much of the world refuse to acknowledge this mission, painting the whole country with the brush of racism and white supremacy. They are wrong. America is needed by the world today as much, if not more, than ever before.

Chapter 19

The Triumph of Good

The Case for Personal Responsibility

The Providence of Restoration

This book has traced the story of human beings from our origin as the apex creation endowed with Divine attributes of goodness and free will, through our alienation from the Creator, and slow, painful process of regaining our original innocence and goodness by overcoming evil. We have pointed out that despite the prevalence of evil in the world, there is always a path for goodness to advance and for men and women to fulfill their original purpose. We have identified Cain and Abel as the archetypal figures of evil and good, respectively, and explained how Abel's path of service and sacrifice is the key to the positive transformation of Cain and the restoration, or salvation, of fallen humanity. As noted, human history is at heart a providential "history of restoration" that stretches from the Garden of Eden to the present day.

We have shown that providential history advances according to the Cain-Abel paradigm, which is evident throughout history and in all cultures. This paradigm explains conflicts within ourselves, as well as between individuals, families, nations and ideologies: in other words, between forces of good and evil. Representing good, Abel is humble and forgiving and willing to sacrifice himself for those in need. Representing evil, Cain is arrogant and resentful and quick to blame others for his problems rather than confronting

240

his own inadequacies, resentments and selfishness. For both, the challenge is to fulfill their responsibilities as human beings to their Creator, to others and to nature. As individuals, we achieve spiritual growth when our Abel nature dominates our Cain nature. For humanity as a whole, progress is achieved when Abel-type individuals, ideas and institutions prevail over their Cain-type counterparts. But is there an end goal for this process? Can Abel's incremental successes lead to a final success in which good permanently triumphs over evil?

The Triumph of Good Over Evil

Given the prevalence and power of evil, it is only natural to wonder how good can ever triumph over it. Most people likely believe that permanently defeating evil is a quixotic quest, a pipe dream of the irrational. This view, supported by the fact of millennia of conflicts between good and evil, undoubtedly helps explain the widely held belief among Christians and members of other faiths that good will only triumph over evil through an apocalyptic intervention by a vengeful God who can no longer tolerate the world remaining under the dominion of Satan. One such scenario is presented in Revelation, the final chapter of the Christian Bible. It says that after the evil world has been totally destroyed by the forces aligned with God, a Kingdom of Heaven will descend upon the earth in which God and humanity will live in peace and harmony. The faithful hope their virtue will be rewarded by being accepted into that Kingdom. The trouble with this belief is that already 2,000 years have passed since Jesus spoke of such a Kingdom. His disciples clearly thought its advent was imminent, especially after Jesus indicated some of them would see it in their lifetimes. (Mark 9:1) Why, then, is the apocalypse so delayed, and when, if ever, can we expect it to occur?

In this book we have pointed out that the realization of Divine purpose is destined to occur, but the timing of its fulfillment is conditioned on people being responsible: doing their part to make it happen. This law of human responsibility is as ironclad as Divine destiny itself. The Cain-Abel paradigm translates the abstract need for responsible behavior into very specific obligations for Cain and for Abel. As we have shown, history demonstrates that successful resolution of Cain-Abel relationships has resulted in a steady evolution of enlightenment in both religion and science. This is hopeful. It means that if we are willing to learn from the past and take responsibility for our actions in the present, we can improve ourselves and approach the point when our Creator can indeed intervene in the affairs of the world to enable us to do good and do away with evil.

Seen from this perspective, the great moral leaders of history all serve as Abel-type teachers and role models who have built on the work of previous Abel figures. Thus Abraham came on the foundation of Noah, and Isaac, Jacob, Moses and Jesus came on Abraham's foundation. In another line, Ishmael and Mohammed also came on Abraham's foundation. The measure of progress from one to the other is reflected in the ever-greater depth of understanding they reveal over time. Thus in the Sermon on the Mount (Matthew 5-7), the moral standard set out for believers is no longer based on a servant's obedience to a master and his laws, as in the Old Testament, but to a son's filial piety to his parents.

For Christians, then, a life of faith is not aimed at fulfilling the dictates of law but rather living according to a high moral standard that is automatically consistent with the law. As Saint Paul wrote in Romans 2:15: "...what the law requires is written on their hearts, while their conscience also bears witness..." And as the author of Hebrews wrote in 10:16: "I will put my laws on their hearts, and write them on their minds." As Paul explained, for the law to become internalized (in hearts and minds rather than written in books) meant that anyone, Jew or Gentile, could be a good Christian if they followed the dictates of their conscience. If they truly loved others, they would naturally refrain from committing sins proscribed by the Mosaic Law.

A Final Contest Between Cain and Abel

The Axial Age (Chapter 6) preceded the advent of Jesus, bringing with it worldwide enlightenment, in religion and science. In recent centuries, a similar enlightenment has swept across the entire world, bringing great advances in all fields of human knowledge. As we have noted, from the dawn of human existence, the false has preceded the true, and evil has preceded good. (For example, slavery preceded freedom, and tyrannies have preceded democracies.) Furthermore, the false typically foreshadows the true, seeking to preempt the true with a deceptive imitation of the authentic version. Hence, the rapid spread of Marxism and Neo-Marxism can be seen as Cain ideology reaching its apogee, with both Communism and Postmodernism embodying all the worst, inhuman traits of Cain-type ideology and behavior even as they claim to offer a Utopian solution to all the world's problems.

The actual outcomes of Leftist ideologies, with their tens of millions of deaths and decades of human suffering, are now undeniably evident before us. With all this proof of their failure to deliver on their promises, it is now time for righteous people to expose and debunk once and for all their falsehoods and deceptions and to provide credible alternatives. We have seen how erroneous and unscientific the Left's theories actually are, and we should be confident that the record of free societies and free markets is infinitely superior to anything proposed or implemented by the Left. We cannot accept Leftist narratives and Cancel Culture but must join forces to defeat the Left and create an environment in which a godly alternative can emerge.

Providence Assures the Final Triumph of Good

The greatest hope for a triumph of good over evil lies in the fact of Divine providence. As we have shown, a belief in this providence was a very important element in the founding of America, imbuing the founders' efforts with a sense of transcendent purpose. The root of providence is the purpose of creation—the fact that we humans did not merely evolve from apes but are the work of a perfect and purposeful Creator. The implication of this is that, despite the prevalence of evil in human history, the ultimate purpose of our existence is to finally embody the image of our Creator, who is only good. History has shown that Divine purpose inexorably works itself out in human affairs over time, regardless of how much time and how much patience is required. That Divine providence will ultimately prevail is the basis for our hope. (For a chart summarizing the central providence of restoration see Appendix 25, p469.)

The intersection of history and providential purpose have reached their culminating point; we are at the moment that will determine human destiny, good or bad. This moment looks dark because we have reached the final battle between the two great forces that have shaped history. If we hold firm to our course, if we keep our trust in Divine providence, and if we invest ourselves fully in the fight, we can expect to see the long-awaited triumph of good over evil.

Chapter 20

Translating Words Into Action

Building an Alliance to Defeat Evil

When bad men combine, the good must associate; else they will fall, one by one, an unpitied sacrifice in a contemptible struggle.[121]

Edmund Burke

The Work That Must Be Done

There is much work to be done. Evil will not voluntarily surrender its current position of power and privilege in the world. And, as we have noted, it is not sufficient for good people only to pray for an invisible, Divine force to deliver us from evil. Rather, we have to combine prayer with taking the initiative to challenge and defeat evil wherever it manifests, trusting that this action will catalyze the necessary forces of good, spiritual and otherwise, to defeat our common enemy. Each of us faces this challenge in our own lives, and by joining forces with others of goodwill, we can create an effective alliance to expose evil and replace it with good.

The goal is not just to win another political contest or another election—with the probability that victory will be fleeting—but to defeat permanently the ideologies and practices that are destroying America and world civilization as a whole. We have more than enough evidence that Marxism and Critical Theories are poisonous—they produce no lasting good but only more chaos, violence, poverty and death. The goal, then, is to draw the necessary conclusions from this evidence and to take the necessary actions to save and strengthen civilization.

The Enemy as a Two-Headed Beast

Tolkien's *The Lord of the Rings* trilogy is a very popular story because it is such an insightful depiction of the conflict between good and evil. The good side is made up of various sentient creatures, including humans, who set aside their differences to confront the common enemy; they are willing to sacrifice themselves in the war to defeat evil. Their leaders, like King Arthur's knights, are noble and chivalrous. The humbler participants in the fight, such as the Hobbits, are often simple and unimpressive to behold, but they too are animated by love and willingness to sacrifice for others. Frustrating their cause, however, are those who have for too long listened to the whisperings of the enemy and are compromised. They are easily disheartened and often lured into making disastrous compromises with evil, betraying their confederates and sacrificing the lives of others to secure their own safety.

The enemy never rests. He is always on the move, plotting the defeat and destruction of those allied against him. His main strategy is to sow discord and enmity among the allies, trying to turn them against one another. He targets those lacking moral fiber and the resolve to fight for goodness. The ugliness of his servants and soldiers is essentially spiritual, but it extends from the depths of their rancid, twisted characters to the gross contours of their grotesque faces and bodies. His evil abode, Mordor, is literally shrouded in black clouds of death, and he keeps his forces in line with a brutal regime of intimidation and terror. And, in the same way that the Iron Curtain prevented East Europeans from escaping their totalitarian regimes, Mordor is surrounded by impenetrable mountains with massive towers located at the passes to prevent escape to the outside world.

Our enemy is not much different in substance, but very different in appearance. The Two-Headed Beast has internal and external manifestations, both of which are kept in disguise for as long as possible. The ugly Leftist beast wraps itself in the deceptively attractive language of "love and peace." It claims to champion the poor and vulnerable, the workers and peasants, the minorities and disenfranchised. But once firmly in power, the Beast abandons its disguise, and the hideous reality of its totalitarian regimes is revealed. The enemy we face today is found at both stages of its typical evolution: the stage of deception on the way to taking power, and the stage of exercising dictatorship to maintain and expand its grip on power. If we are to avert destruction, we need to confront and overcome both.

The Cancerous Ideology of the Left

Throughout this book we have endeavored to expose the dangers of Marxism and Neo-Marxism. These cancerous theories have insinuated themselves deep into our culture and society, infecting education, media, corporations and government. They have already caused extensive damage to traditional societies built on spiritual and religious foundations. Allowed to continue, the armies of the Left will completely take over our institutions of learning and communication. From that position of strength they will no longer need to disguise their real intentions and will turn to dictating to all of us their fascistic rules, crushing our independence and freedom.

We must do whatever we can to fight the spread of the pernicious theories of the Left. We must fight for free speech; we must fight for religious and intellectual freedom; we must fight to get the ideologies of the Left out of education, media, corporations and government. The future of our children and their children is at stake.

The Totalitarianism of Communist China

In 2021, the Chinese Communist Party became 100 years old. It has been in power for seventy-two years. In that time, it has caused the death of as many as 80 million Chinese. Today it is persecuting ethnic and religious minorities on a massive scale. Its leaders dream of overtaking America and establishing a global hegemony by 2049. To achieve this goal, they continue to steal intellectual property from industrialized states. With the information they have stolen and the capital they have gained from naïve foreign investors, the CCP has been able to extend its economic reach throughout the world and build up its armed forces.

We must do whatever we can to stop the rise of Communist China. We must persuade our government to start treating China as an enemy, not an innocuous trading partner. We must campaign to get US and other international banks and corporations to disinvest from China and relocate their money and factories to the United States or other free countries. We must expose and block Chinese subversion in our country. We must limit the freedom of Chinese students and businesspeople to take advantage of our free societies to advance the CCP agenda. And we must maintain our military superiority so that China is never permitted to dominate the Free World and impose its dictates on America and other nations.

An Alliance for Good

Tackling the spread of materialist ideologies has to be the priority for all good people, irrespective of race, religion or nationality. We can no longer permit our differences in color, ethnicity and belief to excuse us from joining forces against evil. This alliance for good must provide a clear alternative to the Left, which always tries to exploit diversity to create conflicts and seduce good people to engage in bad behavior. This is a time for wise men and women to transcend their differences in order to save the world from the relentless advance of evil.

An Interfaith Mission

All too often, religious groups are obsessed with how they differ from other religious groups, based on issues of doctrine or practice. These differences don't matter at all if you are unable to practice your faith freely or at all, as is the case in all totalitarian states. Within Christianity, for example, the many denominations have no excuse for attacking one another in the face of an atheistic enemy that will destroy them all if left to wield power as it wishes. In the same vein, anti-Semitism and anti-Islamic impulses and biases have to be set aside for the sake of creating an alliance of the faithful and the good to counter and defeat evil. Think of it this way: When fighting in a war, the race, religion or ethnicity of the soldier fighting beside you is of no consequence. The same principle should apply in the battle of good against evil. To build an effective alliance against evil, it is necessary for those on the side of good to find allies and thereby multiply their strength and effectiveness.

The interfaith movement is now over a century old, and dialogs among people of faith are now far advanced. These groups can contribute greatly to the common cause by turning their focus on the materialist threats to all religions. As we have seen in the history of Communism, all religions are a prime target of totalitarian regimes, and once Marxists have taken power, it is too late to prevent the destruction of religious institutions. This is a matter of religions surviving, and therefore it should be a priority for interfaith organizations.

A Multidimensional Engagement with the Left

Our response to the Left should match its multidimensional character. We are not just confronted with bad policy and misguided political parties but also by truly poisonous ideas and an extremely dangerous regime in Communist China. Hence, we must integrate political/economic and ideological responses with spiritual and providential alternatives. The Left derives its power from ideology and the cooperation it enjoys from academic, media and political institutions and groups that have embraced that ideology. To reduce the power of the Left, this cooperation must be cut off. At the same time, the Leftist theories must be replaced with virtuous ideas and effective solutions to society's ills. (See Appendix 26, p473, for a chart showing the three dimensions of effective engagement with the Left.)

Here are some general considerations that can serve to guide our multidimensional response to the Left.

I. The Political and Economic Dimension

A wise political strategy begins with recognizing how you have gone wrong, and then fixing your approach accordingly. The goal should not be to revert to "the good old days" when you were in power but to recognize that you have to do better if you are to avoid future reversals. In the present time, this means recognizing that the contest we are engaged in is not just a matter of Republicans versus Democrats, but of fundamentally different ways of looking at our existence and the world. The immediate evidence of that is in the Democratic Party agenda, which is increasingly influenced by radical socialist ideology and programs and threatens to undermine the individual freedoms that have been purchased and protected so dearly by our ancestors. Since the Democrats like to claim the mantle of America's founding principles, we cannot expect that making that claim ourselves will be effective. We need to bring other arguments to bear.

Domestic Policy

In a war, it is treachery to side with an enemy that is bent on your demise. In politics, too, it is not a virtue to be a maverick and side with the opposition (in the name of bipartisanship) if doing so means compromising basic principles of government and individual freedom. Those who truly believe in freedom and democracy must be firmly united and unequivocal in their opposition to the Left. Socialist policies must be overturned, at all costs, because they inevitably lead to authoritarianism, injustice and the loss of personal freedoms.

A righteous political party must provide a big tent for people of all races, religions, classes and ethnic origins to work together towards shared goals, but it should not embrace ideas that are inimical to freedom in order to capture a constituency. The agenda of the Left must be defeated so that all future differences between parties fall within the wide compass of shared values and principles of government. Until that is achieved, the conservative movement must vigorously oppose the ideas and agenda of the Left. (For one proposal for a winning political program for conservatives in 2021 America, see Trevor Loudon's article: *Nine 'Starter Steps' to Save America From Socialism*, Appendix 27, pp474-482.)

Foreign Policy

At the same time, government policy must be aimed at cutting off the oxygen to our foreign enemies. The model for this should be the way we treated Hitler's Germany: as a pariah. Right now we are dealing with Communist China as if it were a neutral player in world affairs. It is not. It is our deadly enemy, our nemesis. Multinational companies, banks and other investors have made China technologically advanced and enabled it to grow into a financial and military powerhouse. There is no stigma or punishment for Western and other international corporations investing in China. Imagine if Communist China was Nazi Germany! Only the truly blind or politically prejudiced could think that continued financial support for China is a good idea.

We have to start treating China as the enemy it is. The huge investments in China's economy by America and other industrialized nations that seek to capitalize on its vast market and labor resources must stop, at least until China becomes a responsible member of the world community. More than that, it is high time for international investments in China to end, and multinationals established there to relocate to America or to other countries that share America's democratic and free-market values. (For example, India could be substituted for China, given its democratic government, religious culture—Hinduism, Islam, Buddhism, Jainism, Sikhism, Christianity—and free markets.)

Visas for Chinese students, tourists and businesspeople should be strictly limited. All fentanyl shipments must be blocked and Chinese suppliers identified and shut down. Espionage or other work for China by Americans should be severely punished. (Why was US Representative Eric Swalwell allowed to remain on the House Intelligence Committee after it was discovered that he had consorted with a Chinese spy who seduced him?) Trade should be strictly limited to goods and services that cannot be used to harm us, and Chinese theft of intellectual property must be treated as a crime. The goal is to crush the Chinese Communist Party—and to liberate the Chinese people from its oppression, giving them a chance to have the same personal freedoms that we enjoy.

At the same time, America should lead a global initiative to build new partnerships with countries that are still relatively undeveloped economically. These partnerships cannot depend on aid but should be based on investment and trade that respects others. In particular this applies to Africa, which by the end of this century will be home to one-third of the world's population. China has already made deep inroads in Africa and many other developing countries through its Belt and Road initiative and other "aid" programs. The strings attached to Chinese investment and trade can only mean trouble for these countries, and a proactive campaign by America and other democracies to replace China as the leading business and development partner for emerging economies will bring those countries new hope and protect the world from further Communist Chinese influence.

II. The Intellectual and Ideological Dimension

Ideas of the Left have gained unprecedented influence in academia, media and politics. These ideas come primarily from Marxism and Neo-Marxist Critical Theories, which are based on atheism and anti-capitalism, and promote conflict as the way to progress. These ideas have no basis in science but have spread deep within society, shaping everything from educational curricula to media bias and government policies. They must be pulled up by their roots.

This means they must be fully understood and explained critically, from their philosophical foundations to their malign influence in changing social norms and shaping radical policy prescriptions. They must be countered and replaced with credible alternative theories that are based on faith and science. Educational curricula must be overhauled to remove the damaging and false Marxist and Postmodernist theories; media must be held to account for its Leftist biases; and government must be held to account for the harm caused by its radical policies and laws.

We cannot hope to succeed in the political and economic arenas without simultaneously reversing the pernicious influence of Leftist ideology that shapes them and replacing it with sound, principled ideas. In America, the Democratic Party is heavily influenced by Leftist ideology, as reflected in the Socialist policies of senators like Bernie Sanders and Elizabeth Warren, as well as House members such as Alexandria Ocasio-Cortez and Ilhan Omar. Their radical policy prescriptions, such as the Green New Deal and massive social welfare programs, were incorporated in the Democratic Platform in the 2020 election and are largely being carried out by President Joe Biden.

Simply put, the side of good must starve the Left of its support by boycotting all its intellectual and ideological products and replacing them with good alternatives.

III. The Spiritual, Religious and Providential Dimension

By denying the existence of a Creator and a purpose for creation, the Left makes itself the enemy of the Divine and the good. This atheism is the root of the evil that besets the world and has caused immeasurable injustice and suffering. It is the cause of division, conflict and war. The spiritual nature of humanity is not only the wellspring of love and goodness, it is also what gives us the capacity to become fully human, to fulfill our potential.

Our culture is flooded with the unhealthy and outright harmful influences of the Left, which by design are intended to undermine the religious foundations and morality of society. Movies and TV programs are full of politically correct language and unprincipled behavior that promotes the sexual revolution and encourages disbelief in the Divine. Pornography has deeply infected society, snaring many faithful believers. Advocates of normalizing homosexuality and transgenderism have had enormous success in getting their agendas accepted by Hollywood and the mass media, while homosexuality and pedophilia have had a devastating effect on Catholic seminaries and the priesthood. Even sports teams and competitions are now held hostage by radical Leftists who are trying to use them to divide society and undermine patriotism. These culturally destructive influences can be made to die out only if our consumption of them ends.

In their place, it is time to reintroduce a spiritual agenda to the nation—reawaken a sense of the transcendent forces that have shaped our history and continue to shape our lives and our world. This means renewing a common awareness of America's providential founding and mission and honoring the sacrifices that have been made on behalf of moral and patriotic ideals. The "America First" and "Make America Great Again" slogans were aimed at mobilizing a renewed patriotism in America as founded, but we cannot simply go back to the place where we lost our way once before. Rather, we should recognize that America's providential mission is not just for itself but also for the world, and that it is the fulfillment of that broader purpose that will secure the values we treasure for future generations. We need to regain our hope for a better world. For too long, we have had to suffer the dystopian portrait of the world painted by the Left. The miserable people behind that dark future, from Rousseau and Marx to Marcuse and Foucault, can never provide the vision of a bright future that is so close to the hearts and minds of good people everywhere. We need a new Great Awakening!

A Personal Mission

Throughout this book we have focused, again and again, on the vital importance of personal responsibility as the key to the fulfillment of Divine providence. But what does that mean for us today? It means, first and foremost, learning the truth about the agendas and ideas of the Left; it means exposing and opposing their ideas whenever possible; it means boycotting their educational and cultural products; and it means calling out policymakers who promote the prescriptions of the Left. Finally, it means having the courage of our convictions and standing up to criticism and even ridicule.

In summary, our primary responsibilities at this time are:

1. *To educate ourselves so that we are truly enlightened* and understand what lies behind the ideas and activities of the Left; we must learn to recognize and oppose them wherever they manifest.

2. *To do whatever we can to stop the spread of Marxist and Neo-Marxist ideas* and replace them with constructive, godly alternatives.

3. *To do whatever we can to end the regime of the Chinese Communist Party* and its network of institutions and corporations that are so harming the world—and to support the liberation of the Chinese people from Communist rule.

To Fulfill America's Providential Purpose

The belief that America was founded for a providential purpose is a powerful source of inspiration that should guide our choice of ideology and shape our political agenda. America has in many ways already lived up to its promise, as we have discussed, and the fact that it has not been perfect should not deter us from being confident in its continued importance for the world. After all, there is no other country that can play the Abel role needed at this time.

There is now a new war to be fought by America and its allies. It is a war of ideas, of good versus evil ideologies and systems of government, and it is a war against the Communist juggernaut China. America's current mission is its most daunting yet, and the world needs America to lead in the creation of an alliance of good forces to counter and defeat evil once and for all. This is a responsibility for America, but it is also a responsibility shared by the rest of the world.

It is all too easy for other countries to criticize America, but when trouble strikes it is always to America that the less powerful look for help. So far, America has not used its enormous wealth and power to conquer countries and build an empire. On the contrary, it has used them to help those in need. Other countries should follow this lead and share in the common mission to rid the world of destructive materialist ideologies and regimes and replace them with ideas and governments that contribute to human well-being and authentic progress towards universally desirable goals.

We are at a critical moment in the long course of human existence. Do we just accept the corruption and relentless decline of our civilization as our most cherished institutions are subverted and destroyed? Or do we turn and fight? The future of our children and grandchildren is truly in our hands. We must fight. This is the moment for righteous men and women of courage to stand up for true justice and true equality in the face of the perfected Cain ideologies of the Marxist and Neo-Marxist Left. This is a moment for individuals like King David and Gideon, Saint Paul and Luther, Joan of Arc, Patrick Henry, George Washington, Abraham Lincoln and Winston Churchill: men and women who are ready to risk their all for the sake of God's providence.

Perhaps Joan of Arc is the most inspiring example for us today. She was an unlikely hero, an illiterate French peasant girl who lacked the education or connections to influence anyone. Yet, guided by instructions from above, she was so convinced of her purpose that she moved her whole nation into action, leading it in a fight for freedom. As Churchill wrote of her:

Joan was a being so uplifted from the ordinary run of mankind that she finds no equal in a thousand years. She embodied the natural goodness and valor of the human race in unexampled perfection. Unconquerable courage, infinite compassion, the virtue of the simple, the wisdom of the just, shone forth in her.[122]

It was Joan's unbending determination to obey God that changed the course of French history. It was a similar commitment by America's Founders that prompted them to sign the Declaration of Independence that concluded with these words: "with a firm reliance on the protection of divine Providence, we mutually pledge to each other our Lives, our Fortunes and our sacred Honor." The noble spirit of America's Founders still lives on, but it must be rekindled and refocused on the real enemy today. We need modern-day heroes with the courage to confront false ideologies and harmful policies in all fields of endeavor, from politics to science, academia, media, sports and the corporate world.

In World War II, young men stepped forward to defend Britain when it seemed impossible to prevent a Nazi invasion. Many died and many more were gravely injured, but Britain was miraculously saved. Today, we need the same type of courage to prevent the further advance of the Left and Communist China and to turn the tide of human events towards the fulfillment of Divine providence. We are not yet called to race to our Spitfires and Hurricanes and take to the skies to prevent invading armies from overrunning our country. But we must be willing to be criticized, ridiculed and cancelled by those who are destroying our country and the world. We might lose our job or our reputation, but this is the hour of decision. We must stand up and fight the Left so that our children and their children can live free in a world of goodness.

As Winston Churchill said:

What is the use of living, if it be not to strive for noble causes and to make this muddled world a better place for those who will live in it after we are gone?[123]

Chapter 21

Conclusion

The End of Marxism and the Dawn of a New Day

This is Our Mission

The thesis of this book is that humanity is not destined to suffer an eternal existence under a dominion of evil, but that we are in fact destined to see good triumph over evil. We are creations of God, while Marxism and Neo-Marxism are merely the creations of several corrupt and immoral people. They will pass away, but only if we choose to reject them. It is not the Creator's work to destroy these destructive theories and the institutions that promote them. It is our work. We must expose the fraud they represent, and we must deny them the support they depend on for their existence. Marxism and Critical Theories will end when no one believes in them, and no one follows their prescriptions.

In this respect, it should be remembered that although Leftist ideologies seem so prevalent in the world today, they themselves are derivative of deeper wells of evil intent and behavior. Ultimately, to rid the world of evil we must recognize and reject the thinking and behavior of Cain, which itself embodies the malignant influence of Lucifer.

Use the Cain-Abel Paradigm

The Cain-Abel paradigm, which we have elaborated and applied throughout this book, is the key to understanding our own struggles with evil as well as the manifestations of good and evil in other people and institutions. It is also the key to judging the relative benefit or harm of government domestic and foreign policies. The Cain-type nature is fundamentally self-centered. It is jealous, resentful, vindictive, power-hungry and inclined to employ violence to get its way. The Abel nature, by contrast, is faithful, patient, humble, forgiving and sacrificial. It only uses violence as a last resort, to protect the vulnerable and innocent from the predations of Cain. We all experience both Cain and Abel influences and impulses in our lives, but we all have the free will to reject Cain and choose the Way of Abel. Likewise, we all have the freedom to oppose Cain-type individuals and institutions in the world around us and to support their Abel-type counterparts.

The nature of Cain itself is the result of the satanic influence of Lucifer, who, out of his resentment for the blessings being bestowed on Adam and Eve by God, initiated a series of illicit actions that destroyed the original family. Lucifer's seduction of Eve was the point at which self-centered nature was translated into destructive action. Ever since, sexual immorality has been the root of evil behavior. It has destroyed families, institutions, nations and empires. Furthermore, it is a feature of the lives and theories of the proponents of atheistic materialism that we have discussed in this book. It is the most deeply entrenched weakness that we all have to contend with.

The Dawn of a New Day

We live for the dawn of a new day, a new era that is not overshadowed by selfish people driven by atheistic and anti-family ideas. We live for a time when we can worship our Creator and speak our minds as we see fit, free from the chains of censors. We live for a time when all tyrants are vanquished and all governments are limited to their proper role as protectors of individual rights, family values and shared prosperity. To reach that day has been the purpose of history and is our purpose now. We believe that the goodness planted in men and women by our Creator will surely prevail in the end and that the day we all long for will surely dawn.

We must become the good, loving and responsible parents that Cain and Abel never had.

Appendices

Appendix 1

The Manifesto of the Communist Party

By Karl Marx and Friedrich Engels

(From the English edition of 1888, edited by Friedrich Engels. First published in 1848.)

A specter is haunting Europe—the specter of Communism. All the Powers of old Europe have entered into a holy alliance to exorcise this specter: Pope and Czar, Metternich and Guizot, French Radicals and German police-spies.

Where is the party in opposition that has not been decried as Communistic by its opponents in power? Where is the Opposition that has not hurled back the branding reproach of Communism, against the more advanced opposition parties, as well as against its reactionary adversaries?

Two things result from this fact.

I. Communism is already acknowledged by all European Powers to be itself a Power.

II. It is high time that Communists should openly, in the face of the whole world, publish their views, their aims, their tendencies, and meet this nursery tale of the Specter of Communism with a Manifesto of the party itself.

To this end, Communists of various nationalities have assembled in London, and sketched the following Manifesto, to be published in the English, French, German, Italian, Flemish and Danish languages.

I. BOURGEOIS AND PROLETARIANS

The history of all hitherto existing societies is the history of class struggles.

Freeman and slave, patrician and plebeian, lord and serf, guild-master and journeyman, in a word, oppressor and oppressed, stood in constant opposition to one another, carried on an uninterrupted, now hidden, now open fight, a fight that each time ended, either in a revolutionary re-constitution of society at large, or in the common ruin of the contending classes.

In the earlier epochs of history, we find almost everywhere a complicated arrangement of society into various orders, a manifold gradation of social rank. In ancient Rome we have patricians, knights, plebeians, slaves; in the Middle Ages, feudal lords, vassals, guild-masters, journeymen, apprentices, serfs; in almost all of these classes, again, subordinate gradations.

The modern bourgeois society that has sprouted from the ruins of feudal society has not done away with class antagonisms. It has but established new classes, new conditions of oppression, new forms of struggle in place of the old ones. Our epoch, the epoch of the bourgeoisie, possesses, however, this distinctive feature: it has simplified the class antagonisms. Society as a whole is more and more splitting up into two great hostile camps, into two great classes, directly facing each other: Bourgeoisie and Proletariat.

From the serfs of the Middle Ages sprang the chartered burghers of the earliest towns. From these burgesses the first elements of the bourgeoisie were developed.

The discovery of America, the rounding of the Cape, opened up fresh ground for the rising bourgeoisie. The East-Indian and Chinese markets, the colonization of America, trade with the colonies, the increase in the means of exchange and in commodities generally, gave to commerce, to navigation, to industry, an impulse never before known, and thereby, to the revolutionary element in the tottering feudal society, a rapid development.

The feudal system of industry, under which industrial production was monopolized by closed guilds, now no longer sufficed for the growing wants of the new markets. The manufacturing system took its place. The guild-masters were pushed on one side by the manufacturing middle class; division of labor between the different corporate guilds vanished in the face of division of labor in each single workshop.

Meantime the markets kept ever growing, the demand ever rising. Even manufacture no longer sufficed. Thereupon, steam and machinery revolutionized industrial production. The place of manufacture was taken by the giant, Modern Industry, the place of the industrial middle class, by industrial millionaires, the leaders of whole industrial armies, the modern bourgeois.

Modern industry has established the world-market, for which the discovery of America paved the way. This market has given an immense development to commerce, to navigation, to communication by land. This development has, in its time, reacted on the extension of industry; and in proportion as industry, commerce, navigation, railways extended, in the same proportion the bourgeoisie developed, increased its capital, and pushed into the background every class handed down from the Middle Ages.

We see, therefore, how the modern bourgeoisie is itself the product of a long course of development, of a series of revolutions in the modes of production and of exchange.

Each step in the development of the bourgeoisie was accompanied by a corresponding political advance of that class. An oppressed class under the sway of the feudal nobility, an armed and self-governing association in the mediaeval commune; here independent urban republic (as in Italy and Germany), there taxable "third estate" of the monarchy (as in France), afterwards, in the period of manufacture proper, serving either the semi-feudal or the absolute monarchy as a counterpoise against the nobility, and, in fact, corner-stone of the great monarchies in general, the bourgeoisie has at last, since the establishment of Modern Industry and of the world-market, conquered for itself, in the modern representative State, exclusive political sway. The executive of the modern State is but a committee for managing the common affairs of the whole bourgeoisie.

The bourgeoisie, historically, has played a most revolutionary part.

The bourgeoisie, wherever it has got the upper hand, has put an end to all feudal, patriarchal, idyllic relations. It has pitilessly torn asunder the motley feudal ties that bound man to his "natural superiors," and has left remaining no other nexus between man and man than naked self-interest, than callous "cash payment." It has drowned the most heavenly ecstasies of religious fervor, of chivalrous enthusiasm, of philistine sentimentalism, in the icy water of egotistical calculation. It has resolved personal worth into exchange value, and in place of the numberless and indefeasible chartered freedoms, has set up that single, unconscionable freedom—Free Trade. In one word, for exploitation, veiled by religious and political illusions, naked, shameless, direct, brutal exploitation.

The bourgeoisie has stripped of its halo every occupation hitherto honored and looked up to with reverent awe. It has converted the physician, the lawyer, the priest, the poet, the man of science, into its paid wage laborers.

The bourgeoisie has torn away from the family its sentimental veil, and has reduced the family relation to a mere money relation.

The bourgeoisie has disclosed how it came to pass that the brutal display of vigor in the Middle Ages, which Reactionists so much admire, found its fitting complement in the most slothful indolence. It has been the first to show what man's activity can bring about. It has accomplished wonders far surpassing Egyptian pyramids, Roman aqueducts, and Gothic cathedrals; it has conducted expeditions that put in the shade all former Exoduses of nations and crusades.

The bourgeoisie cannot exist without constantly revolutionizing the instruments of production, and thereby the relations of production, and with them the whole relations of society. Conservation of the old modes of production in unaltered form, was, on the contrary, the first condition of existence for all earlier industrial classes. Constant revolutionizing of production, uninterrupted disturbance of all social conditions, everlasting uncertainty and agitation distinguish the bourgeois epoch from all earlier ones. All fixed, fast-frozen relations, with their train of ancient and venerable prejudices and opinions, are swept away, all new-formed ones become antiquated before they can ossify. All that is solid melts into air, all that is holy is profaned, and man is at last compelled to face with sober senses, his real conditions of life, and his relations with his kind.

The need of a constantly expanding market for its products chases the bourgeoisie over the whole surface of the globe. It must nestle everywhere, settle everywhere, establish connections everywhere.

The bourgeoisie has through its exploitation of the world-market given a cosmopolitan character to production and consumption in every country. To the great chagrin of Reactionists, it has drawn from under the feet of industry the national ground on which it stood. All old-established national industries have been destroyed or are daily being destroyed. They are dislodged by new industries, whose introduction becomes a life and death question for all civilized nations, by industries that no longer work up indigenous raw material, but raw material drawn from the remotest zones; industries whose products are consumed, not only at home, but in every quarter of the globe. In place of the old wants, satisfied by the productions of the country, we find new wants, requiring for their satisfaction the products of distant lands and climes. In place of the old local and national seclusion and self-sufficiency, we have intercourse in every direction, universal inter-dependence of nations. And as in material, so also in intellectual production. The intellectual creations of individual nations become common property. National one-sidedness and narrow-mindedness become more and more impossible, and from the numerous national and local literatures, there arises a world literature.

The bourgeoisie, by the rapid improvement of all instruments of production, by the immensely facilitated means of communication, draws all, even the most barbarian, nations into civilization. The cheap prices of its commodities are the heavy artillery with which it batters down all Chinese walls, with which it forces the barbarians' intensely obstinate hatred of foreigners to capitulate. It compels all nations, on pain of extinction, to adopt the bourgeois mode of production; it compels them to introduce what it calls civilization into their midst, i.e., to become bourgeois themselves. In one word, it creates a world after its own image.

The bourgeoisie has subjected the country to the rule of the towns. It has created enormous cities, has greatly increased the urban population as compared with the rural, and has thus rescued a considerable part of the population from the idiocy of rural life. Just as it has made the country dependent on the towns, so it has made barbarian and semi-barbarian countries dependent on the civilized ones, nations of peasants on nations of bourgeois, the East on the West.

The bourgeoisie keeps more and more doing away with the scattered state of the population, of the means of production, and of property. It has agglomerated production, and has concentrated property in a few hands. The necessary consequence of this was political centralization. Independent, or but loosely connected provinces, with separate interests, laws, governments and systems of taxation, became lumped together into one nation, with one government, one code of laws, one national class-interest, one frontier and one customs-tariff. The bourgeoisie, during its rule of scarce one hundred years, has created more massive and more colossal productive forces than have all preceding generations together. Subjection of Nature's forces to man, machinery, application of chemistry to industry and agriculture, steam-navigation, railways, electric telegraphs, clearing of whole continents for cultivation, canalization of rivers, whole populations conjured out of the ground—what earlier century had even a presentiment that such productive forces slumbered in the lap of social labor?

We see then: the means of production and of exchange, on whose foundation the bourgeoisie built itself up, were generated in feudal society. At a certain stage in the development of these means of production and of exchange, the conditions under which feudal society produced and exchanged, the feudal organization of agriculture and manufacturing industry, in one word, the feudal relations of property became no longer compatible with the already developed productive forces; they became so many fetters. They had to be burst asunder; they were burst asunder.

Into their place stepped free competition, accompanied by a social and political constitution adapted to it, and by the economical and political sway of the bourgeois class.

A similar movement is going on before our own eyes. Modern bourgeois society with its relations of production, of exchange and of property, a society that has conjured up such gigantic means of production and of exchange, is like the sorcerer, who is no longer able to control the powers of the nether world whom he has called up by his spells. For many a decade past the history of industry and commerce is but the history of the revolt of modern productive forces against modern conditions of production, against the property relations that are the conditions for the existence of the bourgeoisie and of its rule. It is enough to mention the commercial crises that by their periodical return put on its trial, each time more threateningly, the existence of the entire bourgeois society. In these crises a great part not only of the existing products, but also of the previously created productive forces, are periodically destroyed. In these crises there breaks out an epidemic that, in all earlier epochs, would have seemed an absurdity—the epidemic of over-production. Society suddenly finds itself put back into a state of momentary barbarism; it appears as if a famine, a universal war of devastation had cut off the supply of every means of subsistence; industry and commerce seem to be destroyed; and why? Because there is too much civilization, too much means of subsistence, too much industry, too much commerce. The productive forces at the disposal of society no longer tend to further the development of the conditions of bourgeois property; on the contrary, they have become too powerful for these conditions, by which they are fettered, and so soon as they overcome these fetters, they bring disorder into the whole of bourgeois society, endanger the existence of bourgeois property. The conditions of bourgeois society are too narrow to comprise the wealth created by them. And how does the bourgeoisie get over these crises? On the one hand enforced destruction of a mass of productive forces; on the other, by the conquest of new markets, and by the more thorough exploitation of the old ones. That is to say, by paving the way for more extensive and more destructive crises, and by diminishing the means whereby crises are prevented.

The weapons with which the bourgeoisie felled feudalism to the ground are now turned against the bourgeoisie itself.

But not only has the bourgeoisie forged the weapons that bring death to itself; it has also called into existence the men who are to wield those weapons—the modern working class—the proletarians.

In proportion as the bourgeoisie, i.e., capital, is developed, in the same proportion is the proletariat, the modern working class, developed—a class of laborers, who live only so long as they find work, and who find work only so long as their labor increases capital. These laborers, who must sell themselves piece-meal, are a commodity, like every other article of commerce, and are consequently exposed to all the vicissitudes of competition, to all the fluctuations of the market.

Owing to the extensive use of machinery and to division of labor, the work of the proletarians has lost all individual character, and consequently, all charm for the workman. He becomes an appendage of the machine, and it is only the most simple, most monotonous, and most easily acquired knack, that is required of him. Hence, the cost of production of a workman is restricted, almost entirely, to the means of subsistence that he requires for his maintenance, and for the propagation of his race. But the price of a commodity, and therefore also of labor, is equal to its cost of production. In proportion therefore, as the repulsiveness of the work increases, the wage decreases.

Nay more, in proportion as the use of machinery and division of labor increases, in the same proportion the burden of toil also increases, whether by prolongation of the working hours, by increase of the work exacted in a given time or by increased speed of the machinery, etc.

Modern industry has converted the little workshop of the patriarchal master into the great factory of the industrial capitalist. Masses of laborers, crowded into the factory, are organized like soldiers. As privates of the industrial army they are placed under the command of a perfect hierarchy of officers and sergeants. Not only are they slaves of the bourgeois class, and of the bourgeois State; they are daily and hourly enslaved by the machine, by the over-looker, and, above all, by the individual bourgeois manufacturer himself. The more openly this despotism proclaims gain to be its end and aim, the more petty, the more hateful and the more embittering it is.

The less the skill and exertion of strength implied in manual labor, in other words, the more modern industry becomes developed, the more is the labor of men superseded by that of women. Differences of age and sex have no longer any distinctive social validity for the working class. All are instruments of labor, more or less expensive to use, according to their age and sex.

No sooner is the exploitation of the laborer by the manufacturer, so far at an end, that he receives his wages in cash, than he is set upon by the other portions of the bourgeoisie, the landlord, the shopkeeper, the pawnbroker, etc.

The lower strata of the middle class—the small tradespeople, shopkeepers, retired tradesmen generally, the handicraftsmen and peasants—all these sink gradually into the proletariat, partly because their diminutive capital does not suffice for the scale on which Modern Industry is carried on, and is swamped in the competition with the large capitalists, partly because their specialized skill is rendered worthless by the new methods of production. Thus the proletariat is recruited from all classes of the population.

The proletariat goes through various stages of development. With its birth begins its struggle with the bourgeoisie. At first the contest is carried on by individual laborers, then by the workpeople of a factory, then by the operatives of one trade, in one locality, against the individual bourgeois who directly exploits them. They direct their attacks not against the bourgeois conditions of production, but against the instruments of production themselves; they destroy imported wares that compete with their labor, they smash to pieces machinery, they set factories ablaze, they seek to restore by force the vanished status of the workman of the Middle Ages.

At this stage the laborers still form an incoherent mass scattered over the whole country, and broken up by their mutual competition. If anywhere they unite to form more compact bodies, this is not yet the consequence of their own active union, but of the union of the bourgeoisie, which class, in order to attain its own political ends, is compelled to set the whole proletariat in motion, and is moreover yet, for a time, able to do so. At this stage, therefore, the proletarians do not fight their enemies, but the enemies of their enemies, the remnants of absolute monarchy, the landowners, the non-industrial bourgeois, the petty bourgeoisie. Thus the whole historical movement is concentrated in the hands of the bourgeoisie; every victory so obtained is a victory for the bourgeoisie.

But with the development of industry the proletariat not only increases in number; it becomes concentrated in greater masses, its strength grows, and it feels that strength more. The various interests and conditions of life within the ranks of the proletariat are more and more equalized, in proportion as machinery obliterates all distinctions of labor, and nearly everywhere reduces wages to the same low level. The growing competition among the bourgeois, and the resulting commercial crises, make the wages of the workers ever more fluctuating. The unceasing improvement of machinery, ever more rapidly developing, makes their livelihood more and more precarious; the collisions between individual workmen and individual bourgeois take more and more the character of collisions between two classes. Thereupon the workers begin to form combinations (Trades Unions) against the bourgeois; they club together in order to keep up the rate of wages; they found permanent associations in order to make provision beforehand for these occasional revolts. Here and there the contest breaks out into riots.

Now and then the workers are victorious, but only for a time. The real fruit of their battles lies, not in the immediate result, but in the ever-expanding union of the workers. This union is helped on by the improved means of communication that are created by modern industry and that place the workers of different localities in contact with one another. It was just this contact that was needed to centralize the numerous local struggles, all of the same character, into one national struggle between classes. But every class struggle is a political struggle. And that union, to attain which the burghers of the Middle Ages, with their miserable highways, required centuries, the modern proletarians, thanks to railways, achieve in a few years.

This organization of the proletarians into a class, and consequently into a political party, is continually being upset again by the competition between the workers themselves. But it ever rises up again, stronger, firmer, mightier. It compels legislative recognition of particular interests of the workers, by taking advantage of the divisions among the bourgeoisie itself. Thus the ten-hours' bill in England was carried.

Altogether collisions between the classes of the old society further, in many ways, the course of development of the proletariat. The bourgeoisie finds itself involved in a constant battle. At first with the aristocracy; later on, with those portions of the bourgeoisie itself, whose interests have become antagonistic to the progress of industry; at all times, with the bourgeoisie of foreign countries. In all these battles it sees itself compelled to appeal to the proletariat, to ask for its help, and thus, to drag it into the political arena. The bourgeoisie itself, therefore, supplies the proletariat with its own instruments of political and general education, in other words, it furnishes the proletariat with weapons for fighting the bourgeoisie.

Further, as we have already seen, entire sections of the ruling classes are, by the advance of industry, precipitated into the proletariat, or are at least threatened in their conditions of existence. These also supply the proletariat with fresh elements of enlightenment and progress.

Finally, in times when the class struggle nears the decisive hour, the process of dissolution going on within the ruling class, in fact within the whole range of society, assumes such a violent, glaring character, that a small section of the ruling class cuts itself adrift, and joins the revolutionary class, the class that holds the future in its hands. Just as, therefore, at an earlier period, a section of the nobility went over to the bourgeoisie, so now a portion of the bourgeoisie goes over to the proletariat, and in particular, a portion of the bourgeois ideologists, who have raised themselves to the level of comprehending theoretically the historical movement as a whole.

Of all the classes that stand face to face with the bourgeoisie today, the proletariat alone is a really revolutionary class. The other classes decay and finally disappear in the face of Modern Industry; the proletariat is its special and essential product. The lower middle class, the small manufacturer, the shopkeeper, the artisan, the peasant, all these fight against the bourgeoisie, to save from extinction their existence as fractions of the middle class. They are therefore not revolutionary, but conservative. Nay more, they are reactionary, for they try to roll back the wheel of history. If by chance they are revolutionary, they are so only in view of their impending transfer into the proletariat, they thus defend not their present, but their future interests, they desert their own standpoint to place themselves at that of the proletariat.

The "dangerous class," the social scum, that passively rotting mass thrown off by the lowest layers of old society, may, here and there, be swept into the movement by a proletarian revolution; its conditions of life, however, prepare it far more for the part of a bribed tool of reactionary intrigue.

In the conditions of the proletariat, those of old society at large are already virtually swamped. The proletarian is without property; his relation to his wife

273

and children has no longer anything in common with the bourgeois family-relations; modern industrial labor, modern subjection to capital, the same in England as in France, in America as in Germany, has stripped him of every trace of national character. Law, morality, religion, are to him so many bourgeois prejudices, behind which lurk in ambush just as many bourgeois interests.

All the preceding classes that got the upper hand, sought to fortify their already acquired status by subjecting society at large to their conditions of appropriation. The proletarians cannot become masters of the productive forces of society, except by abolishing their own previous mode of appropriation, and thereby also every other previous mode of appropriation. They have nothing of their own to secure and to fortify; their mission is to destroy all previous securities for, and insurances of, individual property.

All previous historical movements were movements of minorities, or in the interests of minorities. The proletarian movement is the self-conscious, independent movement of the immense majority, in the interests of the immense majority. The proletariat, the lowest stratum of our present society, cannot stir, cannot raise itself up, without the whole superincumbent strata of official society being sprung into the air.

Though not in substance, yet in form, the struggle of the proletariat with the bourgeoisie is at first a national struggle. The proletariat of each country must, of course, first of all settle matters with its own bourgeoisie.

In depicting the most general phases of the development of the proletariat, we traced the more or less veiled civil war, raging within existing society, up to the point where that war breaks out into open revolution, and where the violent overthrow of the bourgeoisie lays the foundation for the sway of the proletariat.

Hitherto, every form of society has been based, as we have already seen, on the antagonism of oppressing and oppressed classes. But in order to oppress a class, certain conditions must be assured to it under which it can, at least, continue its slavish existence. The serf, in the period of serfdom, raised himself to membership in the commune, just as the petty bourgeois, under the yoke of feudal absolutism, managed to develop into a bourgeois. The modern laborer, on the contrary, instead of rising with the progress of industry, sinks deeper and deeper below the conditions of existence of his own class. He becomes a pauper, and pauperism develops more rapidly than population and wealth. And here it becomes evident, that the bourgeoisie is unfit any longer to be the ruling class in society, and to impose its conditions of existence upon society as an over-riding law. It is unfit to rule because it is incompetent to assure an existence to its slave within his slavery, because it cannot help letting him sink into such a state, that it has to feed him, instead of being fed by him. Society can no longer live under this bourgeoisie, in other words, its existence is no longer compatible with society.

The essential condition for the existence, and for the sway of the bourgeois class, is the formation and augmentation of capital; the condition for capital is wage-labor. Wage-labor rests exclusively on competition between the laborers. The advance of industry, whose involuntary promoter is the bourgeoisie, replaces the isolation of the laborers, due to competition, by their revolutionary combination, due to association. The development of Modern Industry, therefore, cuts from under its feet the very foundation on which the bourgeoisie produces and appropriates products. What the bourgeoisie, therefore, produces, above all, is its own grave-diggers. Its fall and the victory of the proletariat are equally inevitable.

II. PROLETARIANS AND COMMUNISTS

In what relation do the Communists stand to the proletarians as a whole?

The Communists do not form a separate party opposed to other working-class parties.

They have no interests separate and apart from those of the proletariat as a whole.

They do not set up any sectarian principles of their own, by which to shape and mold the proletarian movement.

The Communists are distinguished from the other working-class parties by this only: (1) In the national struggles of the proletarians of the different countries, they point out and bring to the front the common interests of the entire proletariat, independently of all nationality. (2) In the various stages of development which the struggle of the working class against the bourgeoisie has to pass through, they always and everywhere represent the interests of the movement as a whole.

The Communists, therefore, are on the one hand, practically, the most advanced and resolute section of the working-class parties of every country, that section which pushes forward all others; on the other hand, theoretically, they have over the great mass of the proletariat the advantage of clearly understanding the line of march, the conditions, and the ultimate general results of the proletarian movement.

The immediate aim of the Communist is the same as that of all the other proletarian parties: formation of the proletariat into a class, overthrow of the bourgeois supremacy, conquest of political power by the proletariat.

The theoretical conclusions of the Communists are in no way based on ideas or principles that have been invented, or discovered, by this or that would-be universal reformer. They merely express, in general terms, actual relations springing from an existing class struggle, from a historical movement going on under our very eyes. The abolition of existing property relations is not at all a distinctive feature of Communism.

All property relations in the past have continually been subject to historical change consequent upon the change in historical conditions.

The French Revolution, for example, abolished feudal property in favor of bourgeois property.

The distinguishing feature of Communism is not the abolition of property generally, but the abolition of bourgeois property. But modern bourgeois private property is the final and most complete expression of the system of producing and appropriating products, that is based on class antagonisms, on the exploitation of the many by the few.

In this sense, the theory of the Communists may be summed up in the single sentence: Abolition of private property.

We Communists have been reproached with the desire of abolishing the right of personally acquiring property as the fruit of a man's own labor, which property is alleged to be the groundwork of all personal freedom, activity and independence.

Hard-won, self-acquired, self-earned property! Do you mean the property of the petty artisan and of the small peasant, a form of property that preceded the bourgeois form? There is no need to abolish that; the development of industry has to a great extent already destroyed it, and is still destroying it daily.

Or do you mean modern bourgeois private property?

But does wage-labor create any property for the laborer? Not a bit. It creates capital, i.e., that kind of property which exploits wage-labor, and which cannot increase except upon condition of begetting a new supply of wage-labor for fresh exploitation. Property, in its present form, is based on the antagonism of capital and wage-labor. Let us examine both sides of this antagonism.

To be a capitalist, is to have not only a purely personal, but a social status in production. Capital is a collective product, and only by the united action of many members, nay, in the last resort, only by the united action of all members of society, can it be set in motion.

Capital is, therefore, not a personal, it is a social power.

When, therefore, capital is converted into common property, into the property of all members of society, personal property is not thereby transformed into social property. It is only the social character of the property that is changed. It loses its class-character.

Let us now take wage-labor.

The average price of wage-labor is the minimum wage, i.e., that quantum of the means of subsistence, which is absolutely requisite in bare existence as a laborer. What, therefore, the wage-laborer appropriates by means of his labor, merely suffices to prolong and reproduce a bare existence. We by no means intend to abolish this personal appropriation of the products of labor, an appropriation that is made for the maintenance and reproduction of human life, and that leaves no surplus wherewith to command the labor of others. All that we want to do away with, is the miserable character of this appropriation, under which the laborer lives merely to increase capital, and is allowed to live only in so far as the interest of the ruling class requires it.

In bourgeois society, living labor is but a means to increase accumulated labor. In Communist society, accumulated labor is but a means to widen, to enrich, to promote the existence of the laborer.

In bourgeois society, therefore, the past dominates the present; in Communist society, the present dominates the past. In bourgeois society capital is independent and has individuality, while the living person is dependent and has no individuality.

And the abolition of this state of things is called by the bourgeois, abolition of individuality and freedom! And rightly so. The abolition of bourgeois individuality, bourgeois independence, and bourgeois freedom is undoubtedly aimed at.

By freedom is meant, under the present bourgeois conditions of production, free trade, free selling and buying.

But if selling and buying disappears, free selling and buying disappears also. This talk about free selling and buying, and all the other "brave words" of our bourgeoisie about freedom in general, have a meaning, if any, only in contrast with restricted selling and buying, with the fettered traders of the Middle Ages, but have no meaning when opposed to the Communistic abolition of buying and selling, of the bourgeois conditions of production, and of the bourgeoisie itself.

You are horrified at our intending to do away with private property. But in your existing society, private property is already done away with for nine-tenths of the population; its existence for the few is solely due to its non-existence in the hands of those nine-tenths. You reproach us, therefore, with intending to do away with a form of property, the necessary condition for whose existence is the non-existence of any property for the immense majority of society.

In one word, you reproach us with intending to do away with your property. Precisely so; that is just what we intend.

From the moment when labor can no longer be converted into capital, money, or rent, into a social power capable of being monopolized, i.e., from the moment when individual property can no longer be transformed into bourgeois property, into capital, from that moment, you say individuality vanishes.

You must, therefore, confess that by "individual" you mean no other person than the bourgeois, than the middle-class owner of property. This person must, indeed, be swept out of the way, and made impossible.

Communism deprives no man of the power to appropriate the products of society; all that it does is to deprive him of the power to subjugate the labor of others by means of such appropriation.

It has been objected that upon the abolition of private property all work will cease, and universal laziness will overtake us.

According to this, bourgeois society ought long ago to have gone to the dogs through sheer idleness; for those of its members who work, acquire nothing, and those who acquire anything, do not work. The whole of this objection is but another expression of the tautology: that there can no longer be any wage-labor when there is no longer any capital.

All objections urged against the Communistic mode of producing and appropriating material products, have, in the same way, been urged against the Communistic modes of producing and appropriating intellectual products. Just as, to the bourgeois, the disappearance of class property is the disappearance of production itself, so the disappearance of class culture is to him identical with the disappearance of all culture.

That culture, the loss of which he laments, is, for the enormous majority, a mere training to act as a machine.

But don't wrangle with us so long as you apply, to our intended abolition of bourgeois property, the standard of your bourgeois notions of freedom, culture, law, etc. Your very ideas are but the outgrowth of the conditions of your bourgeois production and bourgeois property, just as your jurisprudence is but the will of your class made into a law for all, a will, whose essential character and direction are determined by the economical conditions of existence of your class.

The selfish misconception that induces you to transform into eternal laws of nature and of reason, the social forms springing from your present mode of production and form of property—historical relations that rise and disappear in the progress of production—this misconception you share with every ruling class that has preceded you. What you see clearly in the case of ancient property, what you admit in the case of feudal property, you are of course forbidden to admit in the case of your own bourgeois form of property.

Abolition of the family! Even the most radical flare up at this infamous proposal of the Communists.

On what foundation is the present family, the bourgeois family, based? On capital, on private gain. In its completely developed form this family exists only among the bourgeoisie. But this state of things finds its complement in the practical absence of the family among the proletarians, and in public prostitution.

The bourgeois family will vanish as a matter of course when its complement vanishes, and both will vanish with the vanishing of capital.

Do you charge us with wanting to stop the exploitation of children by their parents? To this crime we plead guilty.

But, you will say, we destroy the most hallowed of relations, when we replace home education by social.

And your education! Is not that also social, and determined by the social conditions under which you educate, by the intervention, direct or indirect, of society, by means of schools, etc.? The Communists have not invented the intervention of society in education; they do but seek to alter the character of that intervention, and to rescue education from the influence of the ruling class.

The bourgeois clap-trap about the family and education, about the hallowed co-relation of parent and child, becomes all the more disgusting, the more, by the action of Modern Industry, all family ties among the proletarians are torn asunder, and their children transformed into simple articles of commerce and instruments of labor.

But you Communists would introduce community of women, screams the whole bourgeoisie in chorus.

The bourgeois sees in his wife a mere instrument of production. He hears that the instruments of production are to be exploited in common, and, naturally, can come to no other conclusion than that the lot of being common to all will likewise fall to the women.

He has not even a suspicion that the real point is to do away with the status of women as mere instruments of production.

For the rest, nothing is more ridiculous than the virtuous indignation of our bourgeois at the community of women which, they pretend, is to be openly and officially established by the Communists. The Communists have no need to introduce community of women; it has existed almost from time immemorial.

Our bourgeois, not content with having the wives and daughters of their proletarians at their disposal, not to speak of common prostitutes, take the greatest pleasure in seducing each other's wives.

Bourgeois marriage is in reality a system of wives in common and thus, at the most, what the Communists might possibly be reproached with, is that they desire to introduce, in substitution for a hypocritically concealed, an openly legalized community of women. For the rest, it is self-evident that the abolition of the present system of production must bring with it the abolition of the community of women springing from that system, i.e., of prostitution both public and private.

The Communists are further reproached with desiring to abolish countries and nationality.

The working men have no country. We cannot take from them what they have not got. Since the proletariat must first of all acquire political supremacy, must rise to be the leading class of the nation, must constitute itself the nation, it is, so far, itself national, though not in the bourgeois sense of the word.

National differences and antagonisms between peoples are daily more and more vanishing, owing to the development of the bourgeoisie, to freedom of commerce, to the world-market, to uniformity in the mode of production and in the conditions of life corresponding thereto.

The supremacy of the proletariat will cause them to vanish still faster. United action, of the leading civilized countries at least, is one of the first conditions for the emancipation of the proletariat.

In proportion as the exploitation of one individual by another is put an end to, the exploitation of one nation by another will also be put an end to. In proportion as the antagonism between classes within the nation vanishes, the hostility of one nation to another will come to an end.

The charges against Communism made from a religious, a philosophical, and, generally, from an ideological standpoint, are not deserving of serious examination.

Does it require deep intuition to comprehend that man's ideas, views and conceptions, in one word, man's consciousness, changes with every change in the conditions of his material existence, in his social relations and in his social life?

What else does the history of ideas prove, than that intellectual production changes its character in proportion as material production is changed? The ruling ideas of each age have ever been the ideas of its ruling class.

When people speak of ideas that revolutionize society, they do but express the fact, that within the old society, the elements of a new one have been created, and that the dissolution of the old ideas keeps even pace with the dissolution of the old conditions of existence.

When the ancient world was in its last throes, the ancient religions were overcome by Christianity. When Christian ideas succumbed in the 18th century to rationalist ideas, feudal society fought its death battle with the then revolutionary bourgeoisie. The ideas of religious liberty and freedom of conscience merely gave expression to the sway of free competition within the domain of knowledge.

"Undoubtedly," it will be said, "religious, moral, philosophical and juridical ideas have been modified in the course of historical development. But religion, morality philosophy, political science, and law, constantly survived this change."

"There are, besides, eternal truths, such as Freedom, Justice, etc. that are common to all states of society. But Communism abolishes eternal truths, it abolishes all religion, and all morality, instead of constituting them on a new basis; it therefore acts in contradiction to all past historical experience."

What does this accusation reduce itself to? The history of all past society has consisted in the development of class antagonisms, antagonisms that assumed different forms at different epochs.

But whatever form they may have taken, one fact is common to all past ages, viz., the exploitation of one part of society by the other. No wonder, then, that the social consciousness of past ages, despite all the multiplicity and variety it displays, moves within certain common forms, or general ideas, which cannot completely vanish except with the total disappearance of class antagonisms.

The Communist revolution is the most radical rupture with traditional property relations; no wonder that its development involves the most radical rupture with traditional ideas.

But let us have done with the bourgeois objections to Communism.

We have seen above, that the first step in the revolution by the working class, is to raise the proletariat to the position of ruling as to win the battle of democracy.

The proletariat will use its political supremacy to wrest, by degrees, all capital from the bourgeoisie, to centralize all instruments of production in the hands of the State, i.e., of the proletariat organized as the ruling class; and to increase the total of productive forces as rapidly as possible.

Of course, in the beginning, this cannot be effected except by means of despotic inroads on the rights of property, and on the conditions of bourgeois production; by means of measures, therefore, which appear economically insufficient and untenable, but which, in the course of the movement, outstrip themselves, necessitate further inroads upon the old social order, and are unavoidable as a means of entirely revolutionizing the mode of production.

These measures will of course be different in different countries.

Nevertheless in the most advanced countries, the following will be pretty generally applicable.

1. Abolition of property in land and application of all rents of land to public purposes.

2. A heavy progressive or graduated income tax.

3. Abolition of all right of inheritance.

4. Confiscation of the property of all emigrants and rebels.

5. Centralization of credit in the hands of the State, by means of a national bank with State capital and an exclusive monopoly.

6. Centralization of the means of communication and transport in the hands of the State.

7. Extension of factories and instruments of production owned by the State; the bringing into cultivation of waste-lands, and the improvement of the soil generally in accordance with a common plan.

8. Equal liability of all to labor. Establishment of industrial armies, especially for agriculture.

9. Combination of agriculture with manufacturing industries; gradual abolition of the distinction between town and country, by a more equable distribution of the population over the country.

10. Free education for all children in public schools.

    Abolition of children's factory labor in its present form.

    Combination of education with industrial production, &c., &c.

When, in the course of development, class distinctions have disappeared, and all production has been concentrated in the hands of a vast association of the whole nation, the public power will lose its political character. Political power, properly so called, is merely the organized power of one class for oppressing another. If the proletariat during its contest with the bourgeoisie is compelled, by the force of circumstances, to organize itself as a class, if, by means of a revolution, it makes itself the ruling class, and, as such, sweeps away by force the old conditions of production, then it will, along with these conditions, have swept away the conditions for the existence of class antagonisms and of classes generally, and will thereby have abolished its own supremacy as a class.

In place of the old bourgeois society, with its classes and class antagonisms, we shall have an association, in which the free development of each is the condition for the free development of all.

III. SOCIALIST AND COMMUNIST LITERATURE

1. REACTIONARY SOCIALISM

A. Feudal Socialism

Owing to their historical position, it became the vocation of the aristocracies of France and England to write pamphlets against modern bourgeois society. In the French revolution of July 1830, and in the English reform agitation, these aristocracies again succumbed to the hateful upstart. Thenceforth, a serious political contest was altogether out of the question. A literary battle alone remained possible. But even in the domain of literature the old cries of the restoration period had become impossible.

In order to arouse sympathy, the aristocracy were obliged to lose sight, apparently, of their own interests, and to formulate their indictment against the bourgeoisie in the interest of the exploited working class alone. Thus the aristocracy took their revenge by singing lampoons on their new master, and whispering in his ears sinister prophecies of coming catastrophe.

In this way arose Feudal Socialism: half lamentation, half lampoon; half echo of the past, half menace of the future; at times, by its bitter, witty and incisive criticism, striking the bourgeoisie to the very heart's core; but always ludicrous in its effect, through total incapacity to comprehend the march of modern history.

The aristocracy, in order to rally the people to them, waved the proletarian alms-bag in front for a banner. But the people, so often as it joined them, saw on their hindquarters the old feudal coats of arms, and deserted with loud and irreverent laughter.

One section of the French Legitimists and "Young England" exhibited this spectacle.

In pointing out that their mode of exploitation was different to that of the bourgeoisie, the feudalists forget that they exploited under circumstances and conditions that were quite different, and that are now antiquated. In showing that, under their rule, the modern proletariat never existed, they forget that the modern bourgeoisie is the necessary offspring of their own form of society.

For the rest, so little do they conceal the reactionary character of their criticism that their chief accusation against the bourgeoisie amounts to this, that under the bourgeois regime a class is being developed, which is destined to cut up root and branch the old order of society.

What they upbraid the bourgeoisie with is not so much that it creates a proletariat, as that it creates a revolutionary proletariat.

In political practice, therefore, they join in all coercive measures against the working class; and in ordinary life, despite their high-falutin phrases, they stoop to pick up the golden apples dropped from the tree of industry, and to barter truth, love, and honor for traffic in wool, beetroot-sugar, and potato spirits.

As the parson has ever gone hand in hand with the landlord, so has Clerical Socialism with Feudal Socialism.

Nothing is easier than to give Christian asceticism a Socialist tinge. Has not Christianity declaimed against private property, against marriage, against the State? Has it not preached in the place of these, charity and poverty, celibacy and mortification of the flesh, monastic life and Mother Church? Christian Socialism is but the holy water with which the priest consecrates the heart-burnings of the aristocrat.

B. Petty-Bourgeois Socialism

The feudal aristocracy was not the only class that was ruined by the bourgeoisie, not the only class whose conditions of existence pined and perished in the atmosphere of modern bourgeois society. The mediaeval burgesses and the small peasant proprietors were the precursors of the modern bourgeoisie. In those countries which are but little developed, industrially and commercially, these two classes still vegetate side by side with the rising bourgeoisie.

In countries where modern civilization has become fully developed, a new class of petty bourgeois has been formed, fluctuating between proletariat and bourgeoisie and ever renewing itself as a supplementary part of bourgeois society. The individual members of this class, however, are being constantly hurled down into the proletariat by the action of competition, and, as modern industry develops, they even see the moment approaching when they will completely disappear as an independent section of modern society, to be replaced, in manufactures, agriculture and commerce, by overlookers, bailiffs and shopmen.

In countries like France, where the peasants constitute far more than half of the population, it was natural that writers who sided with the proletariat against the bourgeoisie, should use, in their criticism of the bourgeois regime, the standard of the peasant and petty bourgeois, and from the standpoint of these intermediate classes should take up the cudgels for the working class. Thus arose petty-bourgeois Socialism. Sismondi was the head of this school, not only in France but also in England.

This school of Socialism dissected with great acuteness the contradictions in the conditions of modern production. It laid bare the hypocritical apologies of economists. It proved, incontrovertibly, the disastrous effects of machinery and division of labor; the concentration of capital and land in a few hands; overproduction and crises; it pointed out the inevitable ruin of the petty bourgeois and peasant, the misery of the proletariat, the anarchy in production, the crying inequalities in the distribution of wealth, the industrial war of extermination between nations, the dissolution of old moral bonds, of the old family relations, of the old nationalities.

In its positive aims, however, this form of Socialism aspires either to restoring the old means of production and of exchange, and with them the old property relations, and the old society, or to cramping the modern means of production and of exchange, within the framework of the old property relations that have been, and were bound to be, exploded by those means. In either case, it is both reactionary and Utopian.

Its last words are: corporate guilds for manufacture, patriarchal relations in agriculture.

Ultimately, when stubborn historical facts had dispersed all intoxicating effects of self-deception, this form of Socialism ended in a miserable fit of the blues.

C. German, or "True," Socialism

The Socialist and Communist literature of France, a literature that originated under the pressure of a bourgeoisie in power, and that was the expression of the struggle against this power, was introduced into Germany at a time when the bourgeoisie, in that country, had just begun its contest with feudal absolutism.

German philosophers, would-be philosophers, and beaux esprits, eagerly seized on this literature, only forgetting, that when these writings immigrated from France into Germany, French social conditions had not immigrated along with them. In contact with German social conditions, this French literature lost all its immediate practical significance, and assumed a purely literary aspect. Thus, to the German philosophers of the eighteenth century, the demands of the first French Revolution were nothing more than the demands of "Practical Reason" in general, and the utterance of the will of the revolutionary French bourgeoisie signified in their eyes the law of pure Will, of Will as it was bound to be, of true human Will generally.

The world of the German literate consisted solely in bringing the new French ideas into harmony with their ancient philosophical conscience, or rather, in annexing the French ideas without deserting their own philosophic point of view.

This annexation took place in the same way in which a foreign language is appropriated, namely, by translation.

It is well known how the monks wrote silly lives of Catholic Saints over the manuscripts on which the classical works of ancient heathendom had been written. The German literate reversed this process with the profane French literature. They wrote their philosophical nonsense beneath the French original. For instance, beneath the French criticism of the economic functions of money, they wrote "Alienation of Humanity," and beneath the French criticism of the bourgeois State they wrote "dethronement of the Category of the General," and so forth.

The introduction of these philosophical phrases at the back of the French historical criticisms they dubbed "Philosophy of Action," "True Socialism,"

"German Science of Socialism," "Philosophical Foundation of Socialism," and so on.

The French Socialist and Communist literature was thus completely emasculated. And, since it ceased in the hands of the German to express the struggle of one class with the other, he felt conscious of having overcome "French one-sidedness" and of representing, not true requirements, but the requirements of truth; not the interests of the proletariat, but the interests of Human Nature, of Man in general, who belongs to no class, has no reality, who exists only in the misty realm of philosophical fantasy.

This German Socialism, which took its schoolboy task so seriously and solemnly, and extolled its poor stock-in-trade in such mountebank fashion, meanwhile gradually lost its pedantic innocence.

The fight of the German, and especially, of the Prussian bourgeoisie, against feudal aristocracy and absolute monarchy, in other words, the liberal movement, became more earnest.

By this, the long wished-for opportunity was offered to "True" Socialism of confronting the political movement with the Socialist demands, of hurling the traditional anathemas against liberalism, against representative government, against bourgeois competition, bourgeois freedom of the press, bourgeois legislation, bourgeois liberty and equality, and of preaching to the masses that they had nothing to gain, and everything to lose, by this bourgeois movement. German Socialism forgot, in the nick of time, that the French criticism, whose silly echo it was, presupposed the existence of modern bourgeois society, with its corresponding economic conditions of existence, and the political constitution adapted thereto, the very things whose attainment was the object of the pending struggle in Germany.

To the absolute governments, with their following of parsons, professors, country squires and officials, it served as a welcome scarecrow against the threatening bourgeoisie.

It was a sweet finish after the bitter pills of floggings and bullets with which these same governments, just at that time, dosed the German work-ing-class risings.

While this "True" Socialism thus served the governments as a weapon for fighting the German bourgeoisie, it, at the same time, directly represented a reactionary interest, the interest of the German Philistines. In Germany the petty-bourgeois class, a relic of the sixteenth century, and since then con-stantly cropping up again under various forms, is the real social basis of the existing state of things.

To preserve this class is to preserve the existing state of things in Germany. The industrial and political supremacy of the bourgeoisie threatens it with certain destruction; on the one hand, from the concentration of capital; on the other, from the rise of a revolutionary proletariat. "True" Socialism ap-peared to kill these two birds with one stone. It spread like an epidemic.

The robe of speculative cobwebs, embroidered with flowers of rhetoric, steeped in the dew of sickly sentiment, this transcendental robe in which the German Socialists wrapped their sorry "eternal truths," all skin and bone, served to wonderfully increase the sale of their goods amongst such a public. And on its part, German Socialism recognized, more and more, its own call-ing as the bombastic representative of the petty-bourgeois Philistine.

It proclaimed the German nation to be the model nation, and the Ger-man petty Philistine to be the typical man. To every villainous meanness of this model man it gave a hidden, higher, Socialistic interpretation, the exact contrary of its real character. It went to the extreme length of directly opposing the "brutally destructive" tendency of Communism, and of pro-claiming its supreme and impartial contempt of all class struggles. With very few exceptions, all the so-called Socialist and Communist publications that now (1847) circulate in Germany belong to the domain of this foul and en-ervating literature.

2. CONSERVATIVE, OR BOURGEOIS, SOCIALISM

A part of the bourgeoisie is desirous of redressing social grievances, in order to secure the continued existence of bourgeois society.

To this section belong economists, philanthropists, humanitarians, improvers of the condition of the working class, organizers of charity, members of societies for the prevention of cruelty to animals, temperance fanatics, hole-and-corner reformers of every imaginable kind. This form of Socialism has, moreover, been worked out into complete systems.

We may cite Proudhon's *Philosophie de la Misere* as an example of this form.

The Socialistic bourgeois want all the advantages of modern social conditions without the struggles and dangers necessarily resulting therefrom. They desire the existing state of society minus its revolutionary and disintegrating elements. They wish for a bourgeoisie without a proletariat. The bourgeoisie naturally conceives the world in which it is supreme to be the best; and bourgeois Socialism develops this comfortable conception into various more or less complete systems. In requiring the proletariat to carry out such a system, and thereby to march straightway into the social New Jerusalem, it but requires in reality, that the proletariat should remain within the bounds of existing society, but should cast away all its hateful ideas concerning the bourgeoisie.

A second and more practical, but less systematic, form of this Socialism sought to depreciate every revolutionary movement in the eyes of the working class, by showing that no mere political reform, but only a change in the material conditions of existence, in economic relations, could be of any advantage to them. By changes in the material conditions of existence, this form of Socialism, however, by no means understands abolition of the bourgeois relations of production, an abolition that can be effected only by a revolution, but administrative reforms, based on the continued existence of these relations; reforms, therefore, that in no respect affect the relations between capital and labor, but, at the best, lessen the cost, and simplify the adminis-trative work, of bourgeois government.

Bourgeois Socialism attains adequate expression, when, and only when, it becomes a mere figure of speech.

Free trade: for the benefit of the working class. Protective duties: for the benefit of the working class. Prison Reform: for the benefit of the working class. This is the last word and the only seriously meant word of bourgeois Socialism.

It is summed up in the phrase: the bourgeois is a bourgeois—for the ben-efit of the working class.

3. CRITICAL-UTOPIAN SOCIALISM AND COMMUNISM

We do not here refer to that literature which, in every great modern revo-lution, has always given voice to the demands of the proletariat, such as the writings of Babeuf and others.

The first direct attempts of the proletariat to attain its own ends, made in times of universal excitement, when feudal society was being overthrown, these attempts necessarily failed, owing to the then undeveloped state of the proletariat, as well as to the absence of the economic conditions for its eman-cipation, conditions that had yet to be produced, and could be produced by the impending bourgeois epoch alone. The revolutionary literature that accompanied these first movements of the proletariat had necessarily a reac-tionary character. It inculcated universal asceticism and social levelling in its crudest form.

The Socialist and Communist systems properly so called, those of Saint-Simon, Fourier, Owen and others, spring into existence in the early undeveloped period, described above, of the struggle between proletariat and bourgeoisie (see Section 1. Bourgeois and Proletarians).

The founders of these systems see, indeed, the class antagonisms, as well as the action of the decomposing elements, in the prevailing form of society.

But the proletariat, as yet in its infancy, offers to them the spectacle of a class without any historical initiative or any independent political movement.

Since the development of class antagonism keeps even pace with the development of industry, the economic situation, as they find it, does not as yet offer to them the material conditions for the emancipation of the proletariat. They therefore search after a new social science, after new social laws, that are to create these conditions.

Historical action is to yield to their personal inventive action, historically created conditions of emancipation to fantastic ones, and the gradual, spontaneous class-organization of the proletariat to the organization of society specially contrived by these inventors. Future history resolves itself, in their eyes, into the propaganda and the practical carrying out of their social plans.

In the formation of their plans they are conscious of caring chiefly for the interests of the working class, as being the most suffering class. Only from the point of view of being the most suffering class does the proletariat exist for them.

The undeveloped state of the class struggle, as well as their own surroundings, causes Socialists of this kind to consider themselves far superior to all class antagonisms. They want to improve the condition of every member of society, even that of the most favored. Hence, they habitually appeal to society at large, without distinction of class; nay, by preference, to the ruling class. For how can people, when once they understand their system, fail to see in it the best possible plan of the best possible state of society?

Hence, they reject all political, and especially all revolutionary, action; they wish to attain their ends by peaceful means, and endeavor, by small experiments, necessarily doomed to failure, and by the force of example, to pave the way for the new social Gospel.

Such fantastic pictures of future society, painted at a time when the proletariat is still in a very undeveloped state and has but a fantastic conception of its own position correspond with the first instinctive yearnings of that class for a general reconstruction of society.

But these Socialist and Communist publications contain also a critical element. They attack every principle of existing society. Hence they are full of the most valuable materials for the enlightenment of the working class. The practical measures proposed in them—such as the abolition of the distinction between town and country, of the family, of the carrying on of industries for the account of private individuals, and of the wage system, the proclamation of social harmony, the conversion of the functions of the State into a mere superintendence of production, all these proposals, point solely to the disappearance of class antagonisms which were, at that time, only just cropping up, and which, in these publications, are recognized in their earliest, indistinct and undefined forms only. These proposals, therefore, are of a purely Utopian character.

The significance of Critical-Utopian Socialism and Communism bears an inverse relation to historical development. In proportion as the modern class struggle develops and takes definite shape, this fantastic standing apart from the contest, these fantastic attacks on it, lose all practical value and all theoretical justification. Therefore, although the originators of these systems were, in many respects, revolutionary, their disciples have, in every case, formed mere reactionary sects. They hold fast by the original views of their masters, in opposition to the progressive historical development of the proletariat. They, therefore, endeavor, and that consistently, to deaden the class struggle and to reconcile the class antagonisms. They still dream of experimental realization of their social Utopias, of founding isolated "phalansteres," of establishing "Home Colonies," of setting up a "Little Icaria"—duodecimo editions of the New Jerusalem—and to realize all these castles in the air, they are compelled to appeal to the feelings and purses of the bourgeois. By degrees they sink into the category of the reactionary conservative Socialists depicted above, differing from these only by more systematic pedantry, and by their fanatical and superstitious belief in the miraculous effects of their social science.

They, therefore, violently oppose all political action on the part of the working class; such action, according to them, can only result from blind unbelief in the new Gospel.

The Owenites in England, and the Fourierists in France, respectively, oppose the Chartists and the Reformists.

4. POSITION OF THE COMMUNISTS IN RELATION TO THE VARIOUS EXISTING OPPOSITION PARTIES

Section II has made clear the relations of the Communists to the existing working-class parties, such as the Chartists in England and the Agrarian Reformers in America.

The Communists fight for the attainment of the immediate aims, for the enforcement of the momentary interests of the working class; but in the movement of the present, they also represent and take care of the future of that movement. In France the Communists ally themselves with the So-cial-Democrats, against the conservative and radical bourgeoisie, reserving, however, the right to take up a critical position in regard to phrases and illusions traditionally handed down from the great Revolution.

In Switzerland they support the Radicals, without losing sight of the fact that this party consists of antagonistic elements, partly of Democratic Socialists, in the French sense, partly of radical bourgeois.

In Poland they support the party that insists on an agrarian revolution as the prime condition for national emancipation, that party which fomented the insurrection of Cracow in 1846.

In Germany they fight with the bourgeoisie whenever it acts in a revolutionary way, against the absolute monarchy, the feudal squirearchy, and the petty bourgeoisie.

But they never cease, for a single instant, to instill into the working class the clearest possible recognition of the hostile antagonism between bourgeoisie and proletariat, in order that the German workers may straightaway use, as so many weapons against the bourgeoisie, the social and political conditions that the bourgeoisie must necessarily introduce along with its supremacy, and in order that, after the fall of the reactionary classes in Germany, the fight against the bourgeoisie itself may immediately begin.

The Communists turn their attention chiefly to Germany because that country is on the eve of a bourgeois revolution that is bound to be carried out under more advanced conditions of European civilization, and with a much more developed proletariat, than that of England was in the seventeenth, and of France in the eighteenth century, and because the bourgeois revolution in Germany will be but the prelude to an immediately following proletarian revolution.

In short, the Communists everywhere support every revolutionary movement against the existing social and political order of things.

In all these movements they bring to the front, as the leading question in each, the property question, no matter what its degree of development at the time.

Finally, they labor everywhere for the union and agreement of the democratic parties of all countries.

The Communists disdain to conceal their views and aims. They openly declare that their ends can be attained only by the forcible overthrow of all existing social conditions. Let the ruling classes tremble at a Communistic revolution. The proletarians have nothing to lose but their chains. They have a world to win.

WORKING MEN OF ALL COUNTRIES, UNITE!

Appendix 2

The Death Toll of Communism

From The Black Book of Communism

According to *The Black Book of Communism*, the number of people killed by Communist governments in the 20th century amounts to more than 94 million. The statistics of victims include deaths through executions, man-made hunger, famine, war, deportations and forced labor. The breakdown of the number of deaths is given as follows:

65 million in the People's Republic of China

20 million in the Soviet Union

2 million in Cambodia

2 million in North Korea

1.7 million in Ethiopia

1.5 million in Afghanistan

1 million in the Eastern Bloc

1 million in Vietnam

150,000 in Latin America

10,000 deaths "resulting from actions of the international Communist movement and Communist parties not in power"

Appendix 3

A Marxist's Explanation of Dialectical Materialism

By Ian Birchall, a Marxist historian

This is excerpted from an article in the December 1982 issue of *Socialist Review*.

Lenin's Interest

Between September and December 1914, the months immediately following the outbreak of the First World War and the collapse into patriotic treachery of most of the international labor movement, Lenin spent a good deal of his time in the reading hall of the library at Berne, in Switzerland. He was reading Hegel's *Science of Logic*, and judged it sufficiently important to fill several school exercise-books with notes and comments. These notes take up some 160 pages of Lenin's *Collected Works*, Volume 38.

Lenin throughout his life insisted on the importance of Hegel and the dialectical method he initiated. He argued that it was impossible to understand Marx's *Capital* without having studied the whole of Hegel's *Logic*; and in his *Testament* notes that Bukharin has never understood the dialectic. The reason why it is so difficult to explain Lenin's interest in dialectics is that in the last fifty years the whole question got fouled up with a number of red herrings. Before any attempt to explain what dialectics *is*, it is necessary to clear the ground and explain what it *is not*.

Stalin's Quasi Religion

Firstly, Stalinism transformed Marxism from a critical revolutionary theory into the ideology of the Russian ruling class. As part of this process, Stalin invented something called "dialectical materialism" (snappily abbreviated to "Diamat"), a set of quasi-religious formulae. (Marx never used the term "dialectical materialism"; Stalin took it from Plekhanov.)

In the hands of a pig-ignorant bureaucrat like Stalin, dialectics was a gift for explaining away the barbarities of the new regime. In 1930 Stalin told the Sixteenth Party Congress:

> "We are for the withering away of the state, and yet we also believe in the proletarian dictatorship which represents the strongest and mightiest form of state power that has existed up to now. To keep on developing state power in order to prepare conditions for the withering away of state power—that is the Marxist formula. Is it 'contradictory'? Yes, 'contradictory.' But the contradiction is vital, and. wholly reflects the Marxist dialectic."

The Great Helmsman, Chairman Mao, added his contribution to the great tradition by inventing the concept of "non-antagonistic contradiction," as a nice way of saying "class collaboration" (the bourgeoisie are the class-enemy, but we won't fight them.)

Dialectics of Nature

The second problem that has dogged the argument is the famous debate about the "dialectics of nature." Engels was fond of illustrating his account of dialectics from quantity to quality by comparing it to the boiling or freezing or water; water gets progressively warmer or colder, then at a given point turns to ice or steam.

The Stalinists eagerly latched on to this method. The French philosopher Georges Politzer tells us that when a chicken comes out of an egg, it negates the egg; but then the chicken grows into a hen and negates itself. So here we have the "negation of the negation."

The trouble with all this is that it both oversimplifies and mystifies. Making a revolution is, after all, rather more complex than making a cup of tea—or even than breeding chickens. And for dialectics to claim to be rooted in the natural sciences allows it to bask in the reflected glory of "Science," thus fudging the issue of what its true status is.

The question of the "dialectics of nature" must be handled carefully. In his last year Engels, a keen but amateur student of natural science, wrote extensive notes on dialectics in relation to various branches of science. Since he rightly gave priority to working on Marx's unfinished *Capital*, Engels never completed these notes for publication. The posthumous volume that appeared under the title *Dialectics of Nature* should be seen as no more and no less than the interesting but fragmentary speculations of a gifted thinker.

Since Engels' time, many notable scientists, from J.D. Bernal to the French physicist J.P. Vigier, have claimed that the dialectical method has helped them in their work. It would be foolish to claim that dialectics has no place in the study of natural science—but equally dangerous to claim that the validity of dialectics as a method of social enquiry depends on the correctness or incorrectness of a theory about nature.

After all, it is conservative, bourgeois thought that tries to see society as subject to the same laws as nature. We've all heard of the economic "climate," something unchangeable, for which no one is responsible. As Marx, quoting Vico, points out, "human history differs from natural history in this, that we have made the former, but not the latter." To derive the laws of dialectics from inanimate nature leads to denying the role of human agency in the historical process.

From Plato to Hegel

What, then, is dialectics? The term was first used by the Greek philosopher, Plato. For him it meant the process by which pure thought advances towards the achievement of coherent knowledge. Over two thousand years later, Hegel took up the term to refer to the movement of ideas which, for him, was the driving force of human history. For Marx and Engels, dialectics came to be the processes by which human history itself developed.

Since Marx's day, many people have tried to codify dialectics into a set of laws. However, no two seem to agree as to what the laws are, nor even whether there are three or four of them. Dialectics is in fact an extraordinarily slippery subject; attempts to explain it almost always end up in either incomprehensible jargon or banal platitudes.

So why bother? It is very easy to sympathize with socialists who say they are far too busy with the struggle to spend time on philosophy, and that they will rely simply on common sense. But unfortunately socialists cannot rely on common sense.

For common sense is the ideas shared by most people. And as Marx pointed out: "The ideas of the ruling class are in every epoch the ruling ideas." Most people trust appearances. For thousands of years it was common sense that the sun went round the earth. Today, Stalinists and Free-World fanatics will agree that it is obvious that Russia and the United States have totally different social systems. Only a study in depth will reveal that both are governed by the same laws. It is the common-sense view of our society that capitalism is a fair system in which everyone is free. It is precisely our job to undermine that common sense.

The Point is to Change the World

Dialectics, then, is the study of how things change. The imperative underlying all dialectical thought is Marx's eleventh thesis on Feuerbach: "The philosophers have only *interpreted* the world, in various ways; the point, however, is to *change* it." Or, as Engels was to put it:

> "Just as the bourgeoisie by large-scale industry, competition and the world market dissolves in practice all stable time-honored institutions, so this dialectical philosophy dissolves all conceptions of final, absolute truth and of absolute states of humanity corresponding to it. For it (dialectical philosophy) nothing is final, absolute, sacred. It reveals the transitory character of everything and in everything; nothing can endure before it except the uninterrupted process of becoming and passing away, of endless ascendancy from the lower to the higher."

This implies the need for a theory of history. There are, of course, a good number of theories of history already available, both in elaborated form, and embodied in the attitudes held by most people. Basically, they can be summed up under three headings: "You can't really change things"; "You can't stop Progress"; and "Things ain't what they used to be." All of these are fundamentally reactionary. There is nothing progressive about "Progress," as should be obvious in an age when millions of people are being thrown out of their jobs by machines. So revolutionary socialism needs an alternative view of history.

Hegel's Problem

And this is where Hegel comes in. Hegel (1770–1831) was one of a group of German philosophers who lived through the period of the French Revolution. These philosophers had a problem. They were greatly inspired by the Revolution, but they lived in a country which was far less socially developed than France. They couldn't mobilize the masses to overthrow the kings, for there were no masses to mobilize. So they made revolution inside their own heads, translating the real changes of the French Revolution into philosophical abstractions.

What Hegel tried to show was that history was not a series of accidents but had a logic running through it. As he put it: "All that is real is rational; and all that is rational is real." Now, as Engels pointed out, this is a double-edged formulation. On the one hand it can be used to defend the *status quo*; but on the other it can be used to justify the forcible overthrow of that *status quo*. Hence the followers of Hegel rapidly split into left and right wings. For Marx and Engels the important thing was to reintegrate Hegel's insights into a materialist view of history. As Engels put it, Hegel's dialectic was standing on its head and had to be put back on its feet.

One of the key categories that Marx takes from Hegel is that of totality. As the great Hungarian Marxist Georg Lukács wrote (in the days before he became a Stalinist hack):

> "It is not the primacy of economic motives in historical explanation that constitutes the decisive difference between Marxism and bourgeois thought, but the point of view of totality. The category of totality, the all-pervasive supremacy of the whole over the parts is the essence of the method which Marx took over from Hegel ..."

As Lukács pointed out, bourgeois thought sees the organization of social and economic life from the standpoint of competing capitalists, and hence cannot see It as a whole. Moreover, bourgeois ideology tries to force this fragmented view on the rest of us, precisely because it mystifies the process of change.

So, rather than the whole being a simple sum of its parts, the parts can be understood only in the context of the whole. As Lenin points out, a hand is only really a hand if it is part of a body. Likewise, the working class is not produced by simply adding up individual workers. A worker is a worker only if she or he is part of the working class. (Hence the bourgeois enthusiasm for secret ballots, which add up individuals rather than taking the class as a collective.)

Similarly, failure to see every process as part of a totality leads to political errors in the movement. Trade union struggle is important, but if we fail to see it as part of the totality, we lapse into "economism": Building the party is vital, but detached from the totality [it] leads to sectarianism, and so on.

Contradictions

Now, if human society is perceived as a whole, the agency of change must be inside that whole. It cannot be something "outside," like God, or a benevolent elite seen as standing outside society.

For once, an analogy with the natural sciences may be permissible. For many centuries it was assumed that the natural state of matter was immobility. This left an enormous problem—what made things move? One of the most intelligent thinkers of European Middle Ages, Dante, could find no other explanation of how the sun, moon and stars moved than to assume that they were being pushed by angels. But once it is understood that motion is the natural state of matter, then the problem is transformed.

It was this question that Marx confronted in his *Third Thesis on Feuerbach*, one of the most profound passages he ever wrote:

"The materialist doctrine that men are products of circumstances and upbringing, and that, therefore, changed men are products of other circumstances and changed upbringing, forgets that it is men that change circumstances and that the educator himself needs educating. Hence, this doctrine necessarily arrives at dividing society into two parts, of which one is superior to society."

In other words, if we see society as a single whole, the dynamic for change must be contradictions within that single whole. The shortest, but probably the most accurate, definition of dialectics I know is Raya Dunayevskaya's "development through contradiction."

Thus Hegel insists that "Contradiction is the very moving principle of the world." Of course, to identify contradiction as the dynamic of change is only the beginning of the problem. Marx went on to spend the remaining thirty-eight years of his life studying the specific contradictions of capitalist society—capital and labor, use value and exchange value, and so on.

This argument also enables us to avoid another stumbling-block of bourgeois philosophy, the relation of "is" and "ought." Bourgeois philosophy denies that we can ever get logically from "is" to "ought," from statements of fact to statements of value. But if society is transformed by contradictions internal to it, then it is no use looking for change unless that change can be identified with an agency already present in the social system. Likewise, it is no good trying to prefigure socialism on the basis of moral ideas. Capitalism will be destroyed only by the existing working class, with all its flaws and weaknesses. In Lenin's words: "We have to build socialism with people who have been thoroughly spoiled by capitalism."

A World of Processes

As a result, in Engels' words, the dialectical approach means that "the world is not to be comprehended as a complex of ready-made *things*, but as a complex of *processes*." This is crucial for an understanding of the historical role of classes. In looking at any class's place in history, we have to consider it, not in terms of its actual state at a given moment in time, but in terms of its potential for development. In Marx's words:

> "The question is not what goal is *envisaged* for the time being by this or that member of the proletariat, or even by the proletariat as a whole. The question is *what is the proletariat* and what course of action will it be forced historically to take in conformity with its own *nature*."

In the light of what has been said so far, Trotsky's theory of Permanent Revolution is one of the supreme examples of the application of the dialectical method. Firstly, Trotsky stresses that we must see the world as a single totality, and not as a collection of separate nation-states, each with its own history of class development. Secondly, in looking at the role of the working class, in the coming Russian Revolution, Trotsky argues that we must go beyond the facts, such as the small size of the working class (smaller than in many Third World countries today) and its low level of organization compared with Western Europe and focus instead on the potential historical role of the class.

On the basis of the foregoing it is possible to see how the dialectical method can enable us to overcome some of the dilemmas of bourgeois thought.

Firstly, the false alternative which bourgeois critics of Marxism often throw up: is Marxism a "science" or a moral critique of society. As Lukács points out in his essay on *The Marxism of Rosa Luxemburg*, this is a problem only if we see society as something outside ourselves, like the weather.

Ends and Means

If we do, then there are two alternatives: Either we look for technical means of manipulating immutable laws, or we can take a purely inward-directed moral attitude. Thus if we can't stop it raining, we can either respond technically (by using an umbrella) or morally (by deciding rain is good for us). But if we see society as a totality, then the false dichotomy evaporates; the historical process is not governed by immutable laws independent of us, but our actions are precisely part of that process. In the words of the old Sixties slogan: "If you're not part of the solution, you must be part of the problem."

Secondly, the relation between knowledge and action. Hegel tells the story of a philosopher who made the "wise resolution ... not to venture into the water until he had learned to swim." Once again, the dialectical approach sees this as a false dichotomy. The working class in particular is deprived of knowledge by capitalist society. It cannot educate itself before fighting for power. Even the cadre of the revolutionary party cannot be educated in advance of the struggle. Knowledge is achieved only in the course of participation in revolutionary practice.

Thirdly, there is the age-old problem of ends and means. Once again, the way the question is normally posed ("Does the end justify the means?") suggests that the two can be separated and balanced against each other. Discussing this question in *Their Morals and Ours*, Trotsky quotes a passage from a play by Ferdinand Lassalle:

"Show not the *goal*
But show also the *path*. So closely interwoven
Are path and goal that each with other

Ever changes, and other *paths* forthwith
Another *goal* set up."

Ends and means cannot be separated, for both are part of the same process. Thus, for example, the ultimate reason why there can be no parliamentary road to socialism is that socialism is, by definition, the self-emancipation of working people, and one cannot delegate one's own emancipation to a parliamentary representative.

Finally, a few words on two of the famous laws of dialectics.

Quantity to Quality

Firstly, the transition from quantity to quality. It was argued above that boiling kettles don't have much to do with revolution. Nonetheless, the distinction between quantitative and qualitative change is an important one for understanding the process of historical development. Just because history is driven along by contradictions, its progress is not smooth and in a straight line, but rather through sudden jolts and upheavals. Just because society is a totality, it can't be changed bit by bit. As R.H. Tawney pointed out, you can't skin a tiger claw by claw; you must do it in one go, or you will be the victim.

The same thing applies to the progress of revolutionary organizations. These too do not grow in a smooth upward ascent. On the contrary, they stagnate or even decline for years, and then at a moment of crisis expand rapidly. But it is no good simply waiting for the qualitative leap. It is slow quantitative growth that decides whether the qualitative leap will be possible. Thus, at the beginning of 1968, the International Socialists (forerunners of the SWP) had some 450 members. During the massive upheavals of that year we grew to one thousand. But if we had had only two hundred at the start of the year, it is quite probable we should have been too thinly spread to intervene anywhere, and we might have come out of the year no bigger than we began it.

Negation of Negation

Secondly, the negation of the negation. In chapter XXXII of the first volume of *Capital*, Marx describes how the growth of capitalist property destroys individual private property and replaces it by a more developed form of co-operative labor. But at the same time capitalist exploitation produces a discontented working class which will eventually destroy the whole system.

> "The capitalist mode of appropriation, the result of the capitalist mode of production, produces capitalist private property. This is the first negation of individual private property, as founded on the labor of the proprietor. But, capitalist production begets, with the inexorability of a law of Nature, its own negation. It is the negation of negation. This does not re-establish private property for the producer, but gives him individual property based on the acquisitions of the capitalist era; *i.e.* on co-operation and the possession in common of the land and of the means of production."

Abolition of the Working Class

To this Marx might have added another dialectical twist. For when the working class destroys capitalism, the source of its exploitation, it also negates itself. The aim of socialist revolution is not the triumph of the working class, but its abolition.

This, incidentally, is an easily comprehensible proposition to most workers, who didn't choose to be members of the working class and would be quite happy to change their status. It is, however, quite incomprehensible to the bureaucracy of the Labor movement whose whole status as mediators depends on the continued existence of an exploited class and hence of exploitation.

To conclude: dialectics is not a set of "laws" independent of human will. It is simply a means of describing how human beings make their own history. In Marx's words:

> "History does nothing; it does not possess immense riches, it does not fight

battles. It is mean, real living men, who do all this, who possess things and fight battles. It is not 'history' which uses men as a means of achieving—as if it were an individual person—its own ends. History is nothing but the activity of men in pursuit of their ends."

Appendix 4

The Genesis Account Of Eden and the Fall

From the Revised Standard Version of the Bible

Relevant Passages:

Chapter 1: Human beings are created in the image of God

²⁶Then God said, "Let us make man in our image, after our likeness; and let them have dominion over the fish of the sea, and over the birds of the air, and over the cattle, and over all the earth, and over every creeping thing that creeps upon the earth." ²⁷So God created man in his own image, in the image of God he created him; male and female he created them. ²⁸And God blessed them, and God said to them, "Be fruitful and multiply, and fill the earth and subdue it; and have dominion over the fish of the sea and over the birds of the air and over every living thing that moves upon the earth." ²⁹And God said, "Behold, I have given you every plant yielding seed which is upon the face of all the earth, and every tree with seed in its fruit; you shall have them for food. ³⁰And to every beast of the earth, and to every bird of the air, and to everything that creeps on the earth, everything that has the breath of life, I have given every green plant for food." And it was so. ³¹And God saw everything that he had made, and behold, it was very good. And there was evening and there was morning, a sixth day.

CHAPTER 2: Adam and Eve are created innocent

So it reads: [7]then the Lord God formed man of dust from the ground, and breathed into his nostrils the breath of life; and man became a living being. [8]And the Lord God planted a garden in Eden, in the east; and there he put the man whom he had formed. [9]And out of the ground the Lord God made to grow every tree that is pleasant to the sight and good for food, the tree of life also in the midst of the garden, and the tree of the knowledge of good and evil.

[15]The Lord God took the man and put him in the garden of Eden to till it and keep it. [16]And the Lord God commanded the man, saying, "You may freely eat of every tree of the garden; [17]but of the tree of the knowledge of good and evil you shall not eat, for in the day that you eat of it you shall die."

[18]Then the Lord God said, "It is not good that the man should be alone; I will make him a helper fit for him." [19]So out of the ground the Lord God formed every beast of the field and every bird of the air, and brought them to the man to see what he would call them; and whatever the man called every living creature, that was its name. [20]The man gave names to all cattle, and to the birds of the air, and to every beast of the field; but for the man there was not found a helper fit for him. [21]So the Lord God caused a deep sleep to fall upon the man, and while he slept took one of his ribs and closed up its place with flesh; [22]and the rib which the Lord God had taken from the man he made into a woman and brought her to the man. [23]Then the man said,

"This at last is bone of my bones
and flesh of my flesh;
she shall be called Woman,
because she was taken out of Man."

[24]Therefore a man leaves his father and his mother and cleaves to his wife, and they become one flesh. [25]And the man and his wife were both naked, and were not ashamed.

Chapter 3: The Fall of Adam and Eve

[1]Now the serpent was more subtle than any other wild creature that the Lord God had made. He said to the woman, "Did God say, 'You shall not eat of any tree of the garden'?" [2]And the woman said to the serpent, "We may eat of the fruit of the trees of the garden; [3]but God said, 'You shall not eat of the fruit of the tree which is in the midst of the garden, neither shall you touch it, lest you die.'" [4]But the serpent said to the woman, "You will not die. [5]For God knows that when you eat of it your eyes will be opened, and you will be like God, knowing good and evil." [6]So when the woman saw that the tree was good for food, and that it was a delight to the eyes, and that the tree was to be desired to make one wise, she took of its fruit and ate; and she also gave some to her husband, and he ate. [7]Then the eyes of both were opened, and they knew that they were naked; and they sewed fig leaves together and made themselves aprons.

[8]And they heard the sound of the Lord God walking in the garden in the cool of the day, and the man and his wife hid themselves from the presence of the Lord God among the trees of the garden. [9]But the Lord God called to the man, and said to him, "Where are you?" [10]And he said, "I heard the sound of thee in the garden, and I was afraid, because I was naked; and I hid myself." [11]He said, "Who told you that you were naked? Have you eaten of the tree of which I commanded you not to eat?" [12]The man said, "The woman whom thou gavest to be with me, she gave me fruit of the tree, and I ate." [13]Then the Lord God said to the woman, "What is this that you have done?" The woman said, "The serpent beguiled me, and I ate." [14]The Lord God said to the serpent,

"Because you have done this,
   cursed are you above all cattle,
   and above all wild animals;
upon your belly you shall go,
   and dust you shall eat
   all the days of your life.
[15]I will put enmity between you and the woman,
   and between your seed and her seed;

he shall bruise your head,
> and you shall bruise his heel."

[16]To the woman he said,

"I will greatly multiply your pain in childbearing;
> in pain you shall bring forth children,

yet your desire shall be for your husband,
> and he shall rule over you."

[17]And to Adam he said,

"Because you have listened to the voice of your wife,
> and have eaten of the tree

of which I commanded you,
> 'You shall not eat of it,'

cursed is the ground because of you;
> in toil you shall eat of it all the days of your life;

[18]thorns and thistles it shall bring forth to you;
> and you shall eat the plants of the field.

[19]In the sweat of your face
> you shall eat bread

till you return to the ground,
> for out of it you were taken;

you are dust,
> and to dust you shall return."

[20]The man called his wife's name Eve, because she was the mother of all living. [21]And the Lord God made for Adam and for his wife garments of skins, and clothed them.

[22]Then the Lord God said, "Behold, the man has become like one of us, knowing good and evil; and now, lest he put forth his hand and take also of the tree of life, and eat, and live for ever"—[23] therefore the Lord God sent him forth from the garden of Eden, to till the ground from which he was taken. [24]He drove out the man; and at the east of the garden of Eden he placed the cherubim, and a flaming sword which turned every way, to guard the way to the tree of life.

Chapter 4: Cain murders Abel

[1]Now Adam knew Eve his wife, and she conceived and bore Cain, saying, "I have gotten a man with the help of the Lord." [2]And again, she bore his brother Abel. Now Abel was a keeper of sheep, and Cain a tiller of the ground. [3]In the course of time Cain brought to the Lord an offering of the fruit of the ground, [4]and Abel brought of the firstlings of his flock and of their fat portions. And the Lord had regard for Abel and his offering, [5]but for Cain and his offering he had no regard. So Cain was very angry, and his countenance fell. [6]The Lord said to Cain, "Why are you angry, and why has your countenance fallen? [7]If you do well, will you not be accepted? And if you do not do well, sin is couching at the door; its desire is for you, but you must master it."

[8]Cain said to Abel his brother, "Let us go out to the field." And when they were in the field, Cain rose up against his brother Abel, and killed him. [9]Then the Lord said to Cain, "Where is Abel your brother?" He said, "I do not know; am I my brother's keeper?" [10]And the Lord said, "What have you done? The voice of your brother's blood is crying to me from the ground. [11]And now you are cursed from the ground, which has opened its mouth to receive your brother's blood from your hand. [12]When you till the ground, it shall no longer yield to you its strength; you shall be a fugitive and a wanderer on the earth." [13]Cain said to the Lord, "My punishment is greater than I can bear. [14]Behold, thou hast driven me this day away from the ground; and from thy face I shall be hidden; and I shall be a fugitive and a wanderer on the earth, and whoever finds me will slay me." [15]Then the Lord said to him, "Not so! If any one slays Cain, vengeance shall be taken on him sevenfold." And the Lord put a mark on Cain, lest any who came upon him should kill him.

Appendix 5

The Cain-Abel Paradigm in Old Testament History

The stories of the Old Testament in the Bible take on a whole new meaning when looked at through the prism of the Cain-Abel paradigm. From this perspective, there is a law of restoration (salvation) at work that governs the progress humanity makes towards the desired destination: men and women achieving the state of purity and oneness with the Creator that was lost in the fall. The working of this law translates into a pattern of restoration. In this appendix we examine that law in some detail, and then apply it to the history of restoration described in the Bible.

Why is the Biblical account important? We contend that while all people are important in the eyes of the Creator, for the purposes of restoration there is a central providence. In other words, in the same way that humanity originated in one family, so too the restoration of humanity begins in one family and then expands through stages to encompass the whole world. The Old Testament focuses on the stories of the individuals, families, tribes and nations chosen to play a part in this central providence. As we will show, the Cain-Abel paradigm plays out from the individual level to the global level through a series of successes achieved when Cain and Abel unite on Abel's terms. This process is prolonged when Cain wins out over Abel, in which case conditions have to be repeated by new representatives of Cain and Abel.

The Pattern of Restoration

Cain-type and Abel-type people are all children of God and loved by the Creator, but they have different functions in the providence, which unfolds in the real world of two dominions: the original world of good created by God and the world of Satan's dominion created by Lucifer's disobedience. Fallen humanity is trapped in a midway position between these two dominions. As the Creator, God has an eternal claim on all people. But because Adam and Eve freely chose to disobey God and follow Lucifer, Satan has a claim on them as well, albeit a claim that can be settled by us, as we explain below. Thus every person experiences struggles between these two influences that each seek exclusive dominion over his or her life.

Saint Paul described this inner struggle as a Christian:

> So I find it to be a law that when I want to do right, evil lies close at hand. For I delight in the law of God, in my inmost self, but I see in my members another law at war with the law of my mind and making me captive to the law of sin which dwells in my members. Wretched man that I am! Who will deliver me from this body of death? Thanks be to God through Jesus Christ our Lord! So then, I of myself serve the law of God with my mind, but with my flesh I serve the law of sin. (Romans 7:21-25)

As the first fruit of Adam and Eve's love under the influence of Lucifer, Cain was claimed by Satan and came to represent evil. Satan's claim was strengthened by the fact that Eve's first relationship of love had been with Lucifer, not Adam. This meant that God could then claim Abel as the representative of good. Thus the fundamental pattern for the Cain-Abel paradigm was established in which Cain, the older son, represented Satan's dominion and Abel, the second son, represented God's dominion. In other words, "Abel" means the person, family, tribe, nation or ideology that is relatively closer to God than is "Cain". God uses Abel's relatively better and more faithful nature to win Cain away from Satan so that they can both ultimately be reunited with their Creator. In this way, the relatively superior moral standard of Abel is used to elevate the overall standard of human morality, paving the way for the eventual appearance of an absolute standard good as embodied in a perfected Adam, a title belonging to Jesus.

God's purpose is to rescue all humanity, all the children of the loving Creator, by separating them from Satan's dominion. This is the meaning of salvation or restoration. However, because of free will, this separation from Satan can only be achieved through the cooperation of human beings who have to fulfill their own portion of responsibility, as explained in Chapter 2. Put another way, to end Satan's dominion, people must choose on their own to leave Satan for God. (It is the struggle to do this that Paul describes above.) Under God's dominion, we can be restored to God's original, sinless ideal for men and women and be free of Satanic influence. How we can accomplish this follows.

Restoration Through Indemnity

We cannot leave Satan's dominion by our own efforts alone. After all, one can't clean dirty laundry with dirty water. Satan can always make claims on us through our fallen nature, which we inherited from the original sin committed by Adam and Eve, a sexual sin that was the culmination of a process through which Lucifer became increasingly jealous and resentful towards Adam and then disobeyed God. The providence of restoration provides a way for us to separate from Satan's dominion by fulfilling commitments of faith (prayer, meditation, fasting, study of scriptures) and accomplishing symbolic or representative tasks that translate our faith into action through service to others on behalf of the providence. The first commitments establish a conditional demonstration of resolve to return to oneness with God. The subsequent accomplishments establish a conditional rejection of Satan and willingness to sacrifice through service to others in order to separate from his dominion.

A helpful way to understand this is to think of conditions as the price fallen people must pay to become free from Satan, to pay off his claim. When we fulfill the necessary conditions, God can accept us as conditionally separated from Satan and can grant us Divine blessings. If we fail to fulfill necessary conditions, Satan can renew his claim on us, and restoration is postponed until new conditions can be set. These conditions can be seen, then, as a form of payment, or indemnity, that fallen people must make through commitments of faith and suffering. It should be noted that indemnity conditions are required of us by Satan—not by God—in exchange for our freedom from his cruel dominion. In history, these conditions have been made voluntarily, through prayer, fasting and service, or involuntarily through suffering and penance. (Another, little-used word for indemnity is assythment.) Indemnity can be paid for oneself or for others.

As evidenced in the history of restoration, when "Abel" fulfills an indemnity condition, he receives God's blessing and the providence advances to the next stage. However, when Abel fails to fulfill an indemnity condition, Satan claims that person and unleashes torment and suffering on them that is far greater than the original condition. Furthermore, the next time a condition has to be met, it is much more difficult. This explains the seemingly interminable delays in the progress of the restoration providence over the course of millennia.

God does not preempt the Divine laws of indemnity and restoration because that would violate the most basic Divine principle of human existence: men and women have to fulfill their individual portions of responsibility. Thus as frustrating as it is to see evil rampant in the world, it will only come to an end when, with the help of our Creator, we reject it and choose good instead.

Significant People, Conditions and Time Periods

In the restoration providence, indemnity conditions are fulfilled by chosen people completing specific tasks in specific time periods. In the broadest sense, we are all part of that providence and are all called to make indemnity conditions to restore ourselves, our families, our nations and the world. But, as indicated above, there is also always a central providence that ultimately impacts all of us. The Old Testament is an account of that central providence to restore Adam's family up to the arrival of Jesus. It is full of significant people who are tasked with fulfilling specific conditions in specific time periods. This is not the place to examine these in detail but suffice it to say here that there is indeed profound meaning behind the stories of chosen individuals and the efforts they made and suffering they faced to advance the providence.

The basis for significant numbers in the providence can be found in the very nature and structure of the created world, in which the trinity of Creator, subject and object form the foundation for existence and multiplication: Three represents the number necessary for creation and existence and four the number for multiplication of existence. (Subject and object are the two essential elements of all beings, as explained in Chapter 2.) Three also represents the stages of growth, from foundation through a growing period to completion. Three and four combine to make the significant number seven, and three multiplied by four yields the significant number twelve. Thus these are the 'prime numbers' of restoration. Our lives are ordered accordingly. Our days are comprised of two twelve-hour periods, our weeks of seven days and our years of twelve months.

Here are some examples of their use in the Bible. Three: the trinity of God, Adam and Eve; the trinity of God, Jesus and the Holy Spirit; the three key children in the providential families (Cain, Abel and Seth; Shem, Ham and Japheth); the three key generations of Abraham's family; the three types of animals Abraham sacrificed (heifer, goats, turtle doves); the three main disciples of Jesus (Peter, James and John); and Jesus' three days in the tomb. Four: God, subject, object, new existence; forty-day flood; 400 years of slavery in Egypt; three forty-year periods in Moses' life; Moses' two forty-day fasts on Mount Sinai; the forty years the Israelites wandered in the wilderness; the 400 years of Judges, the 400 years of Divided Kingdoms; Jesus' forty-day fast. Seven: days in the week; Jacob's course in Haran (3 x 7 years); the Babylonian exile (7 x 10 years), which was repeated symbolically in the seventy year exile of the Papacy in Avignon. Twelve: the number of Jacob's sons; the number of the tribes of Israel; the number of Ishmael's sons; the number of Jesus' disciples; the number of gates into heaven.

The periods of indemnity fall into a pattern that can be seen repeating in history. In particular, using Biblical chronologies, the first two millennia stretch from Adam's family to Abraham's and the next two millennia from Abraham to Jesus. From this point history reveals yet a third set of parallel developments unfolding in the two millennia from Jesus to the present. (These parallels of providential history are summarized in a chart in Appendix 25, p469.)

Adam's Family

In the Old Testament, restoration began in Adam's family. When Cain killed Abel, the fall of Adam's entire family was complete. The descendants of Adam and Eve lived in the ignorance of profound alienation from God. After murdering his brother, Cain was banished by God. Seth, the third son, was then chosen to establish a new lineage in which the Cain-Abel relationship could be restored and a new Adam and Eve could appear. It was from Seth's lineage that eventually Noah's family was chosen to replace Adam's.

Noah's Family

Resembling Adam's family, Noah's family had eight key members: Noah and his wife in the place of Adam and Eve; Shem, Ham and Japheth with their wives in the place of Cain, Abel and Seth with their wives. Noah was called by God to establish a condition to separate his family from the fallen world by building an Ark, which would save them when a flood inundated the earth. In the pattern of the first family, the second son, Ham, was destined for Abel's position and mission, but failed in a test of faith, angering Noah and causing the loss of this opportunity to restore the Cain-Abel relationship and Adam's family. Consequently, because Satan claimed Ham, God could claim Shem. It was out of Shem's lineage that God would raise up Abraham's family to restore the families of Adam and Noah.

Abraham's Family

Abraham was called to leave his Chaldean home in Ur, to separate from the fallen world in preparation for his mission. He traveled north to Haran, where he was later told to go west to Canaan. As he sought a place of settlement in this new land, he and his wife Sarah were tested. In Egypt, Abraham was afraid that Pharaoh would have him killed and take his beautiful wife, Sarah, for himself. So Abraham told her to say that she was his sister. Pharaoh did take Sarah, but when his household consequently suffered plagues he realized who she really was and returned her to Abraham. The meaning of these events is that Pharaoh represented Lucifer in relation to Abraham and Sarah, who represented Adam and Eve. Sarah's safe return to Abraham established a condition to separate Abraham's family from Satan's dominion by overcoming the seduction of Lucifer (Pharoah).

Abraham was then called to make a condition of sacrificing animals. He was to divide them in two, representing the separation of good from evil, and then make them into burnt offerings. He halved the larger animals (a heifer, ram and female goat) but failed to halve the two turtle doves, falling into a deep sleep instead. On waking he was chastised by God for this mistake and told his descendants would suffer 400 years of slavery, a much greater condition of indemnity. Furthermore, he was then called to offer the much greater sacrifice of his son, Isaac, to make up for the failed sacrifice of animals. Abraham was on the point of plunging a knife into Isaac when an angel called out to him that his faith had saved Isaac. Abraham's willingness to undertake this seemingly impossible task made a condition to restore his earlier mistake and secure his family in the central providence. The obedience of Isaac to his father, even at the cost of his life, enabled Isaac to inherit the mission from Abraham of restoring the families of Adam and Noah. And it enabled him to inherit the position of father of faith from Abraham.

Isaac's Family

Now Isaac stood in Abraham's position and his twin sons, Esau and Jacob, replaced Ishmael and Isaac as representatives of Cain and Abel. The Bible records God expressing his preference for Jacob: "'Is not Esau Jacob's brother?' says the Lord. 'Yet I have loved Jacob but I have hated Esau.'" (Malachi 1:2-3) Esau was born first and, as Cain, was the enemy of God's providence. After the brothers had reached adulthood, Jacob traded some bread and lentils for a hungry Esau's birthright and later, when Isaac was blind, tricked his father into giving him the blessing that traditionally would have been Esau's. Bitter with resentment, Esau determined to kill Jacob: "Now Esau hated Jacob because of the blessing with which his father had blessed him, and Esau said to himself, 'The days of mourning for my father are approaching; then I will kill my brother Jacob.'" (Genesis 27:41) This would have been a repetition of Cain's murder of Abel.

Jacob's Victory

Facing Esau's anger, with the help of his mother Rebekah Jacob went to stay with his uncle Laban in Haran. There he prospered. After seven years he had earned the hand of Laban's daughter, Rachel, but Laban tricked him by sending her sister Leah to him on their wedding night. He worked another seven years to win Rachel. Finally, after twenty-one years under Laban, he returned to Canaan, where he met Esau who was still resentful and wanted revenge for the loss of the birthright and blessing. Jacob wisely offered his wealth to Esau. His brother was moved by this gesture, and they were reconciled. This marked the first significant time in the providence when Abel won over Cain through service and love. It marked a victory over Satan and the successful establishment of a condition for restoration on the family level. This victory was confirmed when, shortly before meeting Esau, Jacob encountered an angel who tested his resolve in what the Bible describes as a wrestling match. Jacob prevailed, and after this victory—which reversed the angel Lucifer's dominion of Adam—Jacob was given a new name, "Israel", meaning "triumphant with God". This would be the name used by Jacob and his descendants—the children of Israel—as well as the nation they established.

Twelve Sons Become Twelve Tribes of Israel

Because Jacob had been successful in overcoming Esau's resentment and anger by humbling himself before his older brother, he was a victorious Abel figure whom God chose to establish a foundation for what would become a chosen nation at the center of God's providence of restoration.

Jacob had twelve sons and one daughter, Dinah, born to Leah, his first wife. The first four sons came from Leah. They were Reuben, Simeon, Levi and Judah. His next two sons, Dan and Naphtali, were born to Bilhah, the servant of Rachel who could not at first have children. Then two sons, Gad and Asher, were born to Zilpah, the servant of Leah, who had also become unable to bear children. However, Leah was later able to once more have children, and gave birth to Issachar and Zebulun. Finally, Rachel too was able to conceive and she gave birth to Joseph and Benjamin.

These twelve sons would become the twelve tribes of the nation of Israel. Their positions in the family, as well as their behavior, would determine the roles the sons, and later the tribes, played in building a chosen nation. The assumption of specific roles began when Reuben made the mistake of defiling his father's concubine, resulting in his birthright as the oldest being given to Joseph, much as Esau's birthright had gone to Jacob.

Joseph's Victory

Jacob had a special love for Joseph, which caused his brothers to hate him, and seek to kill him, much as Cain had envied and hated Abel, and then murdered him:

> Now Israel loved Joseph more than any other of his children, because he was the son of his old age; and he made him a long robe with sleeves. But when his brothers saw that their father loved him more than all his brothers, they hated him, and could not speak peaceably to him. (Genesis 37:3-4)

This jealousy and hatred increased when Joseph told his brothers he had dreamed of them as sheaves of wheat bowing down to his sheaf. In a second dream, he saw the sun, moon and stars likewise bowing down to him, which they understood to mean his father, mother and brothers. They brothers determined to kill him: "But they saw him in the distance, and before he reached them, they plotted to kill him." (Genesis 37:18) Reuben and then Judah intervened to save his life, but his brothers still sold him to Ishmaelite traders who then sold him on as a slave in Egypt. The brothers then lied to Jacob that Joseph had been killed by a wild animal, causing their father great grief.

However, Joseph would come to the attention of Pharaoh and eventually be elevated to the position of Egypt's prime minister. When famine struck Canaan, Joseph brought his parents and siblings with their families to Egypt, saving them from starvation. Joseph's Abel-type forgiveness of his brothers for their treachery, and his substantial act of love in saving his family healed the rift among Jacob's children. Thus as Jacob's victory had laid the foundation for individual-level restoration, Joseph's victory expanded that foundation to family-level restoration. Together, father and son laid the foundation for the children of Jacob's family to become the twelve tribes of the chosen nation of Israel. To forge a nation out of the tribes would require the Israelites to make additional conditions of faith, a challenge which they faced during their slavery in Egypt and the period after their escape from Egypt.

Judah Chosen as the Abel Son and Tribe

Nearing death, Jacob called his sons to him and told them the roles they were to take in the providence. In Genesis 49:4, Jacob tells his oldest, Reuben: "...you shall not have pre-eminence because you went up to your father's bed; then you defiled it." Simeon, Jacob's second son, and Levi, the third, had also angered Jacob when they took violent revenge against the people of Shechem for the defiling of their sister Dinah, brutally killing many. In Genesis 49:6-7, Jacob says of them: "...in their anger they slay men, and in their wantonness they hamstring oxen. Cursed be their anger, for it is fierce; and their wrath, for it is cruel!" Simeon and Levi had repeated the crime of Cain by murdering innocents.

Thus with the first three sons of Jacob disqualified from assuming an Abel position among the sons, and after Joseph had married Asenath, an Egyptian, rather than an Israelite, Jacob chose his fourth son, Judah, and his tribe to be in the Abel position among the children of Israel: "Judah, your brothers shall praise you; your hand shall be on the neck of your enemies; your father's sons shall bow down before you." (Genesis 49.8) Out of the lineage of Judah came King David, his son Solomon and the Kings of Judah, and it was from this lineage that the messiah was prophesized to come.

The Twelve Tribes of Ishmael

The providence of restoration had been set back when Abraham had failed to complete the sacrifice of animals. Not only did it become necessary for Isaac to inherit Abraham's position as father of faith, but Abaham and Sarah were unable to help Ishmael and Isaac restore the Cain-Abel relationship. This was largely due to Sarah's inability to embrace her Egyptian servant Hagar and Hagar's son, Ishmael. Instead, Sarah twice persuaded Abraham to send Hagar away, the first time when Hagar was pregnant with Ishmael and the second time when Ishmael was a fourteen-year-old boy.

The first time, an angel encouraged Hagar to humble herself and reconcile with Sarah: "Return to your mistress and submit to her." (Genesis 16:9). At the same time, the angel warned that Ishmael would be a Cain-like son: "He shall be a wild ass of a man, his hand against every man and every man's hand against him; and he shall dwell over against all his kinsmen." (Genesis 16:12) Nevertheless, the angel promised that Ishmael would be blessed: "I will so greatly multiply your descendants that they cannot be numbered for multitude." (Genesis 16:10) The second time, after Sarah gave birth to Isaac, she said to Abraham: "Cast out this slave woman with her son; for the son of this slave woman shall not be heir with my son Isaac." (Genesis 21:10) Abraham reluctantly agreed: "And the thing was very displeasing to Abraham on account of his son." (Genesis 21:11). With Ishmael on the verge of death in the desert, Hagar was once more encouraged by an angel: "Arise, lift up the lad, and hold him fast with your hand; for I will make him a great nation." (Genesis 21:18)

Consequences of Ishmael's Separation from Isaac

There would be far-reaching consequences that flowed from the failure to establish a condition of unity between Ishmael and Isaac. Instead of the two half-brothers growing up peacefully together within a single family, they were separated long before they faced the inevitable Cain-Abel struggles that are typical of fallen lineage and must be overcome to further the providence. Ishmael was not to blame. Thus Abraham was reassured about Ishamel: "As for Ishmael, I have heard you; behold, I will bless him and make him fruitful and multiply him exceedingly; he shall be the father of twelve princes, and I will make him a great nation." (Genesis 17:20) Ishmael would father twelve sons who became twelve tribes. He also had daughters, one of whom became a wife of Jacob's son Esau.

There would be many conflicts between the lineage of Isaac through Jacob and that of Ishmael, and these continue to this day. The need for these two branches of Abraham's family to reconcile has remained an unfulfilled condition. Today this failure is manifest in the difficulties and conflicts that afflict the relationship between Jacob's physical and spiritual descendants (Jews and Christians), on the one hand, and Ishmael's descendants (Muslims) on the other, since it was to the descendants of Ishmael that the prophet Mohammed was sent to fulfill the age-old promises of God to Abraham and Hagar.

400 Years of Slavery in Egypt

In time, Jacob's descendants lost their privileges in Egypt and were reduced to slavery. After they fulfilled a condition of indemnity by suffering 400 years of bondage in Egypt, they were sent a liberator in the person of Moses. Although raised in the royal palace, Moses was educated by his Israelite mother and was loyal to his enslaved people. Called by God, he led them out of captivity in Egypt towards the promised land of Canaan, home of their ancestors. Once in Sinai, Moses fasted forty days and received the Ten Commandments on two tablets. Because the people lost faith while he was on Mount Sinai, he smashed the tablets in anger and made a second forty-day fast. He received the commandments once more, although with greater difficulty, and later was given the instructions for building a Tabernacle to contain the Ark of the Covenant and the two tablets on which the commandments were written.

Moses and Aaron Take Abel Positions

The Ten Commandments marked the first revelation of God's truth as law. Moses would receive many additional revelations and the law would be greatly expanded in scope. And while Moses was the lawgiver, his older brother Aaron was appointed the high priest. Based on Moses' conditions of faith, the Levite tribe, of which he and Aaron were members, became the priestly tribe. Significantly, Aaron's obedience to his younger brother Moses established a condition to reverse Cain's killing of Abel; this made a condition to restore the mistake of their ancestor Levi that Jacob had referred to when deciding on the missions to be fulfilled by his sons. Moses would be the most significant person in the providence of restoration until Jesus appeared, some 1600 years later.

40 Years of Purification in the Wilderness

In the course of restoration, the establishment of a tribal foundation was to be followed by a national foundation. This step became possible after the 400 years of slavery in Egypt, when the seventy members of Jacob's family who had moved there at the time of Joseph had now multiplied greatly; some 600,000 men with their wives and children left for Sinai with Moses. Many of these million-plus exiles had been infected with Egyptian paganism and it took a condition of forty years of purification in the desert before the new generation of Israelites was able to enter the home promised to them: Canaan.

Among the leaders of the twelve tribes were two men, Joshua and Caleb, who stood out for their faith, and eventually Joshua led the people across the Jordan River into Canaan. (The pattern of Abel being represented by two of the twelve sons/tribes of Israel was established by Joseph and Benjamin, the two sons of Rachel. It was evident in the choice of descendants of Judah and Levi to play a central role under Moses, and again during the period of Divided Kingdoms.)

400 Years of Judges

There followed a 400-year period during which the Israelites sought to suppress the small kingdoms in Canaan and for the first time forge a nation of their own. The territory of Palestine and Transjordan was divided among twelve tribes. Because of Moses' faith, God had chosen his tribe, the Levites, to serves as priests to the other tribes. They would not get a portion of the promised land, but instead would be given special privileges in designated cities, as well as tithes from the rest of the Israelites. The land was divided among the descendants of the other brothers, except in the case of Joseph, whose twin sons, Ephraim and Manasseh, were counted as heads of separate tribes.

120 Years of the United Kingdom of Israel

Finally, at the request of the people, the prophet Samuel anointed Saul as the first king of Israel. He was not an effective leader and after forty years Saul was replaced by David, a young man of great faith and talent. David established Jerusalem as Israel's capital, and extended the boundaries of his kingdom. However, because he had shed so much blood during his life, he was not permitted to build a temple, and, after ruling forty years he died and was replaced by his son Solomon, who built the Temple to replace the Tabernacle and ushered Israel into a golden era. Solomon ruled for forty years.

400 Years of Divided Kingdoms: Cain and Abel

Solomon, however, had fatal flaws as a ruler. He married 700 women and had another 300 concubines. He sought to please some of them by setting up alters to their gods, whom he also worshiped. Idolatry become a major threat to the purity of the Israelite faith, and Solomon lost his Abel position as David's heir to the throne. Thus instead of Israel receiving God's blessing through Solomon, the kingdom was divided upon his death. Two tribes (Judah and Benjamin) formed the Southern Kingdom of Judah, based in Jerusalem, and the other ten tribes formed the Northern Kingdom of Israel, based in Shechem and then Samaria. Solomon's son, Rehoboam, became the first king of Judah, and a former servant of Solomon, Jeroboam, became the first king of Israel. The Kingdom of Judah inherited the Abel position from Judah and David, and the Kingdom of Israel the position of Cain. While the north was deeply infected by idolatry, the south was less so, thanks in large measure to the work of great prophets—like Elijah, Elisha, Isaiah and Jeremiah—who called the people to repent for their idolatry.

70 Years of Babylonian Exile

The Kingdom of Judah was never able to win the Kingdom of Israel back to God's side. Eventually, Israel was conquered by the Assyrians and underwent the permanent destruction of the kingdom and scattering of the ten tribes, never to be reconstituted. (These became known as the Lost Tribes of Israel.) Later, Judah itself succumbed to an invasion. The Babylonian king, Nebuchadnezzar II, defeated the Jews, ransacked Jerusalem and neighboring cities, and destroyed the Temple, taking many captives as slaves to Babylon. Some 400 years of divided kingdoms had ended. Living in captivity for seventy years served to humble and purify the people of Judah, and when Cyrus the Great of Persia conquered Babylon in 539 BC he allowed them to return to their homeland. The return to Judah and Jerusalem would be extended over some 140 years.

400 Years Preparation for Jesus

Under the firm hand of Jerusalem's governor, Nehemiah, and guided back to the law by the scribe Ezra, the Temple was rebuilt and the walls of the city repaired. A purified nation—centered on the external Abel, Nehemiah, and internal Abel, Ezra—made conditions that launched the nation of Israel on a final 400-year period of preparation for the advent of an absolute Abel, Jesus.

Appendix 6

The Cain-Abel Paradigm in the Life of Jesus

The birth of Jesus was in humble circumstances but of momentous importance. It marked the culmination of a foundational period for the restoration of the lineage descended from Adam and Eve. Preparations for this moment had been taking place for centuries in Israel, and more recently through worldwide enlightenment brought about by the developments in religion, philosophy and science of the Axial Age. Jesus appeared as the absolute Abel with the mission to restore the dominion of good, the broken relationship between the Creator and fallen humankind, and the original family that had been corrupted in the Garden of Eden.

Mission of the Messiah

The Messiah comes to restore the failure of Adam as the central figure for the creation. Thus he must first establish God's dominion on earth, in the physical world, and then to establish God's dominion in the spirit world. The condition to establish God's dominion on earth is for the prepared nation to receive him and unite around him. The Messiah comes to the nation to become its physical and spiritual leader, its king and high priest.

The nation of Israel had long been prepared for a special salvific mission of global importance, to be fulfilled under the leadership of a Messiah, or Christ. For Jesus, Israel was Cain. Jesus' mission was to win the nation over to the new providence unfolding through him, so that Israel could become a nation fully under God's dominion, separated from Satan. Israel could then stand as the Abel nation to all other nations in the world, which would be in the Cain position to it.

As the victorious, absolute Abel, Jesus would have been able to restore the position of Adam and establish a new central family in the place of Adam and Eve, inaugurate a new, sinless lineage which would multiply God's dominion throughout the world, and eventually separate the entire world from Satan's dominion.

However, as we have seen throughout the history of restoration, the fulfillment of God's providence is tied to the achievements of Abel but also to the cooperation of Cain with Abel, on Abel's terms. Thus for the mission of Jesus to succeed, Israel would have to accept him as the prophesied Messiah they awaited. The key people responsible to help Jesus included his family, John the Baptist, his disciples and the religious and political establishments. From a Christian perspective, one would expect all of these key people and institutions to have recognized Jesus as the Messiah and supported him. But is that what happened? And was the life of Jesus culminating in his crucifixion the fulfillment of the Messiah's mission or was it another instance of Cain murdering Abel?

A Difficult Early Life

From his childhood, Jesus was remarkable. Quick to learn the scriptures, he developed a profound understanding of the providence and, once he started his public mission at age thirty, he taught a whole new revelation of the truth, an understanding that flowed from his evident intimacy with the Creator. His words had authority because his life was one of moral perfection and unstinting sacrifice for God and humanity. However, from beginning to end, Jesus's life was one of loneliness and betrayal. As absolute Abel, Jesus was constantly challenged by Cain-type elements of society, including some people in his family and among his disciples, as well as the political and religious establishments in Israel.

At the time of Jesus' birth, Israel was ruled by Herod the Great. Herod had been raised as a Jew, but his ancestry combined two primary strains of Cain lineage: His father was an Edomite (descendant of Esau) and his mother was a Nabatean Arab (descendant of Ishmael). The Bible records that when Herod was warned of the imminent birth of a king in Bethlehem, he had all the town's male infants killed, out of fear of a rival. (Matthew 2:16) An angel warned Joseph of Herod's murderous intentions and encouraged him to escape with Mary and Jesus to Egypt: "...an angel of the Lord appeared to Joseph in a dream and said, 'Rise, take the child and his mother, and flee to Egypt, and remain there till I tell you; for Herod is about to search for the child, to destroy him.'" (Matthew 2:13) The family would eventually return to Israel and Joseph's hometown of Nazareth, where Jesus grew up helping with Joseph's carpentry business.

Let Down by His Family

Jesus was apparently little understood by his own parents. Joseph and Mary forgot him in the Temple when he was just twelve years old, seemingly unaware that his was a historic mission closely tied to the destiny of Israel. This occurred even though angels had appeared to both of Joseph and Mary, clearly explaining Jesus' providential mission.

They had four more sons and two daughters, distracting them from their primary responsibility to support Jesus in his mission. In fact, there is no record at all of Joseph supporting Jesus in his public mission. And, at one point, when Jesus's mother and brothers visited him while he was teaching, he expressed his frustration with his family:

> While he was still speaking to the people, behold, his mother and his brothers stood outside, asking to speak to him. But he replied to the man who told him, "Who is my mother, and who are my brothers?" And stretching out his hand toward his disciples, he said, "Here are my mother and my brothers! For whoever does the will of my Father in heaven is my brother, and sister, and mother." (Matthew 12:46-50)

When Jesus faced his final showdown with the religious and political establishment of Israel, his father, mother and siblings seemed to be missing. Only John's Gospel says Mary was present at the crucifixion and then only to record Jesus asking John to take care of Mary. (John 19:26-27). None of the Gospels record any of his family at Jesus' tomb. Furthermore, there is no Biblical evidence at all that Mary played a mother's role to Jesus and the disciples during his public ministry, although several other women did serve Jesus and the disciples. (Luke 8:1-3) It was only some time after Jesus' death that Mary was elevated to the role of mother of the church by some believers. (Mary is even revered as "mother of God" in some traditions.)

The Importance of John the Baptist

The very last words of the Old Testament foretell the return of the prophet Elijah to prepare the way for the expected judgment of God through the advent of a savior or messiah:

> Behold, I will send you Elijah the prophet before the great and terrible day of the Lord comes. And he will turn the hearts of fathers to their children and the hearts of children to their fathers, lest I come and smite the land with a curse. (Malachi 4:5-6)

This prophecy was important because Elijah had been a major figure in Israel and his return was expected by the people to make clear to them who the Messiah would be.

If Jesus was the Messiah, who then was Elijah? Scripture records that it was John, the son of the priest Zechariah and a close relative to Jesus, born just six months before him. John's birth was miraculous, since his mother, Elizabeth, like Abraham's wife Sarah, was barren. Zechariah, at first unable to believe his wife could conceive, was told by the angel Gabriel that his son should be called John and would fulfill the mission of Elijah:

> And he will turn many of the sons of Israel to the Lord their God, and he will go before him in the spirit and power of Elijah, to turn the hearts of the

335

fathers to the children, and the disobedient to the wisdom of the just, to make ready for the Lord a people prepared. (Luke 1: 16-17)

John's mission represented the culmination of preparations for a second Adam, for the chosen nation to receive and follow the person chosen by God to fulfill the providence of restoration. John became a preacher and prophet:

In those days came John the Baptist, preaching in the wilderness of Judea, "Repent, for the kingdom of heaven is at hand." For this is he who was spoken of by the prophet Isaiah when he said, "The voice of one crying in the wilderness: Prepare the way of the Lord, make his paths straight." (Matthew 3:1-3)

He was an ascetic wearing a camel hair garment and living off locusts and honey. He was well respected in Israel, and developed a significant following. As Cain to Jesus' Abel, John's mission was to lay all of the recognition and respect he enjoyed at the feet of Jesus, and to become Jesus' first and main disciple. His own disciples would then have become disciples of Jesus. In doing so, John would immediately have elevated Jesus to the position of spiritual leader of Israel, paving the way for him also to assume the political leadership implied in inheriting the throne of King David. In his preaching, John set the stage for the arrival of Jesus:

I baptize you with water for repentance, but he who is coming after me is mightier than I, whose sandals I am not worthy to carry; he will baptize you with the Holy Spirit and with fire. (Matthew 3:11)

The day arrived when John was to declare Jesus as the expected Messiah and unite with him to help Jesus fulfill the Messiah's mission. John's baptism of Jesus represented the transfer of the providential foundation of the central history of restoration to Jesus, the person chosen to fulfill the messianic mission. Thus when Jesus met John, he asked to be baptized by John, even though John recognized that Jesus was the one chosen by God to fulfill the most important role in history:

"I need to be baptized by you, and do you come to me?" But Jesus answered him, "Let it be so now; for thus it is fitting for us to fulfil all righteousness." Then [John] consented. And when Jesus was baptized, he went up immediately from the water, and behold, the heavens were opened and he saw the Spirit of God descending like a dove, and alighting on him; and lo, a voice from heaven, saying, "This is my beloved Son, with whom I am well pleased." (Matthew 3:15-17)

John the Baptist Betrays Jesus

The day arrived when John was to declare Jesus as the expected Messiah and unite with him. John's baptism of Jesus was the condition that John had to fulfill as the prophet chosen to ready the people for the Messiah. At that point, John should have joined with Jesus so that—as united Cain and Abel— they could together lead the nation to salvation. However, soon after the baptism, John came to doubt Jesus' messiahship. He had likely heard rumors surrounding Jesus' mysterious birth, and must have doubted that his poor relative from a very humble household could be the long-awaited and glorious Messiah, the man who would inherit the throne of the great King David.

John's doubts caused him to hesitate, and he did not immediately join with Jesus. Instead he continued to baptize as if nothing had happened. He spoke of Jesus as someone who would overshadow him, not someone who would show him the way to the Kingdom of Heaven: "He must increase but I must decrease." (John 3:30)

He then became entangled in the personal affairs of King Herod Antipas and was thrown into jail. From there he sent disciples to ask Jesus if he was indeed the Messiah:

Now when John heard in prison about the deeds of the Christ, he sent word by his disciples and said to him, "Are you he who is to come, or shall we look for another?" (Matthew 11:2-3)

In response, Jesus rebuked John:

> And Jesus answered them, "Go and tell John what you hear and see: the blind receive their sight and the lame walk, lepers are cleansed and the deaf hear, and the dead are raised up, and the poor have good news preached to them. And blessed is he who takes no offense at me." (Matthew 11:2-6)

After John's disciples had left, Jesus explained the great importance of John's mission to his own followers:

> As they went away, Jesus began to speak to the crowds concerning John: "What did you go out into the wilderness to behold? A reed shaken by the wind? Why then did you go out? To see a man clothed in soft raiment? Behold, those who wear soft raiment are in kings' houses. Why then did you go out? To see a prophet? Yes, I tell you, and more than a prophet. This is he of whom it is written, "Behold, I send my messenger before thy face, who shall prepare thy way before thee."

> Truly, I say to you, among those born of women there has risen no one greater than John the Baptist; yet he who is least in the kingdom of heaven is greater than he. From the days of John the Baptist until now the kingdom of heaven has suffered violence, and men of violence take it by force. For all the prophets and the law prophesied until John; and if you are willing to accept it, he is Elijah who is to come." (Matthew 11:7-14)

Despite all of his spiritual training, when the time came for John to complete his mission, he could not overcome his Cain-like nature. He repeated Cain's sin. John's rejection of Jesus was the death knell for Jesus' mission. Now Jesus had to create his own foundation and gather his own disciples from the only ones who would not judge him: poor fisherman, farmers and people with good hearts who could unite with Jesus even though they could not fully understand his purpose.

John failed in his mission and no longer had God's protection. He was executed at the behest of Herod's stepdaughter Salome, on behalf of her mother, Herodias.

Judas Betrays Jesus

Another significant betrayal came from Judas, one of Jesus' twelve closest disciples. For thirty pieces of silver, Judas betrayed Jesus to the religious authorities, leading to Jesus' arrest and crucifixion. Judas soon recognized his sin and committed suicide in shame. But the damage had been done. Jesus' period of public mission had lasted some three years, and, in that time, he had been let down by his family, John the Baptist and one of his close disciples. If these people, the closest to Jesus, had been true and faithful, Jesus would have had a foundation for overcoming the crushing hostility of Israel's establishment.

Persecution by the Political Establishment

Once Jesus started his public mission, the political establishment, now headed by Herod Antipas, son of Herod the Great, plotted with Israel's religious leadership to get rid of Jesus: "The Pharisees went out, and immediately held counsel with the Herodians against him, how to destroy him." (Mark 3:6) Jesus warned his disciples of these conspiracies: "And he cautioned them, saying, 'Take heed, beware of the leaven of the Pharisees and the leaven of Herod.'" (Mark 8:15)

On another occasion, Jesus was warned that Herod was seeking to kill him:

> At that very hour some Pharisees came, and said to him, "Get away from here, for Herod wants to kill you." And he said to them, "Go and tell that fox, 'Behold, I cast out demons and perform cures today and tomorrow, and the third day I finish my course. Nevertheless I must go on my way today and tomorrow and the day following; for it cannot be that a prophet should perish away from Jerusalem.'" (Luke 13:31-34)

It was the Cain-like Herod Antipas who executed John the Baptist and later condemned Jesus to death by allowing the Roman governor Pontius Pilate to crucify Jesus without any cause:

> And when [Pilate] learned that [Jesus] belonged to Herod's jurisdiction, he

sent him over to Herod, who was himself in Jerusalem at that time. When Herod saw Jesus, he was very glad, for he had long desired to see him, because he had heard about him, and he was hoping to see some sign done by him. So he questioned him at some length; but he made no answer. The chief priests and the scribes stood by, vehemently accusing him. And Herod with his soldiers treated him with contempt and mocked him; then, arraying him in gorgeous apparel, he sent him back to Pilate. And Herod and Pilate became friends with each other that very day, for before this they had been at enmity with each other. (Luke 23: 7-12)

Persecution by the Religious Establishment

The religious establishment of Israel was uniformly hostile to Jesus. Its members were constantly trying to find Jesus in violation of the Mosaic Law and colluded with the political authorities to have him killed, as we have pointed out above. There were two main factions within the Jewish hierarchy, the Pharisees and Sadducees, who differed over interpretation of the scriptures. The scribes, who were experts on the scriptures, were generally aligned with the Pharisees. With the chief priests, members of these groups composed the Sanhedrin, the judicial body that convicted Jesus of violations of the law and sent him to Pilate to be condemned and executed:

And [Pilate] answered them, "Do you want me to release for you the King of the Jews?" For he perceived that it was out of envy that the chief priests had delivered him up. But the chief priests stirred up the crowd to have him release for them Barabbas instead. And Pilate again said to them, "Then what shall I do with the man whom you call the King of the Jews?" And they cried out again, "Crucify him." And Pilate said to them, "Why, what evil has he done?" But they shouted all the more, "Crucify him." So Pilate, wishing to satisfy the crowd, released for them Barabbas; and having scourged Jesus, he delivered him to be crucified. (Mark 15: 9-15)

Members of the religious establishment had tried to trip Jesus up by asking him leading questions about the Sabbath, marriage and various points of the Mosaic Law. His answers inevitably pointed to their insincerity—they were not interested in a deeper understanding of scriptures but only looking for a way to be able to condemn Jesus as a heretic. There are many passages in the Gospels in which he castigates the religious leaders as Cain-type hypocrites, as serpents and vipers.

The Critical Turning Point in Jesus' Mission

The significance of the betrayals of those most critical to his mission, combined with his rejection by Israel's religious and political establishments, resulted in Jesus reaching a critical turning point in his mission. No longer could he expect to be accepted as Messiah and inherit the throne of David; he would now have to go a course of suffering to lay a foundation for the future realization of these prophesized missions for a second Adam.

Jesus began to speak about having to suffer death at the hands of his enemies. He went up what is called the Mount of Transfiguration with his three closest disciples to meet with Moses and Elijah in spirit. These two men represented the heart of the providence centered on Israel and the foundation that Jesus was to inherit as Messiah. They knew that Israel was rejecting Jesus and what that would mean for the providence.

It was after this meeting that Jesus spoke extensively about the failure of the religious establishment, in particular, to fulfill its mission, to recognize and follow him, despite all the centuries of preparation for this moment, including the law given by God to Moses and the many prophecies and punishments that had been handed down to the chosen people by Elijah and many others.

Jesus' most adamant condemnation of the "Scribes and Pharisees" is found in Matthew 23:

> The scribes and the Pharisees sit on Moses' seat; so practice and observe whatever they tell you, but not what they do; for they preach, but do not practice. They bind heavy burdens, hard to bear, and lay them on men's shoulders; but they themselves will not move them with their finger. They do all their deeds to be seen by men; for they make their phylacteries broad and their fringes

long, and they love the place of honor at feasts and the best seats in the synagogues, and salutations in the market places, and being called rabbi by men. (Matthew 23:2-7)

But woe to you, scribes and Pharisees, hypocrites! because you shut the kingdom of heaven against men; for you neither enter yourselves, nor allow those who would enter to go in. Woe to you, scribes and Pharisees, hypocrites! for you traverse sea and land to make a single proselyte, and when he becomes a proselyte, you make him twice as much a child of hell as yourselves. (Matthew 23:13-15)

Woe to you, blind guides, who say, "If any one swears by the temple, it is nothing; but if any one swears by the gold of the temple, he is bound by his oath." You blind fools! for which is greater, the gold or the temple that has made the gold sacred? And you say, "If any one swears by the altar, it is nothing; but if any one swears by the gift that is on the altar, he is bound by his oath." You blind men! for which is greater, the gift or the altar that makes the gift sacred? (Matthew 23:16-19)

Woe to you, scribes and Pharisees, hypocrites! for you tithe mint and dill and cumin, and have neglected the weightier matters of the law, justice and mercy and faith; these you ought to have done, without neglecting the others. You blind guides, straining out a gnat and swallowing a camel! (Matthew 23:23-24)

Woe to you, scribes and Pharisees, hypocrites! for you cleanse the outside of the cup and of the plate, but inside they are full of extortion and rapacity. You blind Pharisee! first cleanse the inside of the cup and of the plate, that the outside also may be clean. (Matthew 23:25-26)

Woe to you, scribes and Pharisees, hypocrites! for you are like whitewashed tombs, which outwardly appear beautiful, but within they are full of dead men's bones and all uncleanness. So you also outwardly appear righteous to men, but within you are full of hypocrisy and iniquity. (Matthew 23:27-28)

Jesus Identifies His Persecutors as Cain

Why was Jesus so angry at these leaders of the people? From the perspective of the providence of restoration, they were blocking the way forward. They had inherited the positions of central authority in Israel, yet instead of using their knowledge and privilege to recognize Jesus and support his mission, they only attacked him. Jesus was the fulfillment of the prophecies of Isaiah and others who anticipated the Messiah, but he was rejected by the very people he came so save. He said that because of their faithlessness they would inherit the responsibility for the shedding of innocent blood, from Abel to Zechariah, a priest murdered in the Temple during the Divided Kingdoms era. In other words, Jesus was associating them with Cain and all the Cain-type figures of history who had shed innocent blood. And he was warning them that they would be responsible for his death too:

> Woe to you, scribes and Pharisees, hypocrites! for you build the tombs of the prophets and adorn the monuments of the righteous, saying, "If we had lived in the days of our fathers, we would not have taken part with them in shedding the blood of the prophets." Thus you witness against yourselves, that you are sons of those who murdered the prophets. Fill up, then, the measure of your fathers. You serpents, you brood of vipers, how are you to escape being sentenced to hell? Therefore I send you prophets and wise men and scribes, some of whom you will kill and crucify, and some you will scourge in your synagogues and persecute from town to town, that upon you may come all the righteous blood shed on earth, from the blood of innocent Abel to the blood of Zechariah the son of Barachiah, whom you murdered between the sanctuary and the altar. Truly, I say to you, all this will come upon this generation. (Matthew 23:29-36)

Finally, Jesus lamented the faithlessness of the chosen people:

> O Jerusalem, Jerusalem, killing the prophets and stoning those who are sent to you! How often would I have gathered your children together as a hen gathers her brood under her wings, and you would not! Behold, your house is forsaken and desolate. (Matthew 23:37-38)

Jesus Taught the Way of Abel

Jesus was endowed with unrivalled attributes of purity and goodness and taught a deep interpretation of the truth. He used the model of a family to explain the relationship between God and human beings and described his own relationship with God as that of a child at one with his father: "Believe me that I am in the Father and the Father in me." (John 14:11) And: "He who has seen me has seen the Father." (John 14.9) These bold statements reflect Jesus' conviction that the essential relationship between the Creator and humankind was one of parent and child, and that when united their relationship would be like that between a harmonious spirit and body. And while Jesus was the first to manifest this intimacy with the Divine, he taught that all people should strive to achieve it: "You, therefore, must be perfect, as your heavenly Father is perfect." (Matthew 5:48)

This intimate relationship with God was of the same nature as the relationship between Adam and God before the Fall corrupted the first humans. It was a nature of innocence and purity to which Abel aspired, albeit against the forces of the fallen world that surrounded him. In all of history, only Jesus had the depth and purity to be an absolute Abel, a man who was wholly with God and thus capable of living a morally perfect life. It is this depth of heart that gave Jesus such wisdom and the ability to reveal the nature and purpose of the Creator so fully. Jesus' teaching resonates with our original nature and his words have continued to echo down through the centuries. No one before him had understood so fully the pain the Fall of Adam and Eve caused God, the pain of parents who had lost their children. And no one before him had understood so fully the requirements of Abel, the sacrifices he was called to make on the path of restoration.

The power of Jesus' words was complemented by his power of healing. He was able to perform miracles because he was at one with God. Many of these miracles had to do with driving evil spirits out of those so possessed or healing those with illnesses that could be cured with spiritual power. He also raised people from the dead and generally demonstrated a mastery of the physical world. But he knew that for people to change, they had to know the truth: "God is spirit, and those who worship him must worship in spirit and truth." (John 4:24)

This is why his ministry was primarily focused on teaching a new understanding of truth to the people of Israel. He sometimes spoke directly and sometimes in parables, but it was always to lift people's understanding of God's nature and purpose and responsibilities entailed in becoming a child of God. In short, he was teaching the Way of Abel. His teachings are best summarized in his Sermon on the Mount (Matthew 5-7), and in particular the Beatitudes:

Blessed are the poor in spirit, for theirs is the kingdom of heaven.

Blessed are those who mourn, for they shall be comforted.

Blessed are the meek, for they shall inherit the earth.

Blessed are those who hunger and thirst for righteousness,
for they shall be satisfied.

Blessed are the merciful, for they shall obtain mercy.

Blessed are the pure in heart, for they shall see God.

Blessed are the peacemakers, for they shall be called sons of God.

Blessed are those who are persecuted for righteousness' sake,
for theirs is the kingdom of heaven.

Blessed are you when men revile you and persecute you and utter all kinds of evil against you falsely on my account. Rejoice and be glad, for your reward is great in heaven, for in the same way they persecuted the prophets who were before you. (Matthew 5:3-12).

The first six Beatitudes encapsulate the purity and goodness to which believers should aspire, qualities essential for knowing, loving and obeying God. The last three have to do with overcoming the evils of the fallen world, the Cain-type attitudes and behavior that inevitably face Abel as he seeks to manifest God's love in the world.

Jesus elaborated on Abel's path:

> You have heard that it was said, "You shall love your neighbor and hate your enemy." But I say to you, Love your enemies and pray for those who persecute you, so that you may be sons of your Father who is in heaven; for he makes his sun rise on the evil and on the good, and sends rain on the just and on the unjust. For if you love those who love you, what reward have you? Do not even the tax collectors do the same? And if you salute only your brethren, what more are you doing than others? Do not even the Gentiles do the same?" (Matthew 5:43-47)

Cain's False Righteousness

The Way of Abel is the most difficult course one can take in life because it requires self-sacrifice and loving those most difficult to love. Jesus warned his followers that their goodness might be repaid with rejection and even death:

> They will put you out of the synagogues; indeed, the hour is coming when whoever kills you will think he is offering service to God. And they will do this because they have not known the Father, nor me. (Matthew 16:2-3)

This describes behavior typical of Cain: feeling justified and even virtuous in persecuting Abel. Thus Abel suffers because Cain does not understand the heart of the Father and does not know the sadness and grief he gives the Father. In his ignorance and alienation from God, Cain believes himself right and justified in his resentment and violence. Jesus was the first person to fully understand and reveal to the world the suffering nature of God and how this suffering was increased by Cain's ignorance and self-centeredness. It is an understanding that is the basis for our growth into a mature relationship of oneness in heart with God, sharing both the joy and sorrow of the Creator.

As we have shown, the people in Israel with positions of importance and education should have recognized Jesus and accepted his leadership, but they were the ones who turned against him and sought his death. Thus Jesus had to develop a following from among the ordinary people who nevertheless had the heart and humility to see God working through him. They naturally struggled with the demands of discipleship, but they had sufficient faith to follow Jesus. After Jesus died, it would be these sincere men and women who ignited the fire of Christianity, which eventually spread throughout the world. It would also be men and women of this caliber who enabled Christianity to play an important role in civilizing the world.

The Desperate Prayer of Jesus

In his final hours on earth, Jesus was abandoned by his closest twelve disciples. The evening before he was arrested, Jesus had celebrated Passover with the disciples and warned that one of them would betray him. Later that evening, in the Garden of Gethsemane, Jesus had prayed desperately: "My Father, if it be possible, let this cup pass from me; nevertheless, not as I will, but as thou wilt." (Matthew 26:39) This was not a prayer of momentary weakness but of recognition that, despite his unprecedented unity with God and extraordinary efforts to win over Israel, he had been rejected and would be killed by the very people he was sent to save. The traitor Judas arrived with a crowd sent by the Chief Priest, and Jesus was taken away to be tried and convicted by the Sanhedrin and executed by the Romans.

It is believed by most Christians that Jesus came to die for our sins—in other words, that he fulfilled his mission by dying on the cross. There are prophecies in Isaiah that appear to anticipate this: "He was despised and rejected by men; a man of sorrows, and acquainted with grief." (Isaiah 53:3) But why would Jesus be a man of sorrows who prayed desperately, even sweating blood, for "this cup to pass" if his mission was to die on the cross? And why did he call out on the cross: "Father, forgive them; for they know not what they do"? (Luke 23:34)

Everything in Jesus' life tells us that he would have done anything to fulfill his mission. If going to the cross was the way of salvation for all humanity, would he not have done it willingly? Furthermore, when in Biblical history was God's will fulfilled through disobedience and faithlessness? The long passage of time since Jesus' death without the appearance of the heavenly kingdom he spoke of suggests that he was not able to fulfill the victorious prophesies of Isaiah, such as:

> Of the increase of his government and of peace
> > there will be no end,
> upon the throne of David, and over his kingdom,
> > to establish it, and to uphold it
> with justice and with righteousness
> > from this time forth and for evermore.
> The zeal of the LORD of hosts will do this. (Isaiah 9:7)

As we showed in the history of restoration, the model for God's victory is Jacob's course, where the chosen Abel overcomes all challenges from Cain and restores, conditionally at least, the family of Adam and Eve. Surely God and Jesus wanted a similar outcome: a victory for Abel. And surely on that foundation Jesus would have found and married his Eve and established a Godly family and kingdom on earth. How else to restore the fallen lineage?

The Crucifixion Leads to Christianity

Jesus did persevere, against all odds. And, despite his physical death, his pure faith and sacrificial obedience to God resulted in a spiritual victory for Abel: From the life and teaching of Jesus, a new religion, Christianity, would emerge. The power of his spiritual victory soon became evident in the miraculous manifestations of God's Holy Spirit among the disciples, inspiring them to great feats of devotion and service. Several of them received the gifts of healing, driving out spirits and even raising the dead, much as Jesus himself had done.

The first follower to give his life for Jesus was Stephen, who was condemned to death by the Council of the Sanhedrin and killed in the presence of Saul of Tarsus (later Paul), a strict Pharisee and leading persecutor of the new faith. The Bible recounts the impression Stephen made on the Council:

"And gazing at him, all who sat in the council saw that his face was like the face of an angel." (Acts 6.15) Aflame with the love of God, Stephen spoke about the long and difficult history of his people and their frequent disobedience to God, concluding with:

> You stiff-necked people, uncircumcised in heart and ears, you always resist the Holy Spirit. As your fathers did, so do you. Which of the prophets did not your fathers persecute? And they killed those who announced beforehand the coming of the Righteous One, whom you have now betrayed and murdered, you who received the law as delivered by angels and did not keep it. (Acts 7:51-55)

His recitation of their history of Cain-like behavior, and his accusation against them as the murderers of Jesus only angered them more, and he was immediately condemned to die. He was taken outside and stoned to death by a furious mob. Thus from shortly after the death of Jesus, his followers would be called upon to give up their lives for Jesus, and the history of Christianity would be drenched in the blood of martyrs who, like Jesus, faced suffering and death at the hands of Cain.

At Pentecost, fifty days after the death of Jesus, the Holy Spirit descended on the first disciples and there was a great outpouring of spiritual power. Thousands were converted in one day, and the new religion began to grow rapidly. Many of the early Christians were inspired to give up their private property for the sake of the community of believers, expecting that heaven was imminent. Although this trend wasn't sustained for very long by most believers, it did take root in monastic orders and other intentional communities as a sacrificial way of life intended to put the teachings of Jesus into daily practice. Many of the good deeds of Christianity have been carried out by these and similarly dedicated believers.

An Otherworldly Kingdom

How best to practice Christianity is an ongoing issue, especially given that its founder's life was cut short and human nature always tends to corrupt the purity of God's truth and the clarity of God's intentions. If the Kingdom of God is a spiritual realm ruled by Jesus to which we aspire after death but can never expect to experience on earth, what then is the purpose of our life of faith? Jesus said, "My kingdom is not from this world." (John 18:36) This leaves Christians to ponder just what a Godly Kingdom under Jesus would have been and what it might be in the future. Most believe that we must wait for the promised second coming of the Messiah to know the answer.

However, this "otherworldliness" of Christianity can be misused by Christians to excuse them from fulfilling their responsibilities on earth because they believe evil will rule our world until it is vanquished in another, invisible world. Indeed, it was this feature of religion-based Western Civilization that gave Marx, Engels and other materialists an opening to attack Christianity itself. Their attacks have resonated with righteous-minded individuals who believe that the suffering of people on earth must be resolved in the here and now, and not postponed to some future time and place.

The Challenge for Christians

The teachings of Jesus himself are far from otherworldly, however. They are instructions for living the virtuous life of a true Abel, as we have shown. He did promise a reward in heaven for virtuous behavior, but he stressed the importance of living our lives according to God's love and truth, for which he was the model: "I am the way, and the truth, and the life. No one comes to the Father except through me." (John 14:6) This is a very difficult course, the way of absolute Abel, which requires constant dedication and renewal as we strive to overcome our own Cain-like nature and tendencies. Christians who believe that Jesus' high moral standards only apply in another, future life are mistaken.

Nevertheless, it is two full millennia since Jesus walked the earth, and the Christian ideal remains remote. Clearly the life of Jesus did not mark the fulfillment of providential history but rather its most significant milestone.

One might wonder what would have happened had the Jews united with Jesus to make a national foundation for restoration, elevating Israel to the position of a worldwide Abel and enabling it to fulfill the promise given to Abraham and Isaac:

> ... for to you and to your descendants I will give all these lands, and I will fulfill the oath that I swore to your father Abraham. I will make your offspring as numerous as the stars of heaven, and will give to your offspring all these lands; and all the nations of the earth shall gain blessing for themselves through your offspring, because Abraham obeyed my voice and kept my charge, my commandments, my statutes, and my laws. (Genesis 26:3-5)

Jesus was obedient to God's will until the end. However, the faithlessness of the people meant that the nation of Israel could not be restored, and Jesus himself could not complete the work of the Messiah. The mission of Christians is, then, to live according to Jesus' teachings and to build an Abel-type world that is better prepared than Israel was to receive the messengers and messages that God will send as the providence of restoration unfolds. With some 2.4 billion Christians on earth, there are more than enough people to make the dramatic changes for good that are needed today.

Martin Luther's 95 Theses

Nailed to the door of the All Saints Catholic Church in Wittenberg, Germany, on October 31, 1517

Out of love for the truth and from desire to elucidate it, the Reverend Father Martin Luther, Master of Arts and Sacred Theology, and ordinary lecturer therein at Wittenberg, intends to defend the following statements and to dispute on them in that place. Therefore he asks that those who cannot be present and dispute with him orally shall do so in their absence by letter. In the name of our Lord Jesus Christ, Amen.

1. When our Lord and Master Jesus Christ said, "Repent" (Mt 4:17), he willed the entire life of believers to be one of repentance.

2. This word cannot be understood as referring to the sacrament of penance, that is, confession and satisfaction, as administered by the clergy.

3. Yet it does not mean solely inner repentance; such inner repentance is worthless unless it produces various outward mortification of the flesh.

4. The penalty of sin remains as long as the hatred of self (that is, true inner repentance), namely till our entrance into the kingdom of heaven.

5. The pope neither desires nor is able to remit any penalties except those imposed by his own authority or that of the canons.

6. The pope cannot remit any guilt, except by declaring and showing

that it has been remitted by God; or, to be sure, by remitting guilt in cases reserved to his judgment. If his right to grant remission in these cases were disregarded, the guilt would certainly remain unforgiven.

7. God remits guilt to no one unless at the same time he humbles him in all things and makes him submissive to the vicar, the priest.

8. The penitential canons are imposed only on the living, and, according to the canons themselves, nothing should be imposed on the dying.

9. Therefore the Holy Spirit through the pope is kind to us insofar as the pope in his decrees always makes exception of the article of death and of necessity.

10. Those priests act ignorantly and wickedly who, in the case of the dying, reserve canonical penalties for purgatory.

11. Those tares [weeds] of changing the canonical penalty to the penalty of purgatory were evidently sown while the bishops slept. (Mt 13:25)

12. In former times canonical penalties were imposed, not after, but before absolution, as tests of true contrition.

13. The dying are freed by death from all penalties, are already dead as far as the canon laws are concerned, and have a right to be released from them.

14. Imperfect piety or love on the part of the dying person necessarily brings with it great fear; and the smaller the love, the greater the fear.

15. This fear or horror is sufficient in itself, to say nothing of other things, to constitute the penalty of purgatory, since it is very near to the horror of despair.

16. Hell, purgatory, and heaven seem to differ the same as despair, fear, and assurance of salvation.

17. It seems as though for the souls in purgatory fear should necessarily decrease and love increase.

18. Furthermore, it does not seem proved, either by reason or by Scripture, that souls in purgatory are outside the state of merit, that is, unable to grow in love.

19. Nor does it seem proved that souls in purgatory, at least not all of them, are certain and assured of their own salvation, even if we ourselves may be entirely certain of it.

20. Therefore the pope, when he uses the words "plenary remission of all penalties," does not actually mean "all penalties," but only those imposed by himself.

21. Thus those indulgence preachers are in error who say that a man is absolved from every penalty and saved by papal indulgences.

22. As a matter of fact, the pope remits to souls in purgatory no penalty which, according to canon law, they should have paid in this life.

23. If remission of all penalties whatsoever could be granted to anyone at all, certainly it would be granted only to the most perfect, that is, to very few.

24. For this reason most people are necessarily deceived by that indiscriminate and high-sounding promise of release from penalty.

25. That power which the pope has in general over purgatory corresponds to the power which any bishop or curate has in a particular way in his own diocese and parish.

26. The pope does very well when he grants remission to souls in purgatory, not by the power of the keys, which he does not have, but by way of intercession for them.

27. They preach only human doctrines who say that as soon as the money clinks into the money chest, the soul flies out of purgatory.

28. It is certain that when money clinks in the money chest, greed and avarice can be increased; but when the church intercedes, the result is in the hands of God alone.

29. Who knows whether all souls in purgatory wish to be redeemed, since we have exceptions in St. Severinus and St. Paschal, as related in a legend.

30. No one is sure of the integrity of his own contrition, much less of having received plenary remission.

31. The man who actually buys indulgences is as rare as he who is really penitent; indeed, he is exceedingly rare.

32. Those who believe that they can be certain of their salvation because they have indulgence letters will be eternally damned, together with their teachers.

33. Men must especially be on guard against those who say that the pope's pardons are that inestimable gift of God by which man is reconciled to him.

34. For the graces of indulgences are concerned only with the penalties of sacramental satisfaction established by man.

35. They who teach that contrition is not necessary on the part of those who intend to buy souls out of purgatory or to buy confessional privileges preach unchristian doctrine.

36. Any truly repentant Christian has a right to full remission of penalty and guilt, even without indulgence letters.

37. Any true Christian, whether living or dead, participates in all the blessings of Christ and the church; and this is granted him by God, even without indulgence letters.

38. Nevertheless, papal remission and blessing are by no means to be disregarded, for they are, as I have said (Thesis 6), the proclamation of the divine remission.

39. It is very difficult, even for the most learned theologians, at one and the same time to commend to the people the bounty of indulgences and the need of true contrition.

40. A Christian who is truly contrite seeks and loves to pay penalties for his sins; the bounty of indulgences, however, relaxes penalties and causes men to hate them—at least it furnishes occasion for hating them.

41. Papal indulgences must be preached with caution, lest people erroneously think that they are preferable to other good works of love.

42. Christians are to be taught that the pope does not intend that they buying of indulgences should in any way be compared with works of mercy.

43. Christians are to be taught that he who gives to the poor or lends to the needy does a better deed than he who buys indulgences.

44. Because love grows by works of love, man thereby becomes better. Man does not, however, become better by means of indulgences but is merely freed from penalties.

45. Christians are to be taught that he who sees a needy man and passes him by, yet gives his money for indulgences, does not buy papal indulgences but God's wrath.

46. Christians are to be taught that, unless they have more than they need, they must reserve enough for their family needs and by no means squander it on indulgences.

47. Christians are to be taught that the buying of indulgences is a matter of free choice, not commanded.

48. Christians are to be taught that the pope, in granting indulgences, needs and thus desires their devout prayer more than their money.

49. Christians are to be taught that papal indulgences are useful only if they do not put their trust in them, but very harmful if they lose their fear of God because of them.

50. Christians are to be taught that if the pope knew the exactions of the indulgence preachers, he would rather that the basilica of St. Peter were burned to ashes than built up with the skin, flesh, and bones of his sheep.

51. Christians are to be taught that the pope would and should wish to give of his own money, even though he had to sell the basilica of St. Peter, to many of those from whom certain hawkers of indulgences cajole money.

52. It is vain to trust in salvation by indulgence letters, even though the indulgence commissary, or even the pope, were to offer his soul as security.

53. They are the enemies of Christ and the pope who forbid altogether the preaching of the Word of God in some churches in order that indulgences may be preached in others.

54. Injury is done to the Word of God when, in the same sermon, an equal or larger amount of time is devoted to indulgences than to the Word.

55. It is certainly the pope's sentiment that if indulgences, which are a very insignificant thing, are celebrated with one bell, one procession, and one ceremony, then the gospel, which is the very greatest thing, should be preached with a hundred bells, a hundred processions, a hundred ceremonies.

56. The true treasures of the church, out of which the pope distributes indulgences, are not sufficiently discussed or known among the

people of Christ.

57. That indulgences are not temporal treasures is certainly clear, for many indulgence sellers do not distribute them freely but only gather them.

58. Nor are they the merits of Christ and the saints, for, even without the pope, the latter always work grace for the inner man, and the cross, death, and hell for the outer man.

59. St. Lawrence said that the poor of the church were the treasures of the church, but he spoke according to the usage of the word in his own time.

60. Without want of consideration we say that the keys of the church, given by the merits of Christ, are that treasure.

61. For it is clear that the pope's power is of itself sufficient for the remission of penalties and cases reserved by himself.

62. The true treasure of the church is the most holy gospel of the glory and grace of God.

63. But this treasure is naturally most odious, for it makes the first to be last. (Mt. 20:16).

64. On the other hand, the treasure of indulgences is naturally most acceptable, for it makes the last to be first.

65. Therefore the treasures of the gospel are nets with which one formerly fished for men of wealth.

66. The treasures of indulgences are nets with which one now fishes for the wealth of men.

67. The indulgences which the demagogues acclaim as the greatest graces are actually understood to be such only insofar as they promote gain.

68. They are nevertheless in truth the most insignificant graces when compared with the grace of God and the piety of the cross.

69. Bishops and curates are bound to admit the commissaries of papal indulgences with all reverence.

70. But they are much more bound to strain their eyes and ears lest these men preach their own dreams instead of what the pope has commissioned.

71. Let him who speaks against the truth concerning papal indulgences be anathema and accursed.

72. But let him who guards against the lust and license of the indulgence preachers be blessed.

73. Just as the pope justly thunders against those who by any means whatever contrive harm to the sale of indulgences.

74. Much more does he intend to thunder against those who use indulgences as a pretext to contrive harm to holy love and truth.

75. To consider papal indulgences so great that they could absolve a man even if he had done the impossible and had violated the mother of God is madness.

76. We say on the contrary that papal indulgences cannot remove the very least of venial sins as far as guilt is concerned.

77. To say that even St. Peter if he were now pope, could not grant greater graces is blasphemy against St. Peter and the pope.

78. We say on the contrary that even the present pope, or any pope whatsoever, has greater graces at his disposal, that is, the gospel, spiritual powers, gifts of healing, etc., as it is written. (1 Co 12[:28])

79. To say that the cross emblazoned with the papal coat of arms, and set up by the indulgence preachers is equal in worth to the cross of Christ is blasphemy.

80. The bishops, curates, and theologians who permit such talk to be spread among the people will have to answer for this.

81. This unbridled preaching of indulgences makes it difficult even for learned men to rescue the reverence which is due the pope from slander or from the shrewd questions of the laity.

82. Such as: "Why does not the pope empty purgatory for the sake of holy love and the dire need of the souls that are there if he redeems an infinite number of souls for the sake of miserable money with which to build a church?" The former reason would be most just; the latter is most trivial.

83. Again, "Why are funeral and anniversary masses for the dead continued and why does he not return or permit the withdrawal of the endowments founded for them, since it is wrong to pray for the redeemed?"

84. Again, "What is this new piety of God and the pope that for a consideration of money they permit a man who is impious and their enemy to buy out of purgatory the pious soul of a friend of God and do not rather, because of the need of that pious and beloved soul, free it for pure love's sake?"

85. Again, "Why are the penitential canons, long since abrogated and dead in actual fact and through disuse, now satisfied by the granting of indulgences as though they were still alive and in force?"

86. Again, "Why does not the pope, whose wealth is today greater than the wealth of the richest Crassus, build this one basilica of St. Peter with his own money rather than with the money of poor believers?"

87. Again, "What does the pope remit or grant to those who by perfect contrition already have a right to full remission and blessings?"

88. Again, "What greater blessing could come to the church than if the pope were to bestow these remissions and blessings on every

believer a hundred times a day, as he now does but once?"

89. "Since the pope seeks the salvation of souls rather than money by his indulgences, why does he suspend the indulgences and pardons previously granted when they have equal efficacy?"

90. To repress these very sharp arguments of the laity by force alone, and not to resolve them by giving reasons, is to expose the church and the pope to the ridicule of their enemies and to make Christians unhappy.

91. If, therefore, indulgences were preached according to the spirit and intention of the pope, all these doubts would be readily resolved. Indeed, they would not exist.

92. Away, then, with all those prophets who say to the people of Christ, "Peace, peace," and there is no peace! (Jer 6:14)

93. Blessed be all those prophets who say to the people of Christ, "Cross, cross," and there is no cross!

94. Christians should be exhorted to be diligent in following Christ, their Head, through penalties, death and hell.

95. And thus be confident of entering into heaven through many tribulations rather than through the false security of peace. (Acts 14:22)

Appendix 8

Major Denominational Families in Christianity

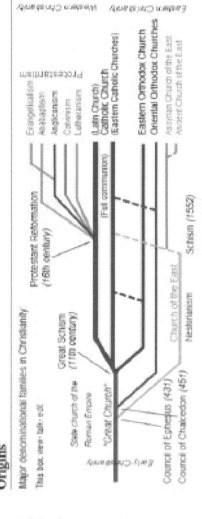

Source: Wikipedia

Appendix 9

English Bill of Rights, 1689

An Act Declaring the Rights and Liberties of the Subject and Settling the Succession of the Crown

Whereas the Lords Spiritual and Temporal and Commons assembled at Westminster, lawfully, fully and freely representing all the estates of the people of this realm, did upon the thirteenth day of February in the year of our Lord one thousand six hundred eighty-eight [old style date] present unto their Majesties, then called and known by the names and style of William and Mary, prince and princess of Orange, being present in their proper persons, a certain declaration in writing made by the said Lords and Commons in the words following, viz.:

Whereas the late King James the Second, by the assistance of divers evil counsellors, judges and ministers employed by him, did endeavour to subvert and extirpate the Protestant religion and the laws and liberties of this kingdom;

By assuming and exercising a power of dispensing with and suspending of laws and the execution of laws without consent of Parliament;

By committing and prosecuting divers worthy prelates for humbly petitioning to be excused from concurring to the said assumed power;

By issuing and causing to be executed a commission under the great seal for erecting a court called the Court of Commissioners for Ecclesiastical Causes;

By levying money for and to the use of the Crown by pretence of prerogative for other time and in other manner than the same was granted by Parliament;

By raising and keeping a standing army within this kingdom in time of peace without consent of Parliament, and quartering soldiers contrary to law;

By causing several good subjects being Protestants to be disarmed at the same time when papists were both armed and employed contrary to law;

By violating the freedom of election of members to serve in Parliament;

By prosecutions in the Court of King's Bench for matters and causes cognizable only in Parliament, and by divers other arbitrary and illegal courses;

And whereas of late years partial corrupt and unqualified persons have been returned and served on juries in trials, and particularly divers jurors in trials for high treason which were not freeholders;

And excessive bail hath been required of persons committed in criminal cases to elude the benefit of the laws made for the liberty of the subjects;

And excessive fines have been imposed;

And illegal and cruel punishments inflicted;

And several grants and promises made of fines and forfeitures before any conviction or judgment against the persons upon whom the same were to be levied;

All which are utterly and directly contrary to the known laws and statutes and freedom of this realm;

And whereas the said late King James the Second having abdicated the government and the throne being thereby vacant, his Highness the prince of Orange (whom it hath pleased Almighty God to make the glorious instrument of delivering this kingdom from popery and arbitrary power) did (by the advice of the Lords Spiritual and Temporal and divers principal persons of the Commons) cause letters to be written to the Lords Spiritual and Temporal being Protestants, and other letters to the several counties, cities, universities, boroughs and cinque ports, for the choosing of such persons to represent them as were of right to be sent to Parliament, to meet and sit at Westminster upon the two and twentieth day of January in this year one thousand six hundred eighty and eight [old style date], in order to such an establishment as that their religion, laws and liberties might not again be in danger of being subverted, upon which letters elections having been accordingly made;

And thereupon the said Lords Spiritual and Temporal and Commons, pursuant to their respective letters and elections, being now assembled in a full and free representative of this nation, taking into their most serious consideration the best means for attaining the ends aforesaid, do in the first place (as their ancestors in like case have usually done) for the vindicating and asserting their ancient rights and liberties declare

That the pretended power of suspending the laws or the execution of laws by regal authority without consent of Parliament is illegal;

That the pretended power of dispensing with laws or the execution of laws by regal authority, as it hath been assumed and exercised of late, is illegal;

That the commission for erecting the late Court of Commissioners for Ecclesiastical Causes, and all other commissions and courts of like nature, are illegal and pernicious;

That levying money for or to the use of the Crown by pretence of prerogative, without grant of Parliament, for longer time, or in other manner than the same is or shall be granted, is illegal;

That it is the right of the subjects to petition the king, and all commitments and prosecutions for such petitioning are illegal;

That the raising or keeping a standing army within the kingdom in time of peace, unless it be with consent of Parliament, is against law;

That the subjects which are Protestants may have arms for their defence suitable to their conditions and as allowed by law;

That election of members of Parliament ought to be free;

That the freedom of speech and debates or proceedings in Parliament ought not to be impeached or questioned in any court or place out of Parliament;

That excessive bail ought not to be required, nor excessive fines imposed, nor cruel and unusual punishments inflicted;

That jurors ought to be duly impanelled and returned, and jurors which pass upon men in trials for high treason ought to be freeholders;

That all grants and promises of fines and forfeitures of particular persons before conviction are illegal and void;

And that for redress of all grievances, and for the amending, strengthening and preserving of the laws, Parliaments ought to be held frequently.

And they do claim, demand and insist upon all and singular the premises as their undoubted rights and liberties, and that no declarations, judgments, doings or proceedings to the prejudice of the people in any of the said premises ought in any wise to be drawn hereafter into consequence or example; to which demand of their rights they are particularly encouraged by the declaration of his Highness the prince of Orange as being the only means for obtaining a full redress and remedy therein. Having therefore an entire confidence that his said Highness the prince of Orange will perfect the deliverance so far advanced by him, and will still preserve them from the violation of their rights which they have here asserted, and from all other attempts upon their religion, rights and liberties, the said Lords Spiritual and Temporal and Commons assembled at Westminster do resolve that William and Mary, prince and princess of Orange, be and be declared king and queen of England, France and Ireland and the dominions thereunto belonging, to hold the crown and royal dignity of the said kingdoms and dominions to them, the said prince and princess, during their lives and the life of the survivor to them, and that the sole and full exercise of the regal power be only in and executed by the said prince of Orange in the names of the said prince and princess during their joint lives, and after their deceases the said crown and royal dignity of the same kingdoms and dominions to be to the heirs of the body of the said princess, and for default of such issue to the Princess Anne of Denmark and the heirs of her body, and for default of such issue to the heirs of the body of the said prince of Orange. And the Lords Spiritual and Temporal and Commons do pray the said prince and princess to accept the same accordingly.

And that the oaths hereafter mentioned be taken by all persons of whom the oaths have allegiance and supremacy might be required by law, instead of them; and that the said oaths of allegiance and supremacy be abrogated.

I, A.B., do sincerely promise and swear that I will be faithful and bear true allegiance to their Majesties King William and Queen Mary. So help me God.

I, A.B., do swear that I do from my heart abhor, detest and abjure as impious and heretical this damnable doctrine and position, that princes excommunicated or deprived by the Pope or any authority of the see of Rome may be deposed or murdered by their subjects or any other whatsoever. And I do declare that no foreign prince, person, prelate, state or potentate hath or ought to have any jurisdiction, power, superiority, pre-eminence or authority, ecclesiastical or spiritual, within this realm. So help me God.

Upon which their said Majesties did accept the crown and royal dignity of the kingdoms of England, France and Ireland, and the dominions thereunto belonging, according to the resolution and desire of the said Lords and Commons contained in the said declaration. And thereupon their Majesties were pleased that the said Lords Spiritual and Temporal and Commons, being the two Houses of Parliament, should continue to sit, and with their Majesties' royal concurrence make effectual provision for the settlement of the religion, laws and liberties of this kingdom, so that the same for the future might not be in danger again of being subverted, to which the said Lords Spiritual and Temporal and Commons did agree, and proceed to act accordingly. Now in pursuance of the premises the said Lords Spiritual and Temporal and Commons in Parliament assembled, for the ratifying, confirming and establishing the said declaration and the articles, clauses, matters and things therein contained by the force of law made in due form by authority of Parliament, do pray that it may be declared and enacted that all and singular the rights and liberties asserted and claimed in the said declaration are the true, ancient and indubitable rights and liberties of the people of this kingdom, and so shall be esteemed, allowed, adjudged, deemed and taken to be; and that all and every the particulars aforesaid shall be firmly and strictly holden and observed as they are expressed in the said declaration, and all officers and ministers whatsoever shall serve their Majesties and their successors according to the same in all time to come. And the said Lords Spiritual and Temporal and Commons, seriously considering how it hath pleased Almighty God in his marvellous providence and merciful goodness to this nation to provide and preserve their said Majesties' royal persons most happily to reign over us upon the throne of their ancestors, for which they render unto him from the bottom of their hearts their humblest thanks and praises, do truly, firmly, assuredly and in the sincerity of their hearts think, and do hereby recognize, acknowledge and declare, that King James the Second having abdicated the government, and their Majesties having accepted the crown and royal dignity as aforesaid, their said Majesties did become, were, are and of right ought to be by the laws of this realm our sovereign liege lord and lady, king and queen of England, France and Ireland and the dominions thereunto belonging, in and to whose princely persons the royal state, crown and dignity of the said realms with all honours, styles, titles, regalities, prerogatives, powers, jurisdictions and authorities to the same belonging and appertaining are most fully, rightfully and entirely invested and incorporated, united and annexed. And for preventing all questions and divisions in this realm by reason of any pretended titles to the crown, and for preserving a certainty in the succession thereof, in and upon which the unity, peace, tranquility and safety of this nation doth under God wholly consist and depend, the said Lords Spiritual and Temporal and Commons do beseech their Majesties that it may be enacted, established and declared, that the crown and regal government of the said kingdoms and dominions, with all and singular the premises thereunto belonging and appertaining, shall be and continue to their said Majesties and the survivor of them during their lives and the life of the survivor of them, and that the entire, perfect and full exercise of the regal power and government be only in and executed by his Majesty in the names of both their Majesties during their joint lives; and after their deceases the said crown and premises shall be and remain to the heirs of the body of her Majesty, and for default of such issue to her Royal Highness the Princess Anne of Denmark and the heirs of the body of his said Majesty; and thereunto the said Lords Spiritual and Temporal and Commons do in the name of all the people aforesaid most humbly and faithfully submit themselves, their heirs and posterities for ever, and do faithfully promise that they will stand to, maintain and defend their said Majesties, and also the limitation and succession of the crown herein specified and contained, to the utmost of their powers with their lives and estates against all persons whatsoever that shall attempt anything to the contrary. And whereas it hath been found by experience that it is inconsistent with the safety and welfare of this Protestant kingdom to be governed by a popish prince, or by any king or queen marrying a papist, the said Lords Spiritual and Temporal and Commons do further pray that it may be enacted, that all and every person and persons that is, are or shall be reconciled to or shall hold communion with the see or Church of Rome, or shall profess the popish religion, or shall marry a papist, shall be excluded and be for ever incapable to inherit, possess or enjoy the crown and government of this realm and Ireland and the dominions thereunto belonging or any part of the same, or to have, use or exercise any regal power, authority or jurisdiction within the same; and in all and every such case or cases the people of these realms shall be and are hereby absolved of their allegiance; and the said crown and government shall from time to time descend to and be enjoyed by such person or persons being Protestants as should have inherited and enjoyed the same in case the said person or persons so reconciled, holding communion or professing or marrying as aforesaid were naturally dead; and that every king and queen of this realm who at any time hereafter shall come to and succeed in the imperial crown of this kingdom shall on the first day of the meeting of the first Parliament next after his or her coming to the crown, sitting in his or her throne in the House of Peers in the presence of the Lords and Commons therein assembled, or at his or her coronation before such person or persons who shall administer the coronation oath to him or her at the time of his or her taking the said oath (which shall first happen), make, subscribe and audibly repeat the declaration mentioned in the statute made in the thirtieth year of the reign of King Charles the Second entitled, _An Act for the more effectual preserving the king's person and government by disabling papists from sitting in either House of Parliament._ But if it shall happen that such king or queen upon his or her succession to the crown of this realm shall be under the age of twelve years, then every such king or queen shall make, subscribe and audibly repeat the same declaration at his or her coronation or the first day of the meeting of the first Parliament as aforesaid which shall first happen after such king or queen shall have attained the said age of twelve years. All which their Majesties are contented and pleased shall be declared, enacted and established by authority of this present Parliament, and shall stand, remain and be the law of this realm for ever; and the same are by their said Majesties, by and with the advice and consent of the Lords Spiritual and Temporal and Commons in Parliament assembled and by the authority of the same, declared, enacted and established accordingly.

II. And be it further declared and enacted by the authority aforesaid, that from and after this present session of Parliament no dispensation by _non obstante_ of or to any statute or any part thereof shall be allowed, but that the same shall be held void and of no effect, except a dispensation be allowed of in such statute, and except in such cases as shall be specially provided for by one or more bill or bills to be passed during this present session of Parliament.

III. Provided that no charter or grant or pardon granted before the three and twentieth day of October in the year of our Lord one thousand six hundred eighty-nine shall be any ways impeached or invalidated by this Act, but that the same shall be and remain of the same force and effect in law and no other than as if this Act had never been made.

Friedrich Engels on Nature And History as Process

From Ludwig Feuerbach and the
End of Classical German Philosophy

The old method of investigation and thought which Hegel calls "metaphysical", which preferred to investigate things as given, as fixed and stable, a method the relics of which still strongly haunt people's minds, had a great deal of historical justification in its day. It was necessary first to examine things before it was possible to examine processes. One had first to know what a particular thing was before one could observe the changes it was undergoing. And such was the case with natural science. The old metaphysics, which accepted things as finished objects, arose from a natural science which investigated dead and living things as finished objects. But when this investigation had progressed so far that it became possible to take the decisive step forward, that is, to pass on the systematic investigation of the changes which these things undergo in nature itself, then the last hour of the old metaphysic struck in the realm of philosophy also. And in fact, while natural science up to the end of the last century was predominantly a *collecting* science, a science of finished things, in our century it is essentially a systematizing science, a science of the processes, of the origin and development of these things and of the interconnection which binds all these natural processes into one great whole. Physiology, which investigates the processes occurring in plant and animal organisms; embryology, which deals with the development of individual organisms from germs to maturity; geology, which investigates the gradual formation of the Earth's surface—all these are the offspring of our century.

But, above all, there are three great discoveries which have enabled our knowledge of the interconnection of natural processes to advance by leaps and bounds:

First, the discovery of the cell as the unit from whose multiplication and differentiation the whole plant and animal body develops. Not only is the development and growth of all higher organisms recognized to proceed according to a single general law, but the capacity of the cell to change indicates the way by which organisms can change their species and thus go through a more than individual development.

Second, the transformation of energy, which has demonstrated to us that all the so-called forces operative in the first instance in inorganic nature— mechanical force and its complement, so-called potential energy, heat, radiation (light, or radiant heat), electricity, magnetism, and chemical energy—are different forms of manifestation of universal motion, which pass into one another in definite proportions so that in place of a certain quantity of the one which disappears, a certain quantity of another makes its appearance and thus the whole motion of nature is reduced to this incessant process of transformation from one form into another.

Finally, the proof which Darwin first developed in connected form that the stock of organic products of nature environing us today, including man, is the result of a long process of evolution from a few originally unicellular germs, and that these again have arisen from protoplasm or albumen, which came into existence by chemical means.

Thanks to these three great discoveries, and the other immense advances in natural science, we have now arrived at the point where we can demonstrate the interconnection between the processes in nature not only in particular spheres but also the interconnection of these particular spheres on the whole, and so can present in an approximately systematic form a comprehensive view of the interconnection in nature by means of the facts provided by an empirical science itself. To furnish this comprehensive view was formerly the task of so-called natural philosophy. It could do this only by putting in place of the real but as yet unknown interconnections ideal, fancied ones, filling in the missing facts by figments of the mind and bridging the actual gaps merely in imagination. In the course of this procedure it conceived many brilliant ideas and foreshadowed many later discoveries, but it also produced a considerable amount of nonsense, which indeed could not have been otherwise. Today, when one needs to comprehend the results of natural scientific investigation only dialectically, that is, in the sense of their own interconnection, in order to arrive at a "system of nature" sufficient for our time; when the dialectical character of this interconnection is forcing itself against their will even into the metaphysically-trained minds of the natural scientists, today natural philosophy is finally disposed of. Every attempt at resurrecting it would be not only superfluous but a *step backwards*.

But what is true of nature, which is hereby recognized also as a historical process of development, is likewise true of the history of society in all its branches and of the totality of all sciences which occupy themselves with things human (and divine). Here, too, the philosophy of history, of right, of religion, etc., has consisted in the substitution of an interconnection fabricated in the mind of the philosopher for the real interconnection to be demonstrated in the events; has consisted in the comprehension of history as a whole as well as in its separate parts, as the gradual realization of idea—and naturally always only the pet ideas of the philosopher himself. According to this, history worked unconsciously but of necessity towards a certain ideal goal set in advance—as, for example, in Hegel, towards the realization of his absolute idea—and the unalterable trend towards this absolute idea formed the inner interconnection in the events of history. A new mysterious providence—unconscious or gradually coming into consciousness—was thus put in the place of the real, still unknown interconnection. Here, therefore, just as in the realm of nature, it was necessary to do away with these fabricated, artificial interconnections by the discovery of the real ones—a task which ultimately amounts to the discovery of the general laws of motion which assert themselves as the ruling ones in the history of human society.

In one point, however, the history of the development of society proves to be essentially different from that of nature. In nature—in so far as we ignore man's reaction upon nature—there are only blind, unconscious agencies acting upon one another, out of whose interplay the general law comes into operation. Nothing of all that happens—whether in the innumerable apparent accidents observable upon the surface, or in the ultimate results which confirm the regularity inherent in these accidents—happens as a consciously desired aim. In the history of society, on the contrary, the actors are all endowed with consciousness, are men acting with deliberation or passion, working towards definite goals; nothing happens without a conscious purpose, without an intended aim. But this distinction, important as it is for historical investigation, particularly of single epochs and events, cannot alter the fact that the course of history is governed by inner general laws. For here, also, on the whole, in spite of the consciously desired aims of all individuals, accident apparently reigns on the surface. That which is willed happens but rarely; in the majority of instances the numerous desired ends cross and conflict with one another, or these ends themselves are from the outset incapable of realization, or the means of attaining them are insufficient. Thus the conflicts of innumerable individual wills and individual actions in the domain of history produce a state of affairs entirely analogous to that prevailing in the realm of unconscious nature. The ends of the actions are intended, but the results which actually follow from these actions are not intended; or when they do seem to correspond to the end intended, they ultimately have consequences quite other than those intended. Historical events thus appear on the whole to be likewise governed by chance. But where on the surface accident holds sway, there actually it is always governed by inner, hidden laws, and it is only a matter of discovering these laws.

Full Circle: The Moral Force of Unified Science

By Edward Haskell, Published 1972

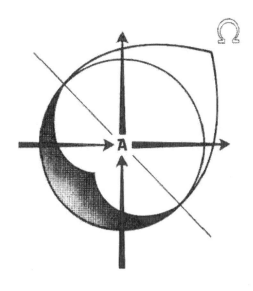

Summary of the Concept

Although his book is long since out of print, the late Edward Haskell developed this diagram to combine the Cartesian Coordinates with his own theory that all science could ultimately be shown to demonstrate a meta order in nature. The intersection of the coordinates becomes the Alpha point, which is both the end of destructive interactions or the beginning of constructive interactions. Where X and Y are both positive, their mutually cooperative interaction is symbiotic, approaching the optimal outcome, Omega. Where both are negative, their interaction approaches mutual destruction. Haskell mapped the Table of Chemical Elements onto this framework (Carbon being the most 'symbiotic' element, due to its greatest combinative structure), as well as biological behavior (symbiotic, predator-prey, parasite-host, and mutually destructive), as well as social interactions (cooperative versus conflictual relations, and degrees in between) and psychological behaviors.

These behaviors, Haskell said, proved that cooperation was rewarded in nature, whereas predation, parasitism and mutual destruction were punished, to varying degrees. (Hence, the moral force of Unified Science.) This view is directly opposite to the Marxist theory of Dialectical Materialism, which holds that conflict is necessary for a higher Synthesis to emerge from a struggle between Thesis and Antithesis.

Appendix 12

Highlights of Khrushchev's 1960 Speeches at the United Nations

Nikita Khrushchev visited the United States to attend the UN General Assembly in 1960. His long-winded speeches there reveal the thinking and policies of the Soviet Union. He decried war, and claimed in lyrical language that his country was opposed to all war and in favor of freedom and peace for all humanity, although he did note that the Soviets needed sufficient weapons to defend themselves against imperialists (i.e. the United States). He claimed that, unlike colonialists, the USSR was only interested in the well-being of African and other poor nations seeking independence. He claimed that the constituent states of the USSR were thrilled to be part of the Soviet Union, and that they had benefited tremendously from their inclusion. He mentioned not a word about the tens of millions killed by Lenin, Stalin and other Soviet leaders, crimes that he himself had been largely responsible for revealing to the world in 1956. As the British ambassador would comment during the debate on October 12, Khrushchev's description of the world situation and Soviet innocence and idealism was a "fairy-tale picture." The Soviet leader simply lied through his teeth.

On September 23, he delivered a speech to the General Assembly calling for the abolition of colonialism and all nuclear weapons. He blamed the United States for disturbing global peace and for all the wasteful spending on weapons. One of the truly remarkable claims he made was that the Soviet states, such as those in Central Asia and Transcaucasia, had been delighted beneficiaries of Soviet benevolence. He said that in Tsarist Russia they were like Europe's colonies, but after being integrated into the Soviet

Union they had experienced rapid economic growth and enjoyed full freedom, including the freedom to leave the USSR if they so chose. He said the Soviet people fully supported the wars of independence, and that the Soviet Union believed it was its moral duty to come to the military aid of independence revolutions, if need be. He omitted to note that the constituent states of the Soviet Union, such as those in Central Asia, had been forced into membership in the USSR by the Red Army after the Russian Revolution, and that the Central and East European states in the Warsaw Pact had been conquered by Stalin after World War II and were more subservient to Moscow than almost any colony had ever been to a European power.

From the tone of his speech, one would have thought that the Soviet Union was bent on nothing other than spreading peaceful coexistence and good neighborliness throughout the world, and that the United States, by contrast, was taking the world to the brink of a Third World War. Applying Marxist doctrine, he said: "…just as in the past the bourgeois order of things came to replace feudalism and as, now, socialism is replacing capitalism, so colonial slavery is giving place to freedom. Such are the rules of human development, and only adventurers can believe that mountains of corpses and millions of victims will delay the advent of a radiant future." Most of those corpses were the result of Communist revolutions in the name of "the people." Tens of millions more victims of Communism would follow in the next few decades.

On October 12, he was once more in the UN General Assembly chamber, seated with the Soviet delegation. The session was to discuss Moscow's proposal for a "Declaration on the granting of independence to colonial countries and peoples." The Soviets wanted a General Assembly debate, where they could depend on votes from Eastern European satellites and client states around the world. The proper procedure, however, was for the matter to first go to committee. The debate was revealing. When Khrushchev spoke, he repeated the claim that Moscow was totally against colonialism and for freedom and independence of all people. His relentless condemnation of colonialism ran into a problem, however, when the representative from the Philippines pointed out that Moscow's East European satellites were far from free, and that they should be included in any UN declaration against colonialism. The Romanian representative leapt to the defense of big brother, trying to get the debate shut down on the grounds that the Philippines representative was insulting East European countries. Khrushchev soon joined in what proved a losing effort to steer clear of this issue. Later, he once again praised the wonders of the Soviet Union and Communism: "There is no greater freedom for man than the freedom to build and develop an independent State— and a socialist State, like ours— into the bargain. The Soviet people have already completed the building of Socialism and has now turned to the building of Communism."

Following are excerpts from Khrushchev's September 23 speech, followed by excerpts from the October 12 debate.

UN General Assembly, September 23, 1960

Speech by Mr. Khrushchev, Chairman of the Council of Ministers of the Union of Soviet Socialist Republics, at the 869th Plenary Meeting of the 15th Session of the United Nations General Assembly, September 23, 1960. Full speech: https:// undocs.org/en/A/PV.869.

97. Naturally, our thoughts are now focused on the matters which most trouble and disturb mankind. Perhaps it is precisely here in this Assembly that the world is seen in all its diversity and, of course, in all its contradictions. It has fallen to our lot to live in the stormiest and yet the most splendid period in the history of mankind; future generations will envy us.

99. Our century is the century of the struggle for freedom, the century in which nations are liberating themselves from foreign domination. The peoples desire a worthwhile life and are fighting to secure it.

100. Victory has already been won in many countries and lands. But we cannot rest on our laurels, for we know that tens of millions of human beings are still languishing in colonial slavery and are suffering grave hardships.

102. It might seem that all was well with the world. Yet can it be said that the world is well ordered in every respect, or that it is free from poverty and deprivation? We should again reflect on the fact that, according to United Nations statistics, hundreds of millions of men and women on different continents drag out an existence at starvation or near-starvation level. Our world is not free from fear for the future; it realizes the dangers of the division into military alliances and of the continuously accelerating nuclear arms race. The great achievements of man's genius may be used either for man's benefit or to his detriment. This is the difficult choice confronting us.

105. This development in international relations, which is fraught with conflict and complications, has not arisen overnight. Even in the early post-

war years there were two clearly antagonistic schools of thought on world affairs. One stood for the reduction of international tension, the halting of the arms race, the development of international cooperation and the elimination of war from the life of society—a fine and laudable approach. It is, indeed, for the triumph of justice that man lives on earth.

106. There is, however, a second school of thought, about which we have no right to remain silent. This school stands for fanning the flames of the cold war, for the unrestricted accumulation of armaments and for the destruction of every basis for international cooperation, with all the dangerous consequences which this entails.

108. The peoples of all countries—workers, peasants, intellectuals and the bourgeoisie, excluding a small handful of militarists and monopolists—want not war but peace, and peace alone. And if, therefore, the peoples actively fight to tie the hands of the militarist and monopolist circles, peace can be ensured.

110. The United Nations was established in the name of the victory of peace and tranquility, in the service of peace and the security of nations. We trust that the decisions reached by the present session of the General Assembly will bring us closer to the realization of peace and justice—the goal of all mankind.

116. A year ago, I had the honor of making a statement from this high rostrum [799ᵗʰ meeting]. At that time, promising prospects of normalizing the international situation were opening up before mankind. Contacts between responsible statesmen in the various countries were increasing. The General Assembly adopted a resolution [1378 (XIV)] on general and complete disarmament. The Ten-Nation Committee on Disarmament began its work. Agreement was reached on holding a summit conference. Definite progress was being made in the negotiations on the discontinuance of nuclear and thermonuclear tests. All this raised high hopes in the hearts of the people of all countries.

117. No one can dispute the fact that the Soviet Union has been unsparing in its efforts to ensure the continuation of this welcome trend in the development of international relations. But the sinister forces which profit from the maintenance of international tension are clinging tenaciously to their positions. Though only a handful of individuals is involved, they are quite powerful and exert a strong influence on the policy of their respective States. A major effort is therefore required to break their resistance. As soon as the policy of easing international tension begins to yield tangible results, they immediately resort to extreme measures in order to ensure that the peoples should feel no relief; they strain every nerve to plunge the world back again and again into an atmosphere of gloom and to exacerbate international tension.

126. Whatever the explanation, one thing remains perfectly obvious: the operations of those responsible for organizing the acts of provocation are designed to create an atmosphere in which the peoples would live in constant fear. Even if such an atmosphere suits the Government of the United States, it certainly does not suit the Soviet Union or the overwhelming majority of other States. We have striven and shall strive to banish all forms of lawlessness from international relations.

127. The Soviet Union is not making any exorbitant demands. We are merely striving to ensure adherence to the most elementary rules of intercourse among States. Our only objective is strict observance of the United Nations Charter which rules out methods of violence, brigandage and aggression and demands respect for the sovereign rights of all States as the basis for lasting peace on earth. Is that asking too much? Is that not the wish of all honest men and women on this earth, who care for the fate of the world and for the sovereignty and independence of their own countries?

132. Fewer and fewer people are prepared to accept the present state of affairs in which any manifestation of the free will of the peoples, any tendency to pursue an independent policy, be it on the part of Indonesia,

Iraq or Guinea, of neutral Austria or of little Iceland, acting to defend its economic interests, encounters fierce opposition and brings down thunder and lightning from the powers grouped together in NATO—this Holy Alliance of our day, which has assumed the ungrateful mission of exorcizing the spirit of freedom in whatever part of the globe it may appear.

136. A new chapter has now begun in Cuba. After expelling the dictator Batista, the Cuban people freed itself from foreign exploitation, took its destiny into its own hands, firmly telling the United States monopolists that they had been robbing the country long enough and that the people themselves would enjoy the fruits of their labor and their soil.

144. The colonialists and their servile supporters say that Mr. Lumumba is a Communist. Mr. Lumumba is, of course, no Communist; he is a patriot and is honestly serving his people in its struggle for freedom from the colonial yoke. But, by putting out this story that he is a Communist, the colonialists are actually helping the colonial peoples to tear off the veil which is being used to obscure their vision. Those peoples will soon see that the Communist Party is the only party which genuinely reflects the will of the peoples struggling for the triumph of justice, the aspirations of all peoples striving for freedom.

146. We have stood, we stand, and always will stand, for the right of the peoples of Africa, just as those of other continents, to establish whatever regime they please in their countries, on attaining their freedom from colonial oppression.

147. Second, we have always been and always will be against any interference by imperialists in the domestic affairs of countries which are emancipating themselves from colonial dependence, against discreditable methods such as those used in the Congo.

149. The people will not stop halfway. They are mobilizing their forces and they will act with still greater foresight and in the knowledge that the struggle for independence is a hard one, that there are many obstacles to be

overcome on the way to genuine freedom, and that it is necessary to learn to distinguish between true friends and enemies.

151. The Soviet State and its Government welcomed and welcomes the struggle of the colonial peoples for independence and is doing all it can to give them moral and material assistance in their just fight.

172. It should be clear to everyone that there is no means and no force which can halt this struggle of the peoples for their liberation, for it is a great historic process, one of ever-growing and invincible power. It may be possible to prolong the dominion of one state over another for a year or two, but just as in the past the bourgeois order of things came to replace feudalism and as now socialism is replacing capitalism, so colonial slavery is giving place to freedom. Such are the rules of human development, and only adventurers can believe that mountains of corpses and millions of victims will delay the advent of a radiant future.

176. The Soviet Union, faithful to the policy of peace and support for the struggle of oppressed peoples for their national independence, the policy proclaimed by Vladimir Ilyich Lenin, founder of the Soviet State, calls upon the United Nations to raise its voice in defense of the just liberation of the colonies and to take immediate steps towards the complete abolition of the colonial system of government.

181. The Soviet Government believes that the time has come to pose the question of the full and final abolition of the colonial system of government in all its forms and varieties in order to make an end of this infamy, this barbarism, this savagery.

190. A positive role in overcoming the age-old backwardness of the countries that are being liberated would be played by economic and technical assistance through the United Nations and on a bilateral basis. Of course, this will require considerable funds. Where can they be obtained without overburdening the population of the industrially developed countries? Once again from this rostrum I draw your attention to the source

which could be provided by disarmament. The allocation of one one-tenth of the funds which the great Powers are now spending for military purposes would increase the amount of assistance to under-developed countries by $10,000 million [$10 billion] a year. Yet the cost of constructing all the units of one of the world's largest power systems, in the Inga region of the Congo, by which a tremendous area in Africa could be made to blossom is estimated at $5,000 million [$5 billion].

191. It is also pertinent to recall that it is the moral duty of the States which possessed colonies in the past to return to the liberated peoples of those countries at least a part of the riches taken from them through cruel exploitation of the people and the plundering of their natural resources.

192. It may be said that it is easy for the Soviet Union to advocate the liquidation of the colonial system, since the Soviet Union has no colonies. Yes, that is so. We have no colonies and no capital in other countries. But there was a time when many of the nationalities inhabiting our country suffered the bitter oppression of Tsarism, of the landlord-bourgeois system. Conditions in remote areas of the Tsarist empire hardly differed from those of colonies because their populations were cruelly exploited by the autocracy, by capitalism. Whereas the autocracy looked upon the peoples of Central Asia and Transcaucasia, and other nationalities inhabiting the Russian Empire, as a source of profit, after the October revolution, when these peoples obtained complete freedom, they quickly improved their economic, cultural and social conditions.

198. In the family of equal socialist republics, the former borderlands of pre-revolutionary Russia, which were threatened with depopulation as a result of malnutrition and disease, have been transformed into flourishing territories where living standards have risen as they have throughout the whole Soviet Union. The wages and salaries of workers and employees there do not differ from those in other republics of the Soviet Union. Like all the citizens of the USSR, they receive pensions, health insurance benefits and

other social benefits.

206. After the great October socialist revolution, the bourgeoisie of the whole world harped incessantly on the inevitability of the collapse of Soviet power because Russia was an ill-educated country and the working class had no experts capable of running the State machinery and the economy of the country. Life has proved the truth of Lenin's statement that the revolution would awaken the initiative of the people, that the Soviet power would produce leaders and organizers from among the masses and that, having taken power, common workers and peasants would learn to govern the State and would master all the achievements of modern science and technology.

207. The Tsarist Government pursued in the borderlands of Russia an essentially colonialist policy which differed little from what can be observed today in colonial countries. Uzbeks, Kazakhs, Tadzhiks and other non-Russian nationalities were scornfully called "aliens". They were not considered human beings and were ruthlessly exploited. National differences, hatred and dissension were fomented between these nationalities, and the Tsarist Empire was held together only by bayonets and oppression. When the peoples of Central Asia and Transcaucasia were given their national freedom and equal rights with the other peoples of Russia, they showed their capabilities in the development of their national economy and culture.

208. Did the development of our country suffer by the granting to the peoples of the right of independence and self-determination? Is there strife and enmity between nationalities in our multi-national country or a disintegration of the State? No, there is nothing of the sort, nor can there be.

209. Under the Constitution, each of our fifteen Union Republics has the right to remain in the Union or to leave it, if it so desires. The existence of nineteen autonomous republics, nine autonomous regions and ten national territories makes it possible to preserve the national characteristics and cultural originality and individuality of each people and nationality.

210. Harmony and unprecedented unity between all nationalities have

been achieved in the Soviet Union. A genuine friendship between nationalities was brought into being, which all the trials of the Second World War could not shake. These great changes benefitted not only the national minorities, but the Russians, Ukrainians and Byelorussians—the nations comprising a majority of the Soviet Union's population.

224. The Soviet Union, for its part, has been giving assistance to economically under-developed countries and will continue to do so in ever-increasing volume. We are genuinely helping the peoples of these countries to establish their independent economies and to develop their own industry, which is the mainstay of true independence and of increasing prosperity for the people.

225. Peoples which oppress others cannot be free. Every free people must help those who are still oppressed to gain their freedom and independence.

227. In September 1959, on the Soviet Government's instructions, I submitted at the fourteenth session of the United Nations General Assembly [799th meeting] the Soviet Union's proposals for general and complete disarmament. The appalling destructive force of modern weapons, the unprecedented pace of the arms race, the accumulation by States of vast stockpiles of weapons of mass destruction, all create a threat to the future of mankind and necessitate a search for an essentially new approach to the problem of disarmament. Our proposals were the practical expression of such an approach.

229. The Soviet Government, which is consistently and resolutely pursuing a peaceful policy, solemnly declares at the present session of the United Nations General Assembly that the Soviet Union maintains armed forces for the sole purpose of defending our country and fulfilling our commitments to our allies and friends in the event of aggression against them. The use of our armed forces for other purposes is precluded because that would be alien to the very nature of our State and to the fundamental principles of our peaceful foreign policy.

230. Our country is compelled to maintain armed forces solely because our proposals for general and complete disarmament have not yet been accepted. We shall do everything in our power to ensure that general and complete disarmament becomes a reality and that mankind is liberated from the arms race and from the threat of a new war of extermination.

233. The facts show that the absence of any progress towards the solution of the disarmament problem is the consequence of the position taken by the United States and by certain other States linked with it through NATO.

236. Acting directly contrary to the General Assembly resolution, the western Powers engaged in meaningless talk on disarmament in the Ten-Nation Committee on Disarmament, trying to impede all progress in the matter and to discredit the idea of general and complete disarmament in the eyes of the world.

237. The Soviet Government, together with the Governments of a number of other States, was compelled to suspend its participation in the work of the Ten-Nation Committee which the Western Powers had turned into a screen for concealing the arms race… It was impossible to tolerate attempts to make the great cause of disarmament an object of speculation for purposes inimical to the interests of universal peace.

240. In submitting the question of disarmament to the General Assembly for consideration in plenary meeting, our basic premise is that a full-scale discussion of this question should finally lead to its solution or, at least, give a more practical direction to the disarmament talks, in which States adhering to a neutral course should now participate, in addition to States belonging to the opposing military group.

252. The Soviet Government is deeply convinced that only a radical solution of the problem of disarmament, providing for the complete prohibition of nuclear weapons together with the cessation of their manufacture, destruction of all accumulated stockpiles of these weapons, can accomplish

the task of delivering mankind from the threat of nuclear war which hangs over it. This is precisely the aim which the Soviet Union is pursuing in consistently and resolutely advocating general and complete disarmament.

254. Soberly appraising the situation and the correlation of forces in the world, the Soviet Government is profoundly convinced that disarmament in our time is not only necessary but possible. The struggle for peace has now become a great watchword mobilizing the peoples. This is a fact to be reckoned with even by those Governments which are still infected with an unhealthy attraction towards the policy of cold war and the armaments race.

257. The peoples of the Soviet Union and the Soviet Government are striving unremittingly to have the principles of peaceful coexistence firmly established in relations between States, and to ensure that these principles become the fundamental law of life for the whole of modern society. There is no Communist-devised "trick" behind these principles, but simple truths dictated by life itself, such as that relations between all States should develop peacefully, without the use of force, without war and without interference in each other's internal affairs.

258. I am revealing no secret when I say that we have no liking for capitalism. But we do not want to impose our system on other peoples by force. Let those, then, who determine the policy of States with a different social system from ours, renounce their fruitless and dangerous attempts to dictate their will. It is time they also recognized that the choice of a particular way of life is the domestic concern of every people. Let us build up our relations having regard to actual realities. That is true peaceful coexistence.

262. Anyone wishing to describe how peaceful co-existence looks in practice might point to the relations maintained by the socialist countries with the new States of Asia, Africa, and Latin America which have freed themselves from colonial oppression and have started to follow an independent policy. These relations are marked by true friendship, great mutual sympathy and esteem, and the granting of economic and technical

assistance to the less developed countries without any political or military strings attached. Another good example might be the relations maintained between the countries of the socialist camp and neutral capitalist States such as, for instance, Finland, Austria, Afghanistan, Sweden and others.

271. Only madmen could think of settling the Korean question by armed force. The only correct proposal, namely to leave the solution of the question of the peaceful reunification of Korea to the Koreans themselves with no interference from outside, is finding ever wider acceptance. An essential condition for this is the immediate and complete withdrawal of all United States troops from South Korea, for their presence poisons the atmosphere not only in Korea but throughout the Far East and has made possible such shameful facts as the rigging of elections in South Korea. The proposal of the Government of the Democratic People's Republic of Korea to establish a confederation of North and South Korea is just as reasonable as the proposal of the Government of the German Democratic Republic to set up a confederation of the two German States. It is the only way to lay a sound foundation for the re-unification of these States.

284. We consider it reasonable and just for the executive organ of the United Nations to consist not of a single person—the Secretary-General— but of three persons invested with the highest trust of the United Nations, persons representing the States belonging to the three basic groups I have mentioned. The point at issue is not the title of the organ but that this executive organ should represent the States belonging to the military bloc of the Western Powers, the socialist States and the neutralist States. This composition of the United Nations executive organ would create conditions for a more correct implementation of the decisions taken.

288. The question arises whether thought should not be given to selecting another place for United Nations Headquarters, a place which would better facilitate the fruitful work of the international body. Either Switzerland or Austria for instance might well be chosen. I can state with full

authority that should it be considered expedient to move the Headquarters of the United Nations to the Soviet Union; we would guarantee the best possible conditions for its work and complete freedom and security for the representatives of all States, irrespective of their political or religious convictions or the color of their skin, for in our country the sovereign rights of all States and the equality of all nations, big and small, receive the highest respect.

302. So let us act in such a way as to make the fifteenth session of the General Assembly not only an Assembly of hopes but also an Assembly of the realization of hopes.

303. The Soviet Government is ready to do its utmost in order that colonial servitude may be destroyed here and now, that here and now the problems of disarmament may find their concrete and effective solution.

304. The Soviet Government is ready to do its utmost in order that the testing of nuclear weapons may be prohibited here and now, that this means of mass destruction may be prohibited and destroyed.

306. In concluding my statement I wish to emphasize once again that the Soviet Government, guided by the interests of the Soviet people, by the interests of the citizens of a free socialist State, once again proposes to all: let us talk, let us argue, but let us settle the questions of general and complete disarmament and let us bury colonialism that is accursed of all mankind.

UN General Assembly, October 12, 1960

Khrushchev's remarks during a UN General Assembly debate at the 902nd Plenary Meeting of the 15th Session of the United Nations General Assembly, October 12, 1960. Full debate: https://undocs.org/en/A/PV.902. (The numbers refer to paragraphs in the transcript.)

4. Mr. KHRUSHCHEV, Chairman of the Council of Ministers of the Union of Soviet Socialist Republics (translated from Russian): The Government of the Soviet Union has requested [A/4501] that the question of the adoption by States Members of the United Nations of a declaration on the granting of independence to colonial countries and peoples should be included in the agenda of the fifteenth session of the General Assembly. In our opinion, it is essential that the question should be discussed by the General Assembly in plenary meeting.

13. If the United Nations does not adopt the proposals aimed at the elimination of the colonial system, the peoples of the colonial countries will have no option but to take up arms. If they are not granted the right to lead an independent existence, to have a political and social system of their own choosing and to organize their life in their own country as they themselves see fit, they will win that right in combat. I have already said, and I now repeat, that the Soviet people are on the side of those who are struggling for liberation from the colonial yoke, for freedom and independence.

19. We appeal to the representatives of the African and Asian countries which recently acquired their independence, because we should like to see them imbued with a due sense of their responsibility at this juncture in history when the struggle of the colonial peoples for their complete liberation is gathering momentum. We address ourselves to the representatives of countries that have acceded to independence and have joined the United Nations on a footing of equality.

20. For centuries the colonialists have been sweating and bleeding your

peoples, exploiting them mercilessly and crushing everything that was vital in your countries. Now that they can no longer pursue their policy of robbery, oppression and murder in your countries, they pretend to be your benefactors; they now pose as magnanimous Christians and are not even averse to censuring oppression and colonialism; they say that by their participation in the colonial system they were merely creating the necessary conditions in which to prepare your countries for independence and self-government. But those are the lies of robbers who know that they are robbers. They now wish to erase their crimes from the memory of the peoples they have been oppressing for centuries. That is why they are now courting you, giving receptions and making honeyed speeches.

22. You must remember that the fate of your brothers in the continent of Africa largely depends on you. The colonialists wish to use you as a cat's paw for their dirty work, namely, to frustrate the adoption of the declaration on the freeing of all the colonial peoples. They wish to use you to tighten the rope round the neck of the colonial peoples and keep a stranglehold upon them. That is why the Soviet Government is calling upon you to show determination and to prove that you can defend other interests in addition to those of your own peoples and States and that, having acceded to independence, you remember those who are still languishing in colonial enslavement.

23. Our countries need not fear the illusory power of the colonialists. Right is on our side and so is the preponderance of force. If you give active support to the countries struggling against colonial oppression, we shall be in the majority. It is necessary to show fortitude and determination and to raise one's voice against the colonialists, whatever guise they may adopt. Every individual sitting in this hall is ultimately answerable to the people. Sooner or later the people will call their representative to account and will ask how he voted in the United Nations and whether he was in favor of the immediate and total abolition of colonial slavery and of freedom for all

peoples, or whether he wavered.

24. We are calling for concerted efforts to combat colonialism. Let the colonial system be ended once and for all by the will of the people, and let all the colonies accede to independence and all peoples become free. The elimination of colonialism would be of paramount importance in easing international tension. The armed conflicts and wars of the post-war period—such as the wars in Indonesia, Indo-China and Algeria, the aggression against Egypt, foreign intervention in Lebanon and Jordan, the plots against Syria and Iraq—developed precisely because the colonialists and the imperialists wished to stifle the liberation movement and frustrate the national development of the countries of Asia, Africa and Latin America. As for the recent intervention against the Republic of the Congo, it has led to a deterioration in the international situation and has presented a threat to peace in Africa and not in Africa alone. That is why we say that the problem of the total liquidation of the colonial system is to a considerable extent bound up with the maintenance and the strengthening of peace and international security.

26. Mr. ORMSBY-GORE (United Kingdom): We have just listened to a speech by the Chairman of the Council of Ministers of the Soviet Union which, in my opinion, was an insult to his audience, in that it assumed that those listening to it had a complete ignorance of the subject about which he was speaking. This is not the occasion for me to try to correct the fairy-tale picture presented this afternoon, for we are now dealing with a purely procedural matter. The purpose of our discussion here is to decide in what forum the Assembly should discuss this item which is already included in the agenda.

27. The Government of the United Kingdom recognizes that this item, entitled "Declaration on the granting of independence to colonial countries and peoples", deals with a subject which is of the greatest interest to most of the Members of this Assembly. The transition of colonial countries and

peoples to the status of sovereign independence is one of the most important political developments at this period of history. It is one with which my Government is deeply and urgently concerned. Indeed, I believe that I can fairly say that there is probably no other Government represented in the Assembly which is more concerned with this problem than the Government of the United Kingdom. For this reason, the United Kingdom representative on the General Committee supported the inclusion of this item in the agenda and advocated that it should be allotted to the First Committee for consideration.

28. We would indeed welcome a serious discussion of this item. It is the hope of the United Kingdom delegation that debate on this subject will be responsible and constructive and that the vital principles involved will be discussed by all delegations in a way which pays proper regard to the real aspirations of all the peoples of the world for independence, peace and prosperity, and individual freedom. We think that this is the spirit in which the majority of the Members of the Assembly will wish to approach this matter.

78. Mr. TARABANOV (Bulgaria) (translated from Russian): The fifteenth session of the General Assembly has assumed exceptional significance mainly because of the importance of three items proposed by the Soviet Union: disarmament and the situation with regard to the non-fulfilment of the relevant resolution [1378(XIV)] of November 1959; the elimination of colonialism, and, in that connection, the submission of the declaration on the granting of independence to colonial countries and peoples; and the menace to peace created by aggressive actions of the United States of America against the Soviet Union.

79. These questions are directly and most intimately connected with the cardinal problems of our time—the problems of peaceful coexistence, of peace and war. For this reason the peoples of all countries rightly expected the General Assembly to proceed to the immediate discussion of the USSR proposals, with a view to arriving at decisions that would open wide the

door to peace with the least possible delay.

81. One of the main features of our time is the collapse of the colonial system. After a long and hard-fought struggle involving many sacrifices, a number of colonial and semi-colonial peoples have freed themselves from colonial bondage. In less than two decades, a tempestuous and irresistible movement for national liberation in the colonies has brought statehood to dozens of new nations; and this movement is so powerful, the sympathies and support it inspires are so universal, that today even the fiercest colonialist diehards are compelled to admit that colonialism is living its last days. However, colonialism is not dead yet. It is even seeking undercover forms which would enable it to preserve its domination and predatory interests.

82. The proposal of the Soviet Government that the United Nations should adopt a declaration on the granting of independence to colonial countries and peoples therefore constitutes an initiative of great humanitarian and immense political significance. The adoption of this declaration by the General Assembly would give the oppressed colonial peoples the assurance that they will gain their freedom and soon be independent. This would make it possible to reduce tensions in those countries and would eliminate many sources of conflict.

94. Mr. TOURE, Ismael (Guinea) (translated from French): My delegation noted with great interest the statement which the United Kingdom representative made from this rostrum a short while ago.

96. I should also like to remind the United Kingdom representative that the African delegations are not afraid of propaganda, especially where the freedom of their peoples is concerned, and that anyone who believes that propaganda can have any effect on us is mistaken. It was not through propaganda that our peoples obtained freedom and it is not by propaganda that they can now be kept under the yoke. On the contrary, we think it shows a lack of understanding to refuse to consider a question of such importance in plenary session, on the mere pretext that it might be made the

subject of propaganda.

134. Mr. SUMULONG (Philippines): My delegation, the Philippine delegation, attaches great importance to this item entitled "Declaration on the granting of independence to colonial countries and peoples", the allocation of which is now under discussion.

135. We have been a colonized country. We have passed through all the trials and tribulations of a colonized people. It took us centuries and centuries to fight, to struggle, and to win our fight for the recognition of our independence, and, therefore, it would only be consistent with our history, our experience and our aspirations as a people that we vote in favor of having this item referred to the highest possible level of the General Assembly.

136. While this is not the occasion to discuss the substance of the item, I would like to place on record my delegation's view on the import as well as on the scope, the extent, the metes and bounds of this item. We feel this to be necessary in view of the statements made at the start of our meeting by the Premier of the Soviet Union. It is our view that the declaration proposed by the Soviet Union should cover the inalienable right to independence not only of the peoples and territories which yet remain under the rule of Western colonial Powers, but also of the peoples of Eastern Europe and elsewhere which have been deprived of the free exercise of their civil and political rights and which have been swallowed up, so to speak, by the Soviet Union.

137. Mr. MEZINCESCU (Romania) (from the floor): Point of order.

138. The PRESIDENT [Frederick Boland (Ireland)]: I would ask the speaker at the rostrum kindly to stand aside or resume his seat while I deal with the point of order which has been raised from the floor.

139. Mr. SUMULONG (Philippines): Mr. President, I shall do so. I had to explain the reasons for our vote on this amendment.

140. Mr. MEZINCESCU (Romania) (from the floor): Point of order.

141. The PRESIDENT: I would ask the speaker at the rostrum kindly

to stand aside for a moment while I hear and deal with a point of order which has been raised from the floor.

142. I call on the representative of Romania on a point of order.

143. Mr. MEZINCESCU (Romania) (translated from French): I appeal to the President and request him to call to order the speaker to whom he gave the floor a few moments ago and who has just been speaking from this rostrum.

144. I protest vigorously because I consider that in this Hall he should not be allowed to address insults to States Members of the United Nations which enjoy sovereign independence and have equal rights as Members of the Organization. I feel that the President should not allow slanderous charges to be made from this rostrum against Members of the United Nations.

145. The PRESIDENT: The Chair did not understand the representative of the Philippines to be actually out of order. The justification of his remarks is a matter for the judgement of the Assembly. I call upon the representative of the Philippines to continue.

146. Mr. SUMULONG (Philippines): Thank you, Mr. President. With the permission of the Assembly may I now proceed?

147. Mr. MEZINCESCU (Romania) (from the floor): Point of order.

148. The PRESIDENT: A point of order has been raised from the floor; I would ask the speaker at the rostrum kindly to stand aside while I deal with it. I give the floor to the representative of Romania on a point of order.

149. Mr. MEZINCESCU (Romania) (translated from French): Mr. President, I was under the impression that it was your duty, as President of the General Assembly, to conduct the discussions in such a way that Members of the United Nations present here are not insulted from this rostrum.

150. I appeal to you again and request you to call to order the speaker who has just occupied this rostrum.

151. We are discussing the abolition of the colonial system and the fate

of peoples and countries which are not represented in this Assembly; there are still dozens of such countries. That is the subject on which we must speak. By allowing independent countries, Members of the Assembly, to be insulted from the rostrum and imposing silence on representatives of countries which not long ago were under colonial domination, you are not upholding the dignity of your office, which is to conduct the debates of this Assembly impartially.

152. I consider that it is your duty to ensure that Member States are treated with respect and to require speakers to keep to the item under discussion, namely, the problem of the peoples and countries which are not represented here and which are at present under the domination of the great and small colonial Powers whose representatives are sitting in this Assembly. The declaration concerning the final abolition of the colonial system has been submitted for discussion by our Assembly in order that they may obtain freedom a little earlier and enjoy the right to sit here side by side with the representatives of all the peoples of the world.

153. The PRESIDENT: There was no element of personal insult in the remarks of the representative of the Philippines. He made a statement of a political and controversial nature with which obviously a large number of delegations do not agree, but it is entirely in order for such statements to be made in the Assembly, and no point of order arises with regard to them. We must be prepared in the Assembly to hear stated views with which we strongly disagree. I would now ask the representative of the Philippines to continue.

154. Mr. KHRUSHCHEV, Chairman of the Council of Ministers of the Union of Soviet Socialist Republics (from the floor): Point of order.

155. The PRESIDENT: I would ask the speaker at the rostrum kindly to stand aside once again while I deal with a point of order which has been raised from the floor. I call on the Chairman of the Council of Ministers of the Soviet Union on a point of order.

156. Mr. KHRUSHCHEV, Chairman of the Council of Ministers of the Union of Soviet Socialist Republics (translated from Russian): I protest against the inconsistent attitude adopted towards representatives of States present in this Assembly. Why, when a gentleman representing his country—the Congo—was speaking here, did the President of the Assembly stop him? Why? He simply referred to a telegram he had received from his brothers who are still suffering under colonial oppression. But the President stopped him, saying that that was a question of substance whereas we were discussing only a procedural question.

157. But why, then, when this toady of American imperialism [he is referring to the Philippines representative] rises and speaks about matters which are entirely non-procedural, does the President, who is evidently in sympathy with colonial domination, not stop him? Is that fair? No, it is not fair.

158. Mr. President, we live on earth not by the grace of God nor, Sir, by your grace, but by the strength and intelligence of the great people of the Soviet Union and of all the peoples which are fighting for their independence.

159. You will not be able to smother the voice of the peoples, the voice of truth, which rings aloud and will go on ringing. Death and destruction to colonial servitude! Away with it! We must bury it, and the deeper the better.

160. The PRESIDENT: I call on the representative of the Philippines to continue.

161. Mr. SUMULONG (Philippines): Before I proceed, Mr. President, I would make it very clear that my delegation and I have no desire to wound the feelings and sensibilities of any Member State or any delegation represented in the General Assembly.

162. But we are here to discuss a very important question. And my delegation feels that we have to express our ideas here freely and without res-

ervation, irrespective of whatever consequences my words may have on the opposing views of any delegation on this particular question. But I repeat: we have no desire to wound, to hurt, the sensibilities of any delegation.

163. We are asked to vote on the allocation of an item entitled: "Declaration on the granting of independence to colonial countries and peoples". And I submit that before my delegation votes on this question we have to make our position crystal clear, our belief as to the meaning and understanding of the word "independence" contained in the declaration.

164. The delegation of Ghana has just recalled to us that all or nearly all of the Western colonial Powers stand committed to a policy of granting independence to the remaining territories under their control. That policy has resulted this year in the accession of no less than seventeen new countries to a sovereign and independent status, and we have no doubt that this process will continue until the last dependent territory is freed from foreign rule. But what of the countries that have fallen under Soviet domination and control?

165. The PRESIDENT: I would ask the speaker at the rostrum to be good enough to avoid wandering out into an argument which is certain to provoke further interventions and which is bound to be very prejudicial to the decorum of this debate.

166. Mr. SUMULONG (Philippines): My delegation would be the first to abide by the rules of this Assembly. But I think the example has been set. Other delegations have come to this rostrum to state their views, mincing no words, and if my delegation has erred in this respect, we are only following the example set by others.

167. If the United Nations is to proclaim a declaration on the right of subjugated peoples to independence, I ask is it fair, is it just, is it moral?

168. The PRESIDENT: The Chair must insist and must really ask delegates to accord a more willing and greater degree of cooperation to the Chair in the interest of the dignity of the Assembly's debates.

169. We are at present discussing a declaration for the granting of independence to colonial territories and peoples. The scope of that proposal is clear. We are concerned solely with the allocation of the item. The suggestion that we should go further and discuss something else which is not comprised within this proposal is not in order, and I must finally ask the representative of the Philippines to try to confine himself to the procedural issue which we are discussing—to what forum this item, which was proposed by the Soviet Union, should be allocated. Anything else is, I am afraid, out of order.

170. Mr. SUMULONG (Philippines): Mr. President, I was in the process of explaining the reasons which will impel my delegation to vote at the proper time in favor of having this item allocated to the highest possible level—to the plenary meeting of this Assembly. But I think we have a right to explain why we are voting in that way. In order to explain our vote and our position in this matter, we have to give our understanding of the meaning of the word "independence".

171. As I said before, we have been a colonized country. We know what it means to be colonized. We know the difference between being a colonized people and being an independent and sovereign people. We have been under the control and subjugation of Spain, the United States and Japan. We understand what it means to be a subjugated people, and we really know the difference between freedom and independence, on the one hand, and colonial subjection and subservience, on the other. We have tasted that which was meant to be a paper independence, and we also know what is meant by real and genuine independence.

172. Now, our position is this: If this item—declaration on the granting of independence to colonial countries and peoples—refers to real and genuine independence, we will certainly vote, one hundred percent, with all our heart and with all our soul, to have this very important item allocated to the highest possible level: the plenary meetings of this General Assem-

bly. But if the meaning to be given to independence is limited to paper independence—where independence is given in form but not in substance, where independence is given without any free exercise of civil liberties and political rights—then I believe that this declaration is not a genuine declaration and, much to my regret, we cannot consider this as important as it purports to be.

173. Indeed, if we are to have a declaration, it should afford the hope of liberation to those peoples who now have no such hope at all rather than to those who almost certain to be free whether or not we adopt the declaration which has been proposed.

174. In the discussion of this item my delegation will be guided by the principles of the Bandung Declaration, under which the countries of Asia and Africa pledged themselves to keep up the struggle against imperialism in any guise or form and from whatever source or direction it may come. We construe this to include all kinds of imperialism, whether that is the old form of imperialism or that is a new form of imperialism.

175. The United Kingdom, which may be said to represent an imperialism that is dying, has accepted the challenge to debate this item. It remains to be seen if other great Powers represented in this Assembly who uphold a point of view opposed to that of the United Kingdom will accept the implied challenge to look at their own faces in the mirror.

176. Since, in our view, this item pertains to a subject which is wider in scope and far more important than the proponents of this draft resolution may have intended, and on the understanding and belief that the word "independence" as contained in the declaration I have quoted means a genuine and real independence and not a mere paper independence, my delegation will support the proposal that the item should be discussed in plenary meeting.

214. The PRESIDENT: That concludes the list of speakers; but one representative has asked for the floor in exercise of the right of reply, and

two to explain their votes before the voting.

215. I call upon the representative of the Soviet Union.

216. Mr. KHRUSHCHEV, Chairman of the Council of Ministers of the Union of Soviet Socialist Republics (translated from Russian): I am pleased in advance at what I hope will be the Assembly's decision to discuss the question of the complete abolition of the colonial system in plenary meeting of the Assembly. If my hope is not fulfilled and the Assembly does not vote for the discussion of this question in plenary meeting, it will be not only I who will be grieved—that is not particularly important—but millions and millions of people who are living in colonial servitude and awaiting their liberation.

217. I am extremely glad about something else, namely the fact that the representative of the United Kingdom, when he spoke here, sharply criticized my position. It is a great satisfaction to me that the colonialists regard me as an enemy of the colonial system. That is a great reward for me, and I take pride in it.

218. I very much like the words of August Bebel, the social democrat and leader of the German workers, who said, more or less, this: If the bourgeoisie praises you, Bebel, think, in that case, what a stupid thing you must have done. If the bourgeoisie reviles you, it means that you are truly serving the working class, the proletariat! If the colonialists now revile me, I am proud of it, because it means that I am truly serving the peoples which are struggling for their independence, for their freedom.

219. The representative of the United Kingdom made a speech here. It would have befitted him better had he drawn a lesson from the wealthy peasants. In our country, when we had private ownership of the means of production, the wealthy man proceeded as follows (this method, of course, is applied in all countries). When he hired a laborer he fed him well the first day. Then he exploited him mercilessly, squeezing everything he could out of him, but when the laborer had finished the work for which he had been

hired the rich man again fed him well so that he would retain a happy memory of this exploiter who had squeezed him dry. The English colonialists, I would remind the United Kingdom representative, drew blood and sweat from the people of India, the people of Burma and the other peoples that they exploited and are still exploiting.

220. You ought to show respect towards these peoples that are now, not by your favor but by their struggles and the decrees of time, securing their independence and freedom. Do not spoil for them this day, which should be a day of celebration for the peoples that have won their independence. Give some moral satisfaction to these people. That is what they have fought for. You cannot rise even to the level of the rich peasant, the exploiter of the poor. You want to squeeze out of these peoples the last drop of sweat.

221. I would say to the United Kingdom representative that when, in my statement today, I said that people were rising and that the English colonialists were sending guns to suppress them, I was using information from your London newspapers. This information was published a day or two ago. So these are quite fresh facts, revealing that the peoples of the colonial countries are rebelling. We applaud them, but we ought to give them assistance from our side, because the colonialists are better armed and are destroying, are annihilating the population in the colonies.

222. I now turn to the statement of the Philippine representative. I have what might be called a "double attitude" to that statement. I protested sharply when he began to stutter, so to speak, in the first half of his speech, but then he recovered himself and came to the right conclusion. I would explain this as follows: He is not a bad man. As he himself said, he and the entire Philippine people suffered for many years under the yoke of the Spaniards. Then the Americans took them over and they have just about received their independence, although God knows what kind of independence it is. You have to look at it very closely, under a magnifying glass, to see it.

223. The representative of the Philippines knows what colonialism is, what colonial oppression is. And it is clear that in the first part of his statement he was not speaking from his heart. What was speaking was that remnant, that thread, which still binds him, so to speak, to the master—the United States of America, which evidently must have tugged at that thread. But then, when he was stopped, he evidently thought to himself: 'Why the devil should I stick my neck out? The Americans themselves are not saying anything, but are hiding, and they have pushed me forward so that I should speak for them.' And so then he gave vent, you might say, to his true feelings and expressed his hatred of colonialists, of colonial oppression. And I heard him with great satisfaction and applauded his words with all my heart.

224. I believe that one day the Philippines will be a truly independent country. Come to our country. We will enable you to visit any of the Republics. We shall ask the Republics to invite you and to allow you to look at them. Look at everything critically, and even with partiality, and you will realize what freedom is and what colonial slavery is. There is no greater freedom for man than the freedom to build and develop an independent State—and a socialist State, like ours—into the bargain. The Soviet people have already completed the building of Socialism and has now turned to the building of Communism.

225. I know that not everyone here will applaud me, because one must mature in order to realize the heights to which human society can attain. But the day will come when you yourselves will be speaking about socialism from this very rostrum if, of course, this rostrum survives, if it is fated to survive. At present the rostrum is a very shaky one.

226. The representative of the United Kingdom and the representative of Colombia have spoken. Englishman and Colombian—that is, virtually, one and the same thing. The Englishman stands for the NATO military bloc, the Colombian for the Monroe Doctrine. It is obvious, therefore,

where that particular current of air is coming from. And you can smell it, too. Smell it! However, Mr. Colombian, we listened to you as the representative of Colombia; but it was your voice, not the voice of the Colombian people. The Colombian people, like all peoples, does not desire the prolongation of colonial servitude. Of that I am convinced. The time will come when the representative of Colombia, speaking from this rostrum, will really speak in the name of the Colombian people.

227. I ask all representatives to pronounce themselves in favor of the discussion of the declaration on independence and freedom for colonial peoples in plenary meeting. The colonialists understand the difference between discussion in a corner and discussion in a large-scale meeting. When I sit in this hall, I am looking at the backs of the Spaniards. Whenever any colonialist makes a remark in support of colonialist policy, they applaud. Why? Because they are colonialists. There is a saying that a devil will never put out another devil's eye with his horn; for devils know how to use their horns. And a colonialist will be supported by colonialists.

228. It is good to live at a time when great events are taking place, when the colonial structure is crumbling. To us falls the honor of taking a spade, digging a deep grave, burying colonialism deep down and driving in a stake so that it shall not rise again: According to popular tradition, if you bury a devil you must drive an aspen stake into his grave so that he will not rise out of his coffin. It is the same with colonialism. It must be buried in accordance with this same popular tradition.

229. I am convinced that we shall find the courage and, more important, sufficient understanding to take a decision in accordance with our conscience and our conscience should tell us that the time has come for every man to be free.

230. I hope that the representatives of the African peoples—the Blacks, as they are called—will pardon and forgive me. I do not know how this sounds to Negroes; perhaps it offends them? I should like to express my

sympathy towards them. It was a pleasure for me to listen to them. The colonialists spoke about these people, saying that they were not yet mature enough to govern themselves. But the representatives of the imperialists who have spoken here have themselves not matured to the level of the human understanding of freedom and of the appreciation of this freedom displayed by these people, the Negroes, who have escaped from oppression and boldly express their thoughts and uphold the interests of their peoples. That is gratifying indeed!

231. Some white people pride themselves on the fact that they are white, and behave haughtily towards the Negroes. But how can you judge people by the color of their skins? One man's skin is black, another's is yellow, yet another's is white. The terrible thing is when a man, whether white or black in skin, has a black soul, a dirty soul. That dirty soul you will never make clean.

232. We salute our brothers the Blacks, the Negroes; we salute all peoples that are striving for their freedom and independence. We are helping them and shall continue to help them, and all peoples should help them. And we earnestly believe that the time is coming when the peoples of all countries will feel that they are brothers, when there will be neither exploited nor exploiters. There will then be only one banner flying—the banner of friendship, of peace and of brotherhood—and that banner will be the words: "Communist Society"!

249. Mr. WILCOX (United States of America): The United States delegation would prefer that this item be dealt with carefully and with due deliberation in the First Committee. But much more important than whether the question is to be considered in the First Committee or in plenary is the substance and the scope of the discussion, wherever it is to be held.

250. Now, some doubt has been cast on the scope of the discussion during one of the interruptions of the debate on a point of order. I believe you said, Mr. President, if my memory serves me correctly, that the discus-

sion of this question was limited by the scope of the memorandum in which the item was proposed. But, Mr. President, are we to rely on the Soviet memorandum [A/4501] and the proposed declaration [A/4502] as the basis for determining the scope of the discussion? I should say, parenthetically, that the proposer of an item cannot bind the Assembly in this respect.

251. If we are to rely on the Soviet memorandum and the declaration, then I must point out that the Soviet Union refers in both documents to "…respect for the sovereign rights and territorial integrity of all States without exception…"

252. Now, this is a statement which raises very many interesting questions. Everyone here in the Assembly is fully aware of the sad fact that there are a number of States in Eastern Europe which do have their complete independence.

253. Mr. MEZINCESCU (Romania) (from the floor): Point of order.

254. The PRESIDENT: I must ask the speaker at the rostrum kindly to stand aside while I deal with the point of order raised from the floor. I call on the representative of Romania on a point of order.

255. Mr. MEZINCESCU (Romania) (translated from French): We are witnessing here a reiteration by the United States representative of attacks against Member States who have equal rights in the United Nations. I insist that you make it clear to the speaker who I am now interrupting that I am here as the representative of the Romanian People's Republic and enjoy the same rights as the United States representative and the representative of any other State. That must be understood by the United States representative as by all other States represented here.

256. Mr. President, although you were elected by a majority of only six votes, you must uphold the rights of all Member States and the dignity of the United Nations.

257. Furthermore, the speaker whom I have just interrupted requested the floor for an explanation of vote. But is this an explanation of vote? Is it

an explanation of vote to launch upon a campaign of slander against other Member States from this rostrum? We are not in the United States Senate where there can be a vote on the organization of a "Captive Nations Week". Here we are among representatives of sovereign States and you, Mr. President, must ensure that they show mutual respect for each other and that the discussion conforms to the elementary rules of courtesy.

258. It is not a question of sympathy for such and such a regime; you are free to sympathize with the colonial countries, that is your right; but I hope that the Irish people and all the peoples represented here...

259. The PRESIDENT: I am sure that the Assembly will feel that, in view of the scene we have just witnessed, the appropriate step is that the Assembly should be adjourned at once, and it is hereby adjourned.

Appendix 13

Map of Socialist and Communist States, by Duration

Color Key (Original color image and key on Wikipedia — link below)

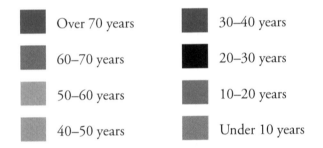

▪	Over 70 years	▪	30–40 years
▪	60–70 years	▪	20–30 years
▪	50–60 years	▪	10–20 years
▪	40–50 years	▪	Under 10 years

Source: Wikipedia
https://en.wikipedia.org/wiki/List_of_socialist_states

Map of Socialist and Communist States, by Duration

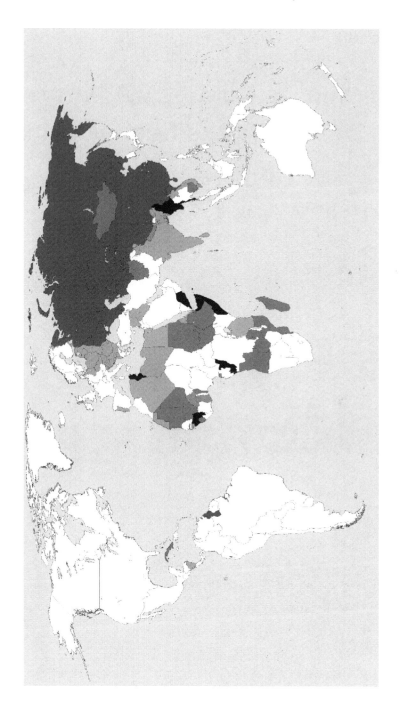

Appendix 14

The Chinese Communist Party Has Destroyed the Best of China

By The Editorial Board of
The Epoch Times, *July 1, 2021*

Reprinted with permission from *The Epoch Times* (www.epochtimes.com)

The Chinese Communist Party (CCP) has taken strict precautions in its preparations to mark its 100th anniversary. Beijing is heavily guarded. Knife stores are required to ask for ID and report customers' information to the police.

Restaurants in restricted areas have been forced to close their doors. The CCP is arresting people going to Beijing and blocking any social media account that might not show enough self-censorship.

The CCP might look strong on the outside, but in reality, it is extremely nervous. Despite decades of tight control and brainwashing, the Chinese people are well aware that the communist system is against human nature and will not last long.

Since its takeover of China, the CCP has killed an estimated 80 million Chinese people. During its existence, it has never stopped its campaigns to purge different groups, every time picking a new group to target. Its primary targets have been those who represented the best of the Chinese people and their culture.

In the 1950s, the CCP took property from landowners, confiscated private businesses from business owners, and killed millions whom they called "capitalists." Many of its victims were the most well educated and the most successful in Chinese society—often those who imparted the best of Chinese culture, handed down to them through a long family history.

The Chinese people have a long tradition of being loyal to their family and their spouses. When CCP officials reached the cities, they divorced their wives and married city girls. The Chinese also had a long history of respecting and supporting those who lived in temples. But the CCP forced monks to marry.

All communist countries have experienced famine. It's an inevitable result of the communist system. In China, the Great Famine from 1958 to 1962 is estimated to have killed around 40 million people. In thousands of cases, people were driven to insanity and turned to cannibalism.

There is one such story that is widely known. A father and his two children, a boy and a girl, were the only ones left in their farmhouse. One day, the father drove his daughter out of the house. When the girl came back, her brother had disappeared. There was a layer of white foam floating in the wok, and a bone had been thrown by the stove. A few days later, the father added water to the wok and then asked his daughter to come over. The girl was so scared that she hid behind the door, crying and begging: "Da, don't eat me. I will tend the grass and keep the fire for you. If you eat me, no one will work for you."

China has a history of 5,000 years of civilization. For most of that time, China was the envy of surrounding countries. The people were civilized and led stylish lives. Even kings from other countries chose to stay and even die in China. Communism, however, has brought famine, poverty, and an endless war against the Chinese people.

The Chinese have a tradition of being extremely respectful toward the elderly, showing respect to their parents, grandparents, and teachers. "One day my teacher, life-long my father," as the old saying goes—he who teaches me for one day is my father for life.

However, in the 1960s during the Cultural Revolution, teenagers were encouraged by communist officials to beat their parents and teachers. In Beijing alone, more than a thousand teachers were beaten to death by their students. As a young man, Bo Xilai—the future mayor of the super city Chongqing who would go on to visit the United States as a high-ranking official—stomped on his father's chest, breaking several of his ribs. This kind of act was unheard of during 5,000 years of Chinese history.

The CCP used teenagers to search civilians' homes and destroy antiques, artwork, and traditional objects they found, as well as public artwork, temples, and so on—anything that could remind people of traditional Chinese culture.

The Chinese culture was always believed to be divinely inspired. But communist ideology is against humanity and against human nature. Anything that represents traditional culture and principles is an obstacle to enforcing its ideology.

After using teenagers to destroy traditional objects and overthrow political opponents, the CCP sent those same teenagers to the remote countryside to get "educated." Doing so prevented a potential revolution and demands from them for employment. These young people faced many years of pain and hopelessness.

The CCP also shut down universities and sent intellectuals to the countryside to do farm work for "reeducation." Many musicians had their hands ruined by hard labor. Countless writers, artists, professors, engineers, scientists, leading experts, and cultural elites—the people who traditionally carry a country's knowledge, skills, and cultural spirit—committed suicide.

Worst of all, when the CCP came to power, it outlawed religion, dismissing it as an "opium of the people." It uses atheism to destroy people's belief in God, taking away people's belief in moral standards.

The most severe religious persecution campaign by the CCP targets Falun Gong practitioners. In terms of the persecution's scale and severity, it is unprecedented, targeting 100 million practitioners of the spiritual discipline, as well as their families and friends. Falun Gong teaches traditional meditation, which has been a core part of Chinese tradition since ancient times, and the principles of truthfulness, compassion, and tolerance.

To carry out the persecution—which is now entering its 23rd year—CCP leader Jiang Zemin promoted anyone who supported this persecution, forcing people to oppose truthfulness, compassion, and tolerance. In promoting people who opposed goodness, the CCP placed those who were most capable of committing evil in the top positions in Chinese society.

The forced organ harvesting from Falun Gong practitioners—whereby healthy individuals are killed for their organs to be sold for profit—has been supported and carried out by the military, police, courts, hospitals, and prison system. As a result, the entire country has become morally bankrupt.

Once the CCP began to profit from killing Falun Gong practitioners for their organs, it could not stop its business of killing for profit. It has continued this practice in Xinjiang Province.

The destruction of Chinese traditions, the damage to the moral standard, and the persecution of people of faith have been the biggest crimes of the CCP.

The Party has killed more people in China than the number who died in the two world wars combined. Beyond killing, it has made every effort to destroy the spirit, culture, and dignity of the Chinese people. Fully aware that it's the enemy of the people, the CCP has always been in an existential crisis.

This is why when top CCP leaders speak at anniversary events, they always try to make a strong appeal, and appear like they represent the Chinese people. Actually, the CCP has taken the Chinese people hostage, for fear that they will rise up and overthrow it.

Appendix 15

The Witness of Whittaker Chambers

In his autobiographical book, *Witness*, a classic exposé of Communism, Chambers describes his own odyssey into and out of the world of Marxism-Leninism. While a student at Columbia, in 1924 he read Lenin's Soviets at Work and became convinced that Communism was the solution to the problems of the world. He joined the Communist Party USA in 1925. A talented writer and editor (he translated Bambi from German), he would work for the Party's Daily Worker newspaper and later its New Masses magazine. He was then recruited by the Party underground and went to work for Soviet military intelligence, the GRU, running networks in Washington, DC.

This was the period of Stalin's Great Terror (1936-1938) and Chambers started to notice that some of the people he knew to be dedicated Communists were being brought before show trials in Moscow, where they were sentenced to death or the Gulag prison camps. Stalin's bloody purges did not comport with his idealistic belief in the Soviet Union, and he began to question his Communist faith. His doubts would turn to disgust. He came to see Communism as a grotesque lie and decided to break away. However, when he shared his disillusionment with members of his espionage network, notably Alger Hiss and Harry Dexter White, they looked at him in puzzlement as if he had suddenly turned irrational.

Chambers and his wife Esther had been friends with Alger and Priscilla Hiss, but after Chambers identified Hiss as a member of the CPUSA, and later as a Soviet spy, the Hisses denied having ever known the Chambers. During 1948 hearings conducted by HUAC, Chambers was asked by the chairman: "I can understand how a young man might join the Communist Party, but will you explain to us how a person who has made a real living in this country, a person with a large income… what, in your mind, would influence them to join the Party here in this country?"[1] Chambers replied:

> "The making of a good living does not necessarily blind a man to a critical period which he is passing through. Such people, in fact, may feel a special insecurity and anxiety. They seek a moral solution in a world of moral confusion. Marxism, Leninism offers an oversimplified explanation of the causes [of world crisis] and a program for action. The very vigor of the project particularly appeals to the more or less sheltered middle-class intellectuals, who feel that the whole context of their lives has kept them away from the world of reality… They feel a very natural concern, one might almost say a Christian concern, for underprivileged people. They feel a great intellectual concern at least, for recurring economic crises, the problem of war, which in our lifetime has assumed an atrocious proportion, and which weighs on them. What shall I do? At that crossroads, the evil thing, Communism, lies in wait for them with a simple answer."[2]

Fearing for his life after defecting from the Communist Party and its underground network of Soviet spies, Chambers went into hiding, only emerging when he thought it safe enough to work as an editor at *Time*. Given FDR's lack of interest in his 1939 report to Berle, Chambers figured he would focus on supporting his family. (When Harry Truman succeeded FDR as president in 1945, he ridiculed accounts of massive Soviet espionage in the US government as a "red herring" being used by his opponents to hide their real agendas.[3]) Chambers would become a devout Quaker, settling on a farm in Maryland to get back to what he discovered was important in life: family and a grounding in nature. In 1950, Hiss would be convicted of perjury and be sent to prison.

Footnotes

1. John Earl Haynes and Harvey Klehr. 1999. *Venona: Decoding Soviet Espionage in America,* Yale University Press, p135.
2. Whittaker Chambers. 2014. *Witness,* Regnery History, p612.
3. *Ibid.* p612.

Appendix 16

Khrushchev's Speech on Stalin's Cult of Personality

Nikita Khrushchev's Secret Speech On the Cult of Personality and Its Consequences *was delivered on February 25, 1956 at the Twentieth Congress of the Communist Party of the Soviet Union.*[1]

Summary: In a secret speech before a closed plenum of the 20th Congress of the CPSU, Khrushchev denounced Stalin's cult of the personality. In addition, he revealed that Stalin had rounded up thousands of people and sent them into a huge system of political work camps (Gulags). This revelation was met with astonishment by many present for the speech and helped to break the power that Stalin still held over the country.

Comrades, in the report of the Central Committee of the party at the 20th Congress, in a number of speeches by delegates to the Congress, as also formerly during the plenary CC/CPSU sessions, quite a lot has been said about the cult of the individual and about its harmful consequences...

---

1. Khrushchev's Secret Speech, 'On the Cult of Personality and Its Consequences,' Delivered at the Twentieth Party Congress of the Communist Party of the Soviet Union," February 25, 1956. Wilson Center Digital Archive. From the Congressional Record: Proceedings and Debates of the 84th Congress, 2nd Session (May 22, 1956-June 11, 1956), C11, Part 7 (June 4, 1956), pp. 9389-9403. https://digitalarchive.wilsoncenter.org/document/115995. Reprinted with permission.

Allow me first of all to remind you how severely the classics of Marxism-Leninism denounced every manifestation of the cult of the individual. In a letter to the German political worker, Wilhelm Bloss, Marx stated: "From my antipathy to any cult of the individual, I never made public during the existence of the International the numerous addresses from various countries which recognized my merits and which annoyed me. I did not even reply to them, except sometimes to rebuke their authors. Engels and I first joined the secret society of Communists on the condition that everything making for superstitious worship of authority would be deleted from its statute...

The great modesty of the genius of the revolution, Vladimir Ilyich Lenin, is known. Lenin had always stressed the role of the people as the creator of history, the directing and organizational role of the party as a living and creative organism, and also the role of the Central Committee.

Marxism does not negate the role of the leaders of the workers' class in directing the revolutionary liberation movement.

While ascribing great importance to the role of the leaders and organizers of the masses, Lenin at the same time mercilessly stigmatized every manifestation of the cult of the individual, inexorably combated the foreign-to-Marxism views about a "hero" and a "crowd" and countered all efforts to oppose a "hero" to the masses and to the people.

Lenin taught that the party's strength depends on its indissoluble unity with the masses, on the fact that behind the party follow the people—workers, peasants and intelligentsia. "Only he will win and retain the power," said Lenin, "who believes in the people, who submerges himself in the fountain of the living creativeness of the people.". . .

During Lenin's life the Central Committee of the party was a real expression of collective leadership of the party and of the Nation. Being a militant Marxist-revolutionist, always unyielding in matters of principle, Lenin never imposed by force his views upon his coworkers. He tried to convince;

he patiently explained his opinions to others. Lenin always diligently observed that the norms of party life were realized, that the party statute was enforced, that the party congresses and the plenary sessions of the Central Committee took place at the proper intervals.

In addition to the great accomplishments of V. I. Lenin for the victory of the working class and of the working peasants, for the victory of our party and for the application of the ideas of scientific communism to life, his acute mind expressed itself also in this that he detected in Stalin in time those negative characteristics which resulted later in grave consequences. Fearing the future fate of the party and of the Soviet nation, V.I. Lenin made a completely correct characterization of Stalin, pointing out that it was necessary to consider the question of transferring Stalin from the position of Secretary General because of the fact that Stalin is excessively rude, that he does not have a proper attitude toward his comrades, that he is capricious, and abuses his power...

Vladimir Ilyich said: "Stalin is excessively rude, and this defect, which can be freely tolerated in our midst and in contacts among us Communists, becomes a defect which cannot be tolerated in one holding the position of the Secretary General. Because of this, I propose that the comrades consider the method by which Stalin would be removed from this position and by which another man would be selected for it, a man, who above all, would differ from Stalin in only one quality, namely, greater tolerance, greater loyalty, greater kindness, and more considerate attitude toward the comrades, a less capricious temper, etc.".

As later events have proven, Lenin's anxiety was justified; in the first period after Lenin's death Stalin still paid attention to his (i.e., Lenin's) advice, but, later he began to disregard the serious admonitions of Vladimir Ilyich.

When we analyze the practice of Stalin in regard to the direction of the party and of the country, when we pause to consider everything which Stalin perpetrated, we must be convinced that Lenin's fears were justified. The negative characteristics of Stalin, which, in Lenin's time, were only incipient, transformed themselves during the last years into a grave abuse of power by Stalin, which caused untold harm to our party...

Stalin acted not through persuasion, explanation, and patient cooperation with people, but by imposing his concepts and demanding absolute submission to his opinion. Whoever opposed this concept or tried to prove his viewpoint, and the correctness of his position was doomed to removal from the leading collective and to subsequent moral and physical annihilation. This was especially true during the period following the 17th party congress, when many prominent party leaders and rank-and-file party workers, honest and dedicated to the cause of communism, fell victim to Stalin's despotism...

Stalin originated the concept enemy of the people. This term automatically rendered it unnecessary that the ideological errors of a man or men engaged in a controversy be proven; this term made possible the usage of the most cruel repression, violating all norms of revolutionary legality, against anyone who in any way disagreed with Stalin, against those who were only suspected of hostile intent, against those who had bad reputations. This concept, enemy of the people, actually eliminated the possibility of any kind of ideological fight or the making of one's views known on this or that issue, even those of a practical character. In the main, and in actuality, the only proof of guilt used, against all norms of current legal science, was the confession of the accused himself, and, as subsequent probing proved, confessions were acquired through physical pressures against the accused...

Lenin used severe methods only in the most necessary cases, when the exploiting classes were still in existence and were vigorously opposing the revolution, when the struggle for survival was decidedly assuming the sharpest forms, even including a civil war.

Stalin, on the other hand, used extreme methods and mass repressions at a time when the revolution was already victorious, when the Soviet state was strengthened, when the exploiting classes were already liquidated, and Socialist relations were rooted solidly in all phases of national economy, when our party was politically consolidated and had strengthened itself both numerically and ideologically. It is clear that here Stalin showed in a whole series of cases his intolerance, his brutality, and his abuse of power. Instead of proving his political correctness and mobilizing the masses, he often chose the path of repression and physical annihilation, not only against actual enemies, but also against individuals who had not committed any crimes against the party and the Soviet Government. Here we see no wisdom but only a demonstration of the brutal force which had once so alarmed V.I Lenin...

Considering the question of the cult of an individual we must first of all show everyone what harm this caused to the interests of our party...

In practice Stalin ignored the norms of party life and trampled on the Leninist principle of collective party leadership.

Stalin's willfulness vis-a-vis the party and its Central Committee became fully evident after the 17th party congress, which took place in 1934...

It was determined that of the 139 members and candidates of the party's Central Committee who were elected at the 17th congress, 98 persons, that is, 70 percent, were arrested and shot (mostly in 1937-38). [Indignation in the hall.] . . .

The same fate met not only the Central Committee members but also the majority of the delegates to the 17th party congress. Of 1,966 delegates with either voting or advisory rights, 1,108 persons were arrested on charges of anti-revolutionary crimes, i.e., decidedly more than a majority. This very fact shows how absurd, wild, and contrary to commonsense were the charges of counterrevolutionary crimes made out, as we now see, against a majority of participants at the 17th party congress. [Indignation in the hall.] . . .

What is the reason that mass repressions against activists increased more and more after the 17th party congress? It was because at that time Stalin had so elevated himself above the party and above the nation that he ceased to consider either the Central Committee or the party. While he still reckoned with the opinion of the collective before the 17th congress, after the complete political liquidation of the Trotskyites, Zinovievites and Bukharinites, when as a result of that fight and Socialist victories the party achieved unity, Stalin ceased to an ever greater degree to consider the members of the party's Central Committee and even the members of the Political Bureau. Stalin thought that now he could decide all things alone and all he needed were statisticians; he treated all others in such a way that they could only listen to and praise him.

After the criminal murder of S. M. Kirov, mass repressions and brutal acts of violation of Socialist legality began. On the evening of December 1, 1934, on Stalin's initiative (without the approval of the Political Bureau, which was passed 2 days later, casually) the Secretary of the Presidium of the Central Executive Committee, Yenukidze, signed the following directive:

I.   Investigative agencies are directed to speed up the cases of those accused of the preparation or execution of acts of terror.

II.   Judicial organs are directed not to hold up the execution of death sentences pertaining to crimes of this category in order to consider the possibility of pardon, because the Presidium of the Central Executive Committee, U.S.S.R, does not consider as possible the receiving of petitions of this sort.

III. The organs of the Commissariat of Internal Affairs are directed to execute the death sentences against criminals of the above-mentioned category immediately after the passage of sentences.

This directive became the basis for mass acts of abuse against Socialist legality. During many of the fabricated court cases the accused were charged with "the preparation" of terroristic acts; this deprived them of any, possibility that their cases might be reexamined, even when they stated before the court that their confessions were secured by force, and when, in a convincing manner, they disproved the accusations against them...

Mass repressions grew tremendously from the end of 1936 after a telegram from Stalin and Zhdanov, dated from Sochi on September 25, 1936, was addressed to Kaganovich, Molotov, and other members of the Political Bureau. The content of the telegram was as follows: "We deem it absolutely necessary and urgent that Comrade Yezhov be nominated to the post of People's Commissar for Internal Affairs. Yagoda has definitely proved himself to be incapable of unmasking the Trotskyite-Zinovievite bloc. The OGPU is 4 years behind in this matter. This is noted by all party workers and by the majority of the representatives of the NKVD." Strictly speaking we should stress that Stalin did not meet with and therefore could not know the opinion of party workers...

The mass repressions at this time were made under the slogan of a fight against the Trotskyites. Did the Trotskyites at this time actually constitute such a danger to our party and to the Soviet state? We should recall that in 1927, on the eve of the 15th party congress, only some 4,000 votes were cast for the Trotskyite-Zinovievite opposition, while there were 724,000 for the party line. During the 10 years which passed between the 15th party congress and the February-March Central Committee plenum, Trotskyism was completely disarmed; many former Trotskyites had changed their former views and worked in the various sectors building socialism. It is clear that in the situation of Socialist victory there was no basis for mass terror in the country ...

The majority of the Central Committee members and candidates elected at the 17th congress and arrested in 1937-38 were expelled from the party illegally through the brutal abuse of the party statute, because the question of their expulsion was never studied at the Central Committee plenum.

Now when the cases of some of these so-called spies and saboteurs were examined it was found that all their cases were fabricated. Confessions of guilt of many arrested and charged with enemy activity were gained with the help of cruel and inhuman tortures...

An example of vile provocation of odious falsification and of criminal violation of revolutionary legality is the case of the former candidate for the Central Committee political bureau, one of the most eminent workers of the party and of the Soviet Government, Comrade Eikhe, who was a party member since 1905. [Commotion in the hall.]

Comrade Eikhe was arrested on April 29, 1938, on the basis of slanderous materials, without the sanction of the prosecutor of the USSR, which was finally received 15 months after the arrest.

Investigation of Eikhe's case was made in a manner which most brutally violated Soviet legality and was accompanied by willfulness and falsification.

Eikhe was forced under torture to sign ahead of time a protocol of his confession prepared by the investigative judges, in which he and several other eminent party workers were accused of anti-Soviet activity.

On October 1, 1939, Eikhe sent his declaration to Stalin in which he categorically denied his guilt and asked for an examination of his case. In the declaration he wrote:

"There is no more bitter misery than to sit In the jail of a government for which I have always fought.". . .

On February 2, 1940, Eikhe was brought before the court. Here he did not confess any guilt and said as follows:

"In all the so-called confessions of mine there is not one letter written by me with the exception of my signatures under the protocols which were forced from me. I have made my confession under pressure from the investigative judge who from the time of my arrest tormented me. After that I began to write all this nonsense. The most important thing for me is to tell the court, the party and Stalin that I am not guilty. I have never been guilty of any conspiracy. I will die believing in the truth of party policy as I have believed in it during my whole life."

On February 4 Eikhe was shot. [Indignation in the hall.] It has been definitely established now that Eikhe's case was fabricated; he has been posthumously rehabilitated...

The way in which the former NKVD workers manufactured various fictitious "anti-Soviet centers" and "blocs" with the help of provocatory methods is seen from the confession of Comrade Rozenblum, party member since 1906, who was arrested in 1937 by the Leningrad NKVD.

During the examination in 1955 of the Kornarov case Rozenblum revealed the following fact: when Rozenblum was arrested in 1937 he was subjected to terrible torture during which he was ordered to confess false information concerning himself and other persons. He was then brought to the office of Zakovsky, who offered him freedom on condition that he make before the court a false confession fabricated in 1937 by the NKVD concerning "sabotage, espionage and diversion in a terroristic center in Leningrad." [Movement in the hall.] . . .

"You, yourself," said Zakovsky, "will not need to invent anything. The NKVD will prepare for you a ready outline for every branch of the center; you will have to study it carefully and to remember well all questions and answers which the court might ask. This case will be ready in 4-5 months, or perhaps a half year. During all this time you will be preparing yourself so that you will not compromise the investigation and yourself. Your future will depend on how the trial goes and on its results. If you begin to lie and to testify falsely, blame yourself. If you manage to endure it, you will save your head and we will feed and clothe you at the government's cost until your death."

This is the kind of vile things which were then practiced. [Movement in the hall.] . .

When we look at many of our novels, films, and historical scientific studies, the role of Stalin in the patriotic war appears to be entirely improbable. Stalin had foreseen everything. The Soviet Army, on the basis of a strategic plan prepared by Stalin long before, used the tactics of so-called active defense, i.e., tactics which, as we know, allowed the Germans to come up to Moscow and Stalingrad. Using such tactics, the Soviet Army, supposedly, thanks only to Stalin's genius, turned to the offensive and subdued the enemy. The epic victory gained through the armed might of the land of the Soviets, through our heroic people, is ascribed in this type of novel, film, and scientific study as being completely due to the strategic genius of Stalin.

We have to analyze this matter carefully because it has a tremendous significance, not only from the historical but especially from the political, educational, and practical point of view...

During the war and after the war, Stalin put forward the thesis that the tragedy which our nation experienced in the first part of the war was the result of the unexpected attack of the Germans against the Soviet Union. But, comrades, this is completely untrue. As soon as Hitler came to power in Germany he assigned to himself the task of liquidating communism. The Fascists were saying this openly; they did not hide their plans. In order to attain this aggressive end, all sorts of pacts and blocs were created, such as the famous Berlin-Rome-Tokyo Axis. Many facts from the prewar period clearly showed that Hitler was going all out to begin a war against the Soviet state and that he had concentrated large armed units, together with armored units, near the Soviet borders...

We must assert that information of this sort concerning the threat of German armed invasion of Soviet territory was coming in also from our own military and diplomatic sources; however, because the leadership was conditioned against such information, such data was dispatched with fear and assessed with reservation...

Despite these particularly grave warnings, the necessary steps were not taken to prepare the country properly for defense and to prevent it from being caught unaware.

Did we have time and the capabilities for such preparations? Yes; we had the time and capabilities. Our industry was already so developed that it was capable of supplying fully the Soviet Army with everything that it needed...

Had our industry been mobilized properly and in time to supply the army with the necessary materiel, our wartime losses would have been decidedly smaller. Such mobilization had not been, however, started in time. And already in the first days of the war it became evident that our Army was badly armed, that we did not have enough artillery, tanks, and planes to throw the enemy back...

Very grievous consequences, especially in reference to the beginning of the war, followed Stalin's annihilation of many military commanders and political workers during 1937-41 because of his suspiciousness and through slanderous accusations. During these years repressions were instituted against certain parts of military cadres beginning literally at the company and battalion commander level and extending to the higher military centers; during this time the cadre of leaders who had gained military experience in Spain and In the Far East was almost completely liquidated...

After the conclusion of the patriotic war the Soviet nation stressed with pride the magnificent victories gained through great sacrifices and tremendous efforts. The country experienced a period of political enthusiasm. The party came out of the war even more united; in the fire of the war party cadres were tempered and hardened. Under such conditions nobody could have even thought of the possibility of some plot in the party.

And it was precisely at this time that the so-called Leningrad affair was born. As we have now proven, this case was fabricated. Those who innocently lost their lives included Comrades Voznesensky, Kuznetsov, Rodionov, Popkov, and others...

Facts prove that the Leningrad affair is also the result of willfulness which Stalin exercised against party cadres...

We must state that after the war the situation became even more complicated. Stalin became even more capricious, irritable, and brutal; in particular his suspicion grew. His persecution mania reached unbelievable dimensions. Many workers were becoming enemies before his very eyes. After the war Stalin separated himself from the collective even more. Everything was decided by him alone without any consideration for anyone or anything.

This unbelievable suspicion was cleverly taken advantage of by the abject provocateur and vile enemy, Beriya, who had murdered thousands of Communists and loyal Soviet people. The elevation of Voznesensky and Kuznetsov alarmed Beriya. As we have now proven, it had been precisely Beriya who had suggested to Stalin the fabrication by him and by his confidants of materials in the form of declarations and anonymous letters, and in the form of various rumors and talks... The question arises: Why is it that we see the truth of this affair only now, and why did we not do something earlier, during Stalin's life, in order to prevent the loss of innocent lives? It was because Stalin personally supervised the Leningrad affair, and the majority of the Political Bureau members did not, at that time, know all of the circumstances in these matters, and could not therefore intervene...

The willfulness of Stalin showed itself not only in decisions concerning the internal life of the country but also in the international relations of the Soviet Union.

The July plenum of the Central Committee studied in detail the reasons for the development of conflict with Yugoslavia. It was a shameful role which Stalin played here. The "Yugoslav affair" contained no problems which could not have been solved through party discussions among comrades. There was no significant basis for the development of this "affair;" it was completely possible to have prevented the rupture of relations with that country.

I recall the first days when the conflict between the Soviet Union and Yugoslavia began artificially to be blown up. Once, when I came from Kiev to Moscow, I was invited to visit Stalin who, pointing to the copy of a letter lately sent to Tito, asked me, "Have you read this?"

Not waiting for my reply he answered, "I will shake my little finger and there will be no more Tito. He will fall.". . .

But this did not happen to Tito. No matter how much or how little Stalin shook, not only his little finger but everything else that he could shake, Tito did not fall. Why? The reason was that, in this case of disagreement with the Yugoslav comrades, Tito had behind him a state and a people who had gone through a severe school of fighting for liberty and independence, a people which gave support to its leaders.

You see to what Stalin's mania for greatness led. He had completely lost consciousness of reality; he demonstrated his suspicion and haughtiness not only in relation to individuals in the USSR, but in relation to whole parties and nations...

Let us also recall the affair of the doctor plotters. [Animation in the hall.] Actually there was no affair outside of the declaration of the woman doctor Timasbuk, who was probably influenced or ordered by someone (after all, she was an unofficial collaborator of the organs of state security) to write Stalin a letter in which she declared that doctors were applying supposedly improper methods of medical treatment.

Such a letter was sufficient for Stalin to reach an immediate conclusion that there are doctor plotters in the Soviet Union. He issued orders to arrest a group of eminent Soviet medical specialists. He personally issued advice on the conduct of the investigation and the method of interrogation of the arrested persons. He said that the academician Vinogradov should be put in chains, another one should be beaten. Present at this Congress as a delegate is the former Minister of State Security Comrade Ignatiev. Stalin told him curtly, "If you do not obtain confessions from the doctors we will shorten you by a head." [Tumult in the hall.] . . .

In organizing the various dirty and shameful cases, a very base role was played by the rabid enemy of our party, an agent of a foreign intelligence service—Beriya, who had stolen into Stalin's confidence. In what way could this provocateur gain such a position in the part), and in the State, so as to become the First Deputy Chairman of the Council of Ministers of the Soviet Union and a member of the Central Committee Political Bureau? It has now been established that this villain had climbed up the government ladder over an untold number of corpses.

Were there any signs that Beriya was an enemy of the party? Yes; there were. Already in 1937, at a Central Committee plenum, former People's Commissar of Health Protection Kaminsky said that Beriya worked for the Mussavat intelligence service. But the Central Committee plenum had barely concluded when Kaminsky was arrested and then shot. Had Stalin examined Kaminsky's statement? No; because Stalin believed in Beriya and that was enough for him. And when Stalin believed in anyone or anything, then no one could say anything which was contrary to his opinion; anyone who would dare to express opposition would have met the same fate as Kaminsky...

Comrades, the cult of the individual acquired such monstrous size chiefly because Stalin himself, using all conceivable methods, supported the glorification of his own person. This is supported by numerous facts. One of the most characteristic examples of Stalin's self -glorification and of his lack of even elementary modesty is the edition of his Short Biography, which was published in 1948.

This book is an expression of the most dissolute flattery, an example of making a man into a godhead, of transforming him into an infallible sage, "the greatest leader," "sublime strategist of all times and nations." Finally no other words could be found with which to lift Stalin up to the heavens.

We need not give here examples of the loathsome adulation filling this book. All we need to add is that they all were approved and edited by Stalin personally and some of them were added in his own handwriting to the draft text of the book...

Comrades, if we sharply criticize today the cult of the individual which was so widespread during Stalin's life and if we speak about the many negative phenomena generated by this cult which is so alien to the spirit of Marxism-Leninism, various persons may ask: How could it be? Stalin headed the party and the country for 30 years and many victories were gained during his lifetime. Can we deny this? In my opinion, the question can be asked in this manner only by those who are blinded and hopelessly hypnotized by the cult of the individual, only by those who do not understand the essence of the revolution and of the Soviet State, only by those who do not understand, in a Leninist manner, the role of the party and of the nation in the development of the Soviet society...

Our historical victories were attained thanks to the organizational work of the party, to the many provincial organizations, and to the self-sacrificing work of our great nation. These victories are the result of the great drive and activity of the nation and of the party as a whole; they are not at all the fruit of the leadership of Stalin, as the situation was pictured during the period of the cult of the individual...

Let us consider the first Central Committee plenum after the 19th party congress when Stalin, in his talk at the plenum, characterized Vyacheslav Mikhailovich Molotov and Anastas Ivanovich Mikoyan and suggested that these old workers of our party were guilty of some baseless charges. It is not excluded that had Stalin remained at the helm for another several months, Comrades Molotov and Mikoyan would probably have not delivered any speeches at this congress.

Stalin evidently had plans to finish off the old members of the political bureau. He often stated that political bureau members should be replaced by new ones...

We can assume that this was also a design for the future annihilation of the old political bureau members and in this way a cover for all shameful acts of Stalin, acts which we are now considering.

Comrades, in order not to repeat errors of the past, the Central Committee has declared itself resolutely against the cult of the individual. We consider that Stalin was excessively extolled. However, in the past Stalin doubtless performed great services to the party, to the working class, and to the international workers' movement...

We should in all seriousness consider the question of the cult of the individual. We cannot let this matter get out of the party, especially not to the press. It is for this reason that we are considering it here at a closed congress session. We should know the limits; we should not give ammunition to the enemy; we should not wash our dirty linen before their eyes. I think that the delegates to the congress will understand and assess properly all these proposals. [Tumultuous applause.]

Comrades, we must abolish the cult of the individual decisively, once and for all; we must draw the proper conclusions concerning both ideological-theoretical and practical work.

It is necessary for this purpose:

First, in a Bolshevik manner to condemn and to eradicate the cult of the individual as alien to Marxism-Leninism and not consonant with the principles of party leadership and the norms of party life, and to fight inexorably all attempts at bringing back this practice in one form or another.

To return to and actually practice in all our ideological work, the most important theses of Marxist-Leninist science about the people as the creator of history and as the creator of all material and spiritual good of humanity, about the decisive role of the Marxist party in the revolutionary fight for the transformation of society, about the victory of communism.

In this connection we will be forced to do much work in order to examine critically from the Marxist-Leninist viewpoint and to correct the widely spread erroneous views connected with the cult of the individual in the sphere of history, philosophy, economy, and of other sciences, as well as in the literature and the fine arts. It is especially necessary that in the immediate future we compile a serious textbook of the history of our party which will be edited in accordance with scientific Marxist objectivism, a textbook of the history of Soviet society, a book pertaining to the events of the civil war and the great patriotic war.

Secondly, to continue systematically and consistently the work done by the party's Central Committee during the last years, a work characterized by minute observation in all party organizations, from the bottom to the top, of the Leninist principles of party leadership, characterized, above all, by the main principle of collective leadership, characterized by the observation of the norms of party life described in the statutes of our party, and, finally, characterized by the wide practice of criticism and self-criticism.

Thirdly, to restore completely the Leninist principles of Soviet Socialist democracy, expressed in the constitution of the Soviet Union, to fight willfulness of individuals abusing their power. The evil caused by acts violating revolutionary Socialist legality which have accumulated during a long time as a result of the negative influence of the cult of the individual has to be completely corrected.

Comrades, the 20th Congress of the Communist Party of the Soviet Union has manifested with a new strength the unshakable unity- of our party, its co-hesiveness around the Central Committee, its resolute will to accomplish the great task of building communism. [Tumultuous applause.] And the fact that we present in all the ramifications the basic problems of overcoming the cult of the individual which is alien to Marxism-Leninism, as well as the problem of liquidating its burdensome consequences, is an evidence of the great moral and political strength of our party. [Prolonged applause.]

We are absolutely certain that our party, armed with the historical reso-lutions of the 20th Congress, will lead the Soviet people along the Leninist path to new, successes, to new victories. [Tumultuous, prolonged applause.]

Long live the victorious banner of our party—Leninism. [Tumultuous, prolonged applause ending in ovation. All rise.]

Appendix 17

Communist Party USA Membership 1922-1950

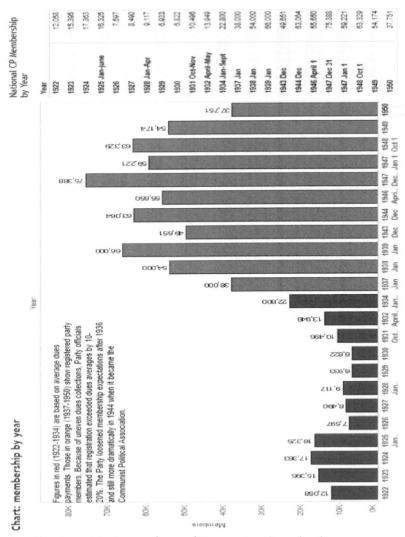

Chart: membership by year

Figures in red (1922-1934) are based on average dues payments. Those in orange (1937-1950) show registered party members. Because of uneven dues collections, Party officials estimated that registration exceeded dues averages by 10-20%. The Party loosened membership expectations after 1936 and still more dramatically in 1944 when it became the Communist Political Association.

National CP Membership by Year

Year	National CP Membership by Year
1922	12,058
1923	15,395
1924	17,363
1925 Jan-June	16,325
1926	7,597
1927	8,490
1928 Jan-Apr	9,117
1929	6,933
1930	6,822
1931 Oct-Nov	10,496
1932 April-May	13,949
1934 Jan-Sept	22,800
1937 Jan	38,000
1938 Jan	54,000
1939 Jan	66,000
1943 Dec	48,861
1944 Dec	63,064
1946 April †	55,660
1947 Dec 31	75,388
1947 Jan †	59,221
1948 Oct 1	63,329
1949	54,174
1950	37,751

https://depts.washington.edu/moves/CP_map-members.shtml

Appendix 18

Socialist/Communist Organizations and Supporters based in America

This list is not comprehensive, but it does show the extent and diversity of organizations in America that are based on Socialist and Communist ideologies, or actively support such groups. Some of these are venerable institutions, like the Ford Foundation and Tides Foundation. Their causes are many, from the environment to racial justice and voter registration, but all are radical and aligned with the Left. Few Americans are aware of the existence and radical orientation of most of these groups. (The Communism Portal on Wikipedia has a great deal of information on the various Socialist and Communist organizations.)

1. ACT UP
   https://actupny.com/

2. Alliance for Retired Americans
   https://retiredamericans.org/

3. Antifa
   https://antifa.com (currently redirects to whitehouse.gov)

4. Asian Americans for Equality
   www.aafe.org/

5. Asian Pacific American Labor Alliance
   www.apalanet.org/

6. Battleground Texas
   www.battlegroundtexas.com/

7. Black Lives Matter
    https://blacklivesmatter.com/

8. Black Leaders Organizing for Communities
    www.blocbybloc.org/

9. Blue Tent
    https://bluetent.us/

10. Brooklyn Commons
    www.thecommonsbrooklyn.org/

11. California Calls
    www.cacalls.org/

12. Carolina Federation
    https://carolinafederation.org/

13. Center for American Progress
    www.americanprogress.org/

14. Center for Tech and Civic Life (Mark Zuckerberg)
    www.techandciviclife.org/

15. Chinese Progressive Association / Boston
    https://cpaboston.org/

16. Chinese Progressive Association / San Francisco
    https://cpasf.org/

17. Coalition of Black Trade unionists
    https://cbtu.nationbuilder.com/

18. Committee of 100
    www.committee100.org/

19. Communist Party USA
    www.cpusa.org/

20. Communist Party of Texas
www.cp-texas.org/

21. Communist Workers League
https://fighting-words.net/

22. Congressional Progressive Caucus
https://progressives.house.gov/

23. Council for a Livable World
https://livableworld.org/

24. Council on American Islamic relations
www.cair.com/

25. Democracy Alliance
https://democracyalliance.org/

26. Democratic Socialists of America
www.dsausa.org/

27. Detroit Action
https://detroitaction.org/

28. Durham for All
https://durhamforall.org/

29. Earth First!
https://earthfirstjournal.news/

30. Ella Baker Center for Human Rights
https://ellabakercenter.org/

31. Emmerson Collective (Powell Jobs)
www.emersoncollective.com/

32. Federation of Southern Cooperatives
www.federation.coop/

33. Fight for $15
    https://fightfor15.org/

34. Ford Foundation
    www.fordfoundation.org/

35. Freedom Road Socialist Organization
    https://frso.org/

36. Highland Research and Education Center
    https://highlandercenter.org/

37. Industrial Workers of the World
    https://iww.org/

38. Institute for Christian Socialism
    https://christiansocialism.com/

39. Institute for Policy Studies
    https://ips-dc.org/

40. Institute of Southern Studies
    www.southernstudies.org/

41. Jobs with Justice
    www.jwj.org/

42. Kentucky Workers League
    https://kentuckyworkersleague.wordpress.com/

43. Korea Policy Institute
    www.kpolicy.org/

44. League of Revolutionaries for a New America
    https://lrna.org/

45. Left Forum
    https://leftforum.org/

46. Left Inside/Outside Project
    https://keywiki.org/Left_Inside/Outside_Project

47. LeftRoots
    https://leftroots.net/

48. Liberation Road
    https://roadtoliberation.org/

49. LUCHA (Living United for Change in Arizona)
    www.luchaaz.org/

50. MalcolmX Grassroots Movement
    https://freethelandmxgm.org/

51. Memphis for All
    www.memphisforall.com/

52. Movement for Black Lives
    https://m4bl.org/

53. NAKASEC (National Korean American Service & Education Consortium)
    https://nakasec.org/

54. Nashville Justice League
    https://nashvillejusticeleague.org/

55. National Nurses United
    www.nationalnursesunited.org/

56. New Black Panther Party
    https://nbpp.org/

57. New Florida Majority
    https://newfloridamajority.org/

58. New Georgia Project
    https://newgeorgiaproject.org/

59. New Students for a Democratic Society
https://newsds.org/

60. New Virginia Majority
www.newvirginiamajority.org/

61. Nodutdol (For Korean Community Development)
https://nodutdol.org/

62. Occupy Democrats
https://occupydemocrats.com/

63. Our Revolution
https://ourrevolution.com/

64. Open Society Foundation (George Soros)
www.opensocietyfoundations.org/

65. OrgUP (Organizing Upgrade)
www.organizingupgrade.com/

66. Our Revolution
https://ourrevolution.com/

67. Party of Communists, USA
https://partyofcommunistsusa.org/

68. Pennsylvania Stands Up
https://pastandsup.org/

69. Peace Action
www.peaceaction.org/

70. Philly Socialists
www.phillysocialists.org/

71. Physicians for a National Health Program
https://pnhp.org/

72.   Physicians for Social Responsibility
www.psr.org/

73.   Progressive Democrats of America
https://pdamerica.org/

74.   Progressive Labor Party
www.plp.org

75.   Project South
https://projectsouth.org/

76.   Refuse Fascism
https://refusefascism.org/

77.   Revolutionary Communist Party, USA
https://revcom.us/en

78.   Richmond for All
http://www.richmondforall.com/

79.   Right to the City Alliance
https://righttothecity.org/

80.   Rockwood Leadership Institute
https://rockwoodleadership.org/

81.   Rosa Luxemburg Foundation
https://rosalux.nyc/

82.   Rosenberg Fund for Children
www.rfc.org/

83.   Socialist Action
https://socialistaction.org/

84.   Socialist Alternative
www.socialistalternative.org/

85. Socialist Unity Party
https://fb.me/e/XOcHNJSg

86. Socialist Party USA
www.socialistpartyusa.net/

87. Socialist Workers Party
https://themilitant.com/

88. Sojourners
https://sojo.net/

89. Southerners on New Ground
https://southernersonnewground.org/

90. State Power Caucus
(No website)

91. Struggle for Socialism
www.struggle-la-lucha.org/

92. Texas Organizing Project
https://organizetexas.org/

93. Tides Foundation
www.tides.org/

94. Union of Concerned Scientists
www.ucsusa.org/

95. Unite Here!
https://unitehere.org/

96. United Students Against Sweatshops
https://usas.org/

97. US Peace Council
https://uspeacecouncil.org/

98.   Venceremos Brigade
       https://vb4cuba.com/

99.   Veterans for Peace
       www.veteransforpeace.org/

100.   Vietnam Agent Orange Relief & Responsibility Campaign
       https://vn-agentorange.org/

UN Global Population Projections to 2021

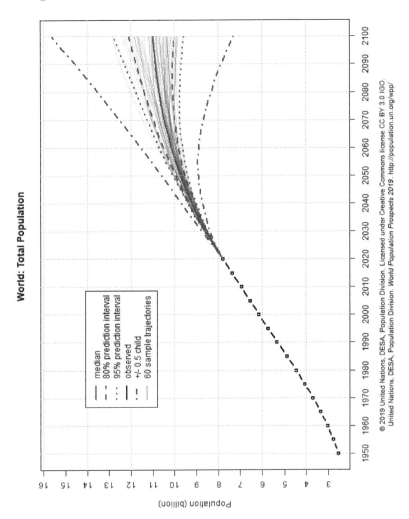

World: Total Population

Population (billion)

Total fertility, 2025-2030 (medium-variant projection)

Total fertility (live births per woman)
- 6.00 to 6.50
- 5.50 to 6.00
- 5.00 to 5.50
- 4.50 to 5.00
- 4.00 to 4.50
- 3.50 to 4.00
- 3.00 to 3.50
- 2.50 to 3.00
- 2.25 to 2.50
- 2.00 to 2.25
- 1.75 to 2.00
- 1.50 to 1.75
- Less than 1.50
- No data

Data source: United Nations, DESA, Population Division. World Population Prospects 2019. http://population.un.org/wpp/

The designations employed and the presentation of material on this map do not imply the expression of any opinion whatsoever on the part of the Secretariat of the United Nations concerning the legal status of any country, territory, city or area or of its authorities, or concerning the delimitation of its frontiers or boundaries. Dotted line represents approximately the Line of Control in Jammu and Kashmir agreed upon by India and Pakistan. The final status of Jammu and Kashmir has not yet been agreed upon by the parties. Final boundary between the Republic of Sudan and the Republic of South Sudan has not yet been determined. A dispute exists between the Governments of Argentina and the United Kingdom of Great Britain and Northern Ireland concerning sovereignty over the Falkland Islands (Malvinas).

Appendix 20

American Bill of Rights

Preamble to the Bill of Rights

Congress of the United States

begun and held at the City of New York, on Wednesday the fourth of March, one thousand seven hundred and eighty nine.

THE Conventions of a number of the States, having at the time of their adopting the Constitution, expressed a desire, in order to prevent misconstruction or abuse of its powers, that further declaratory and restrictive clauses should be added: And as extending the ground of public confidence in the Government, will best ensure the beneficent ends of its institution.

RESOLVED by the Senate and House of Representatives of the United States of America, in Congress assembled, two thirds of both Houses concurring, that the following Articles be proposed to the Legislatures of the several States, as amendments to the Constitution of the United States, all, or any of which Articles, when ratified by three fourths of the said Legislatures, to be valid to all intents and purposes, as part of the said Constitution; viz.

ARTICLES in addition to, and Amendment of the Constitution of the United States of America, proposed by Congress, and ratified by the Legislatures of the several States, pursuant to the fifth Article of the original Constitution.

Note: The following text is a transcription of the first ten amendments to the Constitution in their original form. These amendments were ratified December 15, 1791, and form what is known as the "Bill of Rights."

Amendment I

Congress shall make no law respecting an establishment of religion, or prohibiting the free exercise thereof; or abridging the freedom of speech, or of the press; or the right of the people peaceably to assemble, and to petition the Government for a redress of grievances.

Amendment II

A well regulated Militia, being necessary to the security of a free State, the right of the people to keep and bear Arms, shall not be infringed.

Amendment III

No Soldier shall, in time of peace be quartered in any house, without the consent of the Owner, nor in time of war, but in a manner to be prescribed by law.

Amendment IV

The right of the people to be secure in their persons, houses, papers, and effects, against unreasonable searches and seizures, shall not be violated, and no Warrants shall issue, but upon probable cause, supported by Oath or affirmation, and particularly describing the place to be searched, and the persons or things to be seized.

Amendment V

No person shall be held to answer for a capital, or otherwise infamous crime, unless on a presentment or indictment of a Grand Jury, except in cases arising in the land or naval forces, or in the Militia, when in actual service in time of War or public danger; nor shall any person be subject for the same offence to

Note: The capitalization and punctuation in this version are from the enrolled original of the Joint Resolution of Congress proposing the Bill of Rights, which is on permanent display in the Rotunda of the National Archives Building, Washington, D.C.

be twice put in jeopardy of life or limb; nor shall be compelled in any criminal case to be a witness against himself, nor be deprived of life, liberty, or property, without due process of law; nor shall private property be taken for public use, without just compensation.

Amendment VI

In all criminal prosecutions, the accused shall enjoy the right to a speedy and public trial, by an impartial jury of the State and district wherein the crime shall have been committed, which district shall have been previously ascertained by law, and to be informed of the nature and cause of the accusation; to be confronted with the witnesses against him; to have compulsory process for obtaining witnesses in his favor, and to have the Assistance of Counsel for his defence.

Amendment VII

In Suits at common law, where the value in controversy shall exceed twenty dollars, the right of trial by jury shall be preserved, and no fact tried by a jury, shall be otherwise re-examined in any Court of the United States, than according to the rules of the common law.

Amendment VIII

Excessive bail shall not be required, nor excessive fines imposed, nor cruel and unusual punishments inflicted.

Amendment IX

The enumeration in the Constitution, of certain rights, shall not be construed to deny or disparage others retained by the people.

Amendment X

The powers not delegated to the United States by the Constitution, nor prohibited by it to the States, are reserved to the States respectively, or to the people.

Postcolonial African Countries Which Tried Communism

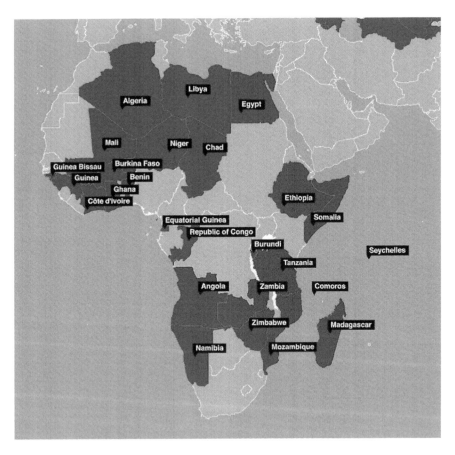

Source: East West Communications

Appendix 22

Black Lives Matter Combines Marxist with Neo-Marxist Ideas

In a 2015 interview with Jared Ball of Real News Network (TRNN.com), Patrisse Cullors, one of three founders of Black Lives Matter, said: "The first thing, I think, is that we actually do have an ideological frame. Myself and Alicia in particular are trained organizers. We are trained Marxists. We are super-versed on, sort of, ideological theories." (A Short History of Black Lives Matter: https://therealnews.com/pcullors0722blacklives with transcript.) She had been trained by Eric Mann of the Labor/Community Strategy Center. Mann, an unabashed Communist revolutionary, had been an activist with the Students for a Democratic Society (SDS) and its more radical offshoot, the Weather Underground.

From the BLM website (blacklivesmatter.com): "… Black activists and organizers are moving forward towards justice, towards visions, towards a world where our families and communities are no longer the sacrifice for a better America, for a better world. We are doing that through our continued fight against elected officials, be it Democrat or Republican, who don't share a vision that is radical and intersectional."

In 2020, BLM activists attacked police and citizens, burned buildings and trashed businesses in the name of seeking justice for George Floyd, who died while in police custody in Minneapolis. Fearing attacks for being racist, major corporations donated millions of dollars to the group, and politicians came out in its support.

The 13 Guiding Principles of BLM include Critical Theory terminology. BLM co-founders Patrisse Cullors and Alicia Garza both self-identify as queer, and their radical sexual agenda is a major part of these principles. (In her TRNN interview, Cullors said: "And so Black Lives Matter was a call for all black lives. And it was important for us as black women, and two of which are queer, was to actually talk about the totality of black life. And that black cis men are not the sum of black people, but rather all black life being the totality of black people. Whether that's black trans folk…") Disturbingly, these principles are at the heart of a school curriculum for elementary through high school students which is now being adopted by schools in many parts of the country.

BLM's 13 Guiding Principles

1. **Restorative Justice**
   We are committed to collectively, lovingly and courageously working vigorously for freedom and justice for Black people and, by extension all people. As we forge our path, we intentionally build and nurture a beloved community that is bonded together through a beautiful struggle that is restorative, not depleting.

2. **Empathy**
   We are committed to practicing empathy; we engage comrades with the intent to learn about and connect with their contexts.

3. **Loving Engagement**
   We are committed to embodying and practicing justice, liberation, and peace in our engagements with one another.

4. **Diversity**
   We are committed to acknowledging, respecting and celebrating difference(s) and commonalities.

5. **Globalism**
   We see ourselves as part of the global Black family and we are aware of the different ways we are impacted or privileged as Black folk who exist

in different parts of the world.

6. Queer Affirming

We are committed to fostering a queer-affirming network. When we gather, we do so with the intention of freeing ourselves from the tight grip of heteronormative thinking or, rather, the belief that all in the world are heterosexual unless s/he or they disclose otherwise.

7. Trans Affirming

We are committed to embracing and making space for trans brothers and sisters to participate and lead. We are committed to being self-reflexive and doing the work required to dismantle cis-gender privilege and uplift Black trans folk, especially Black trans women who continue to be disproportionately impacted by trans-antagonistic violence.

8. Collective Value

We are guided by the fact all Black lives matter, regardless of actual or perceived sexual identity, gender identity, gender expression, economic status, ability, disability, religious beliefs or disbeliefs, immigration status or location.

9. Intergenerational

We are committed to fostering an intergenerational and communal network free from ageism. We believe that all people, regardless of age, show up with capacity to lead and learn.

10. Black Families

We are committed to making our spaces family-friendly and enable parents to fully participate with their children. We are committed to dismantling the patriarchal practice that requires mothers to work "double shifts" that require them to mother in private even as they participate in justice work.

11. Black Villages

We are committed to disrupting the Western-prescribed nuclear family structure requirement by supporting each other as extended families and "villages" that collectively care for one another, and especially "our" children to the degree that mothers, parents and children are comfortable.

12. Unapologetically Black

We are unapologetically Black in our positioning. In affirming that Black Lives Matter, we need not qualify our position. To love and desire freedom and justice for ourselves is a necessary prerequisite for wanting the same for others.

13. Black Women

We are committed to building a Black women affirming space free from sexism, misogyny, and male-centeredness.

Appendix 23

EU Sues Hungary and Poland Over Gay Rights

The European Union Commission starts legal action against Hungary and Poland for violations of fundamental rights of LGBTIQ people

Press Release, Brussels, July 15, 2021
https://ec.europa.eu/commission/presscorner/detail/en/ip_21_3668

"Europe will never allow parts of our society to be stigmatised: be it because of whom they love, because of their age, their ethnicity, their political opinions, or their religious beliefs."
President Ursula von der Leyen, (European Parliament, 7 July 2021)

Equality and the respect for dignity and human rights are core values of the EU, enshrined in Article 2 of the Treaty of the European Union. The Commission will use all the instruments at its disposal to defend these values.

The Commission is launching infringement procedures against Hungary and Poland related to the equality and the protection of fundamental rights.

On Hungary, the cases include the recently adopted law, which in particular prohibits or limits access to content that promotes or portrays the so-called 'divergence from self-identity corresponding to sex at birth, sex change or homosexuality' for individuals under 18; and a disclaimer imposed on a children's book with LGBTIQ content.

In relation to Poland, the Commission considers that Polish authorities failed to fully and appropriately respond to its inquiry regarding the nature and impact of the so-called 'LGBT-ideology free zones' resolutions adopted by several Polish regions and municipalities.

The two Member States now have two months to respond to the arguments put forward by the Commission. Otherwise, the Commission may decide to send them a reasoned opinion and in a further step refer them to the Court of Justice of the European Union.

Hungary: Banning LGBTIQ content and book disclaimer

Access to content that portrays homosexuality for individuals under 18

On 23 June 2021, Hungary published a law that lays down a number of restrictive and discriminatory measures; in particular, it prohibits or limits access to content that propagates or portrays the so-called 'divergence from self-identity corresponding to sex at birth, sex change or homosexuality' for individuals under 18. The protection of minor is a legitimate public interest which the EU shares and pursues. However, in this case Hungary has failed to explain why the exposure of children to LGBTIQ content as such would be detrimental to their well-being or not in line with the best interests of the child.

The Commission has thus decided to send Hungary a letter of formal notice because it considers that the law violates a number of EU rules. First, the Audiovisual Media Services Directive (AVMSD) has been breached as regards standards for audio-visual content and the free provision of cross-border audiovisual media services, as Hungary put in place unjustified restrictions that discriminate against people based on their sexual orientation and are moreover disproportionate. Second, some of the contested provisions infringe the e-commerce Directive (namely the country of origin principle). The law prohibits the provision of services displaying content showing different sexual orientations to minors, even if these services originate from other Member States. Third, Hungary failed to justify the restricting of cross-border information society services. Fourth, Hungary failed to notify in advance to the Commission some of the contested provisions despite the obligation to do so laid down in the Single Market Transparency Directive. Fifth, the Commission considers that Hungary has violated the Treaty principles of the freedom to provide services (Article 56 TFEU) and the free movement of goods (Article 34 TFEU), by failing to demonstrate that the restrictions are duly justified, non-discriminatory, and proportionate. Sixth, the right to data protection laid down in the GDPR and Art. 8 Charter are violated by some of the contested provisions. Finally, the Commission believes that in these fields falling into the area of application of EU law, the Hungarian provisions also violate human dignity, freedom of expression and information, the right to respect of private life as well as the right to non-discrimination as enshrined respectively in Articles 1, 7, 11 and 21 of the EU Charter of Fundamental Rights. Because of the gravity of these violations, the contested provisions also violate the values laid down in Article 2 TEU.

Disclaimer on children's books with LGBTIQ content

On 19 January 2021, the Hungarian Consumer Protection Authority obliged the publisher of a book for children presenting LGBTIQ people to include a disclaimer that the book depicts forms of `behaviour deviating from traditional gender roles'. This equates to restricting the right to freedom of expression and the right to non-discrimination as enshrined in Articles 11 and 21 of the EU Charter of Fundamental Rights and breaches the Unfair Commercial Practices Directive.

The Commission has decided to send Hungary a letter of formal notice because it considers that by imposing an obligation to provide information concerning a divergence from 'traditional gender roles', Hungary restricts the freedom of expression of authors and book publishers, and discriminates on grounds of sexual orientation in an unjustified way. In particular, Hungary failed to justify the restriction of these fundamental rights, nor has it provided any justification as to why exposure of children to LGBTIQ content would be detrimental to their well-being or not in line with the best interests of the child.

Poland: 'LGBT-ideology free zones'

From 2019, several Polish municipalities and regions adopted resolutions on the creation of so-called 'LGBT-ideology free zones'. The Commission is concerned that these declarations may violate EU law regarding non-discrimination on the grounds of sexual orientation. It is therefore necessary to carry out a detailed analysis of the compatibility of the resolutions with EU law. In order to complete this assessment, the Commission needs adequate and comprehensive information from the Polish authorities. Despite a clear call by the Commission in February, to date Polish authorities have failed to provide the requested information, manifestly omitting to answer most of the Commission's requests. Poland is thus hampering the Commission's ability to exercise its powers vested under the Treaties and failing to comply with the principle of sincere cooperation under Article 4(3) TEU, which requires Member States to provide genuine cooperation to the Union's institutions. Therefore, the Commission has decided to send a letter of formal notice to Poland for its lack of cooperation.

Background

Equality and non-discrimination are core principles in the EU, enshrined in its Treaties and in the Charter of Fundamental Rights. In recent decades, legislative developments, case law and policy initiatives have improved many people's lives and helped us build more equal and welcoming societies, including for LGBTIQ people. Still, discrimination against LGBTIQ people persists throughout the EU, which is why the EU has to be at the forefront of efforts to better protect LGBTIQ people's rights.

On 12 November, the Commission presented the first-ever EU Strategy for lesbian, gay, bisexual, trans, non-binary, intersex and queer (LGBTIQ) equality, as announced by President von der Leyen in her 2020 State of the Union Address. The Strategy sets out a series of targeted actions around four main pillars, focused on: tackling discrimination; ensuring safety; building inclusive societies; and leading the call for LGBTIQ equality around the world.

Appendix 24

US Declaration of Independence

In Congress, July 4, 1776

The unanimous Declaration of the thirteen united States of America, When in the Course of human events, it becomes necessary for one people to dissolve the political bands which have connected them with another, and to assume among the powers of the earth, the separate and equal station to which the Laws of Nature and of Nature's God entitle them, a decent respect to the opinions of mankind requires that they should declare the causes which impel them to the separation.

We hold these truths to be self-evident, that all men are created equal, that they are endowed by their Creator with certain unalienable Rights, that among these are Life, Liberty and the pursuit of Happiness.--That to secure these rights, Governments are instituted among Men, deriving their just powers from the consent of the governed, --That whenever any Form of Government becomes destructive of these ends, it is the Right of the People to alter or to abolish it, and to institute new Government, laying its foundation on such principles and organizing its powers in such form, as to them shall seem most likely to effect their Safety and Happiness. Prudence, indeed, will dictate that Governments long established should not be changed for light and transient causes; and accordingly all experience hath shewn, that mankind are more disposed to suffer, while evils are sufferable, than to right themselves by abolishing the forms to which they are accustomed. But when a long train of abuses and usurpations, pursuing invariably the same Object evinces a design to reduce them under absolute Despotism, it is their right, it is their duty, to throw off such Government, and to provide new Guards for their future security.--Such has been the patient sufferance of these Colonies; and such is now the necessity which constrains them to alter their former Systems of Government. The history of the present King of Great Britain is a history of repeated injuries and usurpations, all having in direct object the establishment of an absolute Tyranny over these States. To prove this, let Facts be submitted to a candid world.

He has refused his Assent to Laws, the most wholesome and necessary for the public good.

He has forbidden his Governors to pass Laws of immediate and pressing importance, unless suspended in their operation till his Assent should be obtained; and when so suspended, he has utterly neglected to attend to them.

He has refused to pass other Laws for the accommodation of large districts of people, unless those people would relinquish the right of Representation in the Legislature, a right inestimable to them and formidable to tyrants only.

He has called together legislative bodies at places unusual, uncomfortable, and distant from the depository of their public Records, for the sole purpose of fatiguing them into compliance with his measures.

He has dissolved Representative Houses repeatedly, for opposing with manly firmness his invasions on the rights of the people.

He has refused for a long time, after such dissolutions, to cause others to be elected; whereby the Legislative powers, incapable of Annihilation, have returned to the People at large for their exercise; the State remaining in the mean time exposed to all the dangers of invasion from without, and convulsions within.

He has endeavored to prevent the population of these States; for that purpose obstructing the Laws for Naturalization of Foreigners; refusing to pass others to encourage their migrations hither, and raising the conditions of new Appropriations of Lands.

He has obstructed the Administration of Justice, by refusing his Assent to Laws for establishing Judiciary powers.

He has made Judges dependent on his Will alone, for the tenure of their offices, and the amount and payment of their salaries.

He has erected a multitude of New Offices, and sent hither swarms of Officers to harass our people, and eat out their substance.

He has kept among us, in times of peace, Standing Armies without the Consent of our legislatures.

He has affected to render the Military independent of and superior to the Civil power.

He has combined with others to subject us to a jurisdiction foreign to our constitution, and unacknowledged by our laws; giving his Assent to their Acts of pretended Legislation:

For Quartering large bodies of armed troops among us:

For protecting them, by a mock Trial, from punishment for any Murders which they should commit on the Inhabitants of these States:

For cutting off our Trade with all parts of the world:

For imposing Taxes on us without our Consent:

For depriving us in many cases, of the benefits of Trial by Jury:

For transporting us beyond Seas to be tried for pretended offences

For abolishing the free System of English Laws in a neighboring Province, establishing therein an Arbitrary government, and enlarging its Boundaries so as to render it at once an example and fit instrument for introducing the same absolute rule into these Colonies:

For taking away our Charters, abolishing our most valuable Laws, and altering fundamentally the Forms of our Governments:

For suspending our own Legislatures, and declaring themselves invested with power to legislate for us in all cases whatsoever.

He has abdicated Government here, by declaring us out of his Protection and waging War against us.

He has plundered our seas, ravaged our Coasts, burnt our towns, and destroyed the lives of our people.

He is at this time transporting large Armies of foreign Mercenaries to complete the works of death, desolation and tyranny, already begun with circumstances of Cruelty & perfidy scarcely paralleled in the most barbarous ages, and totally unworthy the Head of a civilized nation.

He has constrained our fellow Citizens taken Captive on the high Seas to bear Arms against their Country, to become the executioners of their friends and Brethren, or to fall themselves by their Hands.

He has excited domestic insurrections amongst us, and has endeavored to bring on the inhabitants of our frontiers, the merciless Indian Savages, whose known rule of warfare, is an undistinguished destruction of all ages, sexes and conditions.

In every stage of these Oppressions We have Petitioned for Redress in the most humble terms: Our repeated Petitions have been answered only by repeated injury. A Prince whose character is thus marked by every act which may define a Tyrant, is unfit to be the ruler of a free people.

Nor have We been wanting in attentions to our British brethren. We have warned them from time to time of attempts by their legislature to extend an unwarrantable jurisdiction over us. We have reminded them of the circumstances of our emigration and settlement here. We have appealed to their native justice and magnanimity, and we have conjured them by the ties of our common kindred to disavow these usurpations, which, would inevitably interrupt our connections and correspondence. They too have been deaf to the voice of justice and of consanguinity. We must, therefore, acquiesce in the necessity, which denounces our Separation, and hold them, as we hold the rest of mankind, Enemies in War, in Peace Friends.

We, therefore, the Representatives of the united States of America, in General Congress, Assembled, appealing to the Supreme Judge of the world for the rectitude of our intentions, do, in the Name, and by Authority of the good People of these Colonies, solemnly publish and declare, That these United Colonies are, and of Right ought to be Free and Independent States;

that they are Absolved from all Allegiance to the British Crown, and that all political connection between them and the State of Great Britain, is and ought to be totally dissolved; and that as Free and Independent States, they have full Power to levy War, conclude Peace, contract Alliances, establish Commerce, and to do all other Acts and Things which Independent States may of right do. And for the support of this Declaration, with a firm reliance on the protection of divine Providence, we mutually pledge to each other our Lives, our Fortunes and our sacred Honor.

Appendix 25

Parallels in Providential History

2000-Year Parallel Periods of Providential History*

Course	P1	Period 1	P2	Period 2	P3	Period 3	P4	Period 4	P5	Period 5	P6	Period 6	P7
Family Restoration Course	Adam & Eve	1600 — Cain / Abel / Seth	Noah	400 — Shem / Ham / Japheth	Abraham	120 — Isaac; Esau/Jacob; Ishmael's 12 Sons become 12 Arab Tribes	Jacob Birthright	40 — Jacob Wins Birthright and Blessing from Isaac	Jacob To Haran	21 — Jacob Marries Rachel and Leah in Haran	Jacob Now Israel	40 — Jacob's 12 Sons Become 12 Tribes of Israel	Joseph to Egypt
Israel's National Course	Jacob/Israel	400 — Slavery of Israelites In Egypt	Moses	400 — Joshua / Judges / Prophets / Samuel	Samuel, Saul	120 — United Kingdom of Israel; Saul, David, Solomon	Solomon	400 — Divided Kingdoms Of Judah and Israel	Nebuchadnezzar	210 — Babylonian Exile and Return to Judah	Nehemiah, Ezra	400 — Axial Age: Judaism, Buddhism, Confucianism, Taoism, Greece	Jesus
Christianity's Worldwide Course	Jesus	400 — Roman Persecution Of Christians	Theodosius	400 — Christianity as a State Religion	Leo, Charlemagne	120 — Holy Roman Empire	Empire Divided	400 — East and West Franks	King Philip IV	210 — Babylonian Exile of Papacy in Avignon, and Return	Luther 1517	400 — Reformation, Great Awakening, Renaissance, Enlightenment	Age of Personal Responsibility
Islam's Worldwide Course			Mohammed	510-532 — Mohammed Establishes Islam In Arabia on Ishmael's Foundation	Harun Al Rashid	120 — Early Abbasid Caliphate	Harun Al Rashid	400 — Middle and Late Abbasid Caliphate	Harun Al Rashid	210 — Abbasid Caliphate in Cairo	1517 Ottoman Cal.	400 — Ottoman Empire; Shah Ismail And Safavid Dynasty	

Biblical time periods are used with the understanding that they are often not precise, especially during pre-history. Some of the time periods are approximations, but others are precise. For example, Pope Leo III crowned Charlamagne in the year 800, and in that year Charlamagne and Harun Al Rashid exchanged gifts. In 1517 Martin Luther nailed his 95 Thesis to the church door in Whittenburg, and in that year too the Caliphate moved from Cairo to Istanbul. Exactly 400 years later the Russian Revolution took place, launching the beginning of 70 years of Soviet rule and worldwide Communism.

Appendix 26

Dimensions of Cain-Abel Engagement

There are two types of human character:
1. Cain-type: Envious, Resentful, Violent
2. Abel-type: Forgiving, Sacrificial, Loving

There are three dimensions of Cain-Abel engagement that can be summarized as follows:

1. **The first dimension** includes political and economic organizations and policies. This is the arena of party politics (Left, Right or Center); and of government economic policies (socialist/statist or capitalist/free market). It is also the dimension of political activism in line with these positions. This dimension includes issues regarding levels of regulation, taxation and state involvement in personal and business affairs.

    Cain-type policies favor government authority over individual rights. These policies translate into big government with more taxes and more regulations, creating more intrusion into personal lives and business affairs.

    Abel-type policies favor individual rights over government authority. These policies translated into small government with limited taxes and fewer regulations, limiting intrusion into personal lives and business affairs.

2. **The second dimension** is theoretical and ideological. This is the arena of theories of government (structure and function) and optimal economic systems (public versus private ownership), based on divergent notions of the nature and purpose of existence. These theories form the basis for government policies and the manner of their implementation.

    Cain-type theories and ideologies deny the existence of a Supreme Being and absolute morality, and instead propose materialist Marxist and Neo-Marxist theories which promote the notion that human identity is established primarily by membership in groups: races, ethnicities, economic classes and others. They advocate for single-party rule with central administration and planning. Put into action, these theories are responsible for totalitarian governments, including Socialist, Communist and Fascist regimes. The most radical of these governments control all the property and means of production, and in none of them is there full political and economic freedom for the people.

    Abel-type theories and ideologies recognize the supremacy of a Creator and propose spiritually-grounded theories which promote the primary importance of the individual and his or her rights, which are granted by God. They advocate for individuals to take responsibility for their own lives and to care for the wellbeing of others. They advocate for multi-party rule with regional and local administration and planning. Put into action, these theories are responsible for democratic governments under the rule of just laws and with the consent of the governed. The economic foundation for these systems is private property and free markets, i.e. capitalism.

3. **The third dimension** is spiritual and providential. This is the arena of belief concerning who we are and why we exist. It is the source of the theories and ideologies that translate into political and economic policies and practices, referred to above.

    Cain-type beliefs are atheistic; they deny that our origin is the work of a loving Creator. They hold that we exist as the result of an evolutionary process that has no transcendent origin or purpose. Thus we are merely advanced animals who must learn to use our brains to build the Utopias we desire. History is the working out of materialist forces, as in Marx's historical materialism, and the best possible destiny for humankind is the realization of a perfect, man-made political and economic system that assures the fair distribution of goods and services to all people.

    Abel-type beliefs are theistic; they recognize that our origin is the work of a loving Creator. They hold that life itself originates with the Divine, and that the intrinsic beauty and goodness of the creation are a reflection of these qualities in the Creator. History is the working out of providential forces: God working through individuals, groups and nations to bring a final end to the dominion of evil so that the original purpose of creation can be fulfilled.

Following is a summary of the three dimensions of Cain-Abel engagement:

Dimensions of Cain-Abel Engagement

	Dimensions	Manifestations	Cain	Abel
1	Political/Economic	Power, Parties, Activism	Leftist Parties, Activists, Statism	Rightist Parties, Activists, Patriotism
2	Theoretical/Ideological	Theory, Science, History	Marxism, Critical Theory, Victimhood	Personal Responsibility, Parenthood*
3	Spiritual/Providential	Revelation, Religion, Belief	Atheism, Materialism, Conflict	Theism, Faith, Harmony, Reconciliation
		Promised Outcome:	Materialist Utopia	Kingdom of Heaven
		Actual Outcome:	Totalitarianism: Socialism, Communism, Fascism	Free People in Free Societies: Fulfillment of the Purpose of Creation

Parenthood represents a state of human maturity.

Nine 'Starter Steps' to Save America From Socialism

By Trevor Loudon, The Epoch Times, March 11, 2021 (Reproduced with permission)

Though I'm a New Zealander, I know America and its people well. I've traveled to every state in the Lower 48 and have addressed more than 500 audiences across this amazing nation. My message has always been the same: The United States is heading toward a brutally tyrannical socialist revolution—and if America goes down, every free country follows.

Well, now it's here, people, unfolding before our very eyes.

So, what can be done? Can the Republic be saved? Honestly, I don't know.

However, I can suggest some steps that would at least give this country a fighting chance.

1. Face Reality

Millions of Americans are still in complete denial. Many think the military is secretly in control—that it's only a matter of time until justice is done and President Donald Trump is restored. There's a "secret plan"—just "have faith." The truth is that Trump was outmaneuvered by an alliance of communists, globalists, and even traitors in his own party. The "deep state" is now almost fully in control.

Trump isn't coming back into office any time before 2024—if we still have meaningful elections by then.

To make sure they can never be voted out of office, the Democrats plan to enfranchise 22 million illegal immigrants, abolish the Electoral College, gain at least four more far-left senators through Puerto Rico and D.C. statehood, and flood the country with tens of millions more refugees and illegal immigrants. They also plan to nationally introduce voting "reforms," i.e., mass mail-in balloting, abolition of ID requirements, etc., that will guarantee eternal Democratic Party control.

If the Democrats can abolish the Senate filibuster and place at least four more leftist "justices" on the Supreme Court, there'll be virtually no way to stop any of this if we rely on traditional political methods.

We're undergoing a Marxist-Leninist revolution driven by China—right now, in real time.

The military can't save us, nor can Trump. On the contrary, it's up to patriots to protect Trump and the Armed Services from unrelenting Democrat/communist attacks.

When enough Americans face the unpleasant truth, then, and only then, can we talk about hope.

2. Stop All Violent Rhetoric

Violence will not save America. The harsh reality is that President Barack Obama had eight years to replace patriotic generals with left-leaning political appointees. He did a great job. If violence breaks out (God forbid), the military will stand with the government, not the insurgents.

Does anyone think Russia and China and Cuba and North Korea and Iran would stand idly by while their Democratic friends are being defeated by a patriotic uprising? They would undoubtedly use the opportunity to finish off their "main enemy" once and for all.

Beware of anyone inciting violence online, at a public gathering, or in a private meeting. Distance yourself fast. They will be at best hopelessly naive, at worst government provocateurs.

The left is praying for "right-wing" violence. It will give them an excuse for a massive crackdown on patriotic Americans. This country will be saved peacefully or not at all. If significant violence breaks out, it's over.

Having said that, the Second Amendment must be preserved at all costs. An armed populace is at least some check on tyranny, even if useless in the face of biological warfare or nuclear attack. Americans should keep their guns and work every day to ensure they never have to use them against their own people.

3. Restore Election Integrity in All Red States

If voter trust isn't restored within months, the Republican Party is doomed. Democrats will continue to vote. Large numbers of Republican voters will stay home. They won't trust the elections and will refuse to participate. We've already seen this play out in the Georgia Senate elections.

Thirty states are currently led by Republican legislatures. Some are already holding inquiries into fixing deficient electoral procedures. Most will be whitewashes unless the public gets heavily involved. If the resulting recommendations don't include the elimination of electronic voting machines and heavy penalties for organized voter fraud, it's likely to be a window-dressing exercise. Be alert.

Patriots must work to restore voting integrity first in the red states, then the red counties of the blue states—then after 2022, the whole nation.

Get involved in this process. It's a top priority.

4. Close the Republican Primaries Immediately

This should be a no-brainer, but no one is talking about it. Only five U.S. states have truly closed Republican primaries. This means that in most states Democrats and independents (even communists) can vote in Republican primaries—and they do. All over the country, the GOP's enemies vote in Republican primaries to pick the weakest, most wimpy candidate they can.

That's why the Republican base is super patriotic but most of their elected representatives in most states vote like "progressive" Democrats.

Close the primaries, Republican patriots. It will transform your party.

5. Organize a Compact of Free States

MAGA folk need to build a "nation within a nation." This doesn't mean secession—Russia and China would be quick to exploit such division. What's needed is a reaffirmation of 10th Amendment rights as already outlined in the U.S. Constitution. The already out-of-control Federal government is about to go on a rampage against every form of independence left in the country. Every red state with the courage to do so must immediately begin working toward a formal compact to collectively oppose all forms of Federal overreach.

Such a formal alliance should start with Florida and Texas, then grow by inviting Oklahoma, the Plains states, most of the Southern states, New Hampshire, the free Midwestern states, and the Republican-led Northern and Western states.

Such an alliance, stretching from the Florida Keys and the Gulf of Mexico all the way to the Great Lakes and the Canadian border and even Alaska, would bisect the entire country.

Adding the red counties of the blue states such as Virginia, Maryland, New Jersey, Massachusetts, Illinois, Minnesota, New Mexico, Colorado, Washington, Oregon, and California, would create a voting and economic bloc that Washington would find exceedingly difficult to challenge.

When the Biden administration recently suggested that Florida Gov. Ron DeSantis close all restaurants in his state to slow the CCP (Chinese Communist Party) virus pandemic, the governor politely refused—citing the ineffectiveness and horrendous economic consequences of mass lockdowns.

Biden then reportedly hinted at an unconstitutional ban on air and road travel to and from Florida. This threat might work against Florida alone. It wouldn't work against Florida plus Texas and Oklahoma and 10 to 25 other states.

The United States is technically a federation of free and independent states. It's time to fully realize that ideal.

Southern states will soon be reeling under a massive new wave of illegal immigration. The Federal government will do nothing to prevent it. Texas, Florida, Arizona, and the free counties of New Mexico and California need to be preparing to defend their borders now. This isn't an immigration issue that is the constitutional preserve of the Federal government—this is a state public welfare issue.

Of course, the Biden-Harris administration plans to pack the Supreme Court with more left-wing justices to make virtually anything they want "constitutional." But this shouldn't even need to go to the courts. State governments already have the power under the 10th Amendment to nullify Federal overreach; they simply have to band together to put Washington back into its constitutionally tiny box.

The Republic will be saved through the courageous application of the First Amendment (free speech) and the 10th Amendment (state sovereignty).

6. Republic Review

Every free state should immediately embark on the adoption of the "Republic Review" process. There's a small but growing movement in some Western and Northern states to review their engagement with the Federal government to eliminate or nullify all unconstitutional relationships.

Under the Constitution, the states are technically superior to the Federal government. They're sovereign under the "equal footing" doctrine and have the legal power to refuse to engage in unconstitutional programs.

For instance, most states only get about 10 percent of their education budget from the feds—but are almost completely subservient to Department of Education dictates. Why not forgo the measly 10 percent in exchange for a return to local control over all public education? America is losing its youths in public schools. Every patriotic parent knows that.

This would give parents more control over their children's education and restore citizens' control over their own government. Is this worth 10 percent of your state's education budget?

If the free states are willing to stand against Federal overreach, they must also be prepared to forgo unconstitutional Federal money.

A thorough Republic Review audit would soon return power to the state legislatures—where it belongs.

7. Form a Multi-State 'America First' Popular Alliance

The left has "Our Revolution," a nationwide alliance of 600 groups operating both inside and outside of the Democratic Party. Operated by Democratic Socialists of America and the Communist Party USA, Our Revolution works in the Democratic primaries to elect far-left candidates such as Reps. Alexandria Ocasio-Cortez (D-N.Y.), Ilhan Omar (D-Minn.), and Rashida Tlaib (D-Mich.) into office. Our Revolution isn't subject to Democratic Party discipline, but it does get to choose Democratic candidates.

We need an "America First" umbrella group to operate both outside and inside the Republican Party—even possibly within the Democratic Party in some areas.

This organization should be all about pushing the MAGA/America First agenda at every level of government, in every state of the union.

Such a movement could harness the energy of 70 million to 80 million Trump voters without being under Republican Party control.

America First could unite the Tea Party and MAGA movements, grass-roots Republicans, patriotic Democrats, and independents to mobilize tens of millions of voters to transform the GOP into the truly populist, patriotic MAGA party it should always have been.

Take that, Mitch McConnell!

Trump is already vetting candidates to stand against Republican House members and senators who betrayed their own base after the 2020 election.

America Firsters should register Republicans by the millions to primary out dozens of Republican sell-outs in 2022. The America First/MAGA movement could "own" every level of the GOP by 2024. The GOP needs the MAGA movement way more than the MAGA movement needs the Republican brand.

Meanwhile, there are almost 70 far-left Democratic members of Congress in red states. Just restoring voter integrity alone could defeat several of them in 2022.

Running MAGA candidates backed by Trump in every one of those races could flip many more. It would be more than feasible to take back the House in 2022 to make Biden a "lame duck" president.

8. Boycott/Buycott Bigtime

Patriots should be abandoning Google, Facebook, Twitter, etc. for more honest platforms. They should also enthusiastically support efforts by DeSantis to heavily fine Big Tech operators who "cancel" patriots. If 25 or 30 free states did the same, Big Tech would soon be little tech.

Patriots need to organize nationwide boycotts of unpatriotic companies and buycotts for loyal American companies like My Pillow and Goya Foods.

Already, local groups are drawing up lists of "unfriendly" local companies and friendly alternatives so patriots can stop supporting their opponents and spend more with their fellow MAGA supporters.

It would also be smart to sequentially target vulnerable unpatriotic companies.

Imagine if 80 million MAGA patriots resolved to begin a nationwide boycott of one such company, starting now. The boycott would go on indefinitely until the target company was broke, or it apologized for "canceling" patriots. If applicable, every MAGA family could simultaneously commit to buying at least one of the canceled person's products this year.

On April 1, another disloyal company could be targeted, then another on May 1, another on June 1, etc.

After two or three companies had collapsed or apologized, we would soon see large companies start to back away from the "Cancel Culture."

Patriots have spending power in this country, people. We need to starve our enemies and feed our friends.

Again, patriots need to build a nation within a nation.

It should be also a given that every U.S. patriot boycotts all communist Chinese goods wherever possible. Check those labels! Buying Chinese communist products in 2021 is like buying Nazi products in 1939. It's immoral and it's suicidal.

The Chinese Communist Party just crippled the U.S. economy with the CCP virus. Then, pro-China communists instigated mass Black Lives Matter rioting. Then, the same people worked to influence the 2020 election.

It's about time Americans stop funding their No. 1 enemy—the CCP.

9. Remove Malign Foreign Influence at State Level

DeSantis has announced legislation to massively curtail communist Chinese activity in Florida. The legislation also targets several other enemy states, including Russia, Iran, Syria, North Korea, Cuba, and Venezuela—all of which interfere in this country's internal affairs.

In December 2020, Trump's Director of National Intelligence John Ratcliffe revealed that the Chinese Communist Party was conducting a "massive influence campaign" focused on dozens of members of Congress and their aides, including through attempted blackmail and bribery.

Currently, thousands of foreign companies from hostile regimes are buying up land, food production facilities, technical companies, educational facilities, and infrastructure. Tens of thousands of foreign agents are co-opting unpatriotic businessmen, unethical politicians, and sympathetic journalists in the interests of China and other malevolent states.

Under the Biden-Harris administration, nothing will be done to stop these activities at a Federal level—but much can still be done by the free states. If every free state cracked down on foreign bribery, corruption, espionage, and subversion, this country would be transformed.

If hundreds of corrupt academics, journalists, businessmen, and politicians (from both parties) were exposed and punished, this country would soon be well on the way to moral, economic, and political recovery.

Trevor Loudon is an author, filmmaker, and public speaker from New Zealand. For more than 30 years, he has researched radical left, Marxist, and terrorist movements and their covert influence on mainstream politics. He is best known for his book "Enemies Within: Communists, Socialists and Progressives in the U.S. Congress" and his similarly themed documentary film "Enemies Within." His recently published book is "White House Reds: Communists, Socialists & Security Risks Running for U.S. President, 2020."

Views expressed in this article are the opinions of the author and do not necessarily reflect the views of The Epoch Times.

Endnotes

1. Aleksandr Solzhenitsyn. 1974. *The Gulag Archipelago, 1918-1956*, Collins, p168.

2. Jordan B. Peterson. 2017. *Biblical Series V: Cain and Abel: The Hostile Brothers*.
   Video: https://www.youtube.com/watch?v=44f3mxcsI50;
   Transcript: https://www.jordanbpeterson.com/transcripts/biblical-series-v/

3. Winston S. Churchill. *Mankind is Confronted by One Supreme Task*, News of the World, November 14, 1937.

4. John F. Kennedy. 1961. *Transcript of Inaugural Address*.
   https://www.jfklibrary.org/learn/about-jfk/historic-speeches/inaugural-address

5. John Stuart Mill. 1867. *Inaugural Address Delivered to the University of St Andrew's*, Longmans, Green, Reader, and Dyer. The original version is: "Bad men need nothing more to compass their ends, than that good men should look on and do nothing." (This saying is often wrongly attributed to Edmund Burke.)

6. C.S. Lewis. 1946. *The Great Divorce*, HarperCollins, p1.

7. *Ibid*. p99.

8. John Adams. 1798. *Letter to the Officers of the First Brigade of the Third Division of the Militia of Massachusetts*, The Works of John Adams, Second President of the United States, Books for Libraries Press, pp228-229.

9. Ronald Reagan. 1964. *Address to the Republican National Convention*.

10. W.E.B. Du Bois quoted by Amity Shlaes. 2007. *The Forgotten Man: A New History of the Great Depression*, HarperCollins, p59.

11. Albert Einstein. *1939. Albert Einstein Solves the Equation: Understanding the Relationship Between Religion and Science, in Princeton's Lapham's Quarterly.*

12. Antony Flew, Roy Abraham Varghese. 2007. *There is a God: How*

the World's Most Notorious Atheist Changed His Mind, HarperCollins, p88.

13. V. I. Lenin. 2013. *Religion*, Dutt Press, p44.

14. V. I. Lenin. 1973. *The Attitude of the Workers' Party to Religion*, Lenin Collected Works, Progress Publishers, Vol. 15, pp402-413.

15. Albert Einstein quoted by H.G. Kessler. 1971. in *Diary of a Cosmopolitan*, Weidenfeld and Nicolson, p157.

16. J.R.R. Tolkien in Humphrey Carpenter. 1977. *J.R.R. Tolkien: A Biography*, George Allen & Unwin, pp197, 198.

17. Albert Einstein. 1950. *Science and Religion*, from *Out of my Later Years*, Philosophical Library, pp41-49.

18. Karl Marx. 1844. *A Contribution to the Critique of Hegel's Philosophy of Right*, Deutsch-Französische Jahrbücher.

19. Karl Marx. 1844. *Estranged Labour*, Economic and Philosophical Manuscripts.

20. Paul Johnson. 2008. In *Intellectuals: From Marx and Tolstoy to Sartre and Chomsky*, HarperCollins Publishers, p3.

21. Maximilien Robespierre. 1792. *On the Fate of the King*, an address to the National Assembly.

22. Maximilien Robespierre. 1794. *On Political Morality*, a speech to the National Assembly. From *The Ninth of Thermidor* by Richard Bienvenu, Oxford University Press, pp32-49.

23. Paul Johnson. 2008. In *Intellectuals: From Marx and Tolstoy to Sartre and Chomsky*, HarperCollins Publishers, p2.

24. *Ibid.* p23

25. *Ibid.* p24

26. *Ibid.* p25

27. *Ibid.* p4

28. *Ibid.* pp25-26

29. Karl Marx and Friedrich Engels. 1975. *Selected Correspondence 1846–1895*, International Publishers, in Marx-Engels Collected Works (MECW) vol. 41, p232.

30. *Ibid.* MECW, vol. 41, pp246–47.

31. Paul Johnson. 2008. *Intellectuals: From Marx and Tolstoy to Sartre and Chomsky*, HarperCollins Publishers, p54.

32. *Ibid.* p60.

33. *Ibid.* p55.

34. See the listing for Karl Popper in *Internet Encyclopedia of Philosophy*, second paragraph: "*Popper's early work attempts to solve the problem of demarcation and offer a clear criterion that distinguishes scientific theories from metaphysical or mythological claims. Popper's falsificationist methodology holds that scientific theories are characterized by entailing predictions that future observations might reveal to be false. When theories are falsified by such observations, scientists can respond by revising the theory, or by rejecting the theory in favor of a rival or by maintaining the theory as is and changing an auxiliary hypothesis. In either case, however, this process must aim at the production of new, falsifiable predictions. While Popper recognizes that scientists can and do hold onto theories in the face of failed predictions when there are no predictively superior rivals to turn to. He holds that scientific practice is characterized by its continual effort to test theories against experience and make revisions based on the outcomes of these tests. By contrast, theories that are permanently immunized from falsification by the introduction of untestable ad hoc hypotheses can no longer be classified as scientific.*"

35. Vladimir Bukovsky. 2019. *Judgement in Moscow: Soviet Crimes and Western Complicity*. Ninth of November Press, pp139-140.

36. Friedrich Engels. 1894. *On the History of Early Christianity*, published in *Die Neue Zeit*.

37. Winston S. Churchill. *The Creeds of the Devil, The Sunday Chronicle*, June 27, 1937.

38. Eugenia Sokolskaya. 2014. *Peace, Land, Bread*, Russianlife.com.

39. Winston S. Churchill. 2013. In Martin Gilbert's *Winston S. Churchill. Vol. IV: 1917-1922*, Hillsdale College Press, p355.

40. *What Was the Great Leap Forward?*, Investopedia, December 1, 2020. https://www.investopedia.com/terms/g/great-leap-forward.asp

41. Winston S. Churchill. *Speech Before the Anti-Socialist and Anti-Communist Union*, February 17, 1933.

42. Richard Weikart. 2004. *From Darwin to Hitler: Evolutionary Ethics, Eugenics, and Racism in Germany*, Palgrave Macmillan, p6.

43. Richard Overy. 2004. *The Dictators: Hitler's Germany, Stalin's Russia*, Allen Lane/Penguin. p281.

44. Whittaker Chambers. 2014. *Witness*, Regnery History, p612.

45. André Gide. 1949. In *The God That Failed*, Columbia University Press. p176.

46.　*Ibid.* p180.

47.　*Ibid.* p177.

48.　David McCullough. 2003. *Truman*, Simon and Schuster, p652.

49.　John Earl Haynes and Harvey Klehr. 1999. *Venona: Decoding Soviet Espionage in America*, Yale University Press, p308.

50.　*Ibid.* p334.

51.　*Ibid.* p 135.

52.　Vivian Gornick. 2020. *The Romance of American Communism*, Verso, p13.

53.　*Ibid.* p10.

54.　*Ibid.* p10.

55.　*Ibid.* p13.

56.　*Ibid.* p230.

57.　*Ibid.* p242.

58.　Arthur Koestler. 1949. In *The God That Failed*, Columbia University Press, p23.

59.　*Ibid.* p50.

60.　*Ibid.* p50.

61.　*Ibid.* p34.

62.　*Ibid.* p62.

63.　*Ibid.* p63.

64.　*Ibid.* p68.

65.　*Ibid.* p71.

66.　*Ibid.* p73.

67.　*Ibid.* p74.

68.　Ignazio Silone. 1949. In *The God That Failed*, Columbia University Press. pp98-99.

69.　*Ibid.* p111

70.　*Ibid.* p112

71.　David Remnick. 1933. *Lenin's Tomb*, Random House, p166.

72.　In *Amoral Politics: The Persistent Truth of Machiavellism*, by Ben-Ami Scharfstein, 2016. State University of New York Press, p215.

73.　Frank Newport. *Public Opinion Review: Americans' Reactions to the Word 'Socialism'*, Gallup, March 6, 2020. https://news.gallup.com/opinion/polling-matters/287459/public-opinion-review-americans-word-socialism.aspx

74.　Freedom House. February 4, 2021. *Transnational Repression Is a*

Growing Threat to Global Democracy.

75. Joe Schoffstall. *Columbia professor who thanked Fauci for Wuhan lab messaging has links to Chinese Communist Party members*, Fox News, July 1, 2021.

76. Peter Mattis. 2021. *Yes, the Atrocities in Xinjiang Constitute a Genocide: Beijing's own words and actions highlight the intent to end the Uyghurs as a people.* Foreign Policy Magazine, April 15 edition.

77. Amnesty International Report. *Like We Were Enemies In A War: China's Mass Internment, Torture and Persecution of Muslims in Xinjiang,* Amnesty International, June 10, 2021. https://xinjiang. amnesty.org/#report

78. Editorial Board of the Nine Commentaries on The Communist Party. 2020. *How the Specter of Communism is Ruling Our World,* An Epoch Times Publication, Vol. 1, pp147-148.

79. Michael Pillsbury. 2015. *The Hundred-Year Marathon: China's Secret Strategy to Replace America as the Global Superpower.* Henry Holt and Co., p269.

80. *Ibid.* pp45-47.

81. *Ibid.* p50.

82. Helen Davidson. *Xi Jinping warns China won't be bullied in speech marking 100-year anniversary of CCP*, The Guardian, June 30, 2021.

83. Arthur Koestler. 1949. In *The God That Failed,* Columbia University Press, p34.

84. Max Horkheimer. 2002. *Critical Theory: Selected Essays,* Continuum, p207.

85. Anonymous. 1926. *The Russian Effort to Abolish Marriage, The Atlantic,* July Issue.

86. Madame Smidovich. 1925. Article in *Pravda,* March Issue.

87. Morris Bowers. 2007. *Secular Humanism: The Official Religion of the United States of America,* American Star Books, Four Mistaken Illusions About Humanism, Chapter 3.

88. Herbert Marcuse. 1969. *An Essay on Liberation,* Beacon Press, pp46-47.

89. Quoted by Patrick Buchanan. 2001. *The Death of the West,* Thomas Dunne Books, p86.

90. Herbert Marcuse, "Repressive Tolerance," in Robert Paul Wolff, Barrington Moore Jr., and Herbert Marcuse. 1969. *A Critique of Pure*

Tolerance, Beacon Press, pp 95-137.

91.   Wilhelm Reich. 1962. *The Sexual Revolution: Toward a Self-Governing Character Structure,* Macmillan, pp77-78, 111, 184.

92.   Saul D. Alinsky. 1989. *Rules for Radicals: A Practical Primer for Realistic Radicals,* Vintage Books, pp126-130.

93.   *Ibid.* p25.

94.   Transcript of Chomsky-Foucault Debate. 1971. https://chomsky.info/1971xxxx/

95.   Peter Wilkin. 1999. *Chomsky and Foucault on human nature and politics: an essential difference?* Social Theory and Practice, pp177–210.

96.   James Miller. 1993. *The Passion of Michel Foucault.* Harvard University Press, pp201-03.

97.   Dalai Lama. 1996. *Beyond Dogma: Dialogues and Discourses.* North Atlantic Books, pp109-110.

98.   Damien Cave, Emma Bubola and Choe Sang-Hun. *Long Slide Looms for World Population, With Sweeping Ramifications,* New York Times, May 22, 2021.

99.   Russell B. Toomey, Amy K. Syvertsen, Maura Shramko. *Transgender Adolescent Suicide Behavior,* Pediatrics, September 11, 2018.

100.   Ralph Northam. 2019. *Ask the Governor with Virginia Governor Ralph Northam,* WTOP radio, January 30.

101.   William J. Broad. 2018. *How the Ice Age Shaped New York,* New York Times, June 5 edition.

102.   Brad Polumbo. *George Floyd Riots Caused Record-Setting $2 Billion in Damage, New Report Says. Here's Why the True Cost Is Even Higher,* Foundation for Economic Education, September 16, 2020.

103.   Estimates of the overall death toll of the Civil War have recently been raised by researcher J. David Hacker to 750,000 from a generally accepted figure of about 620,000. Of these, for the Union side at least 130,000 died in battle while another 300,000 died from injuries and disease. Some 500,000 foreign-born men fought for the north, the vast majority of these from Europe. There were an estimated 36,000 black war dead, according to War Department records. See: Guy Gugliotta. *New Estimate Raises Civil War Death Toll,* New York Times, April 2, 2012.

104.   Isabel Vincent. 2021. *Inside BLM co-founder Patrisse Khan-Cullors' Million-dollar real estate buying binge,* New York Post, April 10, 2021.

105.   Lee Brown. *Author Andy Ngo, who exposed Antifa, says he was beaten*

by 'masked mob', New York Post, June 3, 2021.

106.   Thomas Fuller, Alan Feuer, Serge F. Kovaleski. *'Antifa' Grows as Left-Wing Faction Set to, Literally, Fight the Far Right, The New York Times, August 17, 2017.*

107.   Nancy Rommelmann. *The Conservative Trans Woman Who Went Undercover With Antifa in Portland,* Reason, October 2, 2020.

108.   Andy Ngo. *Antifa: History and Tactics*, Hillsdale College, May 12, 2021.
YouTube: https://youtu.be/yziRK7j0Zpw

109.   Library of Congress. September 11, 2017. *Canada: Senate Passes Landmark Transgender Rights Bill.*

110.   Jordan B. Peterson. *Canadian gender-neutral pronoun bill is a warning for Americans,* The Hill, October 18, 2016.

111.   Karen McVeigh. *Obama tells US officials to use overseas aid to promote gay rights,* The Guardian, December 6, 2011.

112.   William Bradford. 2016. *Of Plymouth Plantation*, Portcullis Books, p35.

113.   *Ibid.* p35.

114.   *Ibid.* p116.

115.   *Ibid.* p116.

116.   *Ibid.* p116.

117.   Thomas Paine. 1776. *Common Sense*, Original Edition: p20.

118.   Abraham Lincoln. 1863. *The Gettysburg Address.*

119.   United States Congress. 1865. *13th Amendment to the Constitution of the United States of America.*

120.   Dwight Eisenhower. 1964. In *D-Day Plus 20 Years - Eisenhower Returns to Normandy,* CBS Reports.

121.   Edmund Burke. 1770. *Thoughts on the Cause of the Present Discontents,* in: Select Works of Edmund Burke, vol. 1, p146 (Liberty Fund ed. 1999).

122.   Winston S. Churchill. 2013. T*he Birth of Britain: A History of the English-Speaking Peoples, Book 1*, Rosetta Books, p260.

123.   Winston Churchill. 1909. In speech on Unemployment, Kinnaird Hall, Dundee, October 10, 1908, in *Liberalism and the Social Problem,* Echo Library, p87.

Glossary of Names and Terms

Adolf Hitler: An Austrian-born German leader who lived from 1889 to 1945. He established the Nazi Party as a socialist party to carry out the racist and German nationalist theories he expounded in his book, *Mein Kampf*. He turned Germany into a Fascist state and launched World War II, which was responsible for some 75 million deaths worldwide. He initiated the Holocaust which was responsible for the deaths of some 6 million Jews.

Anti-Capitalism: Opposition to the economic system of capitalism and advocacy for socialist alternatives.

Anti-Colonialism: Opposition to imperialist colonization of less developed regions of the world, particularly that practiced by European powers. This was also a major argument used by the Soviet Union to justify its support for "wars of national liberation."

Anti-Family: The Leftist view that the traditional family is anti-revolutionary and an oppressive social structure that perpetuates systemic racism, sexism and gender discrimination.

Anti-Imperialism: Lenin believed that imperialism was the final stage of capitalism, and hence the point at which violent revolution is justified.

Anti-Racism: Postmodern theory that policy must actively seek out and destroy systemic racism.

Anti-Religion: The atheistic Leftist view that religion is a harmful force in history and society and must be suppressed and its influences eliminated from society.

Axial Age: Term coined by the German philosopher Karl Jaspers to describe the worldwide era of religious, philosophical and scientific enlightenment between the 8th and 3rd centuries BC.

Buddha: Siddhartha Gautama, the Buddha, lived from 563 to 483 BC and is the founder of Buddhism.

Buddhism: The teachings of Siddhartha Gautama.

Caliphate: The Muslim realm under the rule of the Caliph.

Cancel Culture: The practice of denying others the right to speak in public or publish their ideas. "Others" are those you disagree with because you believe their ideas and language are hateful and must be suppressed.

Capitalism: A market economy based on private ownership of property with prices set by the law of supply and demand. A theoretical basis for capitalism was formulated by Adam Smith in his groundbreaking 1776 book, *The Wealth of Nations*. Capitalism recognizes that private property and the voluntary exchange of goods and services among people create the most wealth for individuals and nations, and that capital is most efficiently managed by private individuals and entities rather than by state bureaucracies. As the basis for economic liberty, capitalism underpins free societies and has greatly diminished poverty around the world.

CCP: Chinese Communist Party, established in 1921 and ruling China since 1949.

Communism: In Marxism, Communism emerges from Socialism as the perfect politico-economic system in which each gives according to their ability and receives according to their need. Citizens are so enlightened that they no longer need a state. They reach this state of enlightenment through their experience of Socialism, the necessary precursor to Communism.

Confucianism: The teachings of Confucius that form the basis for traditional social order in China.

Confucius: A Chinese philosopher who lived from 551 to 479 BC.

CPSU: Communist Party of the Soviet Union, founded by Lenin in 1917 and ruled the USSR until 1990.

CPSUA: Communist Party of the United States, which was founded in 1919.

Critical Race Theory: A Postmodernist concept that race is systemic in America and other Western societies, and that to rid society of racism traditional social institutions have to be deconstructed and replaced with equitable alternatives

Cultural Marxism: Marxist philosophy and its derivatives applied to cultural and social issues. In particular, dialectical materialism is employed (often as Critical Theory) to analyze social ills and conflicts, with the result being a set of cultural norms in line with Marxist and Postmodernist ideology. These norms are characterized by atheism, anti-family thought and sexual liberation, and anti-capitalism. Typically they exert influence through educational curricula, politically correct language, media bias, corporate activism, political activism and government policies that favor the state over the individual. Typically, too, the Marxist and Critical Theory influence behind these forces is veiled behind the language of broadly accepted societal norms.

Dar Al Harb: Arabic phrase meaning "House of War. It refers to the part of the world that has not been conquered for Islam.

Dar Al Islam: Arabic phrase meaning "House of Islam." It refers to the part of the world that is under the control of Islam.

Democratic Centralism: A political system for maintaining a one-party state in which only part-selected candidates are permitted to run for election. This system was introduced by Lenin and is typically employed in Socialist and Communist states to sustain totalitarian rule.

Democratic Socialism: In theory, a socialist economic system managed by a democratic government to achieve equitable income distribution. In practice, parties with this name tend either to be truly democratic and advocate for big government in capitalist societies, or truly socialist and advocate for government ownership of property and means of production. The latter are Socialist states established by Marxist regimes.

Détente: A policy intended to reduce Cold War tensions between the Communist bloc countries, on one hand, and the NATO allies on the other. This was exploited by the Soviets to project a peace-loving image while pursuing the expansion of their power.

Dhimmi: Arabic word meaning a non-Muslim living in a Muslim state.

Dialectical Materialism: This is Stalin's term for the Marxist theory that all existence is material and that it originates and develops through a process of conflict between opposites within all natural and historical entities. The process consists of two stages of conflict: 1. The thesis is contradicted, or negated, by the antithesis; 2. The antithesis is itself contradicted, or negated, by the synthesis. The synthesis represents a higher form of being, but it too contains contractions which must be resolved through the dialectic process.

Divine Providence: The purpose and plan of the Creator to establish a world of love in which men and women live in harmony with God, with one another, and with nature. This is the guiding force of human history.

DPRK: Democratic People's Republic of Korea, or North Korea. It was established in 1948.

Fascism: A socialist system that embraces central planning but eschews secularism or atheism in favor of a state religion. Fascist states are dominated by one party and are totalitarian in practice. The state owns or controls (through favored individuals and companies) most of the capital. This crony capitalism undermines authentic capitalism and strengthens authoritarian rule. In general, fascism is intolerance for the ideas of others. As such, it is displayed by Socialist and Communist regimes and movements.

Feminism: The movement to secure equal rights for women, including the right to vote and hold public office.

Fidel Castro: A Cuban revolutionary who lived from 1926 to 2016. He led the Marxist revolution that took power in 1959 and established the Marxist-Leninist Communist Party of Cuba in 1965. He ruled Cuba from 1959 to 2008, when he turned over power to his brother, Raúl. His regime exercised totalitarian control over Cuba, suppressing all opposition.

Frankfurt School: A group of Leftist thinkers who first worked together in Germany in the 1920s. In the 1930s, the Institute for Social Research at the Goethe University Frankfurt, Germany, became their institutional home. They developed Critical Theory, which, with input from Freud and Nietzsche, adapted the Marxist dialectic to various aspects of society beyond economics and politics. Several escaped Nazism to go to America. Notable among these was Herbert Marcuse, the "Father of the New Left" who rose to prominence in the early 1960s. Their Critical Theory was picked up by the French Postmodernists, especially Michel Foucault, whose Critical Theories are currently favored in Western social science.

Friedrich Engels: A German philosopher, who lived from 1820 to 1895 and worked closely with Karl Marx on the development of Marxism. His family owned industries and he supported Marx financially for most of the latter's later years.

Gender Studies: Postmodernist field of study based on the assumption that there is a difference between biological sex and gender identity. Advocates seek to normalize people's gender self-identification and the language used in this self-identification.

Hafez, Khawje Shams Ad Din: A renowned 14th century AD Sufi and Persian poet.

Hate Crimes: Criminal behavior based on hateful prejudices towards others. It is the inevitable outcome of hate speech, which itself is a form of violence, according to Postmodernist theory.

Hate Speech: Language that is deemed harmful to society. Postmodernism teaches that language itself can be violence, thus hate speech spawns hate crimes.

Helsinki Accords: A 1975 agreement between the Soviet Union, the United States and several other countries that recognized Soviet dominion over Eastern Europe. Signatories committed to a number of principles supposed to govern international relations, including respect for human rights.

Herbert Marcuse: A German philosopher who lived from 1898 to 1979. He was a leading figure of the Frankfurt School who moved to the United States after Hitler came to power in Germany. He has been dubbed the "Father of the New Left" because of the influence of his writings during the 1960s.

Historical Materialism: The Marxist theory that applies Dialectical Materialism to history. Marx believed that all history was a history of class struggle. Thus hunters and gatherers came into conflict with those seeking ownership of land to grow crops. Feudalism resulted, but it was countered by underclasses wanting to own property themselves. The resulting conflict produced capitalist societies pitting proletarians against the bourgeoisie. The proletarians inevitably revolt and create a Socialist state. Under their wise guidance, the state withers away and true Communism appears. (The dialectic ceases to operate as a perfect Socialist state becomes Communist.)

HUAC: House Un-American Activities Committee, which was established in 1938 to investigate individuals and organizations suspected of working for Communist causes.

Identity Politics: Building constituencies based on group identity rather than on individual character and interests.

Imperialism: In Marxist and Neo-Marxist theories, imperialism is the final stage of capitalism. This idea came from Lenin, who said it explained the lack of spontaneous proletarian revolutions in capitalist countries that Marx had predicted. In other words, capitalism has to mature into imperialism before it is ripe for revolution. Attaching the "imperialist" label to countries identifies them as ready for a Marxist revolution.

Intersectionality: The theory that individuals occupy social groups that face disadvantages in society based on the intersection of victim or minority categories, such as race and gender.

ISIS: Islamic State of Iraq and the Levant, or Islamic State for short. This Islamic terror organization claims to be recreating the Caliphate.

Jacques Derrida: An Algerian-born French philosopher who lived from 1930 to 2004. After Foucault, he is the most prominent Postmodernist. His contribution was focused on analyzing the relationship between language and power, and the deconstruction of language to that end.

Jainism: The religion based on the teachings of Mahavira.

Jihad: Arabic word meaning "struggle for righteousness" or more commonly, "holy war." The Dar Al Islam is expanded through Jihad.

Joseph Stalin: A native of the country Georgia, Joseph Vissarionovich Stalin (born Joseb Besarionis dze Jughashvili) lived from 1878 to 1953. He followed

Lenin as leader of the Soviet Union and would become synonymous with totalitarianism and mass murder. He was responsible for the show trials that doomed many of his former colleagues to prison, camps or death, and for the creation of the Gulag Archipelago prison camp system in Siberia. He was likely responsible for the death of some 20 million Soviet citizens and many more in countries where he imposed Soviet hegemony. His Reign of Terror was finally exposed by Nikita Khrushchev in 1956.

Juche: The Marxist-Leninist theory of the Democratic People's Republic of Korea, introduced by the country's first leader, Kim Il Sung. It's basic thesis is self-reliance, although North Korea was established under the protection of the Soviet Union and is today dependent for its survival on Communist China.

Karl Marx: A German philosopher who lived from 1818 to 1883 and is the primary author of Marxism, which he developed in close collaboration with Friedrich Engels.

KGB: The Committee for State Security of the Soviet Union from 1954 to 1991. It was responsible for domestic and international espionage and influence operations as well as suppression of dissidents and similar "secret police" activities.

Kim Il Sung: The founding leader of the Democratic People's Republic of Korea (DPRK), and the founder of Juche theory. His family has ruled North Korea since 1945.

KPD: Communist Party of Germany, which was established in 1918 by Karl Liebknecht and Rosa Luxemburg. It was dissolved in 1946 upon the creation of the German Democratic Republic (GDR) under the East German Communist Party.

Lao Tzu: A Chinese philosopher born between the 4th and 6th centuries BC and the founder of Taoism.

Left: A catchall term to describe ideas, individuals, organizations and governments that espouse or favor Marxism, Socialism, Communism and Critical Theories of the Frankfurt School or Postmodernism.

Leftists: Those who espouse and/or practice the ideologies of the Left.

Liberalism: A 19th century theory that advocates for democracies built by free people enjoying private property rights and participating in free markets under the rule of law. This classical definition has been largely supplanted by a more recent use of liberalism to mean the ideology of the Left. In this new meaning liberals can be defined as people of the Left, or Leftists.

Mahavira: Indian religious leader from the 6th century BC. Founder of Jainism.

Mao Zedong: He was a Chinese native who lived from 1893 to 1976. In the 1920s he became the leader of the Chinese Communist Party, which took power in 1949. He is the author of the Chinese variant of Marxism-Leninism, which is called Marxism-Maoism. His principle ideas are contained in *The Little Red Book*. He was responsible for some 80 million deaths of Chinese people, notably in the Great Leap Forward and the Cultural Revolution.

Marxism A 19th century materialist and revolutionary ideology propounded by Karl Marx and Frederich Engels. Its basic tenets are explained in *The Communist Manifesto*, published in 1848. These are anti-religion, anti-family and anti-capitalism. Marxism holds that private property is the root of injustice and inequality, and that Communism is the solution. The core theories are dialectical and historical materialism. Marxism advocates for violent revolution to overthrow the existing order (a classist society in which the bourgeoisie dominated the proletariat) and the creation of Socialist (and ultimately Communist) states that control all capital, property, and means of production.

Marxism-Leninism: The revolutionary and ruling ideology responsible for the Bolshevik Revolution in 1917 and the seventy-year rule of the Communist Party of the Soviet Union. Marxism itself is a theory that prescribes violent revolution as necessary for the overthrow of capitalism and the establishment of Socialism, followed by Communism. However, Lenin recognized that Marxist theory lacked practical elements that would enable it to produce actual revolutions. He added the theory of imperialism as the final stage of capitalism, the need for a revolutionary party, the need for a revolutionary putsch, and the need for a dictatorship of the proletariat to guide the Socialist state to full Communism. After the October Revolution in Russia, Marxism-Leninism became the revolutionary ideology of the worldwide Communist movement, although some other Communists would add their own flavors to the theory, such as Maoism in China and Juche ideology in North Korea.

Marxism-Maoism: Mao came to believe that Marxism-Leninism could not work in its pure form in China because China's industrial sector, and hence the proletariat, was so small. He simply substituted the peasantry for the proletariat and built the Chinese Communist Party on support from its tens of millions of peasants.

Materialism: Also now called physicalism, is the theory that nothing exists beyond the physical world, and that any phenomena that are considered spiritual are nothing more than the result of physical processes in the brain. This view assumes that there is no invisible creator or invisible spirit world where human spirits dwell after their physical bodies die.

Michel Foucault: A Frenchman who lived from 1924 to 1984, he is the best-known theorist of Postmodernism. He rose to prominence in the late 1960s, and is the most referenced author in social sciences today. He believed there are no moral or other absolutes and that science itself is the product of language and social constructs.

Mohammed: The prophet and founder of Islam. Born in Mecca in 570 AD, died in Medina in 632 AD.

Nazism: The ideology of the National Socialist German Workers' Party, established in 1920 and led by Adolf Hitler. It held that rebuilding Germany after World War I, and preparing it for what would become World War II, could best be achieved by authoritarian government and central planning. Based on the theories in Hitler's book, *Mein Kampf* (My Struggle), the Nazis were fascists and racists who believed that the Aryan race was superior to all others and that racial purification was a mandate for the German people.

Neo-Marxism: Materialist theories that are derived from, or influenced by, Marxism. These include the Critical Theories of the Frankfurt School and of Postmodernists.

NKVD: The Soviet Union's Ministry of the Interior responsible for secret police and other security activities, from 1934 to 1946, before the KGB was established.

PLA: People's Liberation Army of China, which is the military arm of the CCP.

Pol Pot: He was a Cambodian native who lived from 1925 to 1998. Educated by Communists in France, he established the Khmer Rouge, the name given to the Communist Party of Kampuchea (Cambodia) in 1968. After five years of civil war, they took power and ruled Cambodia from 1975 to 1978. They were responsible for the dislocation of the whole population and the death of at least 2 million Cambodians.

Political Correctness: Language that is acceptable to the Left because it conforms to the Left's theories.

Postcolonialism: This was the first target of Postmodernist Critical Theory. It assumed that imperialist powers and their people and institutions had inherited racial and elitist prejudices that influenced their relationships with less fortunate peoples, leading to human and resource exploitation. It advocates for the evils of colonialism to be compensated for through various forms of reparations paid by former colonial powers as well as the industrialized world in general.

Postmodernism: The French school of Critical Theories that rejects absolute truth and traditional science in favor of the view that knowledge is cultural and shaped by language, which enables powerful groups to dominate cultural discourse and social behavior. Michel Foucault is its best-known theorist. He rose to prominence in the late 1960s and is the most referenced author in social sciences today. The theories that have evolved within and from Postmodernism form a matrix of Leftist ideas, including Critical Post-colonialism, Critical Race Theory, Intersectionality, Anti-Racism, White Privilege, White Fragility, social justice, identity politics, political correctness, Cancel Culture, Queer Theory, Transgenderism, radical feminism, gender studies, disability studies and fat studies. All criticize traditional social norms and institutions.

POUM: The Worker's Party of Marxist Unification was established in Barcelona in 1935 and dissolved in 1980. It was the target of attacks by Stalinists because of its Trotskyist ideas. George Orwell joined its ranks to fight Franco.

PRC: People's Republic of China, established by 1949 by the CCP. It is ruled to this day by the CCP.

Queer Theory: A Postmodernist theory that seeks to identify and reverse historical and present-day prejudices against people who identify as belonging to a gender different from their biological nature. In other words, its agenda is to normalize gay, lesbian, transgender and other previously marginalized sexual behaviors.

Quran: The scriptures revealed to the prophet Mohammed in the 7th century

AD. Divided into 114 suras or chapters.

Radical Environmentalism: Use of environmental concerns to justify policy and activism that relies on governmental programs to address environmental issues such as global warming. It generally advocates for the elimination of fossil fuels in favor of renewable energy sources, such as solar, wind and hydro. These policy prescriptions it wants written into domestic government laws and regulations, and to guide foreign policy towards developing countries.

Radical Feminism: Second wave feminism that seeks to rectify historic injustices suffered by women because of male chauvinism and patriarchy, by demanding equity with men for women in all areas of life.

Restoration: The process of salvation through which men and women regain the purity of character of Adam and Eve before the Fall.

Restoration Providence: God's plan for the restoration/salvation of fallen humanity.

Rumi, Jalal Ad Din: A renowned 13th century AD Sufi and poet. Author of the *Methnavi*. Born in Afghanistan and died in Turkey.

Social Justice: The Postmodernist theory of social equity for all people, irrespective of race, religion, ethnicity and gender identity, countering systemic manifestations of these social divisions. In action this means demonstrating for causes, and sometimes mounting violent action in the name of social justice.

Socialism (Marxist): As a Marxist concept, Socialism (we distinguish the Marxist version by using a capital S) is a politico-economic system of authoritarian rule and centralized planning in which capital and property are concentrated in the hands of the state. According to Marxism, Socialism is the bridge between capitalism and Communism, a system that takes property ownership from individuals and gives it to the state. Marxist Socialism took on concrete form through the addition of certain features by Lenin, who believed that the Socialist state could only be established by a revolutionary party which would initiate a revolutionary putsch to destroy the capitalist state it was to replace. Lenin also believed that, post-revolution, the Socialist state had to be governed by the revolutionary party, a dictatorship of the proletariat which he called the Vanguard of the Proletariat. This elite would manage the affairs of the Socialist state so well that eventually there would be a "withering away of the state." In its place would emerge a Communist state of perfect equality and justice in which no state was needed at all.

Socialism (Generic): A politico-economic system of collective ownership or control of property and the means of production, either by a government or a community. In this book we use a lower-case s for this socialism, to distinguish it from its meaning in Marxism, where it is a system of government owner-ship of all property and means of production during an interim stage between capitalism and Communism. Thus many socialist governments are established to manage economies in the belief that by doing so they can achieve a fair dis-tribution of wealth among the citizens. These governments (often thought of as Scandinavian socialism) tend to tax heavily but also provide generous social benefits to citizens, but they do not advocate for the totalitarianism of Marxist Socialism.

SPD: Social Democratic Party of Germany, which was founded in 1863. In 1875, it was officially organized as a Marxist party. After World War II, a fac-tion would split off to form the Communist Party of Germany, and in the late 1950s, the SPD would officially become a social democrat party.

Spiritual Ideology: An ideology based on spiritual principles, in particular those addressing the issues of good and evil.

Structural Violence: The Postmodernist theory that certain social structures are inherently unjust and inflict harm on the less fortunate. Thus, by their very nature, these societies are violent.

Sufi: Muslim mystic. Typically a member of a Sufi order.

Sufism: Muslim mysticism. (Also called Tasawwuf.)

Sura: A chapter of the Quran.

Taoism: The teachings of Lao Tzu that form a basis for traditional Chinese beliefs and traditions.

Theocracy: A government established with a particular religion as the basis for its laws. Its leaders are drawn from that religion's clergy.

Transgenderism: Activism based on normalizing gender dysphoria (in which a biological male identifies as a female, and vice versa) and getting social and political institutions to impose sanctions on those who do not accept transgender ideology and language. Transgenderism typically encourages hormone treatment and sex-change procedures, even for minors; permission for transgender people to have full access to all facilities normally reserved for members of one biological sex only; and permission for transgender people to play in sports that are normally reserved for members of the other biological sex.

USSR: Union of Soviet Socialist Republics, or Soviet Union.

Vladimir Lenin: A Russian native who lived from 1870 to 1924. He led the Bolshevik Party which overthrew the Kerensky government in 1917 in the Russian Revolution and became the first leader of Communist Russia. He is responsible for several additions to Marxism which transformed it from political philosophy to revolutionary ideology. Thus his theory is called Marxism-Leninism, which was the basis for many Socialist and Communist regimes in the 20ᵗʰ century and continues to be the ruling ideology of several nations and Communist parties to this day.

White Fragility: The theory that because racism is systemic, white people are unable to recognize it and deal with it, and therefore have to be shown their racism so that it can be corrected.

White Patriarchy: The Postmodernist theory that racism is closely tied to the historical dominance of white males in Western societies. This legacy must be reversed, and policy should make sure that white males no longer hold undue power in society. This can be achieved by replacing them in positions of power.

White Supremacy: The theory that some white people translate their racism into activism to deny other races their rights. For critical race theorists, white supremacy represents the greatest evil in America and other predominantly white population countries.

Wilhelm Reich: An Austrian psychoanalyst who lived from 1897 to 1957. As a Freudian and Marxist he was associated with the Frankfurt School. He is best known for his book, *The Sexual Revolution*, which helped launch the free sex movement.

Withering Away of the State: The Marxist theory that Socialism will naturally give way to an ideal Communist state in which no state structures will be necessary.

WCC: World Council of Churches, an ecumenical organization that was long influenced by the Soviet Union.

Wokism: Social awareness in line with the ideologies of the Left. This derives from the adjective "woke," itself derived from awake: the need for people to wake up to the need for social justice.

Zarathustra: Also known as Zoroaster, the founder of Zoroastrianism that began to be influential in Persia from the 6th century BC.

Zoroastrianism: The religious teaching of Zarathustra, now practiced by Parsis.

Select Bibliography

Alinsky, Saul D. Rules for Radicals: *A Pragmatic Primer for Realistic Radicals*. New York: Random House, 1971.

Arberry, A.J. *The Koran Interpreted: A Translation*. New York: Touchstone, 1996.

The Holy Bible, Revised Standard Version. New York: Plume, 1974.

Bokhari, Allum. *#Deleted: Big Tech's Battle to Erase the Trump Movement and Steal the Election*. New York: Center Street, 2020.

Breitbart, Andrew. *Righteous Indignation: Excuse Me While I Save the World!* New York. Grand Central Publishing, 2011.

Bukovsky, Vladimir. *Judgement in Moscow: Soviet Crimes and Western Complicity*. California: Ninth of November Press, 2019.

Burke, Edmund. *Selected Works of Edmund Burke*. Indianapolis: Liberty Fund Library, 1999.

Butler, Judith. *Gender Trouble: Feminism and Subversion of Identity*. London: Routledge, 1999.

Cage, Nicholas. *Eleni*. New York: Ballantine Books, 1983

Chambers, Whittaker. *Witness*. Washington: Regnery, 1969.

Chang, Gordon C. *The Coming Collapse of China*. New York: Random House, 2001.

Chang, Jung. *Mao: The Unknown Story*. New York: Anchor, 2006.

Chang, Jung. *Wild Swans: Three Daughters of China*. New York: Simon & Schuster, 2003.

Conquest, Robert. *Harvest of Sorrow: Soviet Collectivization and the Terror-Famine*. Oxford: Oxford University Press, 1987.

Conquest, Robert. *The Great Terror: A Reassessment* (40th Anniversary edition). Oxford: Oxford University Press, 2007.

Cook, Sarah. *The Battle for China's Spirit: Religious Revival, Repression, and Resistance under Xi Jinping*. Washington: Freedom House, 2017.

Crenshaw, Kimberle, Neil Gotanda, Gary Peller and Kendall Thomas. *Critical Race Theory: The Key Writings that Formed the Movement*. New York: The New Press, 1995.

De Tocqueville, Alexis. *Democracy in America*. New York: Library of America, 2004. (Original publication 1835)

DiAngelo, Robin. *White Fragility: Why It's So Hard for White People to Talk About Racism*. Boston: Beacon Press, 2018.

Editorial Board of the Nine Commentaries on The Communist Party. *How the Specter of Communism is Ruling Our World*. New York: An Epoch Times Publication, 2020.

Einstein, Albert. *Albert Einstein Solves the Equation: Understanding the Relationship Between Religion and Science*. Princeton: Lapham's Quarterly, 1939.

Engels, Friedrich. *Dialectics of Nature*. London: Wellred Books, 2012 (Original in German, 1883)

Engels, Friedrich. *Ludwig Feuerbach and the End of Classical German Philosophy*. Beijing, China: Foreign Language Press, 1976 (Original publication in German in 1886)

Evans, M. Stanton. *Blacklisted By History: The Untold Story of Senator Joe McCarthy and his Fight Against America's Enemies*. New York: Crown Forum, 2007.

Flew, Antony. *There Is a God: How the World's Most Notorious Atheist Changed His Mind*. New York: Harper One, 2009.

Foucault, Michel. *Discipline & Punish: The Birth of the Prison*. New York: Vintage Books, 1975.

Foucault, Michel. *The Essential Foucault: Selected from the Essential Works of Foucault, 1954-1984*. New York: The New Press, 2003.

Gertz, Bill. *Deceiving the Sky: Inside Communist China's Drive for Global Supremacy*. New York: Encounter Books, 2019.

Gornick, Vivian. *The Romance of American Communism*. New York: Basic Books Inc. 1977.

Grabar, Mary. *Debunking Howard Zinn: Exposing the Fake History That Turned a Generation Against America*. Washington: Regnery, 2019.

Hamilton, Clive. *Exposing How the Chinese Communist Party is Reshaping the World*. London: One World Publications, 2020.

Hawley, Josh. *The Tyranny of Big Tech*. Washington: Regnery Publishing, 2021.

Hayek, Friedrich A. *The Road to Serfdom*. London: Routledge Press; Chicago: University of Chicago Press, 1944.

Haynes, John Earl and Harvey Klehr. *Venona: Decoding Soviet Espionage in America*. New Haven: Yale University Press, 1999.

Johnson, Adam. *The Orphan Master's Son*. New York: Random House, 2012.

Johnson, Paul. *A History of the American People*. New York: HarperCollins, 1997.

Johnson, Paul. *Intellectuals: From Marx and Tolstoy to Sartre and Chomsky*. New York: HarperCollins, 1989.

Kelly, Edward and Emily Williams Kelly. *Irreducible Mind: Toward a Psychology for the 21st Century*, Lanham, Maryland: Rowman & Littlefield Publishers, 2009.

Kelly, Edward, Adam Crabtree and Paul Marshall editors. *Beyond Physicalism: Toward Reconciliation of Science and Spirituality*, Lanham, Maryland: Rowman & Littlefield Publishers, 2015.

Kengor, Paul. *Takedown: From Communists to Progressives, How the Left Has Sabotaged Family and Marriage*, Washington: WND Books, 2015.

Kengor, Paul. *The Devil and Karl Marx: Communism's Long March of Death, Deception and Infiltration*. Gastonia, North Carolina: TAN Books, 2020

Kennedy, Brian T. *China's War Inside America*. New York: Encounter Books, 2020.

Koestler, Arthur. *Darkness at Noon*. New York: Scribner, 2019 (Original publication 1941)

Koestler, Arthur. *The God that Failed*. New York: Columbia University Press, 2001 (Original publication 1946). Additional authors: Louis Fischer, André Gide, Ignazio Silone, Stephen Spender and Richard Wright.

Levin, Mark R. *American Marxism*. New York: Threshold Editions, 2021,

Levin, Mark R. *Liberty and Tyranny*. New York: Pocket Books, 2009.

Lewis, C.S. *The Great Divorce*. New York: HarperCollins, 2015.

Marcuse, Herbert. *Eros and Civilization: A Philosophical Inquiry into Freud*. Boston: Beacon Press, 1955.

Marcuse, Herbert. *One Dimensional Man: Studies in the Ideology of Advanced Industrial Society*. Boston: Beacon Press, 1964.

Marx, Karl. *Das Kapital (Capital)*. Seattle: Pacific Publishing Studio, 2011 (Original publication 1885).

Marx, Karl and Friedrich Engels. *Manifesto of the Communist Party*. New York: International Publishers, 2014 (Original publication 1848).

McAdams, A. James. *Vanguard of the Revolution: The Global Idea of the Communist Party*. Princeton: Princeton University Press, 2017.

Murray, Douglas. *The Madness of Crowds: Gender, Race and Identity*. London: Bloomsbury Continuum, 2019.

Ngo, Andy. *Unmasked: Inside Antifa's Radical Plan to Destroy Democracy*. New York: Center Street Publishing, 2021.

Nunes, Devin. *Countdown to Socialism*. New York: Encounter Books, 2020.

Orwell, George. *Animal Farm*. Mumbai: Sanage Publishing House, 2020. (Originally 1945)

Orwell, George. *Nineteen Eighty-Four*. New York: Houghton Mifflin Harcourt, 1983. (Originally 1949)

Overman, Dean L. *A Case for the Existence of God*. Lanham, Maryland: Rowman & Littlefield Publishers, 2010.

Paine, Thomas. *Common Sense*. Multiple publishers. 1776.

Panné, Jean-Louis. *The Black Book of Communism: Crimes, Terror, Repression*. (With Andrzej Paczkowski, Karel Bartosek, Jean-Louis Margolin, Nicolas Werth, and Stéphane Courtoisz.) Cambridge: Harvard University Press, 1999.

Peterson, Jordan B. *Twelve Rules for Life: An Antidote to Chaos*. Toronto: Random House Canada, 2018

Pillsbury, Michael. *The Hundred-Year Marathon: China's Secret Strategy to Replace America as the Global Superpower*. New York: Henry Holt and Co., 2015.

Pluckrose, Helen and James Lindsay. *Cynical Theories: How Activist Scholarship Made Everything about Race, Gender, and Identity—and Why This Harms Everybody*. Durham, North Carolina: Pitchstone Publishing, 2020.

Reich, Wilhelm. *The Sexual Revolution: Toward a Self-Regulating Character Structure*. New York: Farrar, Straus and Giroux, 2013. (Originally published in English in 1945).

Romerstein, Herbert and Eric Breindel. *The Venona Secrets: Exposing Soviet Espionage and America's Traitors*. Washington: Regnery, 2000.

Shlaes, Amity. *The Forgotten Man: A New History of the Great Depression*. New York: HarperCollins, 2007.

Shrier, Abigail. *Irreversible Damage: The Transgender Craze Seducing Our Daughters*. Washington: Regnery Publishing, 2020.

Smith, Adam. *The Wealth of Nations*. Mankato, Minnesota: Capstone Publishers, 2010. (Original publication 1776).

Smith, David Livingstone. *Less Than Human: Why We Demean, Enslave, and Exterminate Others*. New York: St. Martin's Griffin, 2012.

Solzhenitsyn, Aleksandr. *The Gulag Archipelago: An Experiment in Literary Investigation*. Paris: Éditions du Seuil, 1974.

Spaulding, Robert. *Stealth War: How China Took Over While America's Elite Slept*. New York: Portfolio, 2019.

Steyn, Mark. *America Alone*. Washington: Regnery Publishing, 2008.

Von Mises, Ludwig. *Socialism: An Economic and Sociological Analysis*. Indianapolis: Liberty Fund Library, 1936.

Von Mises, Ludwig. *The Anti-Capitalist Mentality*. Indianapolis: Liberty Fund Library, 1956.

Ward, Jonathan D.T. *China's Vision of Victory*. Fayetteville, North Carolina: Atlas Publishing and Media Company, 2019.

Wasserstrom, Jeffrey N. and Maura Elizabeth Cunningham. *China in the 21st Century: What Everyone Needs to Know*. Oxford: Oxford University Press, 2013.

Wasserstrom, Jeffrey N. *Vigil: Hong Kong on the Brink*. New York: Columbia Global Reports, 2020.

Weikart, Richard. *From Darwin to Hitler: Evolutionary Ethics, Eugenics, and Racism in Germany*. New York: Palgrave Macmillan, 2004.

Weinstein, Allen. *Perjury: The Hiss-Chambers Case*. Stanford, California: Hoover Institution Press, 1978.

West, Diana. *American Betrayal: The Secret Assault on Our Nation's Character*. New York: St. Martin's Press, 2013.

West, Diana. *The Red Thread: A Search for Ideological Drivers Inside the Anti-Trump Conspiracy*. Washington: Bravura Books, 2019.

Williams, Michael. *The Genesis of Political Correctness: The Basis of a False Morality*. Seattle: Amazon CreateSpace Publishing Platform, 2016.

Wurmbrand, Richard. *Tortured for Christ*. New York: HarperCollins Publishers, 1983.

Zinn, Howard. *A People's History of the United States*. New York: Harper Perennial Modern Classics, 2015.

INDEX